Financial Engineering

von
Michael Bloss
Dietmar Ernst
Joachim Häcker
Daniel Sörensen

Oldenbourg Verlag München

Bibliografische Information der Deutschen Nationalbibliothek

Die Deutsche Nationalbibliothek verzeichnet diese Publikation in der Deutschen Nationalbibliografie; detaillierte bibliografische Daten sind im Internet über http://dnb.d-nb.de abrufbar.

© 2012 Oldenbourg Wissenschaftsverlag GmbH
Rosenheimer Straße 145, D-81671 München
Telefon: (089) 45051-0
www.oldenbourg-verlag.de

Das Werk einschließlich aller Abbildungen ist urheberrechtlich geschützt. Jede Verwertung außerhalb der Grenzen des Urheberrechtsgesetzes ist ohne Zustimmung des Verlages unzulässig und strafbar. Das gilt insbesondere für Vervielfältigungen, Übersetzungen, Mikroverfilmungen und die Einspeicherung und Bearbeitung in elektronischen Systemen.

Lektorat: Thomas Ammon
Herstellung: Sarah Voit, Constanze Müller
Einbandgestaltung: hauser lacour
Gesamtherstellung: Beltz Bad Langensalza GmbH, Bad Langensalza

Dieses Papier ist alterungsbeständig nach DIN/ISO 9706.

ISBN 978-3-486-70551-5

Preface

We strongly believe that regulation does not matter as much as education (cf. testimonial by J. C. Hull). The aim of this book is to provide easy access to the chances, risks and applications of products in financial markets.

Financial Engineering – the development of new financial solutions – covers complex topics seeking both

- a sound academic background and analysis, as well as
- a practical, business-oriented approach.

In addition to providing a detailed analysis of the relevant processes and toolkits, a user-friendly book on financial engineering combines theory and practical examples in a way that enables readers to apply them to the specifics of their engineering case. Financial solutions can refer both to credit and to investment products. Tailor-made financial solutions and products are structured and made available with the help of derivatives and combined products. Financial engineering is thus an interdisciplinary field which seeks to provide innovative and tailor-made solutions that satisfy customer demand. Within the financial sector, financial engineering has developed into a core business area for investment banks and major institutions alike and is among the most important revenue drivers.

It is the aim of this book to train and educate financial experts, investment bankers, traders, financial advisors and natural scientists who are active in financial engineering. Financial engineering is a necessary skill in many sectors of the financial industry. Knowledge of financial engineering improves career opportunities for financial experts and opens doors to new and highly interesting employment opportunities. The book comes with numerous Excel and VBA models and can be used as the basis for a training course.

Since financial engineering and derivatives are increasingly taught at universities, this book is also structured as an academic textbook. The book is optimally suited for classroom instruction due to its scientific foundations, numerous practical applications and case studies.

The didactic approach of the book makes it possible to acquire financial engineering knowledge with only a basic understanding of finance and derivatives and without other prior knowledge. Successful studies and training in the field of financial engineering can be certified and the title "Certified Financial Engineer" can be awarded. The exams are administered centrally by the European Institute for Financial Engineering and Derivatives (EIFD) in cooperation with Deutsche Börse AG. These are the three steps towards the CFE:

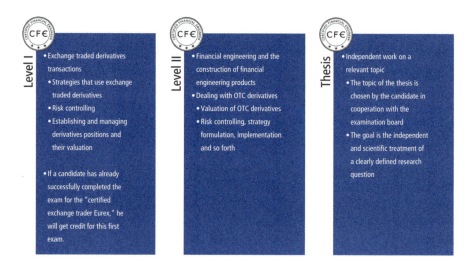

We hope that you will enjoy our book "Financial Engineering" and appreciate the interdisciplinary philosophy that combines a sound academic derivatives framework with real-world financial engineering business practices and global perspectives.

Finally, we would like to thank Michelle Moersch for providing the translation of the entire book into English. Her final editing helped us to specify many technical terms and to point out the American Financial Engineering perspective

Stuttgart and Frankfurt, July 2011

Michael Bloss
Dietmar Ernst
Joachim Häcker
Daniel Sörensen

Questions, comments or inquiries concerning the CFE program can be directed to:

European Institute for Financial Engineering and Derivatives (EIFD)
CFE@EIFD.DE
www.certified-financial-engineer.com

About the authors

Michael Bloss is Director at Commerzbank AG and Director of the European Institute for Financial Engineering and Derivatives (EIFD). He is Associate Professor at the Chair of International Finance of the European School of Finance at HfWU and holds teaching positions at other respected universities.

Dietmar Ernst is Professor for International Finance at the European School of Finance at HfWU. He is Director of the European Institute for Financial Engineering and Derivatives (EIFD). Dietmar Ernst was active at a private equity company and has many years of experience in the field of mergers and acquisitions. Dietmar Ernst has studied international economics at Tübingen University and holds a doctoral degree in both economics and natural sciences. He is the author of numerous standard textbooks.

Joachim Häcker is Professor at Munich University and University of Louisville. He is Director of the European Institute for Financial Engineering and Derivatives (EIFD). His area of specialization is international finance. Mr. Häcker studied business and law at Tübingen University and the Kenan Flagler Business School (USA). He holds doctoral degrees in both subjects.

Daniel Sörensen works as a strategic management consultant at Deutsche Bank. He teaches Financial Engineering at the Frankfurt School of Finance and Management and is an Associate Professor at the European School of Finance (ESF) of HfWU. He holds a doctoral degree in finance from Stuttgart University.

Contents Overview

Preface V
About the authors IX
List of abbreviations and symbols XXIX
List of figures XXXV
List of tables XLIII

Module I   Fundamentals   1

1   Financial engineering – business segment with a future   3
2   Review of the methodological foundations of financial engineering   17
3   Ethical principles for successful financial engineering 73

Module II   Listed options & futures   85

4   Derivatives exchanges and derivatives markets 87
5   Futures – unconditional derivatives contracts 123
6   Options – conditional derivatives contracts 161
7   Derivatives on currencies and commodities 261

Module III   Structured derivatives   297

8   Exotic and non-listed derivatives 299
9   Credit derivatives 357
10   Weather derivatives 375
11   Insurance derivatives 409
12   Real options 415

Module IV Application of derivatives — 437

13 Structuring complex portfolios with the help of derivatives 439

14 Use of derivatives in financial engineering and fund management 457

15 What is a hedge fund? 483

16 Risk controlling and margining 501

In closing 527

17 Appendix 531

References 565

Disclaimer 569

Index 573

Contents

Preface V
About the authors IX
List of abbreviations and symbols XXIX
List of figures XXXV
List of tables XLIII

Module I Fundamentals 1

1 Financial engineering – business segment with a future 3
   1.1 What is the meaning of financial engineering? 3
   1.2 Setup of a financial engineering unit 4
   1.3 Product desks of a financial engineering unit 4
   1.4 Which theories and models are combined in financial engineering? 6
   1.5 The financial engineering process 6
   1.6 How to issue the product 8
       1.6.1   Public Offering 8
       1.6.2   Private Placement 8
   1.7 Flow products 9
   1.8 Issuers 9
   1.9 Which product and when? 10
   1.10 What likely development lies ahead for financial engineering? 12

2 Review of the methodological foundations of financial engineering 17
   2.1 Foundations of probability theory 17
       2.1.1   Laplace probability 18
       2.1.2   Frequentist probability 19
       2.1.3   Subjective probability 19
       2.1.4   Conditional probability 19

2.2	Stochastic processes		23
	2.2.1	Markov process	23
		2.2.1.1 Wiener process	23
		2.2.1.2 Generalized Wiener process	23
	2.2.2	Itō process	25
	2.2.3	The normal distribution	26
	2.2.4	Martingale assumption	28
	2.2.5	Random walk	28
2.3	Correlation analysis		30
	2.3.1	Correlation	30
	2.3.2	Variance, covariance and correlation coefficients	33
2.4	Statistical concepts of security analysis		35
	2.4.1	Calculation of the beta factor	35
	2.4.2	Log-normal distribution of equity prices	37
	2.4.3	Valuation using replication	39
2.5	Value at Risk		40
	2.5.1	Graphical derivation	42
	2.5.2	Analytical models	44
	2.5.3	Simulation models	44
2.6	Foundations and approaches of decision theory		45
	2.6.1	Classical decision theory	45
	2.6.2	Game theory	46
2.7	Who knows what?		47
	2.7.1	Complete information	47
	2.7.2	Perfect information	47
	2.7.3	Transformation of games with incomplete information into games with complete, but imperfect information	47
	2.7.4	Different strategies	47
		2.7.4.1 Pure and mixed strategies	47
		2.7.4.2 Equilibria in dominant strategies	48
		2.7.4.3 Nash equilibrium	48
2.8	Solution strategies for known decision situations		48
	2.8.1	Financial engineering and game theory	49
	2.8.2	Portfolio risk management	50
	2.8.3	Fundamental questions for every investor	51
		2.8.3.1 The different types of investors	53
		2.8.3.2 How to approach derivatives as an inexperienced investor	53
	2.8.4	Portfolio theory	55
		2.8.4.1 Portfolio selection model	55

		2.8.4.2	Single index model	57
		2.8.4.3	Capital Asset Pricing Model (CAPM)	58
			2.8.4.3.1 Assumptions of CAPM	58
			2.8.4.3.2 Main conclusions of CAPM	59
			2.8.4.3.3 Summary of the CAPM	62
	2.8.5		Final assessment of the models	62
	2.8.6		The process of portfolio management	63
2.9			Market psychology and behavioral economics	64
	2.9.1		Market psychology	64
	2.9.2		Behavioral economics	65
	2.9.3		Methods of behavioral finance	66
		2.9.3.1	Herd behavior	67
		2.9.3.2	Group thinking	68
	2.9.4		Closing thoughts	68

3 Ethical principles for successful financial engineering 73
- 3.1 Are ethics enforcable in finance? 74
- 3.2 What is important in financial engineering concerning ethics? 75
  - 3.2.1 The financial engineer as competent partner . . 75
  - 3.2.2 The financial engineer as creator of tangible solutions 76
  - 3.2.3 The financial engineer as judge of the doable . . 76
- 3.3 How to check for ethical principles? 78
- 3.4 Fundamental ethical points of reference for the financial engineer 78

Module II Listed options & futures   85

4 Derivatives exchanges and derivatives markets 87
- 4.1 Historical development of derivatives exchanges 87
- 4.2 What is a derivatives transaction? 91
- 4.3 Why are derivatives transactions mostly standardized today? 94
- 4.4 What are the functions of derivatives exchanges? 97
- 4.5 Who are the market participants at derivatives exchanges? 98
- 4.6 Which other basic concepts are required for an understanding of derivatives exchanges and derivatives markets? 99

4.7	What is the organizational structure of derivatives exchanges?	103
4.8	The working of a computerized exchange	104
4.9	What is the market maker principle?	106
4.10	Trading at Eurex	107
4.11	Who regulates derivatives markets?	109
4.12	Which products can be traded?	110
4.13	The clearing process	110
4.14	How to specify an order	112
4.15	What are the expiration dates at Eurex?	117

5 Futures – unconditional derivatives contracts 123

5.1	What are futures?	123
5.2	Futures markets	124
5.3	Futures trading	125
5.4	Basic futures strategies	125
5.5	Leverage in futures transactions	127
5.6	Settlement	127
5.7	Index futures	128
5.8	Interest rate futures	131
5.9	Currency futures	133
5.10	Commodity futures	133
5.11	Single stock futures	134
5.12	State of the market in futures trading	135
5.13	Determination of futures prices	136
5.14	Pricing of interest rate futures	139
5.15	What is a CTD bond?	141
5.16	What is meant by "final settlement?"	142
5.17	What futures expiration dates exist?	143
5.18	Which futures strategies exist?	144
	5.18.1 Long futures position	145
	5.18.2 Short futures position	145
5.19	Purchasing a spread	148
5.20	Selling a spread	148
5.21	Inter market spread	149
5.22	Inter contract spread and intra contract spread	149
5.23	Cash-and-carry arbitrage	150
5.24	Arbitrage strategies for money market futures (Euribor)	151
5.25	Hedges	152
5.26	Beta-hedging with index futures	153
5.27	Why futures are used for hedging	155
5.28	Hedging with interest rate futures	155

6	Options – conditional derivatives contracts			161
	6.1	What is an option?		161
	6.2	Differences in options		163
	6.3	Option trading		165
	6.4	What are weekly options?		168
	6.5	What is a low exercise price option?		168
	6.6	The closing of a derivatives transaction		169
	6.7	What is a rollover?		171
	6.8	Pricing of options		171
	6.9	Theories of option pricing		172
		6.9.1	Intrinsic value	172
		6.9.2	Time value	174
	6.10	Early exercise of options		177
	6.11	Which factors influence the price of an option?		178
		6.11.1	The value of the underlying	178
		6.11.2	Volatility	179
			6.11.2.1 Historical volatility	179
			6.11.2.2 Implied volatility	180
			6.11.2.3 The Newton procedure	181
			6.11.2.4 The influence of volatility	182
		6.11.3	Market interest rates	183
		6.11.4	Dividend payments	183
		6.11.5	Term to maturity	183
		6.11.6	The effect of corporate actions	184
			6.11.6.1 Mergers and acquisitions	185
			6.11.6.2 Extraordinary dividends	185
			6.11.6.3 Cash settlement of corporate actions	185
	6.12	Greeks – sensitivities of option prices		186
		6.12.1	Delta	186
		6.12.2	Gamma	188
		6.12.3	Rho	189
		6.12.4	Theta	190
		6.12.5	Vega	190
		6.12.6	Derivation of Greeks from the Black-Scholes formula	193
	6.13	What is put-call parity?		195
		6.13.1	Put-call parity relationship	195
		6.13.2	Presentation of the put-call relationship using replication	196
	6.14	Determination of option prices using the Black-Scholes model		197

		6.14.1	Assumptions of the Black-Scholes model	198
		6.14.2	The Black-Scholes formula	198
		6.14.3	The Black-Scholes-Merton model	199
		6.14.4	The Black-Scholes differential equation	200
	6.15	Determination of option prices using the binomial model		202
		6.15.1	Basic assumptions of the binomial model	202
		6.15.2	Setup of a tree	203
		6.15.3	Implementation of the binomial model	204
	6.16	Model critique		208
	6.17	Monte-Carlo simulation		211
	6.18	Tradable option prices		212
	6.19	Strategies using options		212
		6.19.1	What is contained in the four basic strategies in option trading (plain vanilla)?	213
		6.19.2	The strategy LONG CALL	214
		6.19.3	The strategy SHORT CALL	216
		6.19.4	The strategy LONG PUT	219
		6.19.5	The strategy SHORT PUT	220
	6.20	How to hedge with options		222
		6.20.1	Delta hedging	222
		6.20.2	Protective put	223
		6.20.3	Portfolio insurance using calls	224
		6.20.4	Beta hedge	224
	6.21	Which combinations of options are frequently used?		225
		6.21.1	Straddle	225
			6.21.1.1 Long straddle	225
			6.21.1.2 Short straddle	226
			6.21.1.2.1 Straps	227
			6.21.1.2.2 Strips	227
		6.21.2	Strangle	228
			6.21.2.1 Long strangle	228
			6.21.2.2 Short strangle	228
		6.21.3	Spreads	229
	6.22	An overview of plain vanilla option strategies		233
		6.22.1	Strategies for a positive market outlook	233
		6.22.2	Strategies for a neutral market outlook	233
		6.22.3	Strategies for a negative market outlook	234
		6.22.4	Strategies for a volatile market outlook	234
	6.23	Complex option strategies and their implementation		235
		6.23.1	Butterfly	235
		6.23.2	Condor	237

		6.23.3	Ratio spread	238
			6.23.3.1 Ratio call spread	238
			6.23.3.2 Ratio put spread	239
		6.23.4	Back spread	239
			6.23.4.1 Back spread call	239
			6.23.4.2 Back spread put	239
		6.23.5	Box strategies	239
			6.23.5.1 Long box	240
			6.23.5.2 Short box	240
		6.23.6	Time spread or calendar spread	241
			6.23.6.1 Bull calendar spread	241
			6.23.6.2 Bear calendar Spread	242
		6.23.7	Long risk reversal	242
		6.23.8	Short risk reversal	243
	6.24	How to implement a strategy using options	243
	6.25	Options on futures, synthetic derivatives transactions & combinations	247
		6.25.1	How are options on futures constructed and structured?	248
		6.25.2	What is the future-style method?	248
		6.25.3	How to value options on futures with the Black-76 model?	249
		6.25.4	Which strategies are pursued with options on futures?	250
	6.26	What is a synthetic derivatives market position?	253
	6.27	Which combinations and linked strategies are used in practice?	254
7	Derivatives on currencies and commodities			261
	7.1	Development of currency trading		261
	7.2	The fundamentals of currency trading		262
	7.3	Economic determinants of exchange rate formation . . .		264
	7.4	Currency spot transactions		264
	7.5	Currency derivatives transactions		264
	7.6	Currency derivatives transactions of banks		265
	7.7	Calculation of the forward rate		266
	7.8	Currency derivatives transactions at exchanges		267
	7.9	Cross rates		267
	7.10	Tobin tax		268
	7.11	What are currency options?		269

7.12	Pricing of a currency option according to Garman-Kohlhagen		269
7.13	What are currency futures?		270
	7.13.1	Pricing of currency futures	271
	7.13.2	Uses of currency futures	272
	7.13.3	Basic intentions of the investor	272
		7.13.3.1 Hedging	272
		7.13.3.2 Speculation	273
		7.13.3.3 Speculating on spreads or currency pairs	273
7.14	Commodity derivatives transactions versus commodity spot transactions		274
7.15	Commodity futures		275
	7.15.1	Opening, closing and settlement	275
	7.15.2	Application of the different settlement possibilities	276
	7.15.3	Which commodities serve as underlying for derivatives transactions?	277
7.16	Trading in commodity derivatives		279
7.17	When should investors consider commodity derivatives contracts?		279
7.18	Developments and outlook		280
7.19	Price determination of commodity derivatives futures		281
7.20	Prices of commodity futures		281
7.21	What is problematic about contango?		284
7.22	Futures trading		285
7.23	Storage		285
7.24	Which factors can influence pricing?		286
7.25	Strategies in the area of commodity derivatives transactions		288
	7.25.1	Hedging with commodity derivatives	288
	7.25.2	Speculating with commodity derivatives	289
	7.25.3	Arbitrage with commodity derivatives	289
	7.25.4	Spreads with commodity derivatives	289
7.26	What are combinations between currency and commodity derivatives?		290
7.27	What strategies for currency derivatives exist?		291
	7.27.1	Hedging strategies	291
	7.27.2	Speculative strategies	291

Contents   XXI

Module III Structured derivatives   297

8 Exotic and non-listed derivatives   299
   8.1 Derivatives that are not exchange traded   299
        8.1.1 OTC derivatives as "flexible options/futures" at
               Eurex   300
        8.1.2 Caps, floors and collars   301
               8.1.2.1 Caps   301
               8.1.2.2 Caplets   301
               8.1.2.3 Floor   303
               8.1.2.4 Floorlets   303
               8.1.2.5 Valuation of caplets and floorlets   304
               8.1.2.6 Collar   304
        8.1.3 What is a forward?   305
        8.1.4 What is a swap?   306
               8.1.4.1 What are the terms of a swap?   307
               8.1.4.2 Types of swaps and their setup   307
                        8.1.4.2.1 Interest rate swap 308
                        8.1.4.2.2 Constant Maturity Swap (CMS)   309
                        8.1.4.2.3 Currency swap   310
                        8.1.4.2.4 Equity index swap   310
                        8.1.4.2.5 Forward swap   310
                        8.1.4.2.6 Commodity swap   311
               8.1.4.3 Swap trading   312
               8.1.4.4 Valuation of swaps   313
               8.1.4.5 Swaps with variable interest rates   313
               8.1.4.6 Uses of swaps   314
               8.1.4.7 Examples of swaps   314
                        8.1.4.7.1 Inflation swaps 314
                                   8.1.4.7.1.1 Inflation payer swap 314
                                              8.1.4.7.1.1.1 How does the inflation payer
                                                             swap work? 315
                                              8.1.4.7.1.1.2 Payment streams of the inflation
                                                             payer swap 316
                                   8.1.4.7.1.2 Inflation receiver swap 316
                                              8.1.4.7.1.2.1 How does the inflation receiver
                                                             swap work? 316
                                              8.1.4.7.1.2.2 Payment streams of the inflation
                                                             receiver swap 317
                        8.1.4.7.2 Express swap EUR/TRY   318
                        8.1.4.7.3 Second chance swap   322

		8.1.4.7.4	Callable range accrual swap	325
		8.1.4.7.5	FX linked knockout swap	326
		8.1.4.7.6	Step down swap	328
	8.1.4.8	Swap confirmation		331
8.1.5	What are swaptions and interest rate guarantees?			332
	8.1.5.1	Swaptions		332
	8.1.5.2	Receiver or payer swaption		333
	8.1.5.3	Valuation of swaptions		334
	8.1.5.4	Settlement of a swaption		335
8.1.6	What are exotic options?			336
	8.1.6.1	What kinds of exotic options do exist?		337
	8.1.6.2	Types of exotic options		337
		8.1.6.2.1	Barrier options	338
		8.1.6.2.2	Digital options	340
		8.1.6.2.3	Range options	341
		8.1.6.2.4	Bermuda options	342
		8.1.6.2.5	Chooser options	342
		8.1.6.2.6	Compound options	342
		8.1.6.2.7	Window options	342
		8.1.6.2.8	Quanto options	343
		8.1.6.2.9	Rainbow options	344
		8.1.6.2.10	Basket options	345
		8.1.6.2.11	Lookback options	346
		8.1.6.2.12	Cliquet options and ladder options	346
		8.1.6.2.13	Spread options and outperformance options	346
		8.1.6.2.14	Shout options	347
		8.1.6.2.15	Options with delayed premium payment – Boston options	348
		8.1.6.2.16	Multifactor options	348
		8.1.6.2.17	Exchange options	348
		8.1.6.2.18	Asian options (average options)	348

9 Credit derivatives 357
   9.1 Fundamentals of credit derivatives 357
   9.2 What is credit? 357
   9.3 Which capital structures exist? 358
   9.4 Which types of credit derivatives exist? 361
      9.4.1 Classical credit derivatives 361
      9.4.2 Modern credit derivatives 362
   9.5 Valuation of credit derivatives (CDS) 364

9.6	What are iTraxx® futures at Eurex?	365
9.7	What are securitized credit derivatives?	366
9.8	Problems in the securitization market following the financial market crisis in 2007	368
9.9	Complexity of the instruments	369
9.10	Which problems arose during the financial crisis with respect to credit derivatives?	370

10 Weather derivatives — 375

10.1	Fundamentals of weather derivatives	375
10.2	Information on the underlying in weather derivatives	376
	10.2.1 Degree day indexes	378
	10.2.2 Heating Degree Days (HDD) & Cooling Degree Days (CDD)	379
	10.2.3 Gradtageszahlenindex (GTZ)	380
10.3	Structuring of weather derivatives	381
10.4	Conditional weather derivatives	382
	10.4.1 Hedging with call options	383
	10.4.2 Hedging with put options	386
10.5	Unconditional weather derivatives: swaps and futures	390
	10.5.1 Example of a swap between an ice cream parlor and a travel agency	390
	10.5.2 Futures on the HDD for a railroad company	393
10.6	Valuation of weather derivatives	395
10.7	Reasons for the failure of the Black-Scholes model in pricing weather derivatives	395
10.8	Burn analysis or burning cost method	396
10.9	Index Value Simulation Method (IVSM)	398
10.10	Daily Simulation Method (DSM)	398
10.11	Trading in weather derivatives	399
	10.11.1 The first weather derivatives transactions	399
	10.11.2 The markets for weather derivatives	399
	10.11.2.1 Chicago Mercantile Exchange (CME)	400
	10.11.2.2 London International Financial Futures and Options Exchange (LIFFE)	400
	10.11.2.3 Deutsche Börse AG	401
	10.11.2.4 Eurex	401
10.12	The participants in the market for weather derivatives	402
	10.12.1 End user	402
	10.12.2 Trader	402
	10.12.3 Market maker	403

		10.12.4	Broker	403
		10.12.5	Investor	404

11	Insurance derivatives	409
	11.1 What are insurance derivatives?	409
	11.2 Why are they traded and who does the trading?	409

12	Real options	415
	12.1 What are real options?	416
	12.2 How to classify real options	417
	12.3 Real options and financial options	419
	12.4 Valuation of real options	419
	12.5 Valuation of real options in practice	419
	12.6 Can real options be used in practice?	428

Module IV Application of derivatives — 437

13	Structuring complex portfolios with the help of derivatives	439
	13.1 Averaging and pyramiding	439
	13.2 Why should positions be extended?	441
	13.2.1 Extending gains	441
	13.2.2 Position management if investments develop unfavorably	442
	13.3 What is a rollover?	444
	13.3.1 Rollover in case of an adverse market development	444
	13.3.2 Preventing an early exercise	445
	13.3.3 Extension of positions that are favorable to the investor	445
	13.3.4 Cross rollover	446
	13.4 Combinations	447
	13.5 Position management of swaps and other OTC derivatives	447
	13.6 The key to success is liquidity!	448
	13.7 Portfolio structure	449

14	Use of derivatives in financial engineering and fund management	457
	14.1 Considerations when designing new products	458
	14.2 Basic component zero bond	459
	14.3 Financial engineering products and their construction	460
	14.3.1 Discount certificates	460
	14.3.2 Reverse Convertibles	462
	14.3.3 Bonus certificates	463

		14.3.4	Leveraged products	465
		14.3.5	Warrants	466
		14.3.6	Structured financial products with interest rate options	466
			14.3.6.1 Single putable bonds	467
			14.3.6.2 Single callable bonds	468
			14.3.6.3 Bonds with several termination rights . . .	468
			14.3.6.3.1 Multi callable bonds	469
			14.3.6.3.2 Multi putable bonds	469
			14.3.6.4 Reverse floater	469
			14.3.6.5 Leveraged floater	470
		14.3.7	Highly structured financial products	471
			14.3.7.1 Inflation bond	471
			14.3.7.2 Simulation based certificates	472
	14.4	Use of derivatives in fund management	473
		14.4.1	Strategies for the use of derivatives in the portfolio management of a fund	473
			14.4.1.1 Call volatility trade	473
			14.4.1.2 Put volatility trade	474
			14.4.1.3 Combo versus long underlying	474
			14.4.1.4 Put spread versus underlying	476
			14.4.1.5 Conversion versus underlying	476
		14.4.2	Why are these strategies used in fund portfolio management?	477
15	What is a hedge fund?			483
	15.1	What is the aim of a hedge fund?	484
	15.2	Use of leverage	484
	15.3	Legal transparency	484
	15.4	Offshore companies	485
	15.5	Risk attributes of hedge funds	485
		15.5.1	Market risks	485
		15.5.2	Address non-payment risk	486
			15.5.2.1 Issuer risk	486
			15.5.2.2 Counterparty risk	486
			15.5.2.3 Credit risk	486
			15.5.2.4 Country risk	486
		15.5.3	Liquidity risk	487
		15.5.4	Manager risk	487
		15.5.5	Operational risk	487
		15.5.6	Strategic risk	488

- 15.6 Organizational setup of a hedge fund ... 488
  - 15.6.1 Hedge fund company ... 489
  - 15.6.2 Hedge fund management company ... 489
  - 15.6.3 External service providers ... 489
    - 15.6.3.1 Prime broker ... 489
    - 15.6.3.2 Custodian bank ... 490
    - 15.6.3.3 Fund administration ... 490
- 15.7 Strategies ... 491
  - 15.7.1 Convertible bond arbitrage ... 491
  - 15.7.2 Short equity ... 492
  - 15.7.3 Emerging markets ... 493
  - 15.7.4 Market neutral equity ... 493
  - 15.7.5 Event driven ... 493
  - 15.7.6 Fixed income arbitrage ... 494
  - 15.7.7 Global macro ... 494
  - 15.7.8 Long/short equity ... 495
- 15.8 Managed futures ... 495
- 15.9 Single hedge fund versus fund of hedge funds ... 495
- 15.10 Hedge funds as golden calf? ... 497

16 Risk controlling and margining ... 501
- 16.1 Basics of risk controlling ... 501
  - 16.1.1 MaRisk as the basis for risk controlling ... 503
  - 16.1.2 Risk controlling of wealth management clients ... 506
  - 16.1.3 Risk controlling of financial engineering units ... 506
- 16.2 Unforeseeable market events ... 507
- 16.3 What is margin? ... 508
- 16.4 What is risk based margining? ... 510
- 16.5 Why is the deposit of margin required and how is it calculated? ... 510
- 16.6 Which types of margin exist? ... 511
  - 16.6.1 Premium margin ... 511
  - 16.6.2 Additional margin ... 511
  - 16.6.3 Variation margin ... 513
  - 16.6.4 Futures spread margin ... 513
- 16.7 Option margins ... 514
  - 16.7.1 Long positions ... 514
  - 16.7.2 Short positions ... 514
- 16.8 Margin during the time of delivery ... 516
- 16.9 Margin for futures ... 516
- 16.10 Margin for future style options ... 518

16.11	How is the margin calculated for option positions?	519
16.12	Calculating the costs of closing a position	519
16.13	How to provide margin	520
16.14	Settlement price	520
16.15	What is a margin call?	521
16.16	Forced liquidation from the perspective of the bank or the broker	522

In closing 527

17 Appendix 531
    Typical exam questions and problems 531
    Glossary 546
    Table of standard normal distribution 555
    Rating scales 556
    Bond return and rating in context 557
    Internet addresses 559
    Derivatives exchanges globally and their internet addresses 560

References 565

Disclaimer 569

Index 573

List of abbreviations and symbols

A	Any event
ATM	At the money
AVT	Average temperature index
a	Constant
B	Any event
BP	Basis point
B_G	Basis of calculation for the currency quoted (360 or 365 days)
B_Q	Basis of calculation for the other currency (360 or 365 days)
b	Constant
C	Financing costs of the spot position, Caplett
CBOE	Chicago Board Option Exchange
CBOT	Chicago Board of Trade
CCW	Covered Call Writing
CDD	Cooling Degree Days
CDO	Collateralized Debt Obligation
CDS	Credit Default Swap
CHF	Swiss Francs
CLN	Credit Linked Notes
CME	Chicago Mercantile Exchange
CMS	Constant Maturity Swap
CoC	Cost of Carry
COV	Covariance
COV_{im}	Covariance
c	Value of the call option
D	Change, Growth rate, Dividend, Derivative
d	Down-factor
d_M	Monthly down-factor
d_1	Z-value of the standard normal distribution
d_2	Z-value of the standard normal distribution
DAX®	German equity index Deutscher Aktien Index

DCM	Direct Clearing Member
DSM	Daily Simulation Method
DTB	German derivatives exchange Deutsche Terminbörse
dt	Growth rate of t
dz	Change in z
E(..)	Expected value
EE(..)	Expected future return
EUR	Euro
EUREX	European Exchange
F	Function, Density, Floorlet
F_0	Futures price
FDAX®	DAX® future
FGBL	Euro Bund future
FESX	Dow Jones Euro STOXX 50 future
FR	Forward rate
FRA	Forward rate agreement
FTSE	Financial Times Stock Exchange Index
Fw	Forward
FX	Foreign exchange
f	Known return
GCM	General clearing member
GTZ	Temperature index
HDD	Heating Degree Days
HICPexT	Harmonized Index of Consumer Prices excluding Tobacco
IRG	Interest rate guarantee
ISDA	International Swaps and Derivatives Association
ITM	In the money
IV	Intrinsic value
IV_{REL}	Realized implied 30-day volatility at maturity
IV_{EXP}	Expected implied 30-day volatility when entering into the transaction
i	Interest rate
JPY	Japanese Yen
K	Strike price, contract volume
L	Storage cost (net)
LEPO	Low Exercise Price Option
LIFFE	London International Financial Futures and Options Exchange
ln	Natural logarithm

M	Market portfolio, index multiplier, time period between payments
n	Number of units, term to maturity of swaption, measured in periods
NCM	Non clearing member
N(d)	Cumulative standard normal distribution
OGBL	Options on EURO BUND FUTURE
OTC	Over the counter
OTM	Out of the money
p	Value of put option
P	Portfolio
PF	Price factor
Present value$_{cum}$	Present value of the bond including termination right
Present value$_{ex}$	Present value of the bond excluding termination right
Q	Conditional probability
q	Pseudo probability
R	Risk-free rate of interest
R_i	Return
R_f	Risk-free rate of interest
r	Congruent rate of interest for term to maturity
r_f	Risk-free rate of interest
r_G	Interest rate per annum in decimal, quoted currency
r_{im}	Correlation coefficient
r_M	Monthly interest rate
r_Q	Interest rate per annum in decimal, other currency
r_1	Foreign interest rate
r_2	Domestic interest rate
RK	Regression coefficient
S	Strike price, Price of underlying, Spot price, Spread, Discount factor of sum, Project value
SOFFEX	Swiss Options and Financial Futures Exchange
S_0	Starting scenario in $t = 0$
S_d	Down scenario
S_u	Up scenario
T	Time, Remaining term to maturity of the option, Number of days, Term to maturity of the contract
T-Bond	Treasury Bond Future, USA
TV	Time value
t	Time before the option starts
USD	US Dollar
U	Up-factor

u_M	Monthly up-factor
VaR	Value at Risk
WERMA	Weather Risk Management Association
X	Arbitrary variable, Strike swap rate
X-Index	Sample index
X/L/V/C-Aktie	Sample shares
x_i	Share of security i in the portfolio
Y	Variable
y	Convenience yield
Z	Payment from the swaption, coupon returns
z	Random variable
Δ	Delta
Γ	Gamma
P	Rho
Θ	Theta
Λ	Vega, Lambda
β	Beta, Beta factor
δ	Term to maturity of the option
η	Random variable that follows a standard normal distribution
μ	Drift, Mean value
μ_p	Expected portfolio return
μ_i	Expected return of security I, expected return
π	Risk premium
σ	Standard deviation
σ^2	Variance
τ	Remaining term to maturity of the contract

List of abbreviations and symbols

We use symbols in this book which are aimed at facilitating the study of this complex material. The symbols have the following meaning:

 Formula or important scientific statement

 Fundamental statement or fundamental insight

 Chapter information

 Examples and explanations concerning the theory discussed

 Applied pointer concerning the theory discussed

 Literature recommendations and literature used

 Reference to the download area

 Reference to the tools from the download area

 Knowledge transfer with regard to topics covered in the book

List of figures

1.1	Setup of a financial engineering unit	5
1.2	Product categories in financial engineering	5
1.3	Structure of the financial engineering process (simplified)	7
1.4	Private placement (here: regulation in Germany)	8
1.5	Classical business cycle including industry investments	11
1.6	Investment clock	11
2.1	Relative frequency	18
2.2	Law of large numbers following Bernoulli	22
2.3	Wiener process and generalized Wiener process (N 204; Delta t = 1/204; Drift 2)	24
2.4	Normal distribution based on Carl Friedrich Gauss (−1 to 1 correspond to 2/3)	26
2.5	Cumulative normal distribution	27
2.6	Example of a random walk	29
2.7	Positive (first chart) and negative (second chart) correlations of securities	31
2.8	Securities that are uncorrelated	32
2.9	Risk of a portfolio consisting of two assets with different correlations (risk of asset 1 = 15 %, risk of asset 2 = 25 %)	32
2.10	Correlation matrix for the different asset classes (as of August 2009)	33
2.11	Beta of BMW relative to the DAX® Index	36
2.12	Empirical histogram of the DAX® Index, November 3, 2008 – October 31, 2009	38
2.13	Estimated log-normal distribution of DAX® Index on the basis of daily data in the period from December 30, 1998 until October 30, 2009	38
2.14	Definition of Value at Risk and downside risk applied to a density function	41
2.15	Steps in the application of VaR	42
2.16	Graphical representation of VaR	43

2.17	Variance of the portfolio return in relation to the number of securities in the portfolio	51
2.18	Structure of an action plan	52
2.19	Minimum variance portfolio	57
2.20	The capital market line	60
2.21	Structure of portfolio management	63
2.22	Portfolio structure based on investor preferences	64
2.23	Development of a causal chain of market reactions	67
4.1	World map showing today's centers of futures trading (shaded areas)	88
4.2	CBOT trading floor during the founding years (top), 1970 (on the left) and 1999 (on the right)	89
4.3	A historical time line of derivatives	90
4.4	Settlement of spot and forward transaction	92
4.5	Conditional and unconditional derivatives contracts	93
4.6	Conditional and unconditional derivatives contracts	94
4.7	Opening (initial order) and close-out (offsetting order)	95
4.8	Setup of a derivatives exchange with integrated clearing	98
4.9	Market participants at a derivatives exchange	100
4.10	Term structures of interest rates	102
4.11	Types of market making	107
4.12	Eurex trading phases	109
4.13	Derivatives, a list of some products traded	110
4.14	Participants in Eurex trading	111
4.15	Different order specifications	113
4.16	Differences in validity of orders	114
4.17	Eurex order mask ("Sell Order" Eurex @X-ceed Trading GUI)	114
4.18	Order tool for foreign exchanges (UBS SwissKey System; Buy Order)	115
4.19	Dealing with a mistrade	116
4.20	Expiration dates at Eurex (Friday rule)	117
5.1	Unconditional derivatives transactions	124
5.2	The most common types of futures	125
5.3	Timeline of a futures transaction	126
5.4	The basic approaches available to a futures investor	126
5.5	Settlement of futures	128
5.6	Product groups at US commodities exchanges (selection)	134

5.7	Futures contract (above) and index (below) (basis convergence)	137
5.8	Basis convergence of spot and futures price prior to the last trading day	137
5.9	Negative or positive cost of carry of the futures price	138
5.10	Price development of Euro-Bund futures for a normal and an inverted term structure of interest rates	139
5.11	Term structures of interest rates	140
5.12	Cheapest to Deliver bonds for Euro-Bund futures	141
5.13	Rollover losses	144
5.14	Graphical representation of a long futures position	145
5.15	Graphical representation of a short futures position	146
5.16	Inter contract spread and intra contract spread	150
5.17	Cash-and-carry vs. reverse cash-and-carry	151
5.18	Pay-off of the overall position: long hedge	152
5.19	Pay-off of the overall position: short hedge	153
6.1	Options - long and short	163
6.2	Rights and obligations in the case of options	164
6.3	European vs. American options	164
6.4	Settlement possibilities	165
6.5	Movement of the share relative to the zero strike option (including dividend increase and payment)	169
6.6	Opening and closing	170
6.7	The time-value function	175
6.8	Graphical representation of a long call (option price)	176
6.9	Factors influencing the price of an option	178
6.10	Volatility relations	180
6.11	Historical 30-day and 250-day volatility of the DAX® index	182
6.12	Representation of the time value of options (call and put)	184
6.13	Representation of delta (long call, short call, long put, short put)	187
6.14	Gamma of long option (above) and short option (below)	189
6.15	Graphical representation of rho	190
6.16	Theta for long options (above) and short options (below)	191
6.17	Illustration of theta	191
6.18	Vega of long options (above) and short options (below)	192
6.19	Illustration of vega	193
6.20	The option price and its derivatives	195
6.21	Black-Scholes model and Eurex live trading	201
6.22	Binomial step in the one period model	203

6.23	Binomial step (basic structure)	204
6.24	First binomial step	204
6.25	Setup of a multiperiod binomial tree including underlying	207
6.26	Volatility smile versus constant volatility	209
6.27	Volatility surface of a typical equity	210
6.28	Quotes of DAX® options at Eurex	213
6.29	Profit and loss scenario for the long call	215
6.30	Profit and loss scenario for the short call (naked call writing)	217
6.31	CCW payoff including profit and loss statement	218
6.32	Profit and loss scenario for the long put	219
6.33	Profit and loss scenario for the short put	220
6.34	Profit and loss scenario for the long straddle	226
6.35	Profit and loss scenario for the short straddle	227
6.36	Profit and loss scenario for the long strangle	229
6.37	Profit and loss scenario for the short strangle	230
6.38	Basic versions of spreads	230
6.39	Debit bull spread (payoff)	231
6.40	Credit bear spread (payoff)	232
6.41	Overview of strategies including market and volatility assessments (basic strategies)	235
6.42	Long butterfly	236
6.43	Short butterfly	237
6.44	Long condor	237
6.45	Short condor	238
6.46	Ratio call spread	238
6.47	Ratio put spread	239
6.48	Long box	240
6.49	Short box	241
6.50	Long risk reversal	242
6.51	Short risk reversal	243
6.52	DAX® (below) versus DAX® volatility (above)	244
7.1	Share of currency pairs in trading (as of 2007)	262
7.2	Foreign exchange quotations	263
7.3	Possible interest rate relations between two currencies	265
7.4	Currency derivatives transactions	268
7.5	Example of a cross rate	268
7.6	Overview EUR/USD future	273
7.7	Termination of a commodity derivatives transaction	274
7.8	Settlement versions and realizations	276

7.9	Product specifications for physical settlement (here: Sugar No. 11)	277
7.10	Commodities used in commodity derivatives transactions (simplified)	278
7.11	Contango and backwardation	282
7.12	Contango (above) and backwardation (below)	282
7.13	The problem of contango in futures positions	284
7.14	Light sweet crude futures with noticeable contango	284
8.1	Cash flows of a long cap including underlying transaction (variable rate loan)	301
8.2	Upper interest rate limit of a cap	302
8.3	The cap is broken down into individual caplets	302
8.4	Floor is broken down into individual floorlets	303
8.5	Swap	306
8.6	Example of a swap	308
8.7	Swap example with a loan as underlying transaction	308
8.8	Payer and receiver in a swap	309
8.9	Swap, fixed versus variable rate	310
8.10	Payment streams of the diesel fuel swap	311
8.11	Payment streams inflation payer swap	316
8.12	Payment streams inflation receiver swap	317
8.13	EUR/TRY swap	320
8.14	EUR/TRY exchange rate	320
8.15	Possible interest payments	321
8.16	Swap including reference rate and corridors	323
8.17	12 month Euribor from 2000 to 2008 including corridors	323
8.18	3 and 12 month Euribor	324
8.19	Payment streams of the swap transaction	325
8.20	The swap parameters	327
8.21	Analysis of the historical exchange rate development	328
8.22	Graphical scenario analysis of the swap over time	329
8.23	Step down swap	330
8.24	Timeline of a swaption	332
8.25	Possibilities for settling swaptions and their implications	336
8.26	Exotic options	338
8.27	Example of the price development of a down-and-out put	339
8.28	Digital versus standard call: payoff at maturity (long call)	341
8.29	Compound options	343
8.30	Schematic representation of the payout structure of a cliquet option	347

9.1	Tier capital on the bank balance sheet	359
9.2	Credit derivative	361
9.3	Payment streams for the buyer and seller of protection	362
9.4	Credit Default Swap	363
9.5	CDS valuation following DVFA	364
9.6	Structure of a CLN with cash settlement	366
9.7	CLN without credit event	367
9.8	CLN with credit event	367
9.9	New issues in Euro (classical) including spreads over CDS	368
9.10	CDS spreads of the individual banks in basis points	369
10.1	Volume and price risk	376
10.2	Distribution of contracts among different possibilities to measure weather	377
10.3	Relationship between temperature and energy consumption	378
10.4	Temperatures and DD values in Berlin, August 2001	380
10.5	Relationship between precipitation and electrical power use	384
10.6	Payoff profile of a call on precipitation	386
10.7	payoff profile of the HDD put	388
10.8	graphical representation of a CDD swap	392
10.9	Payoff profile of an HDD futures contract	394
10.10	Monthly open interest at CME	400
10.11	Contract volume at CME between 2002 and 2007	401
10.12	Overview of participants in the market for weather derivatives	404
12.1	Features of real options	417
12.2	Classification of real options following Ernst/Thümmel (2000)	418
12.3	Steps in the valuation of real options	421
12.4	Possible states of the project values	424
12.5	Possible values of call in t(5)	425
12.6	Possible values of call in t(4)	426
12.7	Option values for Automotive Vision AG	427
13.1	Schematic representation of averaging	440
13.2	Schematic representation of pyramiding	440
13.3	Schematic representation of the extension strategy used in the example (pyramiding)	443
13.4	Preventing an early exercise by rolling	445
13.5	Closing of the original transaction	446

13.6	Opening of a new transaction to continue the original transaction with a different underlying	447
14.1	Derivatives tree	458
14.2	Payoff of a discount certificate	461
14.3	Payoff of a reverse convertible bond (here: equity linked bond) versus direct investment in shares	463
14.4	Pay-off classical bonus certificate	464
14.5	Pay-off capped bonus certificate	464
14.6	Construction of a reverse floater	470
14.7	Construction of a leveraged floater	471
14.8	Payoff call volatility trade	474
14.9	Payoff put volatility trade	475
14.10	Payoff combo versus long underlying	475
14.11	Payoff put spread versus underlying	476
14.12	Payoff conversion versus underlying	477
14.13	Outperformance protective put versus DAX®	478
14.14	Long DAX® versus DAX® with CCW strategy	478
15.1	Organizational setup of a hedge fund	488
15.2	Price development of a convertible bond	491
15.3	Setup of convertible bond arbitrage	492
15.4	Hedge fund strategies	496
15.5	Fund of hedge funds	496
16.1	Differentiating between various operative units	503
16.2	Typical organizational setup with two members of the management board	504
16.3	Typical organizational setup with four members of the management board	505
16.4	Risk controlling	508
16.5	An overview of the different types of margin	512
16.6	Risk based margin calculation for short puts (150) on Deutsche Telekom	515
16.7	SPAN margin calculation for short calls (3) and short puts (2) on Lonmin	515
16.8	EUR/USD futures at CME, Span method	517
16.9	Margin calculation FDAX® at Eurex, risk based method	517
16.10	Margin call	521
17.1	Relationship between bond return and rating	557
17.2	Correlation of individual markets (Date: July 2009)	558

List of tables

2.1	Correlation of international equity markets (2007)	30
2.2	Correlation coefficients – values and interpretation	35
4.1	Triple witching day	96
4.2	A description of different scenarios for fixed income instruments.	102
4.3	Example of an order book (example: futures on DAX® index)	105
5.1	Opening and closing of futures positions	127
5.2	Frequently traded index futures	130
5.3	Basic expectations of futures investors	130
5.4	Maturity structure of different interest rate futures	132
5.5	Basic expectations when trading interest rate futures	132
5.6	Possible currency futures (currency pairs)	133
5.7	Basic expectations when trading single stock futures	135
5.8	State of the market in futures trading	135
5.9	Futures basis	138
5.10	Overview of possible futures series, the example of the DJ EURO STOXX 50® Futures	143
5.11	Spreads	148
5.12	Values of beta	154
6.1	Rights and obligations of options	163
6.2	Possible values of an option	173
6.3	Dividend payments and their influence on the option price	183
6.4	An overview of the influencing parameters	186
6.5	An overview of the Greeks	186
6.6	Signs on call and put delta	188
6.7	Delta values	188
6.8	Summary of the signs of the Greeks	193
6.9	The four basic option strategies	221
6.10	The four basic strategies and expectations	221
6.11	Overview of options on futures	249
6.12	Trading book with additional trades	252
6.13	Possible combinations	253

7.1	Currency futures and their basic intentions	271
7.2	Opening and closing transactions	275
7.3	Relation between spot and futures price	281
8.1	Data sheet on the collar (individual components)	305
8.2	Comparison between forwards and futures	306
8.3	Scenario analysis	331
8.5	The two positions in a swaption	333
8.6	Swaption and the swap position that exists once the option is exercised	334
8.7	Attributes of swaptions	335
8.8	Knock-in/-out options	338
8.9	Overview of Barrier options	340
8.10	Basket option: Prices at closing and at expiration	346
10.1	Relationship between precipitation and electrical power use	384
10.2	Calculation of the net amount	388
10.3	Uses of CDD/HDD Call/Put	390
12.1	Comparison of the value drivers of financial options and real options	420
12.2	Value of the basic instrument and period-specific strike prices	422
13.1	Sample portfolio and expansion with the help of derivatives transactions	450
17.1	Average cumulative rates of default (%) 1970–2006	557

Module I – Fundamentals

1 Financial engineering – business segment with a future

The following chapter covers these issues:

- What is financial engineering?
- What is the organizational structure of financial engineering departments?
- What are the tasks of these departments?

1.1 What is the meaning of financial engineering?

Financial engineering fundamentally refers to the development of new financial solutions. These financial solutions can refer both to credit and to investment products. Existing problems or demands are solved with the help of derivatives, combined products and innovative ideas. Financial engineering is thus an interdisciplinary field which seeks to provide innovative solutions.

Following the problems of the financial market crisis in 2007 and subsequent years, investment banking was fundamentally restructured. Pure investment banks have become rare. Most financial engineering departments of investment banks are thus integrated into banking groups which work interdisciplinary. It is their task to develop "tailor-made solutions" both for their own institution and for third parties. Financial engineering is thus an important revenue driver and a basic business area for investment banks and major institutions alike.

1.2 Setup of a financial engineering unit

Basically all financial engineering units are set up according to the same principle. The related units are put together in three groups, as shown below:

- Front office
- Middle office
- Back office

The front office, also called the sales desk, is responsible for both the creation of new products and their distribution. This is also where the trading team is located. The middle office focuses on organizational approaches related to the development and planning of new products (daily business). The back office is in charge of clearing transactions, controlling, settlement, matching and maintenance of all accounts. All three groups work together closely, like clockwork, while at the same time maintaining clearly separate responsibilities.

In addition to these "traditional" departments, the following units also interact with financial engineering (but are independent):

- Marketing department
    - Customer liaison (sales support, also event management, and so forth)
    - Active marketing (prospectus, advertising, and so forth)
- Legal department
    - Assure legal conformity
- Staff division
    - Settlement, clearing, maintenance of master file data and so forth

1.3 Product desks of a financial engineering unit

Most financial engineering units are organized around product groups. This allows for targeted controlling as well as efficient and implementable risk controlling. Each product group is additionally divided into the areas of structuring, sales, trading, research, overviews and business management (see Figure 1.1).

The breakdown by product category is usually done as shown in Figure 1.2.

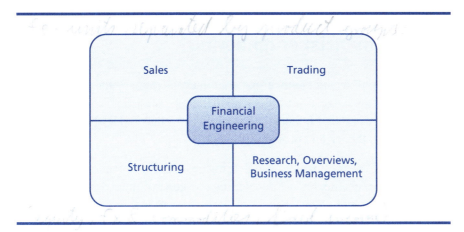

Figure 1.1: Setup of a financial engineering unit

A similar classification also exists for credit products. From time to time, investment products and credit products are combined. Most relevant are mezzanine financing (such as participation certificates, for example), structured finance and syndicated loans (classical syndicated loan, club deal, and so forth) as well as the innovative transfer of credit risks.

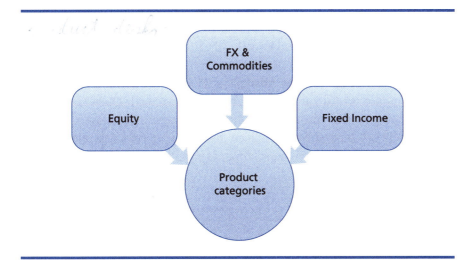

Figure 1.2: Product categories in financial engineering

1.4 Which theories and models are combined in financial engineering?

To begin with, financial engineering is an interdisciplinary field. It draws on specialized knowledge from higher mathematics, statistics, economics and business, the science of financial derivatives as well as model-based theories (such as game theory and probability theory).

The purpose of every financial engineering product is to cover or to represent a certain payoff profile. Before developing this key insight in the course of the book, we first want to take a brief look at the operational process of financial engineering.

> The history of certificates (securitized derivatives) in Germany began in 1989 when Dresdner Bank AG (today Commerzbank AG) issued the first index certificate. It replicated the DAX® Index and thus became the ancestor of all certificates. However, intelligent financial engineering solutions did not really take off until the year 2000. Since then, these customized financial solutions have become a permanent part of financial markets.

1.5 The financial engineering process

A basic idea or a fundamental problem forms the starting point of this process (see Figure 1.3). This could also be called the initial thought[1]. From this initial thought, a payoff diagram is derived which needs to be implemented with the help of derivatives or other financial solutions. In the process, the newly created product is structured and a price is determined. Questions related to costs, margins and resources need to be answered. The next step is the development of a term sheet[2], which contains all important and relevant data of the new product. Thus full transparency is provided. Depending on the kind

---

[1] Initial thought = starting point for every creative process (Creatio ex nihilo = creation out of nothing).
[2] The term sheet is a fundamental instrument of extreme importance. It contains all relevant data on the issue, which are thus available at all times and can be replicated. In many cases, the term sheet is accompanied by a flyer (for sales reasons). An important and required document is the prospectus, which contains extensive information about the offering.

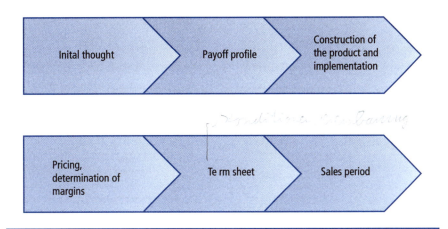

Figure 1.3: Structure of the financial engineering process (simplified)

of product and the target group (retail, wealth management or institutional), it is now handed over to the sales units. The question of target customer (end consumer) of the product is already determined at the beginning of the process.[3] Every new product of a financial engineering unit must pass through this process, often in the context of a new product approval (NPA) procedure. Technical background work required for public placements such as the registration of a security identification number, filing of the securities master data[4] and other tasks are accomplished in parallel. This process is much simpler in the case of a "private placement."

With the creation of a new product, the **financial engineering process** is not yet complete. The financial engineering units are also responsible for after sales support of the products, market making and trading activities (mostly via the trading desk of the same company[5]). The process described above is thus only to be seen as the "**creative process**." The individual units within the financial engineering teams (sales, trading, structuring, etc.) work together on a project and product base and complement each other.

---

[3] The main distinction is made between retail clients and wealth management/institutional investors. Also a distinction between flow product and buy-and-hold product is made. Depending on design, the cost structure of the products varies (among other features, this has to do with the funding of the issuer).
[4] All relevant master data of a security is collected and stored in a database for further processing or as a source of information.
[5] As an alternative, back-to-back trades with external trading desks can be used in cases where internal resources are not available.

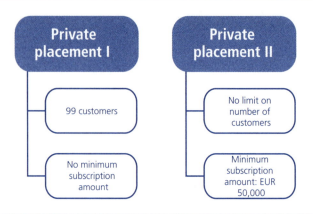

Figure 1.4: Private placement (here: regulation in Germany)

1.6 How to issue the product

There are two major approaches to placing financial engineering products in the market. A distinction is made between a **public offering** on the one hand and a **private placement** (offer that is only available to a select customer group) on the other hand.

1.6.1 Public Offering

In a typical public offering, the securities are made available to a large number of customers. No limits exist concerning customers, subscription volume, etc.

This is the typical and widely used approach when issuing retail products.

1.6.2 Private Placement

For a private placement in Germany,[6] the following conditions must be met (see Figure 1.4):

- The issue may not have more than 99 individual customers.

or

---

[6] This depends on the legal situation in the country where the security is issued.

- The minimum subscription amount cannot be below EUR 50,000. In this case, the number of individuals is not relevant.

Why are these regulations in place? They follow from the premise that the protection of typical retail clients (private customers) must be particularly strong. As a consequence, the requirement to provide them with relevant information is more pronounced than in the case of institutional or major clients. That is why the regulator is limiting the feasibility of private placements.

1.7 Flow products

Products that are not issued via an offering or placement or that are plain vanilla in nature and needed to cover the product range are called classical flow products. These are issued continuously and adjusted in accordance with the market environment. Many of these products are aimed at the classical retail customer segment. As an example, discount certificates are issued continuously and in line with market developments, so that customers can choose from a broad range of certificates.

Following the end of the subscription period and the beginning of classical trading, every product that is initially placed will turn into a flow product. The sole exceptions are products for which no trading is planned (no listing on the stock exchange and no secondary market via the issuer). These are pure private placements.

1.8 Issuers

The question about the appropriate issuer for a securitized product was often raised in connection with the insolvency of Lehman Brothers in 2008. Formally, a certificate is a bearer bond, which, in the case of insolvency, is not backed by separate assets or protected via a deposit guarantee fund.

For this reason, the choice of issuer is of major importance. Basically, the following issuers can be distinguished:

- Governments
- Universal banks
- Investment banks
- Other banks/issuers

Normally, governments issue only bonds and no certificates. This leaves the various types of banks. To get a tangible measure of their credit standing, a look at the ratings and CDS rates of the issuers in comparison to their peers is required. Such an analysis allows a comparison of risks. The same holds for the assessment of counterparty risk among two issuers. It is important to point out in this regard that the choice of issuer constitutes a major value driver of securitized products. This holds both for issuance[7] and secondary markets.

1.9 Which product and when?

This is one of the most decisive questions in the business with new product solutions. A new issue only makes sense when the timing seems right, conditions are favorable and the market environment is stable. Only in the case of plain vanilla products, which are issued continuously, does the issue of timing not play a role (for example in the case of discount certificates or equity-linked bonds). However, products with a specific background, such as an inflation-linked bond, are dependent on the market environment. For these products, the introductory question is relevant.

But how to determine what is favorable? Normally, this is revealed by market demand. Relevant are thus the expectations of market participants. Let us consider the example of an inflation-linked bond. It pays interest according to actual inflation multiplied by a fixed factor (150% for example). It is not very useful to structure such an instrument when declining or steady inflation rates are expected. The market expectation must be an increase in inflation (during the life-span of the product). This is the only case when the coupon payment meets the range of expectations of the investor (inflation multiplied by 150%)[8].

An additional focus should be on the business cycle. With the help of the following two figures (Figures 1.5 and 1.6), it can easily be seen how different industries and investment opportunities should be utilized, depending on the scenario for the economic outlook.

---

[7] This is captured by the "funding spread." Major issuers regularly publish funding tables that list premiums which are influenced by maturity, face value and possibly termination rights.

[8] In general, investors can achieve more favorable multiples if their expectations deviate from market expectations (as captured in forwards, implied volatility levels and correlations).

Which product and when?

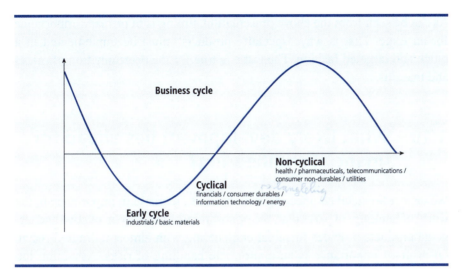

Figure 1.5: Classical business cycle including industry investments

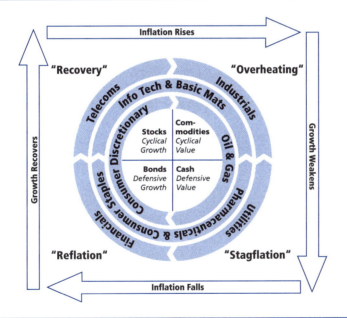

Figure 1.6: Investment clock[9]

---

[9] Source: Merrill Lynch.

As can be seen from the above presentation, timing is of primary importance for an issue. That is why "specialty products" must be implemented in a quick and targeted fashion. The same is true for the determination of prices and margins.

1.10 What likely development lies ahead for financial engineering?

We expect financial engineering to continue to increase in importance in the world of banking. In particular, the opportunity to develop innovative and targeted products provides financial engineering with almost unlimited reach. Of primary importance is an appropriate handling of risks. Assuming too much risk, setting up strategies that are too complex and the combination of complex individual holdings into a new overall position are not only approaches that are devoid of meaning, but also excessively risky. Especially in light of the financial crisis, such strategies will no longer be pursued. At the same time, clean and clearly structured financial engineering continues to be of major relevance and will be able to further enhance its standing.

Literature for this chapter

Hull, John: Options, Futures and Other Derivatives, 7th edition, 2009

Questions and answers on this chapter

Question 1:
Why is financial engineering of such importance for major institutions and investment banks alike?

Question 2:
What is the structure of the financial engineering process?

Question 3:
Why is the approach considered to be interdisciplinary?

Question 4:
What types of offerings exist?

Question 5:
Which product desks are needed in a classical financial engineering unit?

Answer to question 1:
Financial engineering units are innovative departments. Here new products and solutions for problems are created. The revenue share (from internal margin, normal margin and trading result) is an important revenue driver for the entire group.

Answer to question 2:
The process of financial engineering is broken down into several steps. Among these, initial thought, structuring, valuation, sales and after-sales are the most important distinguishing features.

Answer to question 3:
The approach is considered to be interdisciplinary because many aspects of mathematics, statistics, natural sciences, international finance, classical banking and others are combined in financial engineering.

Answer to question 4:
A distinction is made between public offering and private placement. The hurdles for approval are higher for a public offering. In the case of a private placement, either the minimum subscription amount must be EUR 50,000 or above or the maximum number of clients of the product is 99.

Answer to question 5:
The classical product desks are: equity, commodity and fixed income.

2 | Review of the methodological foundations of financial engineering

The following chapter covers these issues:

- Which mathematical basics are required in financial engineering?
- Decision theory – what is it about?
- What are the insights from game theory?
- What are the findings of portfolio theory?
- Why are portfolios formed?
- Which types of models exist?

Financial engineering is based on solid knowledge of mathematics and stochastics. This chapter is structured as a review and explains the methodological foundations needed by a financial engineer.

2.1 Foundations of probability theory

Stochastics is a branch of mathematics that developed in the 20th century when statistics[1] and probability calculus[2] were combined. Probability is interpreted as the relative frequency of an event. The term probability is thus closely linked to the notion of relative frequency and oftentimes the two terms are used as synonyms. Strictly speaking, however, probability has a different meaning than relative frequency. In some sense, it idealizes it. In Figure 2.1, we take a brief look at this issue.

---

[1] Data science.
[2] Description and modeling of random events.

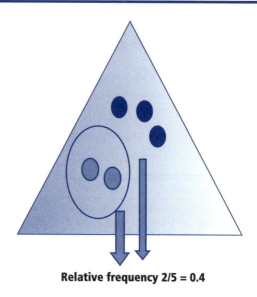

Relative frequency 2/5 = 0.4

Figure 2.1: Relative frequency

 We will deal with stochastic processes again in Chapters 6.14 and 6.15 when pricing options.

2.1.1 Laplace probability

Pierre-Simon Laplace
1749–1827
French mathematician
and astronomer

To derive a **Laplace probability**[3], also called **classical probability**, a random experiment is conducted, that has a finite number of outcomes "with apparently equal probability." In this case, the probability **q** for the event **E** is defined as follows:

$$q(E) = \frac{\text{(Number of outcomes favorable for E)}}{\text{(Number of possible outcomes)}}$$

Typical examples are rolling a die with the possible outcomes 1, 2, 3, 4, 5, 6 or tossing a coin with the outcomes heads or tails. In these cases, the

---

[3] Pierre-Simon Laplace 1749–1827.

probabilities are equal to the expected relative frequency. This presupposes unbiasedness. The computation assumes a fair die or coin, even though these objects may have slightly different probabilities in reality. As we see, there must also be another notion of probability. Even if a coin is not fair, one may be led to believe that a probability for "heads" does exist. For this, we use the frequentist approach to probability.[4]

2.1.2 Frequentist probability

When a "good" or fair coin is tossed very often, it seems that the relative frequency of "heads" converges towards 0.5. When a "bad" coin is tossed, the relative frequency appears to converge towards a different number. While this number is of course unknown, its existance can be assumed. This number is called probability of the event "heads." Once the coin has been tossed repeatedly, this value can be stated.

2.1.3 Subjective probability

In the case of **subjective probabilities**, an assumption is derived from a piece of information, which is used to form an opinion. Here, the term probability is influenced by personal "attitudes." An example would be the outcome of an election or the possible formation of a coalition. Repeatedly, all three definitions of probability are used jointly.

Let us start from the assumption of a federally regulated casino. Many gamblers will hold the subjective opinion that they can expect Laplace or classical probabilities at the roulette table. Once EUR 500,000 has been lost, this belief may give way to skepticism, and an investigation may be demanded. For this, frequentist probabilities would be used.

2.1.4 Conditional probability

The case of **conditional probabilities**[5] deals with the occurrence of a particular event, which is tied to a specific condition. Given the occurrence of Event **B**, the probability of Event **A** will thus be given. Typical examples

---

[4] Source: Prof. Dr. Bernd Hafenbrak.
[5] See: Bayes' theorem – the computation of conditional probabilities, named after Thomas Bayes, 1702–1761.

are found in automotive insurance. The vehicle brand, cylinder capacity and mileage per annum must be provided. Other variables such as the age of the driver, address, use of a garage, home ownership are also requested. They all influence the probability, and thus the amount of the insurance premium.

The conditional probability (q) can be derived for random events **A** and **B** and for $q(B) > 0$ as follows:

$$q(A|B) = \frac{q(A \cap B)}{q(B)}$$

$q(A \cap B)$ is called the joint probability. It refers to the probability that **A** and **B** occur jointly. The joint probability is occasionally referred to as $q(A, B)$.

Rewriting leads to

$$q(A \cap B) = q(A|B)q(B) = q(B|A)q(A).$$

In the case where **A** and **B** are stochastically independent, it holds that

$$q(A \cap B) = q(A)q(B) \Rightarrow q(A|B) = \frac{q(A)q(B)}{q(B)} = q(A).$$

If only the joint probability and the probability of the given event are known, the total probability of **A** can be stated as follows:

$$q(A) = q(A|B)q(B) + q(A|\bar{B})q(\bar{B})$$

where $\bar{B}$ denotes the complement of **B**.

The above case deals with two outcomes. If instead the multivariate case with **n** random outcomes $A_1, A_2, \ldots, A_n$ is considered, the generalization of the above expression for two occurrences leads to the general rule of multiplication of probabilities:

$$\begin{aligned}
& q(A_1 \cap A_2 \cap \ldots \cap A_n) \\
&= q(A_1) \cdot \frac{q(A_1 \cap A_2)}{q(A_1)} \cdot \frac{q(A_1 \cap A_2 \cap A_3)}{q(A_1 \cap A_2)} \cdot \ldots \cdot \frac{q(A_1 \cap \ldots \cap A_n)}{q(A_1 \cap \ldots \cap A_{n-1})} \\
&= q(A_1) \cdot q(A_2|A_1) \cdot q(A_3|A_1 \cap A_2) \cdot \ldots \cdot q(A_n|A_1 \cap \ldots \cap A_{n-1})
\end{aligned}$$

We are assuming two random variables **X** and **Y** with joint density $f_{X,Y}$.

The density f_Y of Y is given as:

$$f_y(y) = \int f_{X,Y}(x,y)dx.$$

In the case where $f_Y(y) > 0$, a joint density $f_{X|Y}$ of X, given $y = y_0$, can be defined:

$$f_{X|Y(x,y_0)} = \frac{f_{X,Y}(x,y_0)}{f_Y(y_0)}.$$

A density for X can be derived as follows:

$$f_X(x) = \int f_{X,Y}(y,y)dy = \int f_Y(y_0)f_{X|Y}(x,y_0)dy_0.$$

With this version of the law of total probabilities, the density f_X can be determined independently of Y from the joint density $f_{X,Y}$ with the help of integration over y.

It is important to keep in mind that densities which lead to the same values of integrals also represent the same probability distributions. A density thus cannot be uniquely determined. A permissible choice for $f_{X,Y}$, f_X and f_Y is every measurable function which provides within the integral the correct probability for $q(X \in A, Y \in B), q(X \in A), q(Y \in B)$, respectively for any A, B. The function $f_{X|Y}$ must satisfy the condition

$$q(X \in A, Y \in B) = \int_B f_Y(y) \int_A f_{X|Y}(x,y) dx\, dy$$

Thus the appropriate choice of densities in the formulas presented above is of great relevance.[6]

The expected value is the probability-weighted average of all possible realizations of the random variable.

Law of large numbers (following Jakob I. Bernoulli)

When a random experiment is repeated (independently and) indefinitely, the probability increases, that the arithmetic mean of the realization equals the expected value.

---

[6] Source: Internet.

Jakob I. Bernoulli
1655–1705
Jakob I. Bernoulli is a member of the Bernoulli family, a highly respected family of scientists and artists.

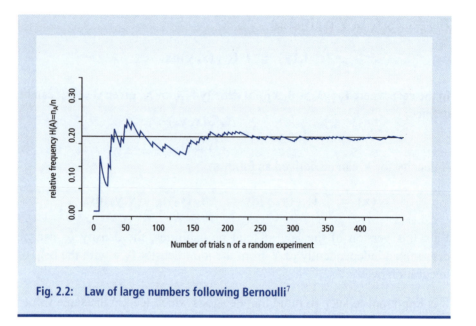

Fig. 2.2: Law of large numbers following Bernoulli[7]

In the **Black-Scholes model**[8] (Chapter 6.14) it is assumed that the underlying asset moves according to a stochastic process of the **Wiener** type. A **Wiener process** is a special case of the **Markov process**.

We will revisit the issue of probabilities repeatedly in the course of the book, especially in Chapters 6.14, 6.15, 6.17, 8.1.4.4, 8.1.5.1.2, 1.1.1.1, 9.5 and 12.4. We will make use of these principles every time we develop a strategy or value a derivative position.

---

[7] Source: Jörg Groß.
[8] Black-Scholes model for the valuation of European options. We will take a more detailed look at the model in the course of the book.

2.2 Stochastic processes

2.2.1 Markov process

In a **Markov process**, the realization of a random variable at a point in time is dependent only on the realization of the random variable in the previous period, but not on realizations in earlier periods. The process thus has no memory[9] and therefore is a requirement for a random walk. It follows for the differences between periods (and thus also for growth rates and rates of return) that they are stochastically independent.

Andrej Andreevič Markov[8]
1856–1922
Russian mathematician

2.2.1.1 Wiener process

The **Wiener process**[11] is a special case of a Markov process, which has the following definition:

$$dz = \eta \sqrt{dt}$$

where:

$$\eta \sim NV(0, 1).$$

z is a random variable and **dz** the change in the random variable during an infinitesimally small time interval. η is a random variable that follows a standard normal distribution. The expected value of **dz** is thus its starting value, in this case **0**. The standard deviation of **dz** is growing over time **t** at the rate of $\sigma\sqrt{dt}$, while the variance is growing at the rate of **t**.

Time and the realizations of the random variable **z** are continuous.

2.2.1.2 Generalized Wiener process

A **generalized Wiener process** for any variable **x** is defined as follows:

$$dx = a\,dt + b\,dz = a\,dt + b\eta\sqrt{dt}$$

where:

$$\eta \sim NV(0, 1)$$

a and **b** are constants.

Norbert Wiener
1894–1964
US mathematician

---

[9] Economically, this assumption can be supported by efficient markets.
[10] Sometimes also Markow. In the original: Андрей Андреевич Марков.
[11] Also known as Brownian motion.

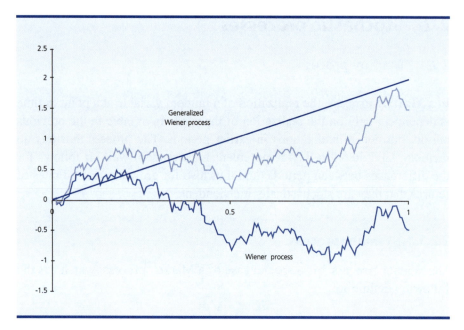

Figure 2.3: Wiener process and generalized Wiener process (N 204; Delta t = 1/204; Drift 2)[12]

dz = rate of change of variable z
dt = growth rate of "time"
η = random variable with a standard normal distribution

When the expected value of **dx** is formed, the second term on the right-hand side is equal to zero. Expected growth is thus driven by the first term alone:

$$dx = a\,dt$$

It therefore follows:

$$\frac{dx}{dt} = a$$

For **x**, the following expression holds:

$$x = x_0 + at (= E(X_t))$$

Consequently, growth of **x** is linear over time.

The second term in the definition of the generalized Wiener process represents the uncertainty with regard to the realization of the random variable. The

---

[12] Source: Thomas Steiner.

expected value of this term is zero and growth of its variance is linear over time.

2.2.2 Itō process

Lifting the assumption of constant parameters **a** and **b** gives rise to the **Itō process**. The generalized Wiener process is thus a specific case in the family of Itō processes, which are defined as follows:

Itō Kiyoshi[13]
1915–2008
Japanese mathematician

$$dx = a(x,t)dt + b(x,t)dz = a(x,t)dt + b(x,t)\eta\sqrt{dt}$$

where:
$$\eta \sim NV(0,1)$$

a and **b** = not constant
dz = rate of change of variable z
dt = growth rate of "time"
η = random variable with a standard normal distribution

Both variance and drift rate can change over time.

In the **Black-Scholes model**, an Itō process (geometric Brownian motion) with parameters that are linear with regard to the process **S**, but independent of time, is assumed for the underlying **S**:

$$dS = \mu S\,dt + \sigma S\,dz = \mu S\,dt + \sigma S\,\eta\sqrt{dt}$$

where:
$$\eta \sim NV(0,1)$$

S = underlying
dz = rate of change of variable z
dt = growth rate of "time"
η = random variable with a standard normal distribution

The **Black-Scholes model** was developed primarily for the valuation of stock options. If a **Wiener process** with constant parameters is assumed, a key aspect of equity trading is neglected: when an investor purchases stocks (or other assets), his expected growth rate is independent of the amount invested, since he is a price taker. In light of this, the geometrical Brownian motion is used for modeling, since it explicitly depends on the underlying.

---

[13] In Japanese: 伊藤 清.

> The basics discussed will be applied when valuing options. This is discussed in detail in Chapter 6. Chapter 6.14 in particular deals with the Black-Scholes model.

2.2.3 The normal distribution

An important probability distribution is the **normal distribution**. Its occurrence is so frequent, that it can be considered "normal." The explanation for the frequent occurrence is the central limit theorem. It states that the sums of random variables are approximately normally distributed ($\eta \to \infty$), regardless of the distribution of the added random variables. The normal distribution is a **continuous distribution**. Its realizations are real numbers.

Carl Friedrich Gauss
1777–1855
German mathematician,
astronomer, physicist
and geometer

The probability distribution in turn is characterized by a **density function**. The density function of the normal distribution is bell shaped and named after CARL FRIEDRICH GAUSS (see Figure 2.4). The normal distribution is characterized with the help of its expected value and its **standard deviation**. The density function with $\mu = 0$ and $\sigma = 1$ is called **standard normal distribution**.

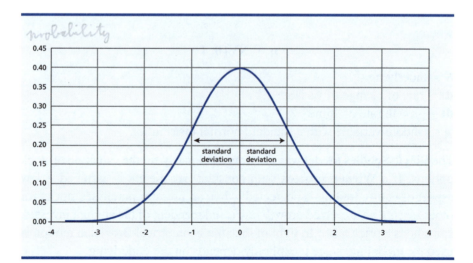

Figure 2.4: Normal distribution based on Carl Friedrich Gauss (-1 to 1 correspond to 2/3)

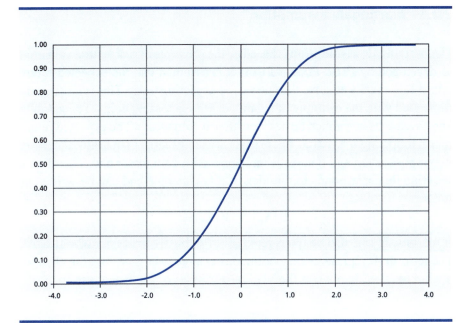

Figure 2.5: Cumulative normal distribution

A random variable with a normal distribution takes on with a probability of **0.6827** $\sim 2/3$ a realization within a **sigma range** between $\mu - \sigma$ and $\mu + \sigma$. In case of the standard normal distribution, therefore, about 2/3 of all realizations fall between -1 and $+1$ (see Figure 2.4). Generally, it can be stated for a normally distributed random variable $\tilde{x}$, that the probability of realizing a value between two numbers x_1 and x_2, $q(x_1 < \tilde{x} \leq x_2)$, is given by the area between x_1 and x_2 below the density function[14]. Formally, this refers to the integral of the density function within the two boundaries x_1 and x_2. $N_{(x)}$ states the probability that a random variable with a standard normal distribution, $\tilde{x}$ ($\mu = 0, \sigma = 1$), takes on a value of less than or equal to x. The function $N(x)$ is also called cumulative normal distribution. A table with the values of the **standard normal distribution** can be found in the appendix to this book.

---

[14] See Spremann (2007).

2.2.4 Martingale assumption

Paul Pierre Lévy
1886–1971
French mathematician.
Coined the term
martingale assumption

The **martingale assumption** is based on the principle of risk neutral valuation as developed by PAUL PIERRE LÉVY. It is assumed that the expected future return **R** is exactly equal to the one we are expecting today. This is most easily illustrated with the example of a gambler who is tossing coins. The gambler knows exactly, how much he has won after **n** coin tosses. The expected future return following **n+1, 2, 3, 4 ....** trials is exactly equal to the value currently in our possession and ignores what happened **n** coin tosses ago. Therefore a **martingale** corresponds to the idea of a fair gamble and can be written as follows:

$$R[X_n] = R[X_{n+1}]$$

A martingale can also be interpreted as a **stochastic process without drift**. The term **drift** represents the continuous change over time. But the changes are not required to possess the Markov attributes or a constant variance.

2.2.5 Random walk

The main idea of the **random walk** can most easily be illustrated with the help of a Galton board[15]. A ball is dropped in the middle of the upper end of the board. From this starting point, the ball always has an equal probability of bouncing to the right or the left. The ball thus has a number of different paths, which all lead to the lower end of the board. The ball will end up more frequently in the middle of the board than on the outside. This has to do with the fact that more paths are available for an exit in the middle, which thus becomes more likely than an exit on the outside. Increasing the number of trials $n \to \infty$, the standard normal distribution is obtained (see Figure 2.4).

A random walk is a discrete stochastic process based on Markov assumptions as previously discussed. It is assumed that the simulated price changes in very small time increments dt by $\emptyset(\mu dt, \sigma\sqrt{dt})$. In order to get to a model for a random walk (see Figure 2.6), it is now assumed that the returns of an asset follow the density function of the normal distribution. It can thus be assumed that the return R_i is composed of the drift μ, the standard deviation σ and a normally distributed random variable z. μ and σ are constant and not equal

---

[15] Following Francis Galton. A mechanical model used to illustrate the binomial distribution.

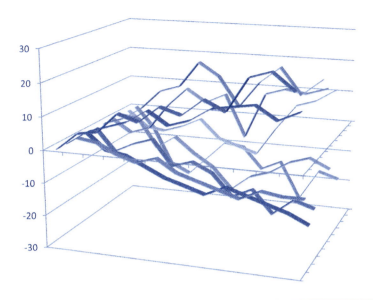

Figure 2.6: Example of a random walk

to zero. Thus the formula reads as follows:

$$R_i = \frac{S_{i+1} - S_i}{S_i} = \mu + \sigma \cdot z$$

R_i = return
μ = drift
σ = standard deviation
z = normally distributed random variable

If we now assume that these returns are happening in very small time increments **dt**, it follows:

Drift $= \mu \, dt$
Standard deviation $= \sigma \sqrt{dt}$

> The models discussed above are required when pricing options and play a large role in this regard. More details about the pricing of options can be found in Chapters 6.14 and 6.15 of this book.

2.3 Correlation analysis

2.3.1 Correlation

Correlation describes the relationship between two or more variables. Even if two series are found to be correlated, it is not clear whether there is a causal relationship between the two, whether both are caused by a third variable or whether a causal relationship exists at all. Furthermore, a strictly non-linear relationship cannot be described with the help of correlations.

A **positive correlation** (see Figure 2.7) is found in cases where an increase in one variable leads to an increase in the other variable. This can be illustrated with reference to the following example: the more fertilizer and water is used on a lawn, the better the grass grows. Frequently correlations are used in order to get an indication whether two statistical series share a common development. This works particularly well in cases where the two variables are tied together via a classical causal relationship, for example an "if ... then" relationship where one variable is only determined by the other one.

The term correlation is of primary importance concerning the overall risk of an investment position. The lower the correlations of the individual holdings are, the lower is the overall risk of the position.

Table 2.1: Correlation of international equity markets (2007)[16]

	US	UK	JP	FR	CH	DE	NL	KA	AU	IT
United States	1.00									
United Kingdom	0.86	1.00								
Japan	0.63	0.62	1.00							
France	0.78	0.82	0.58	1.00						
Switzerland	0.67	0.71	0.50	0.75	1.00					
Germany	0.79	0.78	0.48	0.88	0.70	1.00				
Netherlands	0.78	0.84	0.58	0.87	0.80	0.88	1.00			
Canada	0.87	0.78	0.63	0.78	0.63	0.75	0.74	1.00		
Australia	0.75	0.73	0.70	0.67	0.56	0.69	0.68	0.77	1.00	
Italy	0.66	0.67	0.46	0.78	0.60	0.72	0.74	0.61	0.61	1.00

---

[16] Source: Prof. Herbst, Frankfurt School of Finance and Management, Frankfurt.

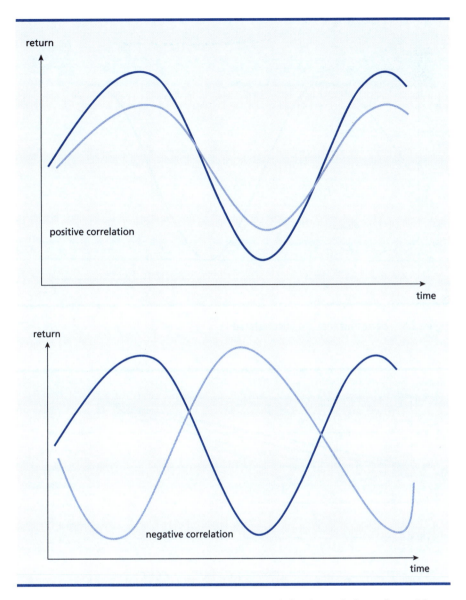

Figure 2.7: Positive (first chart) and negative (second chart) correlations of securities

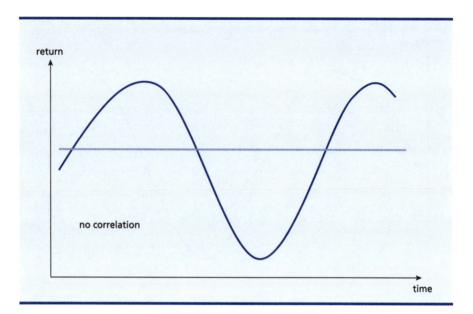

Figure 2.8: Securities that are uncorrelated

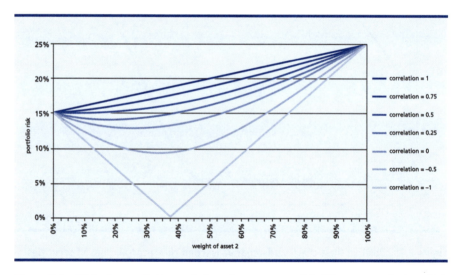

Figure 2.9: Risk of a portfolio consisting of two assets with different correlations (risk of asset 1 = 15 %, risk of asset 2 = 25 %)[17]

---

[17] see Bloss, Ernst, Häcker, Haas, Prexl, Röck: Financial Modeling.

Correlation analysis

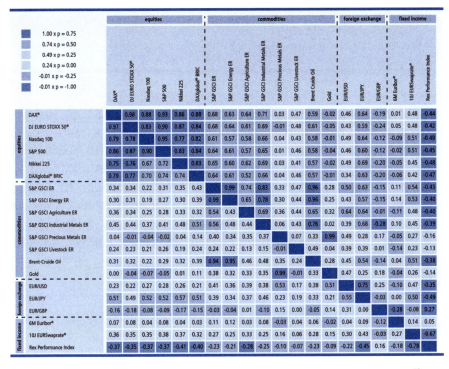

Figure 2.10: Correlation matrix for the different asset classes (as of August 2009)[18]

The correlation among different assets is an important aspect of financial engineering. This topic will be revisited both in the section on hedging of positions and when constructing securitized derivatives (certificates). In particular, Chapters 6.19, 6.20, 6.21, 13 and 15.7 deal with this issue.

2.3.2 Variance, covariance and correlation coefficients

Variance is a statistical measure of **dispersion** of a random variable. Variance is calculated by measuring the distance from the mean of all observations, squaring these values, adding them up and dividing them by the number of observations. In practice the variance of the population is often unknown. It must then be estimated, for example by computing the sample variance.

---

[18] Source: Goldman-Sachs, Bloomberg; left triangle: 5-year correlations, right triangle: 1-year correlations (based on weekly returns).

> Variance measures the dispersion around the mean. It is the sum of squared deviations from the mean, divided by the number of observations.

In statistics, **covariance** measures the relationship, or association, between two statistical series. Covariance will be positive, whenever **X** and **Y** tend to move in the same direction, meaning that large values of **X** will go with large values of **Y** and small values of **X** with small values of **Y**. Covariance will be negative whenever **X** and **Y** tend to move in opposite directions. This means that large values of one random variable go with small values of another variable. When the result is 0, no relationship exists or the relationship is non-linear. An example is a U-shaped relationship between the two variables **X** and **Y**.

> Covariance measures the degree of parallel movement of two series relative to their respective means.

While covariance makes a statement about the direction of the relationship between two variables, nothing is said about the strength of this association. This is due to the fact that the result is dependent on the units of measurement of the variables **X** and **Y**. To spell out interactions more clearly, covariance can be scaled to arrive at the correlation coefficient, which takes on values between −1 and +1. A value of +1 in this context can be interpreted as a complete positive relationship and co-movement. No relationship exists for a value of 0 and −1 means that we can expect a completely contrarian movement.

As already discussed above, scaling of the covariance leads to the **correlation coefficient** of *Bravais* and *Pearson*, which states the strength of the relationship (see Table 2.2). Positive values are indicative of co-movement and negative values of an opposing linear relationship.

Karl Pearson
1857–1936
British mathematician

$$\rho_{im} = \frac{COV_{im}}{\sigma_i \cdot \sigma_m}$$

ρ_{im} = correlation coefficient
COV_{im} = covariance
σ_i = standard deviation **i**

Statistical concepts of security analysis

Table 2.2: Correlation coefficients – values and interpretation

Value	Interpretation
$\rho = +1$	Complete positive relationship and co-movement
$\rho = 0$	No relationship
$\rho = -1$	Completely opposing development

The **correlation coefficient** is a non-dimensional, scaled measure that is restricted to the value range from -1 to $+1$. Positive values indicate a concurrent (correlated) relationship and negative values an opposing (uncorrelated) linear relationship. The relationship is stronger, the closer the correlation coefficient is to the value 1. The closer the correlation coefficient is to zero, the weaker is the relationship.

2.4 Statistical concepts of security analysis

2.4.1 Calculation of the beta factor

The **beta factor** of a security **i** (or a portfolio) with regard to an efficient market portfolio **M** is defined as:

$$\text{Beta factor} = \frac{\text{COV}(r_i, r_M)}{\text{VAR}(r_M)}$$

which is equivalent to

$$\beta = \frac{\sigma_{iM}}{\sigma_M^2} = \rho_{im} \frac{\sigma_i}{\sigma_M}.$$

Figure 2.11 displays the beta of BMW shares relative to the DAX® Index. For the period from September 2007 to September 2009, a beta of 1.053 is recorded. The standard error of the beta of 0.088 implies that beta falls between 0.965 and 1.141 with a probability of approximately 2/3 (see Chapter 2.2.3). The standard error of 0.088 is first subtracted from the estimate of beta to arrive at the lower bound and then added to the estimate of beta to determine the upper bound. In applied work, the raw beta is used (1.053 in this case). Bloomberg in addition provides a value for the adjusted beta. It is

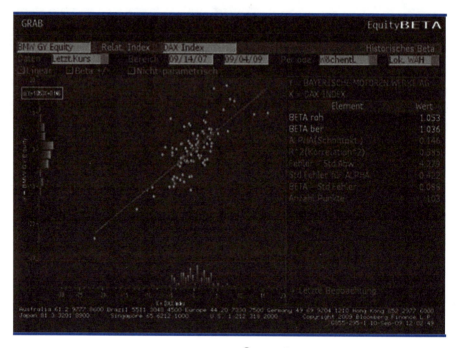

Figure 2.11: Beta of BMW relative to the DAX® Index[19]

calculated as follows: 2/3 · raw beta + 1/3. In the case of BMW, we obtain 2/3 · 1.053 + 1/3 = 1.036.

β > 1 means: the security shows larger fluctuations than the market.

β = 1 means: the security fluctuates in line with the market.

β < 1 means: the security shows smaller fluctuations than the market.

The factors discussed, namely variance, covariance, correlation coefficient, and beta are of primary importance for financial engineering. In this book, we will particularly focus on this aspect with regard to strategy development. The knowledge presented above will be needed particularly for the topics covered in Chapters 8 and 13.

---

[19] Source: Bloomberg.

2.4.2 Log-normal distribution of equity prices

Black, Scholes and Merton assume in their model that equity prices follow a **log-normal distribution**. This characteristic follows from the assumption of a geometrical Brownian motion discussed earlier.

The following is assumed:

μ: expected return of a share
σ: volatility of the share price return
S: starting value of the underlying

It holds that:

$$\frac{dS}{S} \sim \emptyset(\mu dt; \sigma^2 dt)$$

dS is the change in the share price S during the time interval dt and $\phi(\mu, \sigma^2)$ is a normal distribution with mean μ and variance σ^2.

The following can be derived from this model with the help of Itō's lemma:

$$\ln S_T - \ln S_0 \sim \emptyset\left[\left(\mu - \frac{\sigma^2}{2}\right)T; \sigma^2 T\right]$$

It follows that:

$$\ln \frac{S_T}{S_0} \sim \emptyset\left[\left(\mu - \frac{\sigma^2}{2}\right)T; \sigma^2 T\right]$$

and

$$\ln S_T \sim \left[\ln S_0 + \left(\mu - \frac{\sigma^2}{2}\right)T; \sigma^2 T\right]$$

with S_T representing the share price at a future date T and S_0 representing the share price at time 0. The equation shows that $\ln S_T$ follows a normal distribution and thus S_T follows a log-normal distribution. The mean of $\ln S_T$ consequently is equal to $\ln S_0 + (\mu - \sigma^2/2)T$; the standard deviation is $\sigma\sqrt{T}$.

A variable with a log-normal distribution can thus take on values between zero and positive infinity. Negative values are not possible, which is appropriate for the modeling of several asset classes (among them equities). Unlike the normal distribution, the log-normal distribution is **asymmetric**; mean, median and mode are not identical.

The log-normal distribution of equity prices can be ascertained with the help of a probability distribution with continuous compounding between time zero and time T (realized returns). In contrast to the distribution of the absolute values (log-normal distribution), equity returns follow a normal distribution

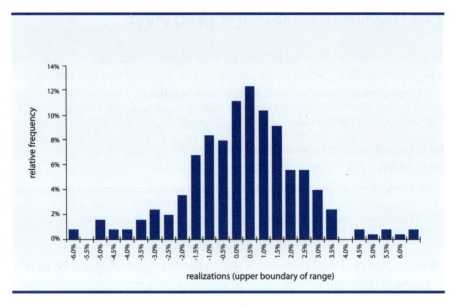

Figure 2.12: Empirical histogram of the DAX® Index, November 3, 2008 – October 31, 2009

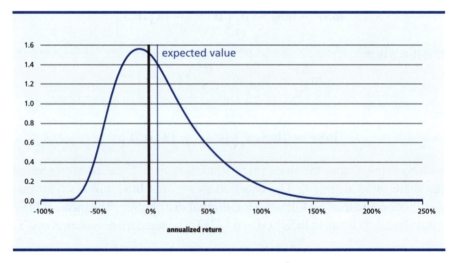

Figure 2.13: Estimated log-normal distribution of DAX®Index on the basis of daily data in the period from December 30, 1998 until October 30, 2009[20]

and can thus also take on negative values. This also is a welcome aspect when it comes to modeling equity prices. Figure 2.12 shows the log-returns of the DAX® Index, and Figure 2.13 shows the estimated log-normal distribution of the DAX® Index.

---

[20] See Bloss, Ernst, Häcker, Haas, Prexl, Röck: Financial Modeling, Stuttgart 2010.

> The log-normal distribution of equity prices is one of the basic assumptions of the model of Black, Scholes and Merton, which we will discuss in Chapter 6.14.

2.4.3 Valuation using replication

Replication is the synthetic derivation of a portfolio with the same cash flows as the instrument to be valued. The requirement of identical cash flows for the replicating portfolio and the instrument to be valued assures that portfolio and security have an identical market value at all times, assuming that the no-arbitrage condition[21] holds. To replicate any security, the possibility of short sales of shares must exist and lending and borrowing must be possible at the same riskless rate. Also the maturities of derivative and portfolio must be identical.

A basic difference is made between **static replication** and **dynamic replication**. In the case of a static replication, adjustments are made only when a change occurs in the instrument to be replicated. A typical example is the valuation of an index. A change is made only in the case of an index adjustment. This is different in the case of options. Here a dynamic trading strategy is required for the duplication, since the relationship between the option price and the price of other securities is not linear. This leads to the requirement of constant portfolio adjustment, so that it replicates the price movement of the derivative at each point in time. Dynamic replication usually relies on parameters such as **delta**, **gamma** and **vega**. They will be explained in depth in Chapter 6 of this book. These parameters are calculated both for the derivative to be duplicated and the individual securities in the portfolio. In the following, the portfolio is adjusted in a way that the individual parameters of the derivative and the portfolio resemble each other. Since the parameters change over time, constant portfolio adjustment is required.

Original underlying	Replication portfolio
x payments on y days in v years	x payments on y days in v years
Original	Synthetic replication of the original underlying with the same profile of cash flows

---

[21] The no-arbitrage assumption is a fundamental tenet of modern financial mathematics. Arbitrage makes use of different prices for an identical good in different markets.

Replication will be used again when valuing derivatives. Particularly in Chapters 6.14, 6.15, 8.1.4.4, 8.1.5.1.2 we will revisit the issue.

2.5 Value at Risk

The risk measure **Value at Risk (VaR)** provides a threshold value for the losses on a risky holding (such as a portfolios of securities) which will not be exceeded with a given probability over a given time horizon[22].

Value at Risk (VaR) is a measure of potential loss, expressed as a sum of money, over a given time horizon and a given confidence level.

But how to determine Value at Risk? The individual risks of an investment object are first identified and then examined with the help of a risk analysis and assessment. The data from the exposure evaluation provides the basis for this exercise for risk managers. This **exposure** is mapped with the constantly changing market factors. The resulting **market price risk** can be interpreted as the possible loss which results from uncertainty concerning the future development of market factors. Deviations of a particular target value from a reference value constitute a downside risk. It is the aim of risk management to quantify this market price risk. For this purpose, Value at Risk (VaR) was established as a quantitative measure in the recent past, especially in the Anglo-American region. VaR was developed in the early 1990s in reaction to a number of financial disasters as a method to measure market risk. Meanwhile it is also utilized to actively control for credit and liquidity risk as well as operative risks as part of financial risks. VaR is defined as the magnitude of a loss which, with a certain probability (for example 95% or 99%) and within a specified time horizon (for example a trading day or a month), will not be exceeded (see Figure 2.14). Risk is thus directly quantified – and as a result may be more easily understood by a lay person – with reference to a monetary value.

---

[22] VaR was developed by J.P. Morgan and is considered to be a standard risk measure.

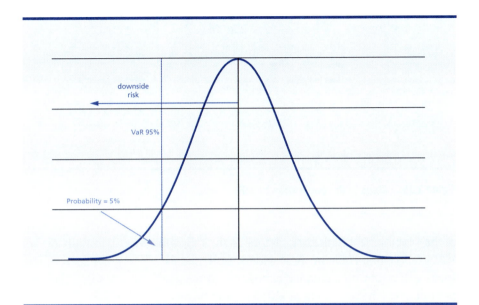

Figure 2.14: Definition of Value at Risk and downside risk applied to a density function[23]

With the help of statistical methods and based on the variability of pre-specified risk factors, the probability of not exceeding this loss is determined. Therefore Value at Risk can also be classified as belonging to the family of **lower partial moments**. The aim of this concept is to integrate all risk factors such as fluctuations in share prices, interest rates and exchange rates into one prominent and easily understood measure. The deviation can be specified either relative to an expected value or to the current market value. Therefore, a reliable assessment of the market value of all positions and of the **variance-covariance matrix** is needed initially. Value at Risk is employed in various areas of financial management. Figure 2.15 provides an overview of input factors, calculations and uses.

In principle, VaR can be computed with the help of two different models: on the one hand with the analytical/parametric approach and on the other hand with the simulation approach. General analytical approaches are the **variance**-covariance model and the **delta**-normal model. Frequently used models of the simulation approach are the historical simulation and the **Monte Carlo simulation**. These modeling approaches differ mainly in two aspects, namely in the sensitivity of the risk positions considered and in the modeling

---

[23] see Bloss, Ernst, Häcker, Haas, Prexl, Röck: Financial Modeling, Stuttgart 2010.

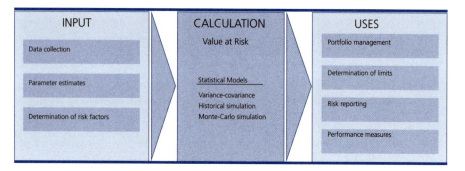

Figure 2.15: Steps in the application of VaR

of the development of the risk factors. In the following we will initially derive VaR graphically. Then the most widely used models will be summarized. The focus will not be on a detailed exposition of the mathematical interrelations, but rather on the relevance of VaR in applied work.

2.5.1 Graphical derivation

The determination of a one-sided fractile α allows the calculation of the probability **q**. It represents the probability that a future absolute change in value of a risk factor will fall below a certain reference value. This reference value therefore also indirectly determines the confidence level. This reference value can be called a negative Value at Risk $(-\text{VaR}_t)$ during the holding period **dt** at a point in time **t** with the confidence level $(1 - \alpha)$:

$$q_t(dV_{t,\,dt} \leq -\text{VaR}_{t,\,dt,\,(1-\alpha)}) = \alpha$$

For the distribution function of the continuous change in market value, this implies:

$$\int_{-\infty}^{-\text{VaR}_{t,dt,(1-\alpha)}} f(dV_{t,\,dt})\,d(dV_{t,\,dt}) = F(-\text{VaR}_{t,\,dt,\,(1-\alpha)}) = \alpha$$

Multiplication by minus one gives a positive number for the Value at Risk, since normally the α-fractile of a distribution takes on negative values. Figure 2.16 once again illustrates VaR.

Depending on the definition of the **holding period** and the **confidence level**, the level of risk can be quantified. In a certain sense, the confidence level is an

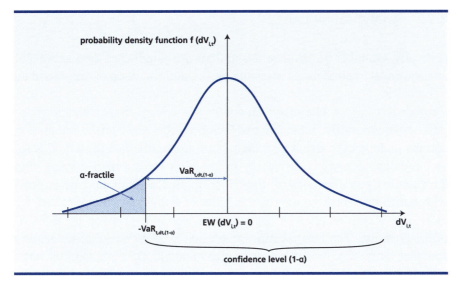

Figure 2.16: Graphical representation of VaR

expression of the degree of risk aversion. Setting this level at 99.9% signifies a relatively high degree of risk aversion. In the applied work of industrial companies, a confidence level of 95 percent is most frequently observed. An additional important factor is the holding period or the time it takes to liquidate a risky position in a crisis situation. VaR thus makes a statement about the maximum loss a company faces as a result of market price risks during a given holding period and with a pre-specified probability.

> At a 95% confidence level, a holding period of 10 days and a VaR of EUR 100,000, the following statement is correct: with a probability of 95%, the company does not lose more than EUR 100,000 over the course of the coming 10 days. In analyzing such values for VaR, it should always be kept in mind that this same statement also implies a probability of 5% of losing more than EUR 100,000. For this reason, the company's willingness and ability to bear risk needs to be considered when setting the input parameters for the analysis.

As already mentioned, two basic approaches are used to calculate VaR: analytical models and simulation models. They are explained in more detail in the following sections.

2.5.2 Analytical models

Normally a number of risk factors simultaneously influence the riskiness of an investment or portfolio of investments. A simple addition of the individual Value at Risk figures would neglect the effects of diversification, which reduce the overall riskiness. The analytical approach therefore deals with known interrelations among the individual risk factors. VaR is based on the assumption that the underlying **market risk factors** are **normally distributed**. VaR for an individual security is derived by multiplying a given market value with the volatility at a given probability. Since applied work in most cases deals with portfolios which consist of a number of individual holdings, VaR for individual securities must be aggregated to get an expression for the VaR of the portfolio. The most significant advantage of the variance-covariance approach is its simple and quick implementation. One assumption, however, is that all risk factors follow a normal distribution. This in turn is the most frequently voiced criticism of the analytical model. When applying the variance-covariance model, it is therefore essential to verify this property for the underlying risk factors.

2.5.3 Simulation models

As an alternative to the analytical approaches, Value at Risk can also be determined with the help of simulation models. They require fewer restrictive assumptions and approximations and can also incorporate non-linear relationships. The estimated distributions of portfolio losses are based on simulated frequency distributions which were generated from a large number of different return scenarios. The historical simulation in contrast, is based on past data and the assumption that the risk factors from the past will continue to influence the holdings in an unchanged manner. Thanks to its low degree of mathematical complexity, the historical simulation can be easily used to quantify risk. Furthermore, no assumptions about risk factors and their distribution are required. A further simplifying feature is the fact that the calculation of VaR with the help of a historical simulation does not require the determination and calculation of volatilities, variances, and correlations. However, a clear shortcoming is the assumption that past influencing factors can simply be carried forward into the future. A further point of contention is the high dependency of the model results on the data available and the time period chosen. Thanks to this criticism, the Monte Carlo simulation has gained increasing influence in the recent past. Monte Carlo simulations, unlike historical simulations, do not use historical data in order to estimate the future development of the risk factors. Instead random numbers are generated. The number of scenarios can be chosen without any restriction. The resulting values from all scenarios are used to derive a probability distribution for future gains and losses. The future market development is thus analyzed and evaluated with the help of simulations. Thanks to the high degree of flexibility, especially in the case of complex portfolio structures, the Monte Carlo simulation is superior to other approaches concerning methodology. A disadvantage is that the computations, even when using modern software, continue to require relatively large amounts of time.

In summary, it can be stated that Monte Carlo simulations are a promising method of modern risk management, especially in cases of complex portfolio structures. Nonetheless, the variance-covariance approach and the historical simulation continue to be sufficient as well, especially in the case of simpler risk structures.

The models discussed will be revisited and applied in Chapter 6 and Chapter 7.

2.6 Foundations and approaches of decision theory

We now want to give a basic introduction to classical game theory and the behavioral patterns that can be observed in practice as well as an overview of standard portfolio theories. In the presentation, we focus on those aspects that are essential for the financial engineer.

2.6.1 Classical decision theory

Classical decision theory is a part of applied probability theory. It analyzes and evaluates the consequences of decisions. Decision theory is thus often used as a managerial instrument. The best known methods are the **cost-utility analysis** and the **analytic hierarchy process**. Decision theory reaches its limits whenever a rational counterpart exists or is constructed. In this case, game theory must be used. We briefly derive its key insights in the following paragraph.

2.6.2 Game theory

John von Neumann[24]
1903–1957
Austro-Hungarian
mathematician

Unlike classical decision theory, **game theory** makes use of the assumption that the success of an individual is not only dependent on his own actions, but also on the actions of others. The first formal analysis of parlor games was provided by JOHN VON NEUMANN in 1928. It continues to be the foundation of game theory to this day.

Game theory is the modeling of various situations as a classical game. In the formal mathematical description, the basic elements of the game are determined. Among others, the following features are identified: How many players are participating? Who are the players? What is the sequence of the game? What are the options available to each player at different stages of the game?

Initially a payoff function is determined. This function assigns a payoff vector to each possible outcome of the game. It determines the profit of each player for a specific outcome of the game. The definition of profit can vary depending on the application. When game theory is applied to the field of economics, the payoff is usually a monetary value; in political science, meanwhile, votes could be at stake and in biology the payoff is interpreted as the ability to reproduce or to survive. Due to this flexibility, every situation can be analyzed with the help of game theory. With the approach, the possibilities and limitations of the strategies of individuals can be assessed. At the same time, scenarios can be derived for the environment in which decisions must be taken.

Games that are not repeated are called **one-shot games**. The sequential repetition of one-shot games gives rise to a **supergame**. In a supergame, the participants can make use of past experiences in all future rounds. Important are the assumptions imposed by game theory at the beginning of the game, namely rationality of all participants and knowledge about this rationality by every participant. A distinction is made between generally known rules of the game and generally known rationality. It is also possible to develop game theoretical models that use bounded rationality.

---

[24] born János von Neumann zu Margitta.

2.7 Who knows what?

A decisive question concerns the knowledge which each individual player possesses. In the following, we will highlight different possibilities for modeling information.

2.7.1 Complete information

A player knows both the structure of the game and the objective functions of the other players, but may not be able to observe all the actions of all the other players.

2.7.2 Perfect information

A player knows both the structure of the game and the objective functions of the other players, and in principle is also able to anticipate the actions of all other players.

2.7.3 Transformation of games with incomplete information into games with complete, but imperfect information

HARSANYI[25] points out that a distinction between games with incomplete information and imperfect information is redundant, since games with incomplete information can be transformed into games with imperfect information.

John Charles Harsanyi[26]
1920–2000
Hungarian-American economist

2.7.4 Different strategies

There are different strategies for every game. In the following, these strategies are presented.

2.7.4.1 Pure and mixed strategies

A strategy is considered to be pure, if a player uses it in every conceivable case. A strategy is called mixed, if a player is forced to choose among two pure strategies based on a random mechanism.

---

[25] John. C. Harsanyi 1967/8. "Games with Incomplete Information Played by Bayesian Players." Parts 1–3 Management Science 14: 159–82, 320–34, 486–502.
[26] properly *János Harsányi*.

2.7.4.2 Equilibria in dominant strategies

In an equilibrium in dominant strategies, each player can determine her strategy independent of the choice of strategy by the opponent. Since by definition no incentive exists to deviate from the equilibrium solution, every equilibrium in dominant strategies is also a Nash equilibrium. Conversely, not every Nash equilibrium is an equilibrium in dominant strategies.

John Forbes Nash jr.
born 1928
American mathematician and recipient of the Nobel Prize in economics

2.7.4.3 Nash equilibrium

In a **Nash equilibrium,** the chosen strategies are optimal, taking into account the strategies of the other players. In this sense, there is no incentive for any of the players to unilaterally change strategy. In the following, we will explain this concept in more detail.

2.8 Solution strategies for known decision situations

It is the aim of the mathematical game theory to develop rational solutions for conflict situations. The inherent difficulty of this task stems from the fact that none of the players know, what the others will decide. Therefore it is completely uncertain for a single player, how his concrete choice will affect strategy.[27]

The Nash equilibrium represents the following idea: considered are all possible combinations of the strategies of all players. A combination of strategies can be considered stable if no individual player has an incentive to deviate from his strategy (this means that the payoff to the player who alone has changed his strategy cannot increase as a result of the change). If this is the case, the strategy combination is called Nash equilibrium.

In general, Nash equilibra are not uniquely determined. However, their existence can be assured for cases where players are allowed to make decisions in the context of so called **mixed strategies**. In these strategies, each player can randomly determine his decisions. In this case, a Nash equilibrium requires that every player follows a mixed strategy. The mixed strategy of every player is the optimal response to the mixed strategies of all the other players.

---

[27] Manfred J. Holler, Gerhard Illing: Einführung in die Spieltheorie, Springer Verlag, Heidelberg, 2008.

Solution strategies for known decision situations

Example

Two players ($1 = X$ and $2 = Y$) possess a black and a white token. The rules are: player **X** wins in case the colors drawn are the same (black-black or white-white). Player **Y** wins in case the colors of the tokens are different (white-black or black-white). Which strategy will be chosen by player **X**? If he chooses the black token, player **Y** will always pick white and player **X** loses. Even in the case where player **X** changes his strategy and settles on the white token, player **B** will also change his strategy and now select black – hence **X** loses again.

If player **Y** starts, player **X** will also adjust strategy. It follows that no player can obtain an advantage from the correct selection of the token. If the opponent guesses the strategy, he can always devise an appropriate counter-strategy which assures victory.

Thus, no Nash equilibrium is possible in this example; at least as long as both players pursue a **pure strategy** (see Chapter 2.7.4.1). This changes if both players switch to a purely random selection of strategy. If both players randomly picked the black or white token with a probability of 50%, and only then, there would be no incentive for either of the players to deviate from this purely random strategy and the inevitable result would be a Nash equilibrium.[28]

2.8.1 Financial engineering and game theory

Now where is the link again between game theory and financial engineering? It is very obvious! And no, we are not talking about gamesters who are active in derivatives markets. We are more concerned about the decisions which are required every day, be it in financial engineering, wealth management or other departments in the financial industry. We admit, it is unlikely that everyday decisions are regularly made with reference to game theoretical approaches, even though subconsciously, these ideas might well be at work (think about the example of the black and white token in Section 2.7.5). In financial markets, daily decisions are reached in favor or against an investment, figures are evaluated and balance sheets researched. But it is also important to know how other investors react to new information. What will determine whether they will buy or sell? What is the likely reaction of my counterpart in a

---

[28] Christian Rieck: Spieltheorie: Eine Einführung, p. 78, Christian Rieck Verlag, Eschborn, 2008.

negotiation? How hard can I press during negotiations? These approaches can be developed and evaluated with the help of game theory. Of course, nobody will always act rationally or follow all rules. But that is exactly why an application of the methods of game theory is so promising. Especially during tough negotiations, this may make the difference. The most important thing is to look at the game situation and all the possible outcomes ahead of time. In this case quick and targeted reactions to changing conditions are possible. It is absolutely mandatory to prepare in this way for all major negotiations.

Let us consider another example from the financial industry. It is assumed by many observers that a dividend payment "increases the wealth" of a shareholder. But this is not true since all he is getting is a profit, which otherwise could be retained by the company and would thus support the share price. Why, then, are companies doing this? There are a number of reasons: on the one hand, an incentive is provided for new providers of capital; on the other hand, the dividend acts as a signaling device. This can be analyzed in the setting of game theory. Bad news, such as a recall of automobiles, job losses and so forth lead to a poor image of the company, while dividend payments on the other hand improve the standing. A manager will always try to match bad news with pieces of good news. But why? Only insiders know whether a company is in good shape. If outsiders receive unfavorable news about a company, this has negative repercussions. But if this is matched with something that a "bad" company could never afford, such as the payment of a dividend, a piece of negative news has been neutralized. The dividend payment thus signals that company insiders know more than outsiders. Apparently the situation of the company must be favorable on balance, even though no concrete information is provided[29].

2.8.2 Portfolio risk management

In the following section we discuss risk management and its application in various hedging strategies. Risk management requires an appropriate definition of risk. A fundamental distinction is made between **unsystematic** risk, which can be linked to individual securities and **systematic** risk, which is also called non-diversifiable risk. Unsystematic risk can be eliminated with

---

[29] See Rieck, Christian: Spieltheorie: Eine Einführung, Christian Rieck Verlag, Eschborn, 2008.

Solution strategies for known decision situations

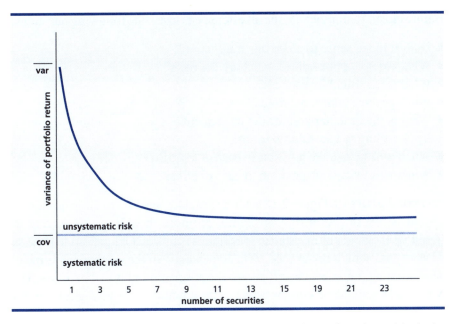

Figure 2.17: Variance of the portfolio return in relation to the number of securities in the portfolio

the help of active management and diversification.[30] In contrast, systematic risk is linked to the overall market and thus affects all assets in this market. It cannot be eliminated via diversification. As can be seen in Figure 2.17, average covariance among the assets remains stable.

> Portfolio risk consists of the weighted sum of all individual risks as well as the correlations among these risks.

2.8.3 Fundamental questions for every investor

It is important for an investor to have clear targets. Before its implementation, every plan should be carefully considered. Hasty decisions should not be taken; in all likelihood they will result in losses.

---

[30] See Harry M. Markowitz, *Portfolio Selection Theory*, 1952.

Before closing a transaction, the investor needs to ask the following questions:

- Does it make sense to close this transaction?
- What are my opportunities, what are the risks?
- What is my initial investment?
- Will I provide additional funds?
- What is the time horizon for the investment?
- Am I willing to take additional risks?
- When will I close the position in case of a profit?
- When will I close the position in case of a loss?

An **action plan** (see Figure 2.18), which provides answers to these questions, should be set up. As a rule of thumb, no more than 20 to 30 percent of liquid assets should be invested in speculative ventures. Obligations to provide fresh capital should not exceed 30 to 50 percent[31] of the original investment. This is a magnitude which still allows the absorption of possible losses. The action plan should be comprehensive; its function is to give guidance for initial investments. It must contain action points concerning the built-up and liquidation of holdings, determine thresholds for realizing a loss or a profit, specify rules on the provision of fresh funds and clarify the basic idea of

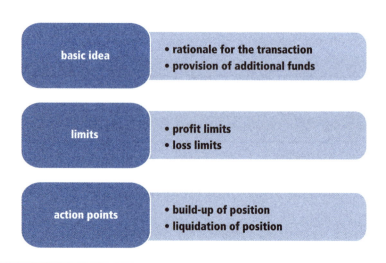

Figure 2.18: Structure of an action plan

---

[31] This does not hold for professional market participants.

the trade. (Why am I entering this trade?) Especially in the beginning, but also for complex strategies, it does make sense to define stop loss limits. The approach also assures the deep involvement of the investor and prevents knee-jerk reactions. Once an investor is fully familiar with the issue, a written action plan is no longer required, since experience can serve as a base for necessary decisions and reactions.

2.8.3.1 The different types of investors

Simply put, a distinction must be made between **retail clients** and **institutional investors**. These two groups in turn can be broken down into a number of subgroups. With regard to the use of derivatives, the two client segments usually differ in the following aspects:

- Expert knowledge
- Holding period
- Liquidity
- Analytical ability and tools
- Market access (OTC and exchanges)
- Regulatory requirements
- Order size

These factors always need to be taken into consideration, as the differences between private clients and institutional investors tend to be rather large. In addition, it is possible that a third party (wealth manager, family office, client adviser, auditor or others) gets involved in a derivatives transaction, either as advisor or agent. Their influence also needs to be considered.

2.8.3.2 How to approach derivatives as an inexperienced investor

Investors who are new to derivatives trading are encouraged to start with a dry run (on paper or using Excel®), setting up strategies and following their development. This dry run should be documented carefully and honestly (do not just count your winning trades). Paper losses are not real, but they might still teach valuable lessons. In this context, the following issues are relevant:

- The strategies need to be tested in different market situations
  - Normal market situation
  - Stress test in an unusual market situation

- All signals for built-up and liquidation of the holding must be realistic and documented
  - Market-based Signals
  - It must always be possible to reproduce all decisions made
- The fundamental laws of statistics must always be applied and considered

Dishonesty with regard to these points will be regretted severely once live trading has begun.

Only after an investor has gained experience in this way, should he start investing in the market. Now he can deal with more confidence with problems that he has already experienced during the trial phase. But it would be an illusion to think that nothing new will be encountered: even the best action plan and the best preparation during the dry run will not prevent hectic and oftentimes emotional decisions. Therefore it is most important to stay calm and to try to reach decisions in a rational manner.

> **"Things are simple at the top!"**
>
> This statement[32] also holds for financial engineering. Not always are complex strategies appropriate. In many instances, simple strategies prove to be a lot more successful than highly complex ones.

At this point, a few observations about the magnitude of the investment are in order. Statistically, a larger number of smaller wagers tend to produce higher returns than a few big ones. This approach is also supported from the perspective of risk. The ability to bear losses depends on the overall level of wealth; the investment volume should definitely not be a function of losses suffered. Do not throw good money after bad!

> The theoretical foundations of portfolio management are relevant in this regard. They will be presented in Section 2.8.4. The issue of risk controlling should not be ignored either. It will be covered in more detail in Chapter 16.1.

---

[32] Alpa of Switzerland.

2.8.4 Portfolio theory

Portfolio theory is concerned with the investment behavior of investors in financial markets and with their return expectations relative to the risks taken. It is the aim of portfolio theory to provide decision rules regarding the most favorable combination of investment alternatives in an optimal portfolio. An optimal portfolio takes into account the preferences of investors concerning risk and return as well as liquidity. In the following we will provide an overview of the most frequently used portfolio theories.

2.8.4.1 Portfolio selection model

The **portfolio selection model**[33] of *H. M. MARKOWITZ*[34] starts from the empirical observation that investors spread their wealth among a number of securities; in other words, they diversify. In order to develop a model for the optimal portfolio choice, Markowitz considers a one-period model. In 1990, Markowitz received the Nobel Prize for this model.

Harry M. Markowitz
Born 1927
American economist and recipient of the Nobel Prize in economics

> **Main insights from the Markowitz model**
>
> - The variables expected return and risk are important when constructing a portfolio.
> - To reduce risk, it makes sense to form security portfolios (diversification).
> - A portfolio is called efficient if there is no other portfolio with lower risk for a given return level, or if there is no other portfolio with a higher return for a given level of risk.
> - Of major importance for the risk of the portfolio is the correlation of returns of the securities in the portfolio. The decisive factor is not so much the number of securities included in the portfolio, but rather the correlation among these securities.
> - The optimal portfolio is an efficient portfolio which satisfies the risk appetite of an individual investor. Every investor chooses a portfolio on the efficient frontier that corresponds to his individual willingness to assume risk.

---

[33] Developed 1952 by Harry Markowitz and published in: Portfolio Selection, Journal of Finance. 7/1952, pp. 77–91.
[34] Born 1927 in Chicago, US economist; recipient of the Nobel Prize in economics 1990.

The risk of security investments is explicitly considered in the **Markowitz model**. The one-dimensional focus on return, which was predominant at the time, is replaced by a two-dimensional approach (return and risk) which is still in use today. Another positive development was the switch from valuing individual securities towards assessing entire portfolios. Still, the portfolio selection model is not without problems, since large amounts of data estimations are required to calculate the efficient frontier. In applied work there is frequently massive uncertainty about the values of the variables used for modeling. And finally the use of historical data is problematic since investors are interested in the structure of future efficient portfolios.

The expected portfolio return is measured with reference to the expected returns of the individual holdings. It is calculated as follows:

$$\mu_p = \sum_{i=1}^{n} x_i \mu_i$$

μ_p = expected portfolio return
x_i = share of security i in the portfolio
μ_i = expected value of the return of security i
n = number of securities contained in the portfolio

The expected portfolio risk is measured with the help of variance. Variance is calculated as follows:

$$\sigma_p^2 = \frac{1}{T} \sum_{t=1}^{T} (R_{pt} - \mu_p)^2$$

σ_p^2 = Variance of returns of portfolio p
T = Number of observed returns in the portfolio (time periods)
R_{pt} = Return of portfolio p in period t
μ_p = Expected value of the portfolio return

Instead of variance, standard deviation can also be used as a measure of risk. Standard deviation is the square root of the variance.

$$\sigma = \sqrt{\sigma^2}$$

In order to calculate the variance of the portfolio return from the returns of the individual securities, the correlation of the returns (which expresses the degree of co-movement) needs to be considered as well. Thus the portfolio variance needs to be calculated in addition to the variance of the individual securities (see Figure 2.19).

Solution strategies for known decision situations

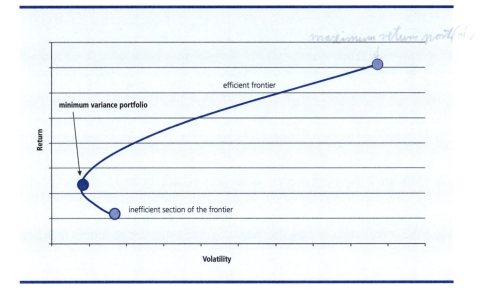

Figure 2.19: Minimum variance portfolio

Main conclusion of the Markowitz model

No other portfolio exists, which

- for a given return expectation has lower risk,
- for a given risk level has a higher return,
- simultaneously has higher expected returns as well as lower risk.

2.8.4.2 Single index model

William Sharpe
born 1934
American economist
and recipient of
the Nobel Prize in
economics

The model created by *SHARPE*[35] has the advantage of requiring fewer data series than the *MARKOWITZ* model. Sharpe assumes that the positive correlation coefficients among securities are caused by fundamentals (for example changes in interest rates by the central bank, political or economic influences). He argues that these joint influences can be captured with the help of an index and that they fully explain the uncertainty of equity returns – apart from an error term which is specific for each individual stock. In his opinion, all relevant information is contained in the index.

---

[35] William F. Sharpe *1934, is an American economist and professor emeritus at Stanford University. He is one of the founding fathers of CAPM.

> **Main conclusion of the single index model**
>
> - The data problem of the Markowitz model can be solved with the help of an index.
>
> - Security prices do not develop independently of each other, but also depend on an index.

The problem of requiring excessive amounts of data for the Markowitz model can be solved with the help of the single index model. This saves money and time. However, the use of the **index model** also leads to a loss of information, since the correlations among the individual securities are no longer included in the model.

2.8.4.3 Capital Asset Pricing Model (CAPM)

CAPM, developed by *Sharpe*, *Lintner* and *Mossin*, makes use of the main insight of portfolio theory, namely the possibility to partly eliminate the risk of securities via diversification. Hence the overall risk of a security cannot be the appropriate basis for valuation. The ultimate aim of **CAPM** is the derivation of equilibrium prices for individual risky investments as parts of a portfolio in an uncertain (risky) environment.

2.8.4.3.1 Assumptions of CAPM

In addition to the known premises of portfolio theory, the following assumptions are introduced:

- A perfect capital market exists. This means that there are no information or transaction costs, no taxes or other impediments such as market regulation.
- Individual investors cannot influence market prices.
- All investments are infinitely divisible and can be bought or sold in the market.
- A risk-free rate of return exists. Investors can borrow or lend at this rate without limitation.
- All investors have homogeneous expectations concerning return and risk of all securities.

2.8.4.3.2 Main conclusions of CAPM

- In equilibrium, the risky portion of the portfolio of all investors – independent of their attitude towards risk – has an identical structure. The risky portion of the portfolio is equivalent to the market portfolio. It contains all risky assets weighted by their capitalization. The introduction of a market portfolio, which is based in the assumption of homogeneous expectations, has one advantage in comparison to portfolio theory: rather than assembling individual portfolios, all investors share the same portfolio composition.

- The expected returns of efficient portfolios are a linear function of the standard deviation of the portfolio return (capital market line). A linear relationship (security market line) exists between the return of a security or a portfolio of securities and its (systematic) risk. This equilibrium relationship provides the basis for the valuation of an individual security in the context of the market portfolio.

- The return of the security is composed of a risk-free rate and a risk premium.

- In the context of a portfolio, only the beta factor is a relevant risk measure for individual securities. Since beta only reflects systematic risk, or that risk which cannot be eliminated with the help of diversification, CAPM does not reward the assumption of unsystematic risk.

While earlier empirical tests of CAPM tended to confirm its basic tenets, more recent evidence leans towards a refutation of the model and its conclusions. Apparent contradictions of CAPM can be observed in capital markets. Evidence relates to the size of a company[36], the price-to-book ratio of a share, the price-earnings ratio or the sensitivity concerning interest rate changes.

Two points determine the position of the **capital market line**. First, the ordinate intercept R_f and second, the point of tangency with the efficient frontier of risky portfolios, which is also called the market portfolio (see Figure 2.20). The following equation can thus be derived:

$$E(R_p) = R_f + \frac{E(R_m) - R_f}{\sigma_m} \cdot \sigma_p$$

---

[36] Especially small and mid cap.

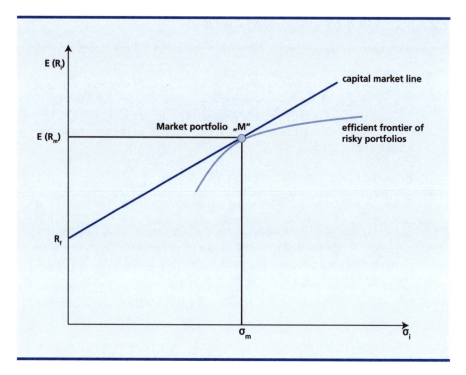

Figure 2.20: The capital market line

$E(R_p)$ = Return expectation for the portfolio **p**
$E(R_m)$ = Return expectation for the market portfolio
σ_p = Standard deviation of the portfolio **p**
σ_m = Standard deviation of the portfolio **m**
R_f = risk-free interest rate (riskless investment)

> The capital market line defines the general relationship between increasing return expectations and increasing portfolio risk.

This relationship can also be stated as follows: investors who are willing to assume risk expect a risk premium to do so. Or put differently: when risk changes, the return expectations of investors are also adjusted. From the capital market line, which illustrates the return expectations for risky portfolios, the security market line can be derived. It states the appropriate equilibrium price of the individual securities which form the market portfolio.

$$E(R_p) = a \cdot E(R_i) + (1-a) \cdot E(R_m)$$

a = share of security **i** in portfolio **p**
$E(R_i)$ = Expected value of the return of security **i**
$E(R_m)$ = Expected value of the return of the market portfolio
$E(R_p)$ = Expected value of the return of the portfolio **p**

It follows that the portfolio risk is given as:

$$\sigma_p = [a^2\sigma_i^2 + (1-a)^2\sigma_m^2 + 2COV_{im}\,a(1-a)]^{1/2}$$

COV_{im} is the covariance between security **i** and the market portfolio.

To study the effects of a variation in the share of security **i** on portfolio risk and portfolio return, both equations can be differentiated with respect to the portfolio share **a**.

$$\frac{dE(R_p)}{da} = E(R_i) - E(R_m)$$

$$\frac{d\sigma_p}{da} = \frac{1}{2} \cdot [a^2\sigma_i^2 + (1-a)^2\sigma_m^2 + 2COV_{im}\,a(1-a)]^{1/2} \cdot$$
$$[2a\sigma_i^2 - 2\sigma_m^2 + 2a\sigma_m^2 + 2COV_{im} - 4aCOV_{im}]$$

To determine an equilibrium solution, the portfolio share of security **i** is set equal to zero since security **i** already has a share of **a** in the market portfolio. Any additional weight would imply disequilibrium. Solving the two equations for **i** results in the capital market line.

$$E(R_i) = R_f + [E(R_m) - R_f] \cdot \frac{COV_{im}}{\sigma_m^2}$$

$E(R_i)$ = Expected value of the return of security **i**
$E(R_m)$ = Expected value of the return of the market portfolio **m**
COV_{im} = Covariance between security **i** and the market portfolio **m**
σ_m^2 = Variance of the market portfolio
R_f = Return of the riskless asset

As can be seen, the return which can be expected for an individual security in **capital market equilibrium** is composed of the risk-free interest rate and a risk premium. The measure for the magnitude of the risk taken is also called beta factor ($= \text{COV}_{im}/\sigma_m^2$). The model can be extended to allow for a multi-dimensional perspective.

> The return of an individual asset is dependent on the size of beta. The higher beta, the higher the return. In CAPM, risk is increasing as return goes up.

2.8.4.3.3 Summary of the CAPM

The CAPM derives a theoretical relationship between expected return and risk of an asset for all investable assets. The return expectation for every asset is equal to the interest rate of a riskless asset plus a risk premium. The risk premium is proportional to the beta of an asset.

2.8.5 Final assessment of the models

The models presented above are most frequently used in applied work. Of course, other models are also relevant as well, such as the **Arbitrage Pricing Theory** (APT)[37] developed by *Ross*[38] and other approaches. Due to the limited relevance for financial engineering, however, we will not discuss these models.

The models presented above are all based on assumptions which can be derived in theory, but which are sometimes not workable or observable in practice. Returns, for example, are not normally distributed in practice; forecasts are less than perfect and so on. As a consequence, every portfolio manager[39] needs to apply his expertise and critical thinking when structuring individual portfolios.

---

[37] Determination of the cost of equity and expected returns of securities.
[38] Professor at MIT (MIT Sloan School of Management)
[39] In our opinion, this holds both for an asset management mandate as well as the direct management of a portfolio.

2.8.6 The process of portfolio management

Let us briefly outline the practice of applied portfolio management. The process is best structured along the following three building blocks:

- Planning
- Implementation
- Control

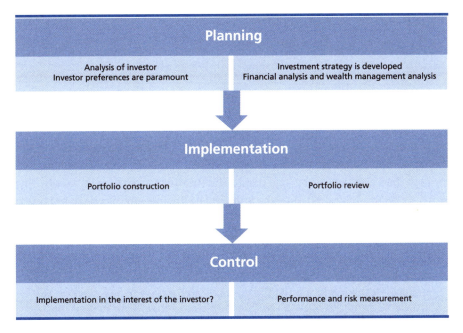

Figure 2.21: Structure of portfolio management

Most mistakes are made in the assessment of the investor (analysis of his preferences, risk assessment, evaluation of the complexity of the portfolio and so forth). It is important to realize that this analysis is about the investor and not the portfolio manager. Especially the question about the appropriate complexity of the portfolio is frequently answered with regard to the competency of the portfolio manager and not the requirements of the investor. The same is true for the performance outlook, which is frequently too optimistic. *"High return, high risk!"* is still a valid concept. This must be clear to the investor (see Figure 2.22). A long and open discussion at the beginning, regular – at least quarterly – updates (higher frequencies for some investors) and a review meeting are recommended. The portfolio manager always needs to

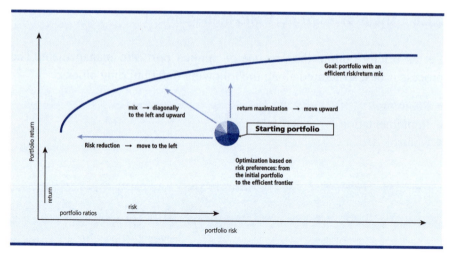

Figure 2.22: Portfolio structure based on investor preferences[40]

adhere to the basic strategy agreed upon, unless he has the explicit permission from the customer for an individual trade. Should a complete change of strategy become necessary as a result of extreme market developments, this can only be implemented once the approval of the investor has been obtained.

Why is the area of portfolio management of such relevance for the financial engineer? At this stage, the various instruments are combined. It requires "thinking in a portfolio context" to be close to the market. The individual products must be in line with each other, so that they can be placed in the market. In Chapters 8 and 13, these basics are assumed and developed further.

2.9 Market psychology and behavioral economics

2.9.1 Market psychology

Market psychology attempts to explain human behavior in a market environment and to derive forecasts based on this behavior. Just as marketing

---

[40] Source: Commerzbank AG Wealth Management.

psychology, market psychology is an applied or practical branch of psychology. The various tasks are clearly structured:

- Explanations of behavior (why does an investor acquire a share, why does a consumer purchase a good)
- Analysis of motives and wants
- Assessment of opinions, conceptions and stereotypes
- Segmentation of target groups
- Forecasts concerning the reaction of investors or consumers

According to *WISWEDE*[41], market psychology as a science is a part of classical economic and business psychology. While the focus of market psychology is mostly on the consumer, behavioral economics is dealing mostly with human behavior in situations of economic decision making.

2.9.2 Behavioral economics

As already mentioned, behavioral economics deals with human reactions (behavior) in different situations that require economic decisions. Of particular interest are constellations where human actions violate the model assumptions of **homo oeconomicus**[42]. In the specific field of behavioral finance, the focus is on irrational behavior in financial and capital markets. In classical economic thought, a close relationship existed between economic theory and psychology[43]. During the age of neoclassical theory, economic theory and human psychology parted ways. Instead the natural sciences served as a model for the development of theories. In this context, the model of homo oeconomicus was developed. Only in the late 1970s did an interest in the psychological aspects of human actions reemerge. Extremely influential in this regard was the work of *KAHNEMAN/TVERSKY*[44] on **"Prospect Theory**[45]: Decision Making Under Risk."

Daniel Kahneman born 1934 Israeli-American psychologist and recipient of the Nobel Prize in economics

Amos Tversky 1937–1996 Israeli-American psychologist

---

[41] Günter Wiswede, born in 1938, Professor Emeritus, Universität zu Köln.
[42] Model used in economic theory. It assumes an individual who exclusively acts and thinks in economic categories. Homo oeconomicus only cares about economic goals and is characterized by a number of features such as rational behavior, utility maximization, complete knowledge of economic alternatives and their consequences, as well as complete information about all markets and attributes of all goods (completely transparent markets). All decisions are reached in a rational manner, free from emotions and without disturbance from the outside.
[43] See Adam Smith: The Theory of Moral Sentiments, 1759.
[44] Daniel Kahneman was awarded the Nobel prize in economics in 2002 (jointly with Vernon L. Smith).
[45] New expectation theory: realistic alternative, grounded in psychology, to the expected utility function of von Neumann-Morgenstern.

2.9.3 Methods of behavioral finance

Initially the focus was almost exclusively on experimental methods. Even functional magnetic resonance tomography was used in order to find out which areas of the brain are used at different stages of the economic decision-making process. Experiments which simulate market situations such as securities trading and auctions turned out to be particularly useful.

As a result of these studies, the following themes turned out to be particularly relevant:

- **Heuristics:** people frequently reach decisions based on gut feelings and not just strict rational thinking.
- **Framing:** the way in which a problem or a decision scenario are presented, affects the decision taken.
- **Incomplete markets:** the assumption of complete markets does not hold in practice.

The existence of widespread **anomalies** cannot be explained with reference to the behavior of individuals, who are prejudiced in a certain way. Individual prejudices are often not sufficiently influential to alter market prices and profits. In addition, it is possible that individual prejudices can cancel out. Cognitive biases will only generate unusual effects, if a societal contamination with very emotional content is found, such as widespread greed or panic. This leads to a number of group phenomena, of which **herd behavior** and **group thinking** will be discussed in more detail.

Homo oeconomicus is a human, who

1. Acts completely rational
2. Attempts to maximize profits or utility
3. Is endowed with "market transparency" and complete foresight with regard to economic affairs
4. Reacts immediately and in a completely rational manner to changes in data[46]

---

[46] see Bongard, 1965.

2.9.3.1 Herd behavior

Herd behavior is a phenomenon that can be observed in financial markets. It describes the fact that investors act like a herd in their investment decisions and that large numbers of investors follow the same investment strategy. Herd behavior can result in large price fluctuations of the investment object. It is a specific case of the so-called contagion effects, and can be explained with reference to the existence of asymmetric information. If an investor thinks that other investors (insiders, professional investors and others) possess information that is superior to their own, he will interpret their market decisions as the result of superior information and duplicate the decisions of the supposedly better informed market participants. He is thus following the leader. Put differently, herd behavior is an indication of market inefficiencies. The consequences of herd behavior can be massive price movements and ultimately even financial and currency crises.

The only reason why investors take action in the case of herd behavior is the expectation of changing prices. But in that way, investors are in fact affecting prices due to their own actions. A self-fulfilling prophecy may be the result. The behavior of the herd can lead to changes in fundamental data of the investment object itself. Such behavior is also present in the case of a bank run. All depositors simultaneously withdraw their deposits for fear that they

Figure 2.23: Development of a causal chain of market reactions[47]

---

[47] Source: J.P. Morgan.

are no longer safe with the bank. The result of this action is the insolvency of the bank, an example of a self-fulfilling prophecy.

2.9.3.2 Group thinking

If a group of competent experts reaches bad or unrealistic decisions, this is often caused by the fact that individual opinions have been adjusted to conform to a supposed group opinion. Independent arguments are often not brought up. This may result in situations where the group approves of actions or compromises that would not be accepted by any individual group member under normal circumstances or outside the group. The inherent dangers of group thinking are stubborn persistence and irrationality. In cases where groups are not in the possession of functional mechanisms to adjust the common patterns of thinking, these are raised to the level of absolute dogma, which can be highly appealing. In the worst case, clinging to such a dogma, which is out of touch with reality, can even lead to the demise of the group. Breaking free from such a situation requires active and intense discussions, possibly including a **devil's advocate**[48] or a system of anonymous suggestions of topics and processes to be discussed.

2.9.4 Closing thoughts

Some financial models make use of the fundamentals of **behavioral finance**. The neoclassical models are modified and augmented to include the effects discussed. But opponents continue to insist that behavioral finance is nothing but a collection of anomalies in an otherwise complete market. Due to the complexity, a final verdict about the actual relevance is impossible at the moment. It must be reiterated, however, that herd behavior and group thinking can be observed in daily economic life and that the effects on markets can be quantified.

---

[48] The "devil's advocate" (advocatus diaboli) was originally the person who presented an opposing view during the beatification and canonization procedures of the Catholic Church. His opponent is the advocatus angeli (or advocatus dei, "advocate of the angels" or "God's advocate"), who represents reasons supporting the motion. Today he is known as the "promoter of justice" (promotor justitiae), renamed 1983 by Pope John Paul II. Outside the church, the term has been established as a description of somebody who holds an opposing opinion in a discussion or debate. It is his responsibility to challenge everything and to cast doubt on other opinions.

> The strength of the influence of the above discussed concepts depends on the actual market environment. The more uncertain the outlook, the stronger the influence. The concepts play a role in all strategies discussed in this book. Particularly affected are the strategies for managing an existing exposure, which are presented in Chapter 13.

Literature for this chapter

Hull, John: Options, Futures and Other Derivatives, 7th edition, 2009

Hager, Peter: Corporate Risk Management: Cash Flow at Risk und Value at Risk, Frankfurt am Main, 2004

Riechmann, Thomas: Spieltheorie, 2nd edition, 2008

Rieck, Christian: Spieltheorie, 8th edition, 2008

Spremann, Klaus: Finance, 3rd edition, 2007

Steiner, Manfred; Bruns, Christoph: Wertpapiermanagement, 9th edition, 2008

Questions and answers on this chapter

Question 1:
What is a martingale?

Question 2:
What is implied by the law of large numbers?

Question 3:
What is Laplace probability?

Question 4:
What topics are looked at in heuristics?

Question 5:
What is the difference between the single index model and the Markowitz model?

Answer to question 1:
In probability theory, a martingale is a stochastic process which has the property that the expected value of an observation is equal to the value of previous observations.

Answer to question 2:
When a random experiment is repeated often, the arithmetic mean of the realizations converges towards the expected value.

Answer to question 3:
Laplace probability is also called classical probability.

Answer to question 4:
Decisions which are reached based on feelings and emotions, but not on rationality.

Answer to question 5:
The main differentiating feature is that the model developed by Sharpe requires fewer data series than the Markowitz model. Sharpe assumes that the positive correlations between securities are caused by fundamentals.

3 | Ethical principles for successful financial engineering

The following chapter covers these issues:

- Are ethics enforceable in finance?
- What is our definition of ethical foundations for financial engineering?
- Which approaches to ethics are relevant for a financial engineer?

Ethics and finance, where is the link? Many newspapers are likely to ask this question in light of discussions about bonus payments to bankers and other issues. But the importance of ethics in finance is becoming increasingly clear. Business ethics is one of the main pillars for a successful operation. In contemporary discussions about business ethics, the term is often used as a synonym for living values. However, what we consider to be indispensable and important for the area of financial engineering is summarized below.

First, we define the term ethics. It is a translation of the classical Greek ἠθική ēthikē and means consciousness of moral importance. Ethics is thus dealing with human actions and in addition looks at morals; in particular at justifications for human behavior. In the classical academic and sociological perspective, ethics is divided into several sub-fields: social ethics, business ethics and company ethics. The latter is dealing with the question of which moral values ought to define a company. This is of relevance for financial engineering. Classical business ethics by comparison is analyzing the behavior of companies and the effects on society or the individual. Social ethics involves societal issues that illustrate an exemplary life and the values "liberty", "tolerance", and "justice."

The term business ethics is of relevance for financial engineering. It was already discussed in the ancient world but defined clearly in modern times only in 1907 by IGNAZ SEIPEL[1]. Business ethics pulls together a number of components, some of which appear rather self-evident for a well educated person. Defined are, among others, interactions with business partners, behavior when closing a transaction, issues of confidentiality and professional and personal qualifications of employees. This work focuses in the following issues:

Ignaz Seipel
1876–1932
Catholic theologist and Austrian politician

1. Morality and profitability of a project are not mutually exclusive.
2. Not everything that can be done must be done.
3. Property rights and environmental resources are to be respected.
4. Confidentiality is of the utmost importance; never abuse it.

During difficult economic times (especially following or during a crisis), calls for business ethics, i.e. for moral behavior, are frequently heard. During the boom, however, this dimension is frequently neglected. What is the reason for this? One explanation is the helplessness of individuals. Simply put, if humans are not feeling well, they are calling for help. God and faith take on a bigger role. However, it should be stated that much of what we refer to as ethics today, i.e. an understanding of values, is a matter of upbringing.

3.1 Are ethics enforcable in finance?

In order to answer this question, a definition of the term finance must be found. We define it as the science of applying financial theory to companies and financial markets. It also deserves mentioning that finance has developed significantly over the past years. Complex issues have gained a greater influence. The integration of these also requires a new understanding of ethics. Financial engineering, which is closely tied to the notion of progress[2], is the science of solving financial problems. Innovative products are to present and provide possible solutions. Not infrequently these possible solutions are characterized by considerable complexity and, for this reason, are considered to be intransparent by many (this does not mean, however, unethical or ethically incorrect). The basic premise must be to give every idea a fair chance. However, the idea needs to be scrutinized not only with regard to its feasibility but also concerning the related ethical dimension.

---

[1] In the context of the Catholic social teachings, see Ordo Socialis; see The Church Fathers' Teaching on Social Ethics.
[2] See Professor Dr. Rainer Stöttner, Kassel University: Lecture on financial engineering.

3.2 What is important in financial engineering concerning ethics?

One approach would be to say that financial engineering is merely the provider of ideas, the producer. But this approach would be inadequate. Where does the ethical inappropriateness of an idea begin – during development or during distribution? We favor the development theory and are therefore of the opinion that strong ethical behavior must be present at every stage of production. Consequently the ethical rules for financial engineering presented must be implemented at all times. Only those who are able to sell a product solution that is clear, transparent and elaborate will be successful over the long term. Financial engineering is not the handmaiden of turbo-capitalism. Today, financial engineering is one of the major revenue drivers of an investment bank. But such a cash cow[3] brings with it the obligation to carefully weigh the question: "Is the decision I am about to reach an ethically correct one?" But what is the ethically correct approach?

We distinguish three issues along the ethically correct route:

- The financial engineer as competent partner.
- The financial engineer as creator of tangible solutions.
- The financial engineer as keeper of the doable.

3.2.1 The financial engineer as competent partner

Initially every financial engineer must subject himself to a personal and internal investigation: "Am I, based on my education, my motives and my fundamental thinking suitable for this profession?" Reputation and character must be beyond doubt at all times. Each client and each employer must be sure that he can rely on a financial engineer. The relationship of trust with these groups of people can be viewed like the relationship between a patient and his doctor. If somebody is unwilling to assume the role of trusted partner and to keep secrets, he is not a competent partner. The fair and at all times truthful handling of the wishes of the client is also of primary importance. Every financial engineer must be aware that his products can contribute to the success or failure of a company. One should not be afraid in this regard that a product does not pan out. This will always happen in a market economy. But those who fundamentally accept such an outcome are acting grossly neg-

---

[3] Also see BCG Matrix (also Boston I Portfolio). Here applied to an in-house perspective.

ligent. A financial engineer should always reach his decisions after careful consideration and free from outside influences.[4]

3.2.2 The financial engineer as creator of tangible solutions

Whenever a client approaches the financial engineer with a problem, a tangible solution needs to be developed. In this regard, the interest of the own company must be subordinated. The client and his demands must take center stage. One thing is true in particular: respect for the client (and his problem) as well as for the product to be developed must always be present. Once respect for either one of these is lost, the development will suffer.

3.2.3 The financial engineer as judge of the doable

There are almost no limits to the possibilities of creating new products. This observation in particular implies that the moral and ethical understanding of the financial engineer must play a key role. Not everything that is doable needs to be implemented. Not all products are suitable for all market environments and all client segments. Furthermore, the setting of margins needs to be watched carefully. It is quite possible to place products with an internal margin of 5%. However, is this first of all correct and secondly defensible on ethical grounds? In this case, as in all others, the interest of the client must come first. The same is true for special products that are so highly complex that a large number of investors will not be able to understand them. Does a market really need such a product? Again, reason needs to win out over the possibility of making money.

On a second level, we extend the basic requirements just discussed as follows:

Ethical behavior vis-à-vis counterparts and end customers
The counterpart is just as important for the financial engineer as the client is for the sales desk. Therefore a relationship of absolute trust is a requirement. It is important not to promise anything that cannot be fulfilled. Agreements must be honored and if an error has crept in, it needs to be disclosed immediately and made fully transparent. In cases where frictions arise, quick and targeted

---

[4] Outside influeces can refer to decisions on business politics, but also to personal differences. A financial engineer should always base his decisions on the adult ego state and not the child ego state, which is often characterized by spitefulness, anger and so forth. On this issue see: Transactional Analysis by Eric Berne (1910–1970).

action is required. The same is true in the relationship with the end customer. It is the customer who is purchasing the products. His wishes and needs must take center stage. He sets the direction that needs to be taken. In this regard, care must be taken that our own road map and that of the client coincide. This illustration nicely shows the value of coordination. Only those who understand their clients, their worries, fears and problems, are in a position to present meaningful solutions.

Productive use of resources instead of Monte Carlo capitalism

There is no free lunch! At times it may appear that there is such a thing. It is important for the financial engineer that he does not cause more problems than he solves with his product solutions. That is why the mentality of a gambler is utterly misplaced in this position. Every decision must be carefully thought through. Resources ought to be used in a meaningful way and not to increase margins of the issuer. The new product is supposed to solve problems and not create new ones. In that sense, the financial engineer is also a protector of Pandora's box[5]. Yes, he can define a product, but it is his choice how he does it and what his intentions are. He has the freedom of design and is the steward of private and commercial wealth.

Reasons for the increasing demand for financial engineering services

The reasons for the increasing demand for financial engineering services can be stated rather easily. It is possible to use them for complex problems. Only 30 years ago, this would have been impossible in many ways. Today it has become daily routine. Of course, this is also driving the demand for such solutions. In addition, a higher degree of efficiency and demand can be reached in a global and interlinked world. New markets and investment opportunities are opening up. But many new questions also appear, such as: "Where do these new resources come from, and what goes on behind the scenes (for example child labor)?" In this regard, the ethical question must be: do we need a product which promises a higher return to a Western investor, while exactly as a result of this product, child labor will increase? Or think about the possibility of launching a product on almost any index. Is it permissible to issue a product that is linked to increasing unemployment, for example?

---

[5] In Greek mythology, the opening of Pandora's box released all evil into the world.

3.3 How to check for ethical principles?

Many investment banks have issued internal compliance regulations, which also list ethical principles and rules. In addition to the basic requirements discussed above, rules of proper conduct with regard to clients, contract partners and counterparts are specified in these documents. The regulations also cover monitoring by supervisors. Such rules clearly spell out the values a company – and thus also its employees – adhere to. Without such a code of conduct, pure cynicisms would surely result. And this in turn would result in a measurable loss of reputation. The famous lines of the sorcerer's apprentice[6] still hold true in this regard: "Sir, my need is sore. Spirits that I've cited, my commands ignore."

3.4 Fundamental ethical points of reference for the financial engineer

It is difficult to formulate rules for the ethically correct behavior of the financial engineer that are generally binding and not case specific. In the following, we venture out by entrusting our point of view into the hands of the reader as a base for critical reflection.

- A financial engineer should be driven by the urge to find a solution to a problem and not by the revenue potential of the product.
- A product solution should not trigger fresh problems.
- Religious, cultural and other demands of the customer must be respected. Use the same map when charting the course with your client.
- The product may not violate public morality.
- Resources must be used in a meaningful and productive manner.
- If conflicts of interest exist, they must be solved before proceeding.
- If you or your company are prejudiced, no product solution is to be provided.
- The question "Who is our client?" is central.
- Will this product or my actions cause harm to somebody else? If yes, the idea is not to be taken further.
- Promises made to third parties (counterparts, end customers) must be met at all times.

---

[6] The sorcerer's apprentice by Johann Wolfgang von Goethe; 1749–1832.

- Am I in violation of the law? If yes, no further action is to be taken.
  - Be careful concerning:
    - Embargoes
    - Child labor
    - Weapons and war trades
    - Transactions with a dubious financial background

In the discussion above, we touched upon the legality of a transaction. But equating ethics and legality would be too simplistic an approach. Behavior in conformity with the law is not sufficient to achieve ethically sound behavior. Otherwise, ethics would only play a minor role in finance; ethics is more than just adherence to legal standards. Ethics demonstrates contemporary positions on issues and the values of a society. Ethics means to launch a product free of hidden agendas and necessities. To be a partner for clients and the marketplace means more than just being a mindless producer; ethics means involvement of all parties. Logos[7], the word, must prevail, must be turned into reason[8] and thus into action[9]. PETER DRUCKER in his book *The five most important questions you will ever ask about your organization*[10] has provided clear definitions, which we want to quote at this point:

Peter Drucker
1909–2005
US economist of
Austrian descent

- What is our mission?
- Who is our customer?
- What does the customer consider value?
- What have been our results?
- What is our plan?

We would like to add two questions to this list:

- What are the values that we stand for?
- What are our motives and goals for the decisions and actions we take?

---

[7] Logos is not sufficiently captured with the term *word*, it means more. It also stands for proof, theorem and teachings, meaning and reason. See also J.W. von Goethe: Faust I, verse 1224ff.; the religious foundation is provided in the Gospel according to John (John 1,1): en archç çn ho Logos kai ho Logos çn pros ton Theon kai Theos çn ho Logos; translated into English: In the beginning was the Word, and the Word was with God, and the Word was God. In this context, it demonstrates the obligation of the spoken and considered word. It thus expresses the purity of the teaching, which is to be considered uncoupled from earnings and margin pressures. It should also be uncoupled from economic and personal profit seeking of individuals or society.

[8] Reason thus means wisdom and insight.

[9] In this case, action means recognizing what is appropriate and implementation with the help of a financial engineering solution.

[10] See "The five most important questions you will ever ask about your organization," Wiley, San Francisco, USA.

It is left to each of us individually to answer these questions. They are the base for reflection and an assessment of our personality and our environment. There is no use in trying to force ethical behavior on a person; it would never be taken seriously. Ultimately, all parties involved must resolve these issues for themselves[11]. This in turn leads to mutual self-commitments, which are desirable at all times.

---

[11] Those unwilling to approach these questions with a strong inner breadth and openness, will always just wear a mask, which is unlikely to be maintained in stress situations.

Literature for this chapter

Seipel, Ignaz: The Church Fathers' Teaching on Social Ethics

Ratzinger, Joseph: Introduction to Christianity

Drucker, Peter: The five most important questions you will ever ask about your organization

Pieper, Annemarie: Introduction to Ethics

Löhr, Albert; Valeva, Milena, v.: Finance & Ethics

Questions and answers on this chapter

Question 1:
In our definition, what is the meaning of ethics?

Question 2:
Is this statement correct? "Morality and profitability of a project are fundamentally at odds with each other."

Question 3:
Why is it often the case that ethics are demanded in economically difficult times?

Question 4:
What are the three points we use to structure the ethically correct behavior of the financial engineer?

Question 5:
Why must ethics become a part of daily life and why is it impossible to mandate it?

Answer to question 1:
Ethics means consciousness of moral importance and is thus dealing with human actions and furthermore with the effects of these actions on the environment.

Answer to question 2:
No, morality and profitability are not mutually exclusive. This was demonstrated clearly in Seipel's work.

Answer to question 3:
One explanation is the helplessness of individuals in dealing with problems.

Answer to question 4:
The financial engineer as competent partner.
The financial engineer as creator of tangible solutions.
The financial engineer as keeper of the doable.

Answer to question 5:

If ethics are simply mandated, there is a massive danger that actors fall back into old patterns of behavior during extreme situations. That is why correct ethical behavior must be part of the education of a financial engineer and must come from within.

Module II – Listed options & futures

4 | Derivatives exchanges and derivatives markets

The following chapter covers these issues:

- The origins of derivatives exchanges
- The organization of derivatives exchanges
- The functions of derivatives exchanges
- Who is active on derivatives exchanges?
- What is a derivative?
- What is required to trade derivatives?
- What are the uses of derivatives?

4.1 Historical development of derivatives exchanges

The origin of the widely used financial derivatives markets can be traced to futures on commodities. They were negotiated in order to hedge against **price risks**. Already around 2000 BC, the first forms of derivatives markets existed in India. Numerous records from the times of the Roman Empire and the Phoenicians also substantiate the existence of derivatives transactions. THALES OF MILETUS is said to have made use of options on olives and olive presses as early as around 500 BC.

Thales of Miletus
624 BC – 546 BC
Philosopher, statesman, mathematician, astronomer

Due to the vagaries of international trade, derivatives contracts appeared early for goods that were transported by sea and delivered from "unsafe" areas. The derivatives contracts served to secure prices. In medieval times, derivatives contracts are reported from England and France. The majority of these were commodity futures for commodities from Asia that were delivered months

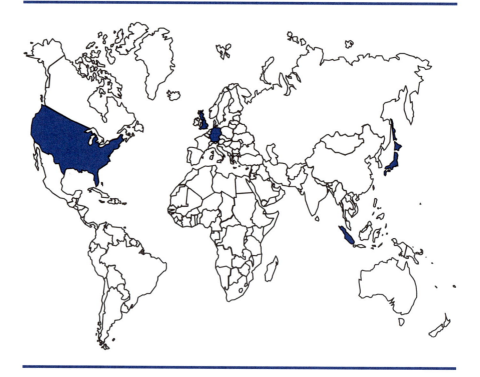

Figure 4.1: World map showing today's centers of futures trading (shaded areas)

later. In these cases as well, the motive was to guarantee prices. Around 1630, the Netherlands witnessed active options trading on tulip bulbs[1]. Similar to the new economy[2], a bubble developed[3]. Due to the excess demand for tulip bulbs, their prices increased steadily and prices spiraled upward. When the first investors decided that it was time to collect their profits and to sell their investments, they triggered a wave of selling. Due to excess supply, the price for tulip bulbs collapsed. Most investors suffered losses in excess of 90 percent.

In Asia (Osaka, Japan) rice and silk were traded actively during that time. The so-called "**Dojima Rice Market**" is considered to be the first organized derivatives market in Asia.

---

[1] Known as tulip mania.
[2] The new economy is an economic system characterized by globalization and technology. In Germany it mainly developed during the late 1990s. (see also: listing of internet companies, introduction of Anglo-American terminology and so forth).
[3] One characteristic of a bubble is excessive trading, for example in stocks. This is observed periodically in an economy and is part of the economic cycle.

Figure 4.2: CBOT trading floor during the founding years (top), 1970 (on the left) and 1999 (on the right)[4]

The **Chicago Board of Trade (CBOT)** can be considered to be the "mother of all derivatives exchanges." It was founded in 1848[5] and for the first time in history allowed the trading of standardized derivatives contracts. Also in Chicago, the "**Chicago Butter and Egg Board**" was founded in 1898. As the name suggests, butter and eggs were traded there. With the expansion of the product offering, the name was changed to **Chicago Mercantile Exchange (CME)** in 1919. In 2007, **CME** and **CBOT** merged to form the **CME Group**.

---

[4] Source: CBOT, Chicago.
[5] Founded on April 3, 1848.

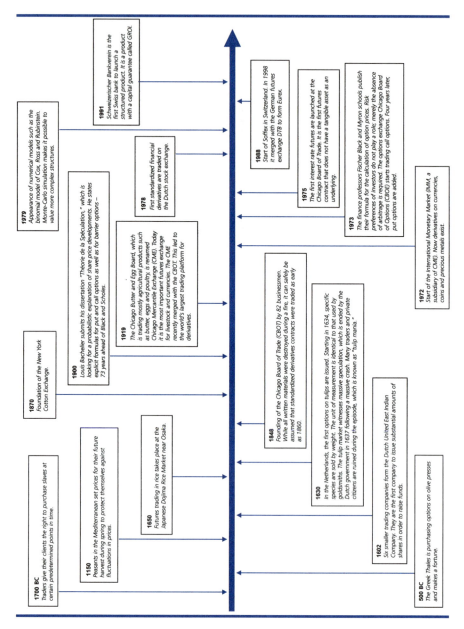

Figure 4.3: A historical time line of derivatives[6]

What is behind the massive increase in derivatives trading? As a result of the sudden increase in government debt in the United States as well as the breakdown of the system of fixed exchange rates (introduction of contracts

---

[6] Source: http://www.4finance.ch/literatur/derivatgeschichte.pdf.

on May 16, 1972 on the **International Monetary Market (IMM)**), a new financial landscape evolved, which was characterized by increased volatility. As a consequence, the first financial derivatives contracts, interest rate futures, were introduced in Chicago in the 1970s. This was the hour of birth of financial futures. In 1972 the first exchange rate futures on the seven major currencies were traded at the CME. The first contracts on the S&P500 were introduced in 1982 at the CME. In 1988, the first German futures exchange **Deutsche Terminbörse (DTB)** was founded. In 1998 it merged with the Swiss **SOFFEX** to form **Eurex**. In 1992, the GLOBEX Trading System (a computerized trading platform) of the CME was introduced. Figure 4.3 displays the development of the derivatives markets.

The current centers of derivatives trading are shown in Figure 4.1.

4.2 What is a derivatives transaction?

A derivatives transaction is a trade agreement in which **closing** (T_0) and **settlement** ($T_0 + x$) are happening at different points in time. In that regard they differ from spot market transactions, where settlement "immediately" follows the closing[7]. A forward transaction is binding for both parties and implies delivery and acceptance of an underlying commodity of a predefined quality and quantity at a predetermined price and date (see Figure 4.4).

An institutional distinction exists between a **forward** and a **future**. Forwards are individually drafted bilateral agreements between the parties. All aspects are determined individually with reference to the underlying. Futures on the other hand are standardized and traded on an exchange. The individual treatment of specific aspects is not possible. Futures can therefore be transferred at any time to another investor. This is not possible in the case of a forward contract due to its very specific nature. Futures and forwards are unconditional in nature: the contract must be honored and executed. No additional declaration of intend is required concerning settlement; it is mandatory.

> Futures/forwards are unconditional transactions. The buyer of futures/forwards benefits from an increase of the underlying, the seller from a decline.

---

[7] The value date can be different in some cases. Securities are bought and sold with a value date of transaction date plus two days.

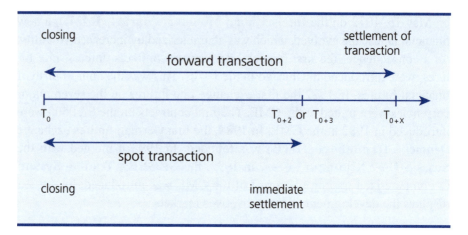

Figure 4.4: Settlement of spot and forward transaction

This is different in the case of **options**, which are also considered to be derivatives. An option is somewhat less concrete. Unlike futures or forwards, options give the buyer a choice: he decides whether or not to exercise.

An option gives the right to purchase or to sell a specified amount of an underlying asset within a predetermined time period or at a fixed point in time, at a price which has been specified in advance.

The **buyer** (long) of an option decides whether he wants to exercise the option or not. The **seller** (short), also called option writer, is asked to deliver once the option is exercised. He therefore does not have the freedom to choose and is completely passive in the agreement. In exchange, he receives financial compensation from the buyer of the option, the **option premium**.

Since the buyer is not required to make use of his right, but can also choose to let it expire, options are so-called conditional forward agreements. In contrast to forwards or futures, a declaration of intent by the buyer is required to exercise an option.

Options which are not standardized and are not traded on a derivatives exchange, but rather agreed individually between the contract parties are called OTC options. They are traded "**Over The Counter**" (see Figure 4.5 and Figure 4.6)

What is a derivatives transaction?

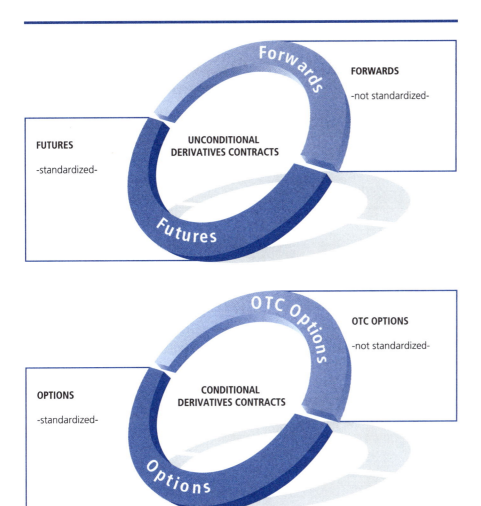

Figure 4.5: Conditional and unconditional derivatives contracts

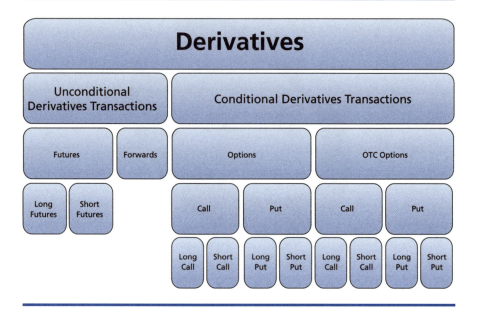

Figure 4.6: Conditional and unconditional derivatives contracts

 In Chapters 5 and 6 we will take a detailed look at futures and options. In Chapter 6.25, we discuss options on futures and Chapter 8 deals with derivatives that are traded over the counter.

4.3 Why are derivatives transactions mostly standardized today?

Most derivatives transactions that take place today are standardized. But why is this? There are a number of reasons in support of standardization:

- On the one hand, it is hard to find potential counterparts for a **forward** (which lacks standardization).
- On the other hand, the closing of a position – meaning to enter into an offsetting position – is very hard to accomplish.

Once a contract is standardized, the party that is closing out the position can be replaced by another party. The contract specifications are given and are not the result of individual negotiations. That is why a third party can easily take the place of the initial contract partner. An additional important point is the access to liquid and quick trading as a result of the standardization. This makes it possible to **open** or **close** a position at all times (a so-called **counter-order** is used to close a derivatives transaction).

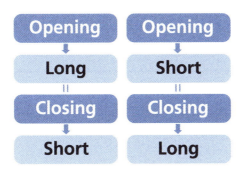

Figure 4.7: Opening (initial order) and close-out (offsetting order)

Standardization of the contracts refers to the following features:

Underlying
The underlying is the object of the derivatives transaction. It can be a financial asset or a commodity for example. The derivatives contract refers to this underlying.

Contract size – quantity
The contract size specifies the amount of the underlying which must be delivered or purchased (for example 100 shares, 5 Euro per index point). Contract size thus specifies the quantity of the derivatives transaction.

Strike price
The strike price is the price at which the underlying must be purchased or sold in case an option is exercised. It is also called the exercise price. Options with different strike prices are provided by the exchange on an ongoing basis. This means that at any point in time, a sufficient number of tradable strike prices are available.

Maturity
Maturity indicates the date at which the contract expires or the time to expiration. Internationally, the third Friday of the month is the expiration date, the last date on which the contract can be traded. The third Friday of the last

Table 4.1: Triple witching day

3rd Friday of the month of expiration	Assessment of the expiration date
January + February	NORMAL EXPIRATION DATE
March	TRIPLE WITCHING DAY
April + May	NORMAL EXPIRATION DATE
June	TRIPLE WITCHING DAY
July + August	NORMAL EXPIRATION DATE
September	TRIPLE WITCHING DAY
October + November	NORMAL EXPIRATION DATE
December	TRIPLE WITCHING DAY

month in the quarter is called triple witching day. On these dates, not only options, but also futures contracts are expiring.

Trading hours and location

Trading hours and location are determined by the derivatives exchange. Trading hours guarantee liquid and ongoing trading. This is true both for an open outcry system[8] and for computerized exchanges[9].

Quality of the underlying

Especially in the case of commodities, the quality of the underlying is of primary importance, since different versions may exist. An exact definition of the underlying (for example Sugar No. 11) is required. The same holds for stocks: it is precisely specified which type of share (preferred or ordinary shares) must be delivered. Mistakes or misunderstandings can be prevented in that way.

If parts of the contract are not specified, they need to be negotiated individually. Such an individual derivatives contract cannot be traded on an exchange, since it is very unlikely that a third party is looking for exactly such a highly individualized specification. In this case, a bilateral and individual derivatives contract is required, which is drawn up specifically for the parties involved.

Standardization also has its drawbacks. It may happen that an investor is unable to exactly hedge his exposure with regard to quantity and maturity, due to the existence of predetermined volumes and expiration dates. In this event, a tailor-made solution in the form of an OTC contract may well be preferable.

---

[8] This includes trading on the floor of the exchange.
[9] Trading takes place in a virtual trading room.

> **Flexible trading due to standardization**
>
> As was shown in the previous section, standardization of derivatives contracts leads to the smooth transfer of ownership as well as easy opening and closing of positions. Standardization makes trading in listed derivatives possible. OTC derivatives are less flexible and harder to handle in many regards. But when non-standard hedging is required, they are a useful addition.

4.4 What are the functions of derivatives exchanges?

The existence of well organized and liquid spot markets is a prerequisite for the successful development of derivatives markets. The exchange provides the necessary organizational infrastructure that makes it possible to initiate and maintain trading in the listed derivatives products.

The main reason for the founding of derivatives exchanges is the **redistribution of risk**, which we already discussed before. Futures markets enable market participants to hedge against unwanted fluctuations in the spot market. Risk is transferred from hedgers (investors who want to shed risk) to speculators (investors who actively seek to assume risk). Speculators in particular are important providers of liquidity and assure a smooth working of the exchange. They absorb existing risks without generating new ones.

Furthermore, derivatives markets generate additional information about prices, which can be used in the spot markets. This leads to more efficient and transparent decision making. Prices in the derivatives markets reveal more information than prices in spot markets. This implies quicker and more active trading in derivatives markets, and through the link between the two, also in the spot market. Figure 4.8 shows the organizational setup of a derivatives exchange, including its clients.

Thanks to low transaction costs and the quick speed of execution, large volumes can be moved inexpensively and quickly. Within a few minutes, vast amounts of money can change hands. Entire markets (via **indexes**) can be traded with only one transaction, for example with an index future. What is more, trading at a derivatives exchange does not require possession of the full amount of the transaction value. Only a deposit, the so called margin pay-

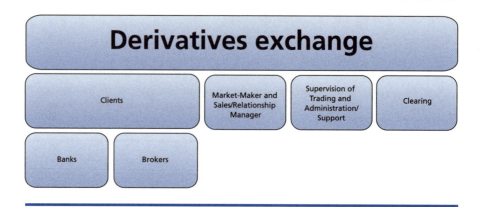

Figure 4.8: Setup of a derivatives exchange with integrated clearing

ment, must be provided. The margin payment assures that the counterparty can always meet all obligations. When purchasing options, a long position in options, the premium paid is only a fraction of the value of the contract. This enables an investor to move large amounts of money with a small capital base. An additional and very important advantage of derivatives exchanges is the ability to speculate on declining prices. While **spot exchanges** only allow speculation on price increases, derivatives exchanges also make it possible for an investor to position himself for a decline in value. This means that money can also be made in times of falling prices. Without the provision of suitable instruments by derivatives exchanges, such strategies would not be possible.

4.5 Who are the market participants at derivatives exchanges?

There are different participants at derivatives exchanges. They are clustered into four groups based on their motivations (see Figure 4.9).

Hedger
His motivation is the elimination of risk for existing holdings. This is the fundamental reason for the existence of derivatives exchanges. He hedges against price risks by transferring the risk to other market participants. He is risk averse. His hedge allows him to secure for example, the profit from a spot transaction. A risk transfer is the result of the transaction. The transfer of price risks to another party was the initial rational for derivatives transactions.

Speculator
He is the counterpart of the hedger. The speculator takes a position with the expectation of making a profit. He actively assumes risk and provides required market liquidity. He accepts risk and in turn expects to profit from his activities.

Arbitrageur
He is motivated by arbitrage opportunities. This means that he makes use of different price quotes on the same underlying at different markets and profits from the difference without taking any risk. Since the contracts are bought and sold simultaneously, there is essentially no risk. The arbitrageur as well provides the market with liquidity. He also helps to move prices towards an appropriate level. Arbitrageurs are mostly banks and brokers. With its implementation, arbitrage, or better the possibility for arbitrage, is self-defeating. Arbitrage activities remove any pricing differences found among identical underlying securities and therefore eliminate future profit opportunities.

Spreader
This investor attempts to make a profit by exploiting pricing differences. He is buying a futures contract which appears cheap to him and sells another one which appears overpriced. The simultaneous opening and closing of positions leads to price differences. The maximal profit is equal to this difference.

4.6 Which other basic concepts are required for an understanding of derivatives exchanges and derivatives markets?

Investors
This book frequently uses the term investor. Therefore, the concept needs to be explained briefly at this point. The investor is active in derivatives contracts and in the underlying securities. He can be either a retail investor or an institutional investor. In our interpretation, the investor can even sell something which he does not possess (short selling[10]) or he can be involved in all kinds of derivative transactions (no limitations on size or barriers to entry). The investor has an unlimited amount of financial assets at his disposal, which

---

[10] Short selling means entering into a negative asset position with the basic intention to repurchase this asset at a later point in time for a lower price, thus closing the negative position.

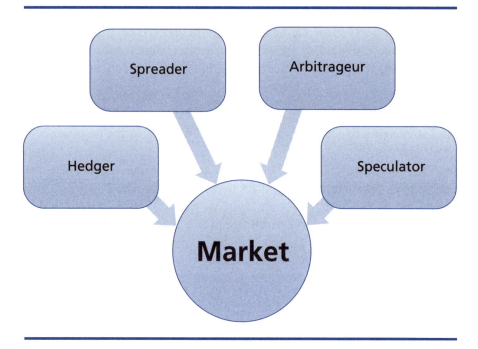

Figure 4.9: Market participants at a derivatives exchange

he can use without limitations concerning timing and location. Furthermore, the investor can draw on a wealth of experience and knowledge and thus is able to make use of all instruments available.

Derivative
We also want to define the term derivative for our purposes. The word derivative can be traced to the Latin "**derivare**" and means descendant. It is thus a financial instrument which is derived from an underlying (such as a share).

The development of the derivative is always linked to the development of the underlying. The underlying itself is largely unaffected by the investment in derivatives, since an investment in derivatives is motivated merely by the expectation or assumption of a change in the underlying. Only in rare cases is the underlying itself part of the strategies. The underlying thus forms the basis and origin of the investment, but is not included directly. This changes when the derivative is exercised. In this case, the derivative ceases to exist and is replaced by the underlying.

Hedging
With the help of a hedging transaction, the investor avoids adverse market developments. Protection is the main motivation for the trade. Hedging al-

ways involves a financial commitment. A hedger[11] is risk averse and values certainty. With the transaction, the risk is transferred to a third party and no longer a concern for the hedger. In exchange, he is willing to pay financial compensation to the party that is willing to bear the risk.

Speculation

Speculative positions have a different background. The Latin word "**speculor**" is equivalent to the English "I peek." To speculate thus means to take a brief look or to seek. Speculation is always a short-term activity aimed at making a profit. In cases where a speculative holding is medium-term to long-term, it is called a strategic investment or a planned future speculation.

This readiness to enter into an investment with a profit motive provides a large part of the liquidity in the derivatives market. The speculator can thus be called the engine of every order. Every closing of a transaction requires the willingness of one party to assume risk. A speculator is aware of the risks he is taking and in most cases assesses them correctly. In our definition, speculation means the generation of returns by accepting risk. In this sense, the speculator absorbs risks which are inherent in the economy and attempts to derive a legitimate profit from this activity.

Dividends and interest rates

Let us take a brief look at interest rates and dividends, which directly or indirectly influence financial derivatives.

Dividends

A dividend is the payment of profits of a stock company. It directly influences the underlying of a financial derivatives transaction and thus the derivatives transaction itself. Part of the profit of a company is paid out to shareholders and thus reduces the capital available to the company[12]. This means that the price of the underlying will decline. As a consequence, the price of a derivative written on the underlying will also change.

Interest rates

The level of interest rates varies with the term to maturity. The graphical representation of interest rates for different maturities is called **term structure of interest rates** (see Figure 4.10). An important issue is the expected change in the term structure of interest rates and its magnitude (see Table 4.2).

---

[11] This is an investor who shuns risk and attempts to keep his holdings at a risk-neutral level.
[12] The payment of a dividend does not enrich the investor. He merely receives a share of the profits of the company and thus obtains liquidity.

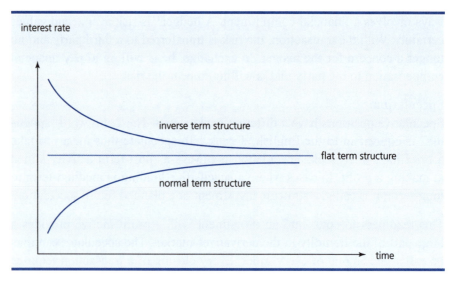

Figure 4.10: Term structures of interest rates[13]

Table 4.2: A description of different scenarios for fixed income instruments.

Scenario	+100 bp	−100 bp	‚Flattening' +100bp/ −50 bp	‚Steepening' −100bp/ +50bp	+300 bp	−300bp
description	Parallel upward movement of the entire yield curve by 100 bp.	Parallel downward movement of the entire yield curve by 100 bp.	money market interest rates increase by 100 bp; 10-year rate declines by 50 bp; 30-year rate declines by 100 bp.	money market interest rates decrease by 100 bp; 10-year rate increases by 50 bp; 30-year rate increases by 100 bp.	Parallel upward movement of the entire yield curve by 300 bp.	Parallel downward movement of the entire yield curve by 300 bp.

A distinction is made between three typical shapes of the term structure:

Flat term structure: The level of interest rates is the same across all maturities. In the case of a flat term structure, central banks have difficulties to control monetary aggregates.

Normal term structure: Interest rates are increasing with maturity. Such a term structure is typical during the onset of an economic recovery.

---

[13] Source: Frankfurt School of Finance "Wertpapiergeschäft für Wertpapierspezialisten."

Inverted term structure: Interest rates are decreasing with maturity. An inverted term structure is often observed during recessions and times of deflation. A decline in inflation is expected and money market rates are high while capital market rates are lower. The central bank has reduced the money supply.

The difference between two interest rates at the short end and the long end of the maturity spectrum is called **term spread**. Below are the formulas for calculating the term spread for Euro and USD.

Term Spread Euro

$$S_{eur} = \left(\frac{10}{1}\right) = i_{10} - i_1$$

S_{eur} = Spread for the Euro-area
i = interest rates

Term Spread USD

$$S_{USD} = \left(\frac{30}{0.5}\right) = r_{30} - r_{0.5}$$

S_{usd} = Spread for the U.S.
r = yields

The term structure is upward sloping in case of a positive term spread. It is an indication of continuing economic growth. On the other hand, a negative or zero value for the term spread signals recessionary tendencies.

> **Note for the United States:**
>
> In the U.S. it is customary to state yields rather than interest rates. This leads to the term yield curve.

4.7 What is the organizational structure of derivatives exchanges?

Derivatives exchanges are either organized as **floor exchanges** or involve **computerized trading**:

- The **floor exchange** is the traditional way an exchange is organized. Trading takes place on the trading floor and among others, the **open outcry system**[14] is used. Hand signals are used for communications.
- This is different on **computerized exchanges** such as Eurex. Trading on these exchanges takes places via the anonymous and noiseless exchange of information on a network. All participants are linked and communicate via data networks. This allows for unobstructed supra-regional and international trading. All participants have simultaneous access to the same market and price information. The placement of orders via the trading screen guarantees extremely quick execution. All orders are cleared in a fully automated fashion. Liquidity is assured due to active market making. The entire system can be thought of as a virtual trading room.

4.8 The working of a computerized exchange

Eurex is a very good example for a fully computerized exchange. It was created in 1998 from a merger between **DTB**[15] and **SOFFEX**[16]. DTB, founded in 1988 as an operating company, was an exchange that exclusively focused on computerized trading. Since derivatives contracts were virtually absent in Germany prior to the founding of DTB due to a lack of a legal framework, the new exchange had a hard time in its early years. But soon the major advantages of derivatives trading were realized and DTB was able to hold its own against the competition in other European and American stock exchange centers. The new exchange is winning over customers thanks to its new structure which is based on high transparency, functionality and security. With the help of the mainframe computer, trading is noiseless and fast. A program immediately assigns all incoming orders to already existing orders whenever possible. In case orders cannot be executed immediately, the main computer puts them into the central order book. As soon as orders can be executed, the system automatically triggers their **matching**. New orders are sorted based on the **price-time-principle**[17]. This means that the order with the earliest time stamp for which an execution is possible is executed first. If further orders can be filled, execution is based on the time stamp as well.

---

[14] Communication system used in floor trading.
[15] DTB: Deutsche Terminbörse.
[16] SOFFEX: Swiss Options and Financial Futures Exchange.
[17] In case several orders can be executed at the same price, the order with the earlier time stamp is executed first. Orders with a better price are filled ahead of orders with a worse price.

The working of a computerized exchange

Table 4.3: Example of an order book (example: futures on DAX® index)

Trading day April 21, 2010	Orders to buy (bid)			Dax futures	Orders to sell (ask)		
Limit	6050	6050	6090		6100	6100	6130
Contract size	30	45	12		45	30	32
Time stamp	11:15	11:05	12:07		10:23	12:05	11:22

Table 4.3 presents the example of an order book for the FDAX®. Shown are the buy and sell orders, contract size and time stamp of the orders.

The quote in the above example is 6090/6100 (12 contracts/75 contracts). If now, for example, an order to sell 20 contracts at 6060 were to arrive, it would be matched with the 12 contracts to buy at 6090 and the remaining 8 contracts would be entered into the order book. The new quote would be 6050/6060 (75/8).

A very important aspect is the security of the system. Eurex therefore introduced three security layers.

Technical security:

- Technical security starts with the core component of Eurex. The mainframe computer is duplicated in order to prevent systems failure. All tasks will immediately be taken over by the second computer, should the first one go down. At the same time, all lines of communication and data lines exist twice. This duplication of all data and orders guarantees a high security standard.

Market security:

- In order to assure market integrity, all suspicious facts concerning manipulations are permanently analyzed and monitored.

Participant security:

- An access authorization is provided by Eurex to every participant, so that only authorized traders can enter orders on a trade screen. Eurex also controls the access of employees to the data sources. Access is possible only to one's own trading and clearing data. Access by third parties is denied.

With this system and these regulations, Eurex is one of the world's leading derivatives exchanges.

> **Computerized exchanges versus floor exchanges**
>
> Summarized briefly, it can be said that computerized exchanges establish purely virtual trading rooms. Trading is executed quickly with the help of computer-based methods. Floor exchanges still have the flair of "traditional" trading. Trading activities are still tangible and take place on the "parquet" of the exchange. Thanks to increasing globalization, increases in volume and the "thrill of speed," the classical trading rooms are increasingly being abandoned in favor of the virtual world.

4.9 What is the market maker principle?

In order to guarantee liquidity in all products traded, Eurex has introduced the principle of **market making**. Market makers are brokers[18] who provide binding price **quotes** for the products they are responsible for, either continuously or on demand. These quotes consist of a **bid** and an **ask** price. When providing these quotes, the market maker needs to adhere to a contract volume and a spread as determined by Eurex. In addition, the market maker is required to reply to at least 50% (depending on the level of market making, this number can be as high as 85%) of the **quote requests** within a minute and to keep open these quotes for at least ten seconds. This gives the counterparty an opportunity to place an order based on the quote received. Once the market maker has replied to 150 quote requests in one day, he can turn down or leave unanswered additional queries. This form of market making is called **regular market making**. It is aimed at less liquid series and means that a quote must be provided **on request**. Without market making it would often be impossible to trade certain products – especially exotic ones. Once a market participant has submitted an order to the system and no quotes are available, the order system automatically sends a query to the market maker. Then the order is either executed or transferred to the central order book.

> Find out about the market making obligations for various product types of Eurex in our download area.

---

[18] They work for banks or brokerages.

Figure 4.11: Types of market making

Permanent market making is available for options (certain strike prices in the "At-the-money" range). The market maker provides **continuous** quotes for the contracts serviced by him. The availability of continuous quotes assures quick and liquid trading. The great importance of the market maker is highlighted by the fact that quick and consistent trading would not be possible without him. Quotes on certain packages (equity options, equity index options as well as options on fixed income futures) are provided in **advanced market making**. Since the quotation is also **continuous**, execution can be assured. In contrast to permanent market making, not only individual series are quoted, but entire packages defined by the exchange, which can contain different products (see Figure 4.11).

4.10 Trading at Eurex[19]

At Eurex, different trading phases can be distinguished.

Pre-Trading Phase
During this phase, all market participants can enter, change and delete orders. No trading takes place.

Opening Phase
Trading at Eurex starts with an opening auction. The first step is to create a balanced order book. The netting process refers to the calculation of opening

---

[19] We use Eurex as an example of a futures exchange in this book. Their market model serves as the basis for explaining derivatives trading.

prices and transactions, if possible. The basis for price determination is the price level that results in the maximum executable order volume. Existing orders and quotes are matched to the extent possible. As soon as this netting process is completed, the trading period commences.

Trading Period
During the trading period, open orders and quotes are compared continuously. All orders and quotes entered during this time that are equal to or better than existing orders and quotes on the corresponding contra-side of the order book are immediately matched. If not immediately matched, orders are held in the central order book, if appropriate. Transactions are confirmed in real time. Orders and quotes can be entered, changed or deleted as required.

Closing Auction
Again the order book is balanced. All open orders and quotes are considered during the closing auction and netted if possible. The closing auction ends as soon as the netting process has been completed for all futures contracts based on that product.

If no market orders exist for any specific futures contracts and matching between limit orders and quotes is not possible, or if market orders exist that are not executable, the closing auction ends without determining a closing price.

Post-Trading Period
The post-trading period is divided into four phases (see Figure 4.12):

- **Post-Trading Full**: Orders may be entered, changed or deleted.
- **Post-Late 1:** The Eurex system does not allow OTC trade entries during that phase.
- **Post-Late 2:** The Post-Late 2 period only applies for interest rate options on the last trading day.
- **Post-Trading Restricted:** Only data inquiries are possible during this phase. Orders may still be entered for the next trading day, but exercises are no longer accepted.

Following these phases, the batch process begins (processing of completed contracts traded) on the Eurex system. Data inquiries are no longer available. The system is maintained and prepared for the next trading day. In theory, 24-hour trading would be possible, since the systems' maintenance could be done in a few minutes. However, Eurex has decided to maintain specific

Figure 4.12: Eurex trading phases

trading hours. This is different at GLOBEX[20]: this system is ready for trading almost 24 hours a day, with only brief downtimes for maintenance.

4.11 Who regulates derivatives markets?

Options and futures markets are subject to strict, in some countries even extremely strict regulation. The respective regulatory bodies differ from country to country and a general assessment is not possible. In the US, for example, the **Securities and Exchange Commission (SEC)** is responsible for options products at the federal level. The **Commodity Futures Trading Commission (CFTC)** is responsible for futures and options on futures. In Germany, meanwhile, there are supervisory bodies for exchanges as well as federal supervisors.

Exchange supervision in Germany	http://www.boersenaufsicht.de
Securities and Exchange Commission (SEC) in the US	http://www.sec.gov
Commodity Futures Trading Commission (CFTC) in the US	http://www.cftc.gov

---

[20] Computerized trading system of the CME in Chicago.

4.12 Which products can be traded?

In principle, a derivatives contract can be written on any underlying. However, liquidity and demand for the listed derivative (as well as the **underlying**) is a major concern and a prerequisite for a listing at a derivatives exchange.

The underlying assets presented in Figure 4.13 are only a selection of all products traded. The complete universe of products can be obtained from the information pages of the derivatives exchanges. Contract specifications such as contract size, multiplier, settlement, trading times, and so forth, are also provided there.

Product information and contract specifications can also be found in our Download Area.

4.13 The clearing process

Clearing is a central issue behind every order. Clearing means the management, provision of collateral and final settlement of cash payments and delivery of securities of the completed trade. Clearing (Central Counterparty) at Eurex is provided by Eurex Clearing AG.

Figure 4.13: Derivatives, a list of some products traded

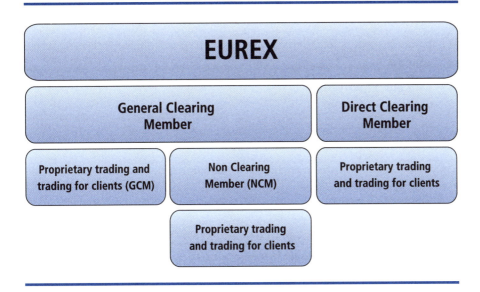

Figure 4.14: Participants in Eurex trading

Members who are allowed to trade on the Eurex platform are distinguished by clearing status (see Figure 4.14).

General Clearing Member (GCM)
This membership is for banking institutions which satisfy the capital requirement of EUR 125 million in liable equity. They have the right to clear transactions for their customers and other members who do not hold a clearing license in addition to their own transactions.

Direct Clearing Member (DCM)
Banking institutions with liable equity in excess of EUR 12.5 million can obtain this status. They can clear their own transactions and those of their customers.

Non-Clearing Member (NCM)
NCM do not undertake independent clearing activities, but can access Eurex trading through a General Clearing Member. This requires a contractual agreement with a General Clearing Member. These contracts are an independent legal relationship, since only clearing members can be contracting parties of Eurex Clearing AG.

4.14 How to specify an order

When placing orders for a derivatives market transaction, the following terms are required:

- What kind of derivative?
    - Options or futures?
    - In the case of options: call or put?
- Is it a buy or sell order?
    - Long
    - Short
- Number of contracts?
- Which underlying?
- Which expiration month and in which year?
- In the case of options: strike price
- Possibly a limit on the price or a market order
- Possibly details about the cancellation of the order (GFD = Good-for-Day, GTC = Good-till-Cancelled, GTD = Good-till-Day)
- Which trading location?
- Other specific features?
- Covered or uncovered?[21]
- Is this a combination order?
- Opening or closing?
- Possibly additional instructions for the order

Orders can either be **limited** or **unlimited**. Unlimited orders are called "market orders", which are executed immediately upon receipt if possible. In the case of limited orders, execution can take time, since a price equal to or better than the limit must first be reached. If an order cannot be filled, it is added to the Eurex order book. The same is true for partial executions: remaining partial orders which cannot be filled are entered into the order book.

Limits

- **Limit order:** A limit must be reached before the order can be executed. The order cannot be executed before a pre-specified price target is reached. This is in contrast to a market order, which is filled at the next available price.
- **Stop order (STP):** These are orders in derivatives trading which are activated once a pre-specified level is breached. This only makes sense for a buy order above the current market price and a sell order below the current

---

[21] In a covered options position, the investor possesses the underlying, for example shares.

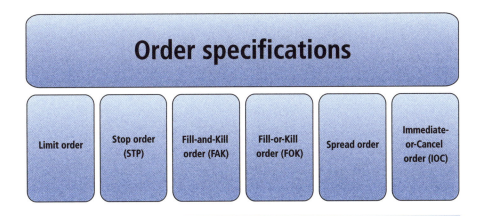

Figure 4.15: Different order specifications

market price. This kind of limit is used for system orders based on technical analysis. At the same time, it is used to define key points in a strategy. An investor can protect himself against losses or target a specific price level for entering the market, based for example on technical analysis.

- **Fill-and-Kill order (FAK):** Immediate execution of the order, also in parts. The order for the parts which were not filled is cancelled.
- **Fill-or-Kill order (FOK):** Fill-or-kill orders are executed immediately and completely, or if this is not possible they are cancelled without execution. Partial execution is not possible.
- **Spread order:** A spread order deals with the entire spread in one order. Purchase and sale are stated in one order. At Eurex, this is possible only for futures.
- **Immediate-or-Cancel order (IOC):** The order is to be filled immediately, partial execution is possible. The parts which remain unfilled are cancelled. This type of order is available at Eurex for combined orders in futures as well as options (see Figure 4.15)

Orders can remain valid for various amounts of time, depending on the specification (see Figure 4.16):

- Orders which are valid only on the day they were placed (Good-for-Day, GFD);
- Orders which remain valid up to a predetermined date (Good-till-Date, GTD);
- Orders which remain valid until cancelled (Good-till-Cancelled, GTC).

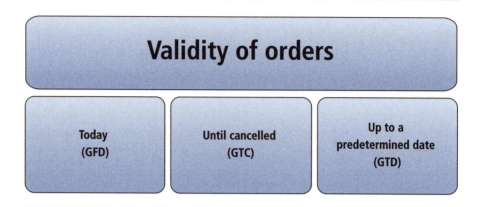

Figure 4.16: Differences in validity of orders

Execution of orders

In order to rule out unwanted sharp price movements, Eurex has determined a maximal price range for futures, within which unlimited orders can be filled. This protects the investor who has placed an order against undesirable jumps in prices.

The **price-time-principle** is used when matching[22] orders. Orders which cannot be filled immediately or only in parts are added to the electronic order book of Eurex and executed when a possibility for a match arises. Partial execution is always possible, unless the order rules this out. Since Eurex is a computerized exchange, the speed of transaction is rather high (see Figure 4.17/ and Figure 4.18). Following execution, the system immediately provides information concerning the contracts traded (underlying of the contract), the price of the transaction and the volume traded.

Figure 4.17: Eurex order mask ("Sell Order" Eurex @X-ceed Trading GUI)[23]

---

[22] Matching means bringing together orders with the aim of trading.
[23] Source: Commerzbank AG CM Derivatives Sales Desk & Eurex.

How to specify an order   115

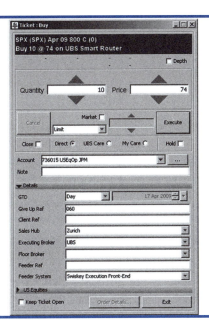

Figure 4.18: Order tool for foreign exchanges (UBS SwissKey System; Buy Order)[24]

Additional order specifications

Additional order specifications with very different features exist at other futures exchanges. A **market if touched order** for example is an order which becomes effective once the stated price is traded. The order becomes a market order at that moment. A **not held order**, also called **take time order**, gives certain leeway to the broker concerning execution: if he expects more favorable pricing later, he can add the order to the order book and fill on his discretion. No possibility of recourse exists in this case. A **cancel former order** always entails the cancellation of a previous order. In contrast to this, several combinations are captured in a **one cancels the other order**. This means that the execution of one of the orders leads to the cancellation of the order which was registered jointly as part of a package. And finally there are orders which become effective only during the market closing or opening. These orders are restricted to these trading periods and are called market opening and market closing orders.

It is important to understand all available order specifications – regardless of which specification is ultimately chosen in a given situation and for a specific position. At the same time, it is important to ask the bank/broker, which

---

[24] Source: Commerzbank AG CM Derivatives Sales Desk.

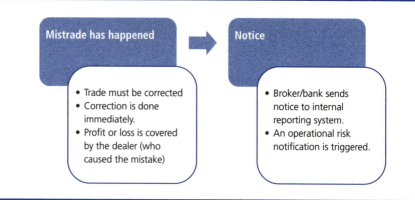

Figure 4.19: Dealing with a mistrade

types of orders are available; not all banks/brokers offer all specifications. One always needs to check as well whether the order makes sense as specified. Meaningless orders or orders that are not in line with current market conditions should not be placed. In many cases they are even rejected by banks/brokers.

When trading in an underlying is halted at the exchange, normally all orders for derivatives transactions on the underlying are deleted at the derivatives exchange. Once trading is resumed, these orders must be entered again.

Mistrade rules

Mistrade rules deal with mistakes that occur during trading in derivatives (see Figure 4.19). Please note: As soon as a mistake is discovered, it must be corrected immediately and without further delay. The attempt to benefit from an order which was incorrectly placed can produce high losses and above all damage a client relationship. A record must be kept on every order that was placed by mistake and steps must be taken to prevent a repetition.

Order systems and placement of orders
It goes without saying that a high degree of familiarity with all order systems is required. But at this point we would like to stress again that there are different kinds of orders and order specifications. The following rule applies: prior to placing an order, it must be determined which types of orders and specifications are required. Then it must be ascertained whether these are offered by the counterpart and can be exercised. These are preparatory measures which must be taken in all cases. If the counterpart has been known for years, an inquiry is often not necessary.

4.15 What are the expiration dates at Eurex?

The expiration date for series of options at Eurex is the third Friday of the month. Index futures in addition are due on the third Friday of the last month in the quarter (both expiration dates are in line with international standards). The last trading day for fixed income futures is two working days prior to the delivery date[25]. Options on fixed income futures are traded for the last time six working days prior to the first calendar day of the expiration month of the option. Weekly options expire on the first, second, fourth and fifth Friday (see Figure 4.20).

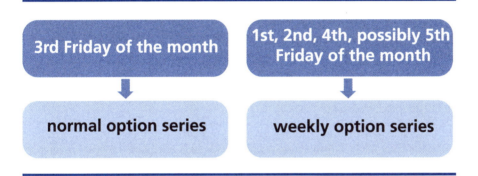

Figure 4.20: Expiration dates at Eurex (Friday rule)

Interview with Thomas Knipping
Head Listed Derivatives Sales – Commerzbank AG

Mr. Knipping, what is your outlook for the derivatives market in the years to come?
In my opinion, the market for derivatives is undergoing significant change at the moment. Following the excesses of the previous years, which have contributed significantly to the financial crisis, we notice heightened interest in plain vanilla derivatives. We also witness increased demand for listed products at the expense of OTC derivatives. The example of Lehman Brothers has shown that counterparty risk should not be taken lightly.

Which percentage differences in the contracts traded can you state for the different types of underlying instruments (fixed income, equity, commodities)?
I think we will witness a structural change in the coming years. So far, demand was strongest for fixed income products, but equity and index products are catching up and will be in the number one position in the foreseeable future. And the demand for commodities is increasing as well.

---

[25] Delivery date, for example in the case of Euro Bund Futures is the tenth day of the expiration month.

Which products (listed options & futures) will be of relevance in the years to come?
Equity and index options for portfolio protection and generation of additional returns by selling calls or puts.

Which product group is likely to see the most dynamic growth in the coming years?
I expect stronger growth in the segment of flexible products, especially with regard to equities and indexes. Products such as the Flex Futures at Eurex enable the investor to implement individual preferences (maturity, settlement and so forth), without counterparty risk.

What will be the importance of hedging transactions relative to speculative trades in the future?
I basically think that there will be fewer speculative transactions. This may mean that markets will become less liquid. But the financial crisis has drastically increased investors' awareness of risk. Therefore, the focus is increasingly on hedging transactions.

How do you assess the upcoming development of futures markets?
It is important to differentiate: structured products and credit derivatives were harshly criticized, but they are still in demand because they fulfill a needed function. But plain vanilla products are clearly becoming more popular.

Which client segment has the highest growth potential in your opinion?
Very clear answer: wealth managers. "Buy and hold" is no longer adequate. Different and better products are out there.

Which additional underlying would you like to see listed?
Quite frankly, I think that the current product range is adequate. Innovations such as weather futures may look interesting at first sight, but they have a big drawback: since the underlying cannot be traded, it is hard to achieve a liquid market.

Looking back on the past years, how would you briefly assess developments in the derivatives markets?
For a long time, the derivatives market has witnessed steady and strong growth in all segments. Unfortunately, not all products were scrutinized with the required diligence. Apparently investors, especially in the retail segment, did not fully understand the products.

Literature for this chapter

Hull, John: Options, Futures and Other Derivatives, 7th edition, 2009

Madura, Jeff: International Financial Management, 6th edition, 2004

Rudolph, Bernd, Schäfer, Klaus: Derivative Finanzinstrumente, 2005

Steinbrenner, Hans-Peter: Optionsrechte in der Praxis, 2002

Questions and answers on this chapter

Question 1:
How do futures and forward transactions differ?

Question 2:
What is an open outcry system?

Question 3:
What is regular market making?

Question 4:
Define General Clearing Member.

Question 5:
What is a Fill-or-Kill (FOK) order?

Answer to question 1:
Futures, unlike forwards are traded on a futures exchange. Futures are standardized and can therefore be transferred to a third party at any time.

Answer to question 2:
This is a trading procedure used in parquet trading in Chicago. It is only used at floor exchanges (for example Chicago).

Answer to question 3:
Regular market making means the continuous provision of quotes in the product group managed by a market maker. Normally at least 150 quotes are provided in this way every day by each market maker.

Answer to question 4:
It is the highest level of membership for clearing at Eurex. GCM have the right to clear their own transactions, transactions for their customers and transactions for third parties who are not clearing members.

Answer to question 5:
The order must be filled completely and immediately. If this is not possible, the order is deleted. Partial execution is thus not possible.

5 | Futures – unconditional derivatives contracts

The following chapter covers these issues:

- What are futures?
- How do futures function?
- How to price futures?
- What kinds of futures exist?
- Which strategies can be developed with the help of futures?

5.1 What are futures?

Classical derivatives contracts, in the following referred to as forwards and futures, are almost as old as trading itself. In the beginning, futures existed mainly on commodities. The first financial futures were traded in August 1977 in Chicago; they were based on the 30-year US Treasury Bond (T-Bond), which continues to be one of the most frequently traded contracts to this date. The multitude of underlying assets and contracts traded today is almost unmanageable. There are index futures, fixed income futures, commodity futures, currency futures and many others.

What are **futures**? Futures are contracts with standardized elements that can be traded on an exchange. They can be easily transferred and are accepted by a third party without problem. Their OTC counterparts are **forwards**, which constitute individual contracts between two parties, in most cases between a bank and its client (see Figure 5.1). A contract is drawn up specifically for the two parties and their demands and therefore cannot be transferred easily to a third party. Both contracts are unconditional commitments that must be honored. The two parties agreed to fulfill all obligations specified during the

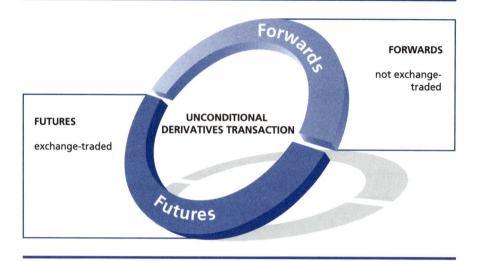

Figure 5.1: Unconditional derivatives transactions

closing of the contract. The main motive of a forward investor is to hedge against risk or to speculate on a medium-term market development. Due to the limited fungibility of forward contracts, they are not suitable for short-term or "true" speculation; instead they are predominantly used to hedge an underlying transaction and its associated cash flows.

A futures contract is a type of derivative that obligates the parties involved to either receive (**long**) or to deliver (**short**) a predetermined underlying, at a pre-specified price, at a set date and in a defined quality and quantity. The derivatives contract must be honored, it is an unconditional agreement.

5.2 Futures markets

Futures exist on a number of underlying assets. Figure 5.2 lists the most common types of futures.

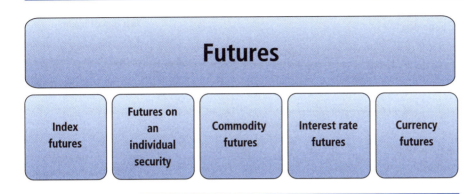

Figure 5.2: The most common types of futures

5.3 Futures trading

In order to trade a futures contract, an investor needs a certain amount of money, which is only a small fraction of the contract value of the contract. This amount is called **initial margin**[1]. Its function is to guarantee that the investor can meet all payment obligations until the next trading day.

During the time an investor holds a futures contract in his account, the **mark-to-market** process assures the daily balancing of profits and losses (see Figure 5.3). This is called **variation margin**. Additional information on the topic of margins can be found in Chapter 16.3.

5.4 Basic futures strategies

Fundamentally, two basic strategies are available to a futures investor:

- He buys a futures contract ("is long"), if he wants to benefit from an upward trend.
- He sells a futures contract ("is short"), if he speculates on a downward trend.

---

[1] Eurex calls this margin additional margin; in the literature it is sometimes referred to as maintenance margin.

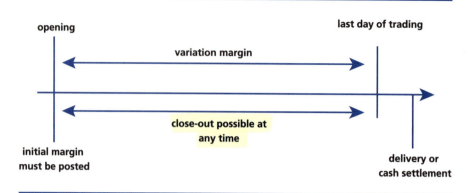

Figure 5.3: Timeline of a futures transaction

Figure 5.4 summarizes these two approaches.

In the case of **long futures**, the investor, as already discussed, benefits from an upward trend of the underlying. The futures contract represents the synthetic purchase of this underlying. He achieves a profit if the underlying, and with it the futures contract, goes up in price and realizes a loss if the underlying declines in value. As stated before, the profits and losses are settled at the close of each trading day in the margin account.

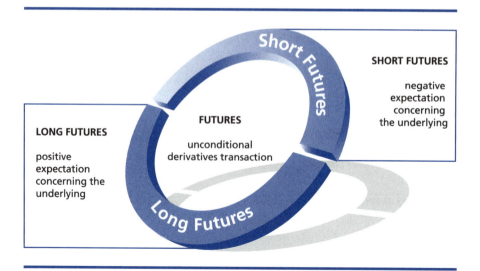

Figure 5.4: The basic approaches available to a futures investor

An investor should only be short the futures contract if he expects a decline in the value of the underlying. Analogous to the above scenario, the **short futures position** is starting to lose money when the underlying increases in value.

Futures are traded the same way as options. They can also be closed by entering into offsetting positions (see Table 5.1). These unconditional derivatives transactions are popular especially among professional investors, since they provide an opportunity to cover or replicate the overall market in a quick and inexpensive fashion.

Table 5.1: Opening and closing of futures positions

Opening	BUY FUTURES **(Long)**
Closing	SELL FUTURES **(Short)**
Opening	SELL FUTURES **(Short)**
Closing	BUY FUTURES **(Long)**

5.5 Leverage in futures transactions

Leverage in a futures transaction arises from the fact that the investor does not have to provide the entire contract value, but merely the initial margin. Since he is moving the same volume as in a spot transaction with a relatively modest amount of money, leverage arises.

$$\text{Leverage of Futures} = \frac{\text{Value of Contract}}{\text{Initial Margin}}$$

5.6 Settlement

There are two possibilities to settle a futures contract. First, classical physical delivery[2], which is used for Euro Bund Futures for example. Second, cash

---

[2] Delivery takes place in the underlying. Obviously, this requires that the underlying can actually be delivered. This is the case, for example, for bonds and stocks.

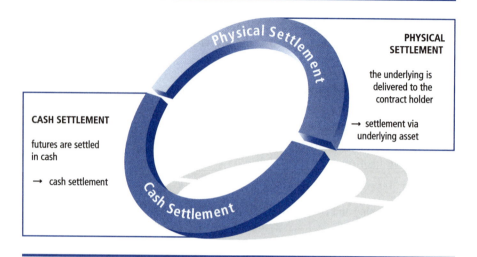

Figure 5.5: Settlement of futures

settlement[3], which involves paying the difference between contract value and market value. It is used for example in the case of index futures, since delivery of the underlying is not possible (see Figure 5.5).

In business practice, physical settlement is usually avoided, as it is generally not the reason for entering into the transaction.

5.7 Index futures

Many futures on indexes exist. In the following, we use futures on the DAX® Index (FDAX®) to illustrate several examples. Detailed knowledge of the underlying is required in the case of an index future. Is it a performance index or a price index? How many individual stocks constitute the index? How is the index calculated? What is the index multiplier? Which trading hours are available? Only after these questions have been answered, should trading in index futures be considered.

---

[3] Cash settlement of the difference in debits and credits.

Let us take the example of the DAX® Index Future:

The underlying is the DAX® performance index of Deutsche Börse AG, which is made up of 30 shares. Each index component is selected according to a set of rules (free float, size, and so forth) which is defined and clearly specified by Deutsche Börse AG. The index is adjusted at predetermined points in time, or if fundamental factors are changing. An adjustment of index weights takes place once every quarter. Since it is a performance index, dividends paid are reinvested in the index. This is different, for example, for the Dow Jones Industrial Average, which is a price index. On the day the share trades ex-dividend, an adjustment factor is used to account for the dividend payment.

Additional important background information refers to the settlement procedure. Since the index cannot be delivered, cash settlement takes place. In practice, the majority of futures contracts are already closed prior to expiration.

Futures on the DAX® (FDAX) are based on a value of EUR 25 per index point. When the FDAX goes up by one point, the investor who is long is credited with EUR 25 while the investor who is short gets debited the same amount. This process is also called **mark-to-market**[4]. The accounts are updated every day until the position is exercised or closed. It assures that all accounts are balanced at the close of the business day. The following day starts again with zero balances on the daily profit and loss statements of all holdings.

An investment in futures involves leverage, since a relatively small margin payment provides access to a rather sizeable investment. Therefore, futures investors tie up significantly less liquidity per transaction than spot market investors.

In the case of index futures, the difference is stated in **points**. With the help of an index multiplier[5] (for the FDAX: EUR 25 per point), it is transformed into the relevant monetary unit.

Example:
An investor buys 10 DAX® Index Futures contracts (long) at 6,700 points. In the evening, the FDAX® is quoted at 6,650. The investor suffers a loss of 50 points. Given an index multiplier of EUR 25 per point[6], this translates into a loss of EUR 1,250 Euro per contract. In our example, the overall loss of the investor on all ten contracts is equal to EUR 12,500.

---

[4] Holdings are valued at the current market price each day.
[5] The specific index multipliers are set by the futures exchanges. They can be found in the fact sheets on the contract.
[6] Example: FDAX traded at Eurex.

Table 5.2: Frequently traded index futures

Index	Futures
DAX®	DAX® Index Futures (FDAX)
Standard & Poor's	S&P 500 Futures
Dow Jones Industrial Average	DJI Futures
FTSE	FTSE Futures
Dow Jones Euro STOXX 50®	Dow Jones Euro STOXX 50® Futures
Nikkei 225	Nikkei 225 Futures
...	...

Table 5.3: Basic expectations of futures investors

Futures position	Expectation
Long futures	Increasing markets
Short futures	Declining markets

Let us take a look at the magnitude involved:

10 FDAX® contracts in our example are valued in the spot market at EUR 1,675,000 ($10 \times 25^7 \times 6{,}700$ points). But the investor is only required to deposit the initial margin (currently 410 points per contract) of EUR 102,500 ($410^8 \times 10 \times 25$).

Thus the investor only needs to deposit EUR 102,500 to control a position with a current spot market value of EUR 1,675,000!

Index futures are a suitable instrument for the implementation of a strategy which is based on a strong opinion concerning the direction of the market. However, it should be kept in mind that the futures position must be closed and that the strategy possibly needs adjustment in case the expected scenario does not materialize.

---

[7] Index multiplier of FDAX: EUR 25 per index point.
[8] The initial margin is set by the futures exchange and is subject to change at any time. See Chapter 16.3.

5.8 Interest rate futures

Things are different for a number of other futures contracts such as the Euro Bund Future (FGBL), for example, which calls for physical delivery. It is based on a synthetic government bond with a nominal coupon of 6 percent and a maturity of 8.5–10.5 years. Physical delivery takes place in this case. Since the contract is based on a fictitious bond, a number of securities are defined, which can be used by the seller to fulfill his obligation at settlement. The most favorable possibility for the seller is the so called **CTD** (**C**heapest **to D**eliver) bond (see Section 5.15). The bonds thus cannot be converted at a rate of 1:1 but need to be adjusted with the help of a conversion factor[9]. This factor serves to align the different coupons and maturities, as well as the standardized contract specifications of the Euro Bund Future. It must be kept in mind that no delivery takes place in the majority of cases, since most futures contracts are either closed or rolled over prior to maturity.

Trading in interest rate futures such as the Euro Bund Future and the 30-year Treasury Bond Future (T-Bond) is both intense and very liquid. Due to the existence of different futures (maturity structure of the bonds), investors can profit from changes in the level of interest rates, disequilibria and movements of the term structure of interest rates. An investor who expects an increase in interest rates (at the long end of the term structure) will sell contracts on the Euro Bund Future. The investor covers both ends of the maturity spectrum with such a transaction. Using modeling, it is also possible to benefit from changes in the entire term structure with such an investment.

Transactions which involve more than one currency are also possible by combining Euro Bund Futures (Euro) and T-Bond futures (USD). If an investor expects a decline in interest rates in the USA and an increase in Europe, he can buy T-Bond futures and simultaneously sell Euro Bund Futures. It might even make sense to also trade currency futures in such a scenario.

The prices of interest rate futures are also an important indicator for the level of interest rates in specific maturity ranges at a given point in time. Changes in the futures price provide an approximation based on duration for the price development of a bond with the same maturity as the underlying of the futures contract. Let us assume that the futures contract has a duration of 7 and the current price is 100. If it is priced at 107 at a later point in time, we can deduce that interest rates have declined by approximately one percent in this maturity segment. Futures prices can thus be interpreted as indications of

---

[9] Makes it possible to compare the different bonds.

interest rate levels when quoting a bid or ask price for a bond. They can also be helpful in understanding why quotes have changed.

Table 5.4 lists a number of interest rate futures and their maturity ranges. Table 5.5 once again summarizes the basic intentions of investors in the area of interest rate futures.

Table 5.4: Maturity structure of different interest rate futures

Futures	Maturity of underlying in years
Euro-Schatz-Futures (EUR)	1.75–2.25 government bonds (Bunds)
Euro-Bobl-Futures (EUR)	4.5–5.5 government bonds (Bunds)
Euro-Bund-Futures (EUR)	8.5–10.5 government bonds (Bunds)
Euro-Buxl-Futures® (EUR)	24.0–35.0 government bonds (Bunds)
Conf-Futures (CHF)	8.0–13.0 Swiss government bonds
T-Bill Futures (USD)	3-month US T-Bills
10-y T-Bond Futures (USD)	10-year US government bonds
30-y T-Bond Futures (USD)	30-year US government bonds
JGB (JPY)	7 – 11-year Japanese government bonds

Table 5.5: Basic expectations when trading interest rate futures

Futures position	Expectation	Settlement
Long futures	Decline in interest rates; Bond prices increase	Must purchase bond
Short futures	Increase in interest rates; Bond prices decline	Must sell bond

We will explicitly revisit trading in currency futures and commodity futures again in Chapter 7.13.

5.9 Currency futures

Currency futures are traded for example at the CME in Chicago (see Table 5.6), where fixed currency pairs such as EUR/USD are offered. Each contract is equivalent to an amount of EUR 125,000[10]. An investor who purchases the futures contract (long) expects an increase of the Euro relative to the USD, an investor who sells the contract (short) expects a decline. The same principle also holds for all other currency pairs. Due to rapid and liquid trading opportunities, these futures are also suitable for quick speculation and not only for a medium and long term investment horizon. The possibility for yield enhancement can be achieved with short-term ancillary trading of derivatives positions.

Table 5.6: Possible currency futures (currency pairs)

EUR	USD
EUR	CHF
EUR	YEN
GBP	USD
AUD	USD
...	...

Derivatives exchanges cover nearly every currency pair (that is reasonable and necessary).

5.10 Commodity futures

Trading in commodity futures is a very exciting and important aspect of derivatives markets. Commodity futures gave rise to the formation of derivatives exchanges and are the initial reason for their existence. Today they are no longer used exclusively for hedging, but also for speculative purposes. In Germany, commodity futures are only poorly represented, and all major commodities exchanges are based in the USA. On July 20, 2009, Eurex inaugurated trading in agricultural futures[11].

---

[10] EUR/USD 125,000 EUR, YEN/USD 12,500,000 Yen, GBP/USD 62,500 GBP, EUR/CHF 125,000 EUR.
[11] Trading in European Processing Potato Futures, London Potato Futures, Piglet Futures and Hog Futures among others.

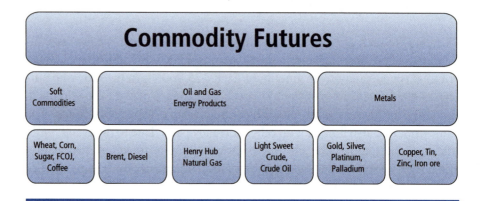

Figure 5.6:   Product groups at US commodities exchanges (selection)

Figure 5.6 displays product groups which are traded on US commodities exchanges.

Here again, one can distinguish between **cash** settlement and **physical** delivery. Mostly both possibilities are offered. For speculative purposes, cash settlement is preferable since physical delivery is ruled out in advance.

When futures are traded at exotic derivatives exchanges, differences in time zones must be kept in mind.

5.11   Single stock futures

Also available are **single stock futures**, in which individual stocks serve as underlying. At Eurex, for example, companies that are components of the Dow Jones EURO STOXX 50® can be traded as single stock futures. As in the case of index futures, it enables investors to position themselves in anticipation of rising or falling prices of the underlying. Holding the futures contract amounts to a synthetic replication of the underlying (in this case a single stock). One advantage of this approach is the possibility to immediately and easily sell the stock short (see Table 5.7).

Table 5.7: Basic expectations when trading single stock futures

Futures position	Expectation
Long futures	Increase in share price
Short futures	Decrease in share price

5.12 State of the market in futures trading

Especially when trading futures and options, it is important to carefully assess the state of the market. Open interest provides important information in this regard. **Open interest** gives the number of contracts that are open: each transaction is counted only once, since every short position requires a long position. Open interest goes up when two market participants enter into a transaction and goes down when they close a position. It remains unchanged when one market participant closes a transaction and is replaced by a third party. Relating open interest to turnover and market prices allows us to draw certain conclusions about the state of the market. Table 5.8 summarizes the state of the market in futures trading.

Table 5.8: State of the market in futures trading

Open interest	Prices	Turnover	State of the market
∧	∧	∧	∧
∨	∧	∨	∨
∧	∨	∧	∨
∨	∨	∨	∧

Trading on derivatives exchanges is anonymous. This means that the two contract partners do not know each other and do not need to know each other in order to close a transaction. The exchange takes on the role of central counterpart. The central counterpart eliminates the risk that the transaction will not be honored and guarantees unobstructed execution.

5.13 Determination of futures prices

Pricing a futures contract is easier than pricing an option. An investor has two distinct choices: He either purchases a portfolio which consists of the assets on which the futures contract is based, or he directly purchases the futures contract. If the investor decides to invest in the portfolio, he is required to purchase all assets in line with the weights they have in the futures contract and to hold those assets for the same time period as the futures position. The purchase of the assets involves transaction costs, but at the same time generates income. A calculation of the futures price under these assumptions and the requirement that the no-arbitrage condition holds, gives rise to identical prices for both approaches. This means that the futures price can be determined with reference to the following formula:

Theoretical Futures Price =
Spot Price + (Financial Costs − Income Lost)

$$F_0 = S_0 + \left[S_0 \left(r\frac{T-t}{360}\right) - d_{t;T}\right]$$

F_0 = Futures price
S_0 = Spot price[12]
r = Risk-free interest rate per annum
$T - t$ = Remaining term to maturity of the futures contract in days
$d_{t,T}$ = Expected income during the period t to T

The net financing costs, which are given by the difference between financing costs and income lost (such as dividends), are called **Cost of Carry** (CoC) or **basis**.

Basis = Spot price − Futures price
Basis = Futures price − Spot price[13]

Cost of Carry (CoC) can be either **positive** or **negative**. It is positive when the return exceeds financing costs and **negative** when financing costs are greater than the return (see Figure 5.9).

---

[12] Current price of the underlying.
[13] Both versions are possible and therefore are shown here. The first version is more common in the literature (due to its logic), see John C. Hull Options, Futures and other Derivatives, 2009.

Determination of futures prices 137

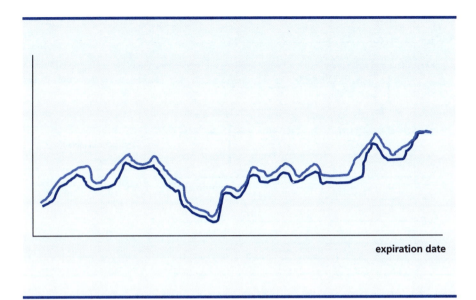

Figure 5.7: Futures contract (above) and index (below) (basis convergence)

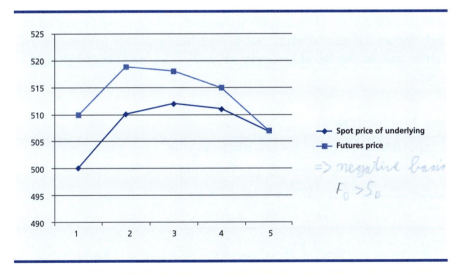

Figure 5.8: Basis convergence of spot and futures price prior to the last trading day

The closer the futures contract comes to the last trading day, the smaller the cost of carry. On the last trading day, the spot price is equal to the futures price. This is called basis convergence. As a result of declines in both financing costs and income from the investment, the basis is equal to zero on the last day of trading. Now the spot price and the futures price are equal (see Figures 5.7 and 5.8).

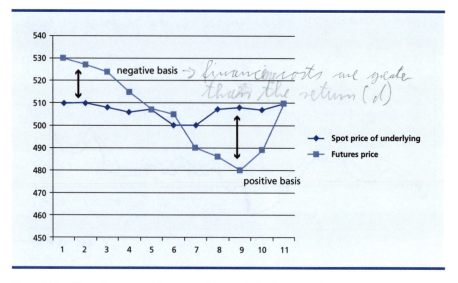

Figure 5.9: Negative or positive cost of carry of the futures price

As we can see, calculating the futures price is not very complicated. All we need to do is add the cost of holding the asset to the price of the underlying and subtract the income which would have been available in case of a spot market transaction. We also see that volatility does not affect the pricing of futures.

Table 5.9: Futures basis

Spot price is …	Futures price is …	Basis is …
… lower than futures price	… higher than spot price	negative
… higher than futures price	… lower than spot price	positive

Futures largely and quickly influence the pricing of spot market instruments, since major investors prefer to trade in futures markets (cost efficient and quick). For that reason, futures markets at times put pressure on spot markets. In this context, models of market psychology and behavioral economics discussed in Chapter 2.9 need to be kept in mind.

5.14 Pricing of interest rate futures

The term structure of interest rates has a large influence on the pricing of interest rate futures. Short-term interest rates determine the refinancing costs of an investment, while longer-term interest rates influence the income in form of the coupon payment. Thus in the case of a normal term structure of interest rates (positive slope of the curve), income received exceeds financing costs. The result is a positive basis: the spot price is above the futures price. Longer maturities therefore tend to lead to more favorable futures prices. The opposite case can be observed for an inverted term structure of interest rates (negative slope of the curve): the basis of the futures contract is negative as financing costs exceed coupon income. Consequently futures prices increase with longer maturities (see Figure 5.10).

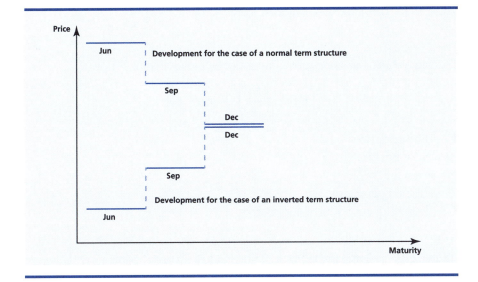

Figure 5.10: Price development of Euro-Bund futures for a normal and an inverted term structure of interest rates

We once again present the three possible shapes of the term structure of interest rates in Figure 5.11.

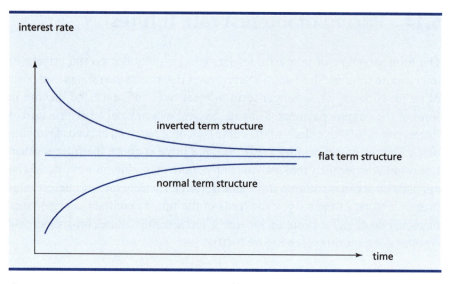

Figure 5.11: Term structures of interest rates[14]

The fair value of interest rate futures can be calculated as follows:

$$F_0 = \left(\frac{S_0}{P}\right) - Z + C$$

F_0 = Futures price
S_0 = Spot position
P = Price factor[15]
Z = Coupon payments
C = Financing cost of the spot position

At the fair value, theoretical and actual basis are equal. Put differently: the futures price is equal to the price of the underlying plus financing costs minus income (coupon payments) received during the holding period.

The relevance of the price factor becomes clear at maturity. It is needed to determine the final settlement price. The price factor is larger than one if the coupon of the actual bond is larger than the coupon of the synthetic bond. It

---

[14] Source: Frankfurt School of Finance and Management "Wertpapiergeschäft für Wertpapierspezialisten."
[15] The price factor makes the bonds that can be delivered comparable. This is necessary as the bonds that can be delivered are not homogeneous. While they are all from the same issuer, they differ with regard to coupon and maturity and are therefore trading at different prices.

is less than one if the coupon of the actual bond is smaller than the coupon of the synthetic bond.

> Delivery price =
> Settlement price of the futures
> · Conversion factor of the bond
> + Accrued interest on the bond

5.15 What is a CTD bond?

The **CTD** (**C**heapest **to D**eliver) bond is that bond among a number of bonds available (see Figure 5.12) that provides the seller of the futures contract with the maximum profit or the minimum loss when delivering the underlying. It will ultimately be used for delivery as it is (synthetically speaking) the best choice. The CTD bond is determined with the help of a conversion factor (W_{phy}/W_{syn}). It equalizes differences in the terms of the different bonds

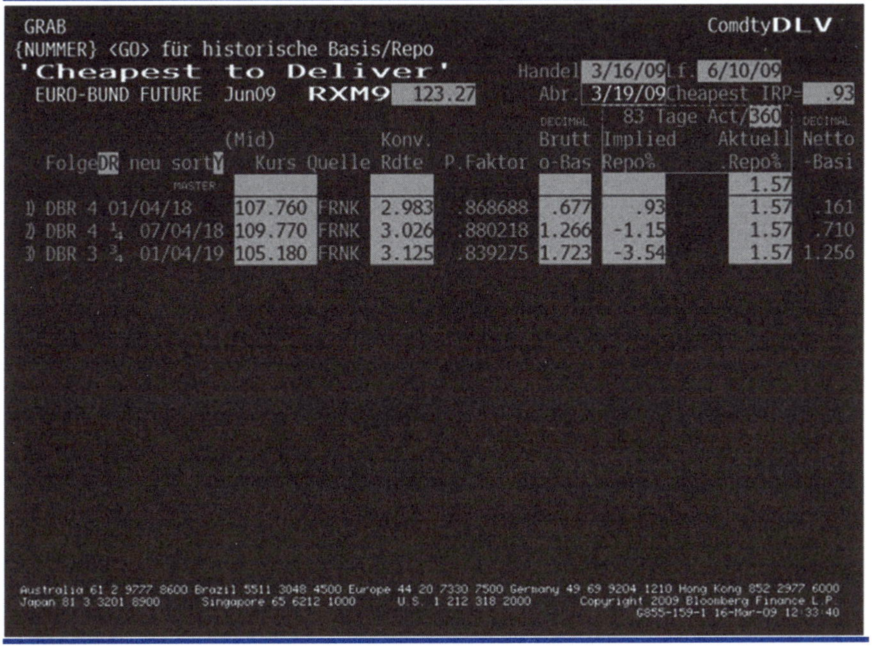

Figure 5.12: Cheapest to Deliver bonds for Euro-Bund futures[16]

---

[16] In this example the expiration date is Jun2009; source: Bloomberg.

(coupon, maturity and so forth). Once all possible delivery options have been calculated, the most favorable bond (this is the CTD bond) will be selected and delivered.

$$\text{Basis} = \text{Spot price of the bond} - (\text{Futures price} \cdot \text{Conversion factor})$$

The basis is equal to zero at the delivery date. The formula can thus be simplified as follows:

$$\frac{\text{Spot price of the bond}}{\text{Conversion factor}} = \text{Futures price}$$

This futures price is also called "zero basis futures price." As can be seen, no arbitrage is possible (by purchasing the bond and delivering the underlying).

It needs to be stated that most investors are not interested in delivery/receipt of the bond and therefore prefer to close out or roll their futures positions prior to expiration. A market participant is required to indicate which bond he intends to deliver if he wants to hold his futures position until final settlement (notification day). Delivery then takes place on the second work day following the last trading day. As in the case of stock options, this is done via the clearing house.

5.16 What is meant by "final settlement?"

The price quoted on the last trading day is also called the **final settlement price**. This price is used for settling the futures contract or delivering the underlying. Before such a transaction is closed, it is determined (and specified in the contract) whether physical delivery of the underlying or cash settlement will be used. This needs to be considered when deciding on an investment. In order to avoid an obligation, it is advisable to close the position on time and thus prevent delivery. If an investor, based on his expectations, intends to prolong the transaction past the initial expiration date, a rollover is an appropriate strategy: he closes the original position and opens a new position with a later expiration date.

5.17 What futures expiration dates exist?

Normally at least three different expiration dates are available. At Eurex, for example, futures on the Dow Jones Euro STOXX 50® are always offered for the last months of the upcoming three quarters. The next futures expiration date is called **"nearby future"** or **"front month."** Futures contracts further away in time are called **"back month"** or **"second nearby"** or **"third nearby**[17]**."** Every derivatives exchange has its own regulations concerning availability of futures expiration dates for the different products. It must be kept in mind that interest rate futures have an expiration date that is out of sequence and that commodity futures often have monthly expiration dates (third Friday of every month).

Table 5.10: Overview of possible futures series, the example of the DJ EURO STOXX 50® Futures[18]

1st possibility	March	June	September
2nd possibility	June	September	December
3rd possibility	September	December	March
4th possibility	December	March	June

If an investor decides to trade a futures contract beyond the front month, he needs to keep in mind that financing costs may develop unfavorably – this means that they are possibly higher (in the case of long futures) or lower (in the case of short futures). This problem may also arise if futures positions are rolled over. Losses which are caused by existing differences in pricing are called rollover losses (see Figure 5.13). Unfortunately there is no way for investors to avoid these losses, since they arise from the pricing process and are independent of the strategy. In the following, an example is presented for a rollover loss (later futures are more expensive).

---

[17] Depending on the order of expiry the second or third expiration date, counting the current (nearby) future.
[18] Three series are always active.

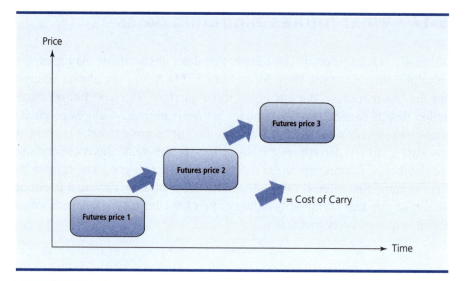

Figure 5.13: Rollover losses

5.18 Which futures strategies exist?

As with all derivatives transactions, the major motives for using futures are the three fundamental investment motives

- speculation
- hedging
- arbitrage

But there are additional reasons for the importance of futures markets for the overall market. One of them is leverage trading. Due to the small amount of capital that is tied up in the transaction, a leverage effect arises; investors can get access to a large investment amount with only a limited capital base. A second advantage is that any transaction can be conducted not only as buyer (long), but also as seller (short). A third advantage is the guarantee that all obligations from the transaction will be met. Counterparty risk is minimized since the clearinghouse of the exchange acts as counterparty. For that reason, trading is quick and old positions can be closed easily. Low prices and high speed of transaction on a wide range of investments are an additional advantage. For investors it is a quick and effective way of trading.

5.18.1 Long futures position

The investor expects an increase in the underlying; he therefore enters into a **long futures position**. His profit is the difference between the lower purchase price and the higher selling price; in case prices decline, he is suffering a loss. The payoff diagram of a long position is equivalent to being long the underlying (see Figure 5.14).

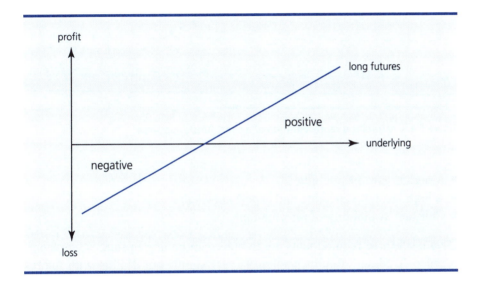

Figure 5.14: Graphical representation of a long futures position

5.18.2 Short futures position

The investor expects a decrease in the underlying; he therefore enters into a **short futures position**. His profit in this case is the difference between the higher selling price and the lower repurchase price of the future. If the futures contract increases in value contrary to the expectation of the investor, he suffers a loss. With short futures positions, the investor conducts a synthetic sale of the underlying (see Figure 5.15).

These two speculative futures positions form the basis for other strategies.

At this point, a few fundamental words about the futures investor are in order. He needs to possess the following three indispensable attributes with regard to his investment:

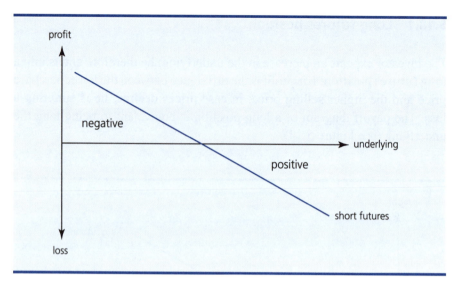

Figure 5.15: Graphical representation of a short futures position

- A high degree of liquidity
- A high level of education and expert knowledge
- Constant availability of information

Only if all three requirements are in place can trading in futures be recommended. Trading a futures position is very simple but dealing with futures is not. Futures positions can be used both for speculation and for hedging. Hedging with classical futures positions is quite straightforward: the aim is to protect either against falling or rising prices.

Protection against falling prices is the baseline scenario: an investor is afraid that his portfolio will lose in value over time. He protects his portfolio by taking a short futures position. Such a typical hedge is only possible if underlying and futures are equivalent. Since this is not usually the case, the largest possible intersection is established and a hedging position is implemented using futures. Such an approach is called a "**cross hedge**." It is based on the idea that the correlation between the futures position chosen and the underlying is as high as possible.

In a first step, the number of futures contracts required is calculated.

$$\text{Hedge Ratio} = \frac{\text{Portfolio}}{\text{Index} - \text{Futures} - \text{Points}} \cdot \frac{1}{\text{Index multiplier}}$$

Example:

An investment portfolio is valued at EUR 1 million. It is to be hedged against price declines. Since the stocks contained in the portfolio are most similar to the Dow Jones (DJ) Euro STOXX 50®, a hedge using DJ Euro STOXX 50 Futures® (FESX) is chosen.

The hedge ratio is calculated first:

$$\frac{\left(\frac{\text{Portfolio}}{\text{Index}}\right)}{\text{Index multiplier}} = x$$

$$\frac{\left(\frac{\text{Portfolio}}{\text{DJ Euro Stoxx 50}}\right)}{\text{Index multiplier}} = x$$

$$\frac{\left(\frac{1000000}{4450}\right)}{10} = 22.47$$

23 contracts of the DJ Euro STOXX 50 Futures® must be sold in order to establish the hedge.

Hedging against price increases initially sounds somewhat confusing but is also worth contemplating. Let us assume that an investor expects to receive a massive inflow of funds in six months; due to the current market environment, however, an investment appears favorable already now. Today, the investor can lock in the price at which he will obtain the shares, even though the actual purchase date is still six months away. This kind of hedge is particularly useful in scenarios where the investor expects a steady inflow of liquidity. He builds a synthetic portfolio position today, but won't receive the required liquidity for six months. In contrast to the scenario above, where the futures are used as protection against falling prices, in this example they serve as a hedge against rising prices.

In both cases, the investor is worried that prices in the spot market will change to his disadvantage. With either strategy, he locks in a purchase or selling price for his investment.

As already discussed in the chapter on pricing futures contracts, the futures price is a function of the spot price and the cost of carry. Therefore the prices of futures on the same underlying but with different expiration dates are not the same. This difference is called **time spread**. It results from variations in net financing costs for the various maturities. The variable is not influenced by expectations about the underlying. This spread can be used strategically by investors.

5.19 Purchasing a spread

A futures investor purchases the earlier contract and sells the contract that matures later in time.

Example:

Purchase X index with expiration March.
Sell X index with expiration December.

5.20 Selling a spread

A futures investor sells the closest contract and purchases a contract which matures later in time.

Example:

Sell X index with expiration March.
Purchase X index with expiration December.

In which cases is this strategy advisable?

There is a fundamental difference in trading a futures contract on a price index and on a performance index. In addition, the investor must concern himself with the price development of the index and the development of net financing costs.

Table 5.11: Spreads

Index type	Prices increase	Prices decrease
Performance index	Sell spread	Purchase spread
Price index, cost of carry > 0	Sell spread	Purchase spread
Price index, cost of carry < 0	Purchase spread	Sell spread

We conclude the following: in the case of performance indexes, the strategic decision is based on the price development alone. The longer the remaining time to maturity of the futures, the higher the futures price (negative basis). An increase in the underlying thus leads to an increase in the basis. As this is the case for both contracts (in the same proportion), the spread increases. Exactly the opposite mechanism is at work in the case of declining prices, where the spread futures investor suffers a loss. Things are more complex for price indexes, where net financing costs need to be assessed. In the case of a futures contract with a positive basis, the behavior is exactly opposite to that of a futures position on a performance index.

5.21 Inter market spread

In an **inter market spread** the investor buys and sells the same contract at two different exchanges. He benefits from pricing differences at different locations.

Example:

Purchase of X index at exchange A at 11,000
Sale of X index at exchange B at 11,010
Due to the high standard of information technologies, this kind of spread is found only rarely today.

5.22 Inter contract spread and intra contract spread

In an **inter contract spread,** two futures with different contract specifications are traded. The investor expects changes in the fundamentals of the two contracts. In an **intra contract spread**, futures on the same underlying, but with different expiration dates are traded (see Figure 5.16). The investor expects changes in the contracts due to the maturity differences.

In both transactions, profits are limited to price differences of the two contracts. Relative changes in prices are the only sources of profit.

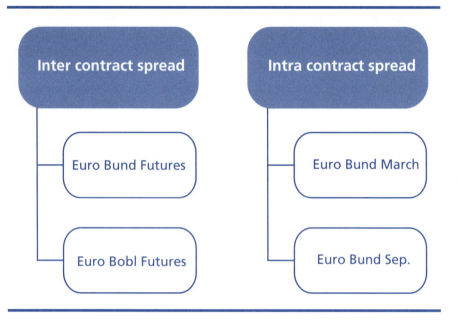

Figure 5.16: Inter contract spread and intra contract spread

5.23 Cash-and-carry arbitrage

The goal of an arbitrage transaction is to obtain a riskless profit from disequilibria in prices. These disequilibria in prices appear whenever there is a difference between the current futures price and the spot price. Any difference between the actual basis and the theoretical basis allows arbitrage. If the futures are too expensive relative to the theoretical fair value, they will be sold and the underlying is bought. This is called a **cash-and-carry arbitrage** (see Figure 5.17). If the situation is reversed, and the futures are too cheap relative to the underlying, the futures are bought and the underlying sold. This is called **reverse cash-and-carry arbitrage** (see Figure 5.17).

An underlying such as an index cannot be bought and sold as easily as a futures contract. Therefore a basket is constructed: all securities with a beta of around one are purchased. If they also have a high correlation coefficient, the index can be replicated. While this is not perfect replication, it is a synchronous synthetic equivalent.

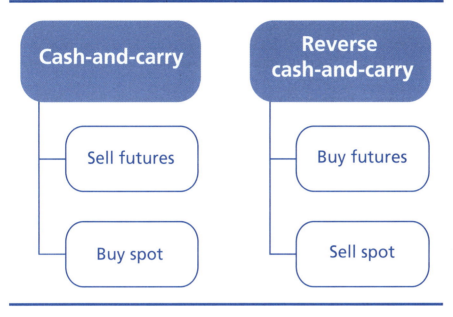

Figure 5.17: Cash-and-carry vs. reverse cash-and-carry

Example:

We construct a basket of shares from the DJ Euro STOXX-50® with stocks that have a beta of about one as well as a high correlation coefficient. This leads to a synthetic replication of the DJ Euro STOXX 50®. Jointly with this replication, we trade DJ Euro STOXX 50® Futures in line with the market situation.

There are several problems with such a transaction:

- Transaction costs will accrue
- Short sales are sometimes difficult to exercise and can be costly
- In the case of bonds, a choice must be made at the exercise date

5.24 Arbitrage strategies for money market futures (Euribor)

Arbitrage in the case of mispriced money market futures works through the construction of corresponding credit and investment transactions. The goal is to develop a synthetic construction of fixed income investment and credit transaction which has exactly the same specification as the underlying. The prices of the synthetic position and the futures ought to be identical. If this is not the case, arbitrage profits are possible. If the interest payment of the futures is higher than that of the synthetic position, long futures positions are established. In the opposite case, the futures are sold and the synthetic construction is purchased. A factor of key importance in this regard is the term structure of interest rates. A careful analysis will reveal interest rates for futures transactions which provide the basis for arbitrage strategies (long or short).

5.25 Hedges

In the case of a long hedge (purchase of futures – see Figure 5.18), the investor protects himself against an increase in prices until he can undertake the investment in time **t + x**. In the case of a short hedge (sale of futures – see Figure 5.19) he protects an investment which was undertaken in time **t − x**.

In the case of a long hedge, a pre-approved investment will always follow at a later point in time.

An investor expects to receive EUR 1 million in three months and plans to invest this amount in the stocks which make up the Dow Jones EURO

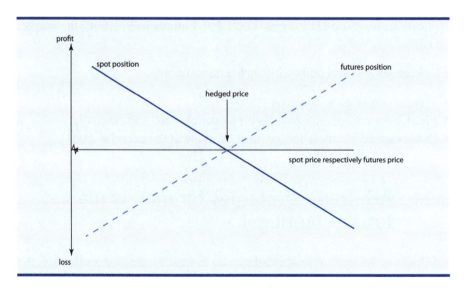

Figure 5.18: Pay-off of the overall position: long hedge

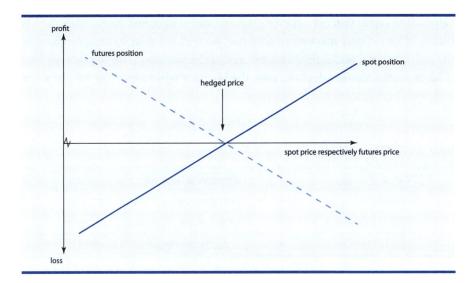

Figure 5.19: Pay-off of the overall position: short hedge

STOXX 50®. As he is worried that the index may be higher in three months, he purchases futures contracts today in order to protect against this scenario. As soon as he receives the cash, he closes the futures position and invests in the market at the spot rate. If the futures have gone up in value, he can compensate the higher costs because of the income from the futures transaction. If the value of the futures has gone down, he has realized the same loss as if he had purchased the underlying three months ago at the spot rate. The purchase price for his investment has been locked in with the help of the transaction.

With a short hedge, the investor protects existing holdings against a decline in market value. He has already invested in the market. Since he expects a decline in prices, but is not certain about timing and magnitude, he uses futures to hedge. If the decline materializes, profits from the futures transaction compensate for the portfolio losses. If it does not materialize, the investor incurs costs for the protection (offsetting futures position), which he has to pay.

5.26 Beta-hedging with index futures

Since a beta factor β can be calculated for every portfolio, it is an optimal target variable for hedging. The beta factor describes the sensitivity of a portfolio relative to the overall market.

Depending on market expectations, an investor will adjust the portfolio's beta factor. If he expects markets to advance, he will increase his equity share in the portfolio and add long index futures to the position. The opposite is true if he expects a market decline: now the investor will reduce the equity share and add short futures to the position.

Table 5.12: Values of beta

Value	Interpretation
Beta (β) 1	Share moves with the market: 1:1
Beta (β) greater 1	Share moves more than the market
Beta (β) smaller 1	Share moves less than the market

Beta-hedge for a negative market outlook

In order to hedge a portfolio, its beta factor β must first be determined. Once it is known, the investor can implement a beta hedge as follows:

$$\text{Futures contracts} = \left(\frac{\text{Portfolio value}}{\text{Index value} \times \text{Contract size}}\right) \cdot \beta$$

Example:

An investor holds a portfolio of the X-index valued at EUR 1.5 million. β is equal to 1.1. The X-index stands at 6,700 points; the index multiplier of X futures is EUR 25 per point. He plans to protect his holding.

$$= (1{,}500{,}000/(6{,}700 \times 25)) \times 1.1$$
$$= 9.8$$

Thus the investor must sell 10 contracts.

If changes occur in the above scenario, the investor needs to adjust the hedge in order to maintain a consistent strategy.

The long hedge works in a similar fashion: the contracts are purchased and not sold.

The formula is the same:

$$\text{Futures contracts} = \left(\frac{\text{Portfolio value}}{\text{Index value} \times \text{Contract size}}\right) \cdot \beta$$

It can also be shown that the method described can be applied to a "cross hedge." Instead of the beta factor, the correlation between the underlying to be hedged and the futures contract is used. An example is the attempt to hedge a grapefruit harvest with the help of orange futures. While the underlying (grapefruits) is not identical to oranges, both are citrus fruit and a highly correlated price development can be expected.

5.27 Why futures are used for hedging

First of all, futures transactions are very inexpensive and transparent. A second very important point concerns the quick and consistent implementation of such a strategy. While the positions require continuous monitoring and adjustment, this can be done using technical equipment and thus does not require much time.

At this point we would like to add a few thoughts on the transparency of futures. Since portfolios are never focused exclusively on the domestic market and since coverage of the domestic markets is not sufficient, futures are a good choice for covering additional markets in a transparent and consistent fashion. The transparency follows from the calculation of futures prices and trading which is supported by market makers. The quick and inexpensive execution of orders is another major and important feature in support of futures markets. A disadvantage, which tends to be relevant mostly when dealing with private clients, is the contract size.

5.28 Hedging with interest rate futures

The following fundamental methods exist for setting up hedges to protect against increasing or declining interest rates:

The **price factor method** and **nominal value method** are used mostly to hedge the CTD.

$$\text{Hedge} - \text{Ratio} = \frac{\text{Nominal value}_{spot}}{\text{Nominal value}_{futures}}$$

The **duration method** attempts to achieve a comparison of the price reaction in relation to the CTD.

$$\text{Hedge} - \text{Ratio} = \left(\frac{\text{Nominal}_{spot}}{\text{Nominal}_{futures}}\right) \cdot \left(\frac{\text{Duration}_{spot}}{\text{Duration}_{futures}}\right) \cdot \text{PF}_{CTD}$$

PF$_{CTD}$ = pricing factor of the CTD

The **basis point value method** calculates the change in the price of the bond for a change in the yield of the bond of one basis point. Once this is done for both the spot market position and the CTD, a ratio is formed.

$$\text{Hedge} - \text{Ratio} = \left(\frac{\text{Nominal}_{spot}}{\text{Nominal}_{futures}}\right) \cdot \left(\frac{\Delta_{spot,bp}}{\Delta_{CTD,bp}}\right) \cdot \text{PF}_{CTD}$$

The value changes can be derived from the return formula.

The **regression method** determines the degree of co-movement between the spot market and the futures market.

$$\text{Hedge} - \text{Ratio} = \frac{\text{Nominal value}_{spot}}{\text{Nominal value}_{futures}} \cdot \text{RC}$$

RC = Regression coefficient

Two sides of the same medal

Hedges provide the opportunity to clearly and transparently identify the risk that remains in a portfolio. As convenient and useful as hedges may be, they are also not free of problems. Every hedge is costly and rules out participation in possible favorable price movements. Furthermore, it can be difficult to cover complex portfolios. This may be attempted with the help of a cross hedge, but a complete coverage is often not possible. Then again, it is questionable whether such a hedge is really required.

Example:

Basic intention of the investor:
The X index is overpriced and based on a technical analysis[19] totally overbought. He expects the index to decline.

---

[19] As determined with the help of a thorough technical analysis.

Holding:
X index portfolio valued at EUR 1 million

Establishing the basic idea:
Short X index contracts, sold at an index value of 7,000

Now the X index goes up due to positive economic news from 7,000 to 7,150! The investor no longer profits from this, as he has already sold the X index at an index value of 7,000. He takes a loss on his futures position. Should the index decline, he makes a profit. But only in the case where the X index declines below 7,000, is he actually making a profit and not just reducing his losses.

This example demonstrates the importance of an adequate assessment of the market environment by the investor. Should the market develop contrary to expectations, losses are the result. Since a futures contract is an instrument with a delta of 1, the investor immediately participates in any gains or losses.

Literature for this chapter

Hull, John: Options, Futures and Other Derivatives, 7th edition, 2009

Madura, Jeff: International Financial Management, 6th edition, 2004

Rudolph, Bernd, Schäfer, Klaus: Derivative Finanzinstrumente 2005

Wiedemann, Arnd: Bewertung von Finanzinstrumenten, 4th edition, 2007

Questions and answers on this chapter

Question 1:
What settlement options exist for futures?

Question 2:
In the case of an inverted term structure, is the front month futures contract more expensive or cheaper than the second nearby?

Question 3:
What is **basis convergence** and when does it occur?

Question 4:
What is reverse cash and carry arbitrage?

Question 5:
What is determined with the help of the **regression method**?

Answer to question 1:

Either the underlying is delivered or cash settlement takes place.

Answer to question 2:
The front month is cheaper than following futures. It would only be more expensive in the case of a normal term structure.

Answer to question 3:
Basis convergence means that futures price and price of the underlying become equal. This is the case on the last day of trading, since no financing costs arise and no income can be expected.

Answer to question 4:
It involves purchasing futures and at the same time selling the position in the spot market.

Answer to question 5:
The regression method determines the degree of co-movement between spot market and futures market which is expressed as a regression coefficient.

6 Options – conditional derivatives contracts

The following chapter covers these issues:

- What is an option?
- What types of options exist?
- How is the fair value of an option determined?
- What factors influence option prices?
- Which theoretical models for pricing options exist and how are they structured?
- Which strategies can be pursued with the help of options?

6.1 What is an option?

At a fundamental level, an option is a bilateral agreement with a limited contract period, which involves the right to choose[1]. Thanks to standardization, these contracts can be traded on derivatives exchanges. As already discussed, options with individual features are called OTC options. They are agreed directly between the contracting parties without a derivatives exchange as intermediary. No matter whether options are traded at a derivatives exchange or OTC, they are always characterized by an asymmetric distribution of risk. In this chapter we will deal with classical options. Next we cover exotic options.

Basically, there are two types of options: **call options and put options**.

---

[1] The word option stems from the Latin "optio," which can be translated as "free will" or "the right to demand."

Call option

A **call option** provides the buyer (long) with the right, but not the obligation, to purchase an underlying, in a specified amount (contract size), within a certain time period (term to maturity) or at a specific point in time (last day of trading) and at a price which is specified when the contract is signed (strike price or exercise price).

Example:

An investor is interested in participating in the price development of the x share. Based on his analysis, he expects increasing prices. Instead of directly investing in the shares, he purchases call options. Due to the lower liquidity requirement, he can purchase significantly more options than shares. Should the expected price development occur, he is profiting disproportionately due to the leverage effect.

Put option

A **put option** provides the buyer (long) with the right, but not the obligation, to sell an underlying, in a specified amount (contract size), within a certain time period (term to maturity) or at a specific point in time (last day of trading) and at a price which is specified when the contract is signed (strike price or exercise price).

Example:

An investor holds y shares. He is afraid that prices might decline but is not absolutely certain. In order to protect his holding, he purchases put options on y shares. This means that he receives compensation for the losses of the underlying in the case of price declines. In case prices advance, the put options will lose value, and the options position will realize a loss. But if the shares advance sufficiently, this can be offset. The alternative of selling the shares rather than purchasing the put option would have eliminated any participation in the increase. The purchase of the put option, meanwhile, makes participation in the upside possible.

Every buyer (**long**) must be matched with a seller (**short**) (see Figure 6.1). The seller is also referred to as option writer. The writer of the option has no choice; he is forced to react to the decision of the buyer. As compensation, he receives

Differences in options

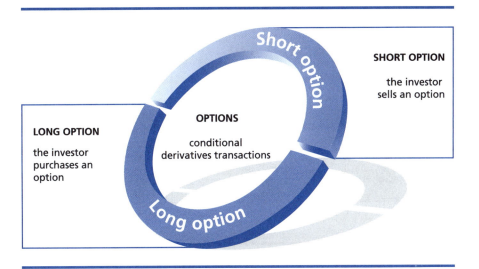

Figure 6.1: Options - long and short

the option premium from the buyer. He thus entered into the obligation to sell (call) or purchase (put) a predefined quantity of the underlying at a specified time and price (see Table 6.1).

Table 6.1: Rights and obligations of options

	Right	Obligation
Buyer	Exercise	Payment of premium
Seller	Receipt of premium	Delivery or receipt of underlying

6.2 Differences in options

Types of options

As stated before, options can be either call or put options (see Figure 6.2).

Options can also be distinguished with regard to their exercise: some options can be exercised on any day up to the expiration day. They are called **American-style options**. In most cases, these are options written on individual stocks. Options that can only be exercised on their expiration day are called **European-style options** (index options are normally European-style options). A summary is provided in Figure 6.3.

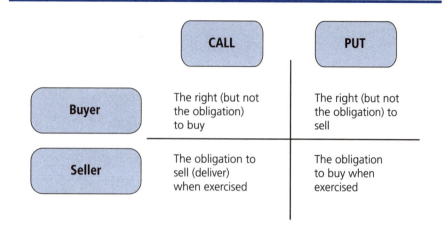

Figure 6.2: Rights and obligations in the case of options

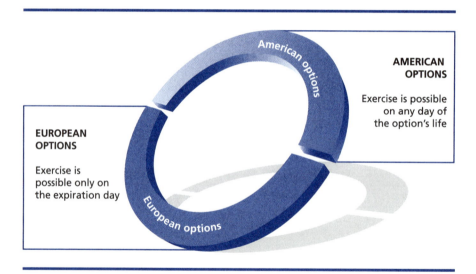

Figure 6.3: European vs. American options

Of course, options also differ with regard to the underlying (the commodity or security, such as a share, the option is based on). The derivative contract is thus defined by the underlying.

Finally there are also differences in the way options contracts can be settled. A distinction is made between **cash settlement** and **physical delivery** (for example of securities). Cash settlement is used whenever physical delivery

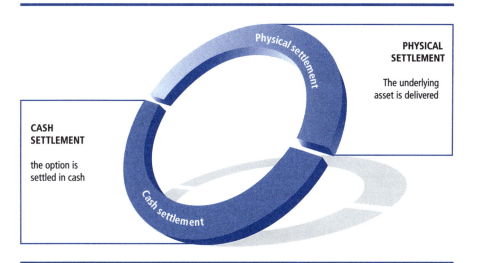

Figure 6.4: Settlement possibilities

is not possible. This is the case for example for index options, where the difference between the underlying and the strike price is paid in cash. In case an underlying needs to be delivered (stock options), physical delivery is arranged by the clearinghouse (see Figure 6.4).

6.3 Option trading

Contract

We often refer to contracts[2] and would now like to briefly discuss and precisely define the term. A contract defines the minimum size of a derivatives transaction. As an example, equity options typically have a contract size of 100 shares. For index options, the options prices are stated in index points and need to be multiplied with the index multiplier to obtain an absolute amount. This varies from index to index. The German stock index DAX®, for example, has an index multiplier for options of EUR 5 per point. The Dow Jones Euro STOXX 50® has an index multiplier of EUR 10 per point[3]. The

---

[2] The word originates from the language of 15th century advocates and describes a binding agreement (lat. contractus = contract).

[3] The relevant multipliers for all products can be obtained from the responsible derivatives exchange and are published on their homepage.

respective multipliers are published by the derivatives exchanges and can be found in their regulations.

Payment or receipt of premium

The **premium** (lat. praemium = gain or advantage) that is paid or received as part of an options transaction is due immediately after the transaction is closed. It is available to the short investor without delay. Liquidity flows from the long investor to the short investor on the same day. This holds for all classical options.

Exercising an option

Once an option has been **exercised**, the order is put into after hours processing. Clearing participants with corresponding short positions are determined, and counterparties are assigned by drawing lots. On the following day, these clients are informed, and the clearing process is started. The active decision is called **exercise**, while a passive one (short investor) is called **assignment**. An assignment is the request to deliver or accept delivery since the option was exercised.

For the actual settlement this means that exercising a long call implies delivery of the underlying by an investor who holds a short call. Delivery is done via the clearing company. In the event of a long put, the person exercising the option delivers the underlying to the option writer who is required to accept. Following the exercise, the option ceases to exist for both parties. The contract was fulfilled and is thus completed. It is not possible to reuse the original option. The only possibility is to open a new position with the derivatives exchange. The investor needs to sign a new contract and is thus also entering into a new derivatives transaction.

Options for which physical delivery of the underlying is not possible are settled in cash, as already stated. In most cases a payment in the amount of the difference[4] is made.

Example:

Exercising DAX® options at Eurex:

Strike price of the DAX® call options:	5,000 points
Settlement price of DAX® on the last trading day:	5,050 points

---

[4] Many index options (depending on the derivatives exchange) are automatically exercised and cash-settled if they are in the money by one point.

One contract for a long call is open and it will be exercised, since the option is in the money. This leads to the following final settlement:

5050 − 5000 = 50 points
50 points × 1 contract = 50
50 × EUR 5 (contract multiplier) = EUR 250.00 credit
Debited is the investor who holds the short call.

What this example nicely illustrates is the fact that the position can be magnified via the number of contracts. An investment in 100 contracts instead of 1 contract would have resulted in a profit of EUR 25,000.

Specifics concerning the exercise

Due to the complications that arise in the case of dividend payments, Eurex has decided that exercises are no longer possible on the day of the annual shareholders' meeting. This used to be possible, combined with a reverse posting for the dividend. Owing to the complexity of this process, it was decided to no longer allow an exercise. Should the day of the annual shareholders' meeting be the last day of trading, the last day to exercise the options series affected is one day earlier. The different derivatives exchanges have regulations for this issue which normally can also be found on their homepage.

Options products

Theoretically, an option strategy can be devised and implemented for every underlying. In practice, options are written on a standard set of liquid shares contained in the large and medium-sized indexes as well as on selected exotic securities. For index options, marketability, respectively market demand is the deciding factor for an admission to trading. As an example, all components of the DAX®30 are offered. It needs to be taken into consideration which derivatives transactions are offered by the broker or bank which is responsible for clearing. Important is the existence of a reliable clearing organization for every derivative transaction conducted. It is a prerequisite for a successful closing by all parties involved. For that reason, banks and brokers only offer contracts which they can administer themselves.

Frequently the same contracts are traded at different exchanges. Therefore investors should take into consideration liquidity and clearing. Due to the higher liquidity, it is preferable in most cases to trade the contracts at the home exchange (US options in the USA and not in Europe). The respective contract specifications are determined by the regulations of the derivatives exchanges and should be studied prior to the first transaction! This prevents negative surprises concerning contract details. At the same time, an investor needs to think in advance about the possibilities for settlement or about an exit strategy.

6.4 What are weekly options?

Outside the normal cycle of expiration dates (third Friday of the month), Eurex, for example, also offers weekly options[5], which expire on the first, second or fourth Friday of the month. They add to the product range by covering maturities within one cycle of expiration dates. There are also options which expire on the fifth Friday of the month. If there is no fifth Friday in a month, the option expires on the next fifth Friday.

Weekly options are particularly useful if the gap between two "regular" expiration dates needs to be covered. This can be helpful, for example, during a time period when quarterly figures are reported. At the same time, many institutional investors use these options because they increase their flexibility. Prior to their listing on an exchange, the weekly options were traded only in the OTC market. Since their maturities are short, weekly options have high **gamma exposure**. This implies a large dynamic of the option price when the underlying changes. Both speculative and hedging strategies can be refined with the help of these series of options. As an example, a speculative position can be established shortly before a company releases new figures. This is also true for hedging transactions in the case of expected negative data.

Currently DAX®, Dow Jones Euro STOXX 50® and SMI® are covered. The contract specifications correspond to those of the "normal, long" series.

6.5 What is a low exercise price option?

Low Exercise Price Options (**LEPOs**) are options with a strike price near zero. For that reason, they are also called **zero strike options** (see Figure 6.5). These options are deep in the money and therefore react similar to the underlying. They are used for example when creating "structured products." Compared to a direct investment, one advantage is the ability to take a short position without having to engage in securities lending. These instruments are thus also available to investors who are unwilling or unable to participate in securities

---

[5] Introduced in April 2006.

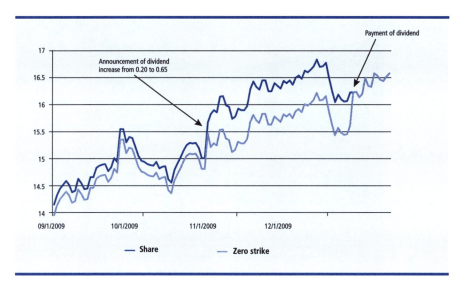

Figure 6.5: Movement of the share relative to the zero strike option (including dividend increase and payment)[7]

lending activities[6]. Many **zero strike options** are also OTC traded, or if the volume is large, as a block trade at an exchange. The daily settlement price is determined using the **fair value method**. If necessary, dividend payments, current interest rates and other distributions are taken into account.

6.6 The closing of a derivatives transaction

If an investor wants to get out of a derivatives transaction, he can do this by **closing** (also **close-out**) the open contracts. He enters into an offsetting transaction which results in the termination of all rights and obligations from the previously opened contract (see Figure 6.6).

Example:

An investor holds an open position of 100 short put contracts on x shares. He wants to eliminate this risk. Therefore he closes the 100 open short put

---

[6] Securities lending means borrowing securities from another broker, working with these and returning them after the lending period. Securities lending involves the payment of a premium to the lender of the securities.
[7] Source: Commerzbank AG.

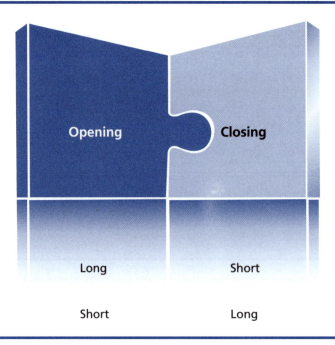

Figure 6.6: Opening and closing

contracts with the help of an offsetting transaction. He purchases 100 long put contracts with identical specifications. The difference between sale and repurchase price is his profit or loss.

Short put 100 × contracts = EUR 15,000
Long put 100 × contracts = EUR 10,000
In this example, the investor realizes a profit of EUR 5,000.

If an investor has purchased a **long option** and intends to close it again, he needs to sell it. If, on the other hand, he has initially sold the option, he needs to repurchase it for **closing** (close-out). We note: every derivatives transaction is cancelled with the help of an **offsetting transaction**.

> Thus there are three different ways of terminating existing transactions:
> - Cancellation via close-out (offsetting transaction)
>   a. Long positions need to be sold
>   b. Short positions need to be repurchased
> - Settlement when the option is exercised
>   a. Delivery of underlying
>   b. Accept delivery of underlying
> - Expiration on the last day of trading (the transaction expires worthless)
>   a. Normally the last trading day is the third Friday of the month.
>   b. In the case of options on futures and other products, this can also be a different day (for example FGBL: the tenth trading day of the expiration month).

6.7 What is a rollover?

A rollover can be used by an investor to extend positions beyond the last day of trading. He closes his existing position and simultaneously opens a new one with a later expiration date. The strike price or the number of contracts can also be amended during the rollover. A rollover is cost-neutral if the investor does not incur net expenses from rolling the position. The rollover thus extends the position past the initial time horizon. By adjusting the number of contracts or the strike price, the investor can modify the options position according to the current market environment.

Example:
Investor A is long 100 contracts on X futures. As he expects a continued increase of the X index, he plans to prolong his position beyond the original expiration date. He simultaneously sells the 100 old contracts and purchases 100 new contracts with a later expiration date. He has thus extended his original position to the new expiration date.

6.8 Pricing of options

The search for the fair value of an investment is one of the fundamental questions of finance. But in the case of an option, which provides the right to either purchase or sell an investment vehicle, this question is even more complex and multilayered than usual. As you can see in the coming sections, the pricing of options, not least because of the asymmetric risk structure and the many factors which influence the price of an option, poses numerous challenges.

Asymmetric distribution of risk

In the case of a call option that was acquired (long call), the opportunity to make a profit is unlimited if the underlying increases. Meanwhile, the risk of making a loss is limited to the option premium paid. We thus have unlimited **upside potential** and limited and known **downside risk**.

In the case of a put option which was acquired (long put), the opportunity to make a profit is limited (**downside potential**) in the case of a decline of the underlying (since zero is the lower bound). In the case of a rising price of the underlying, the risk is limited to the premium paid (**upside risk**). The opportunity and risk profiles of the opposing strategies short call and short put are mirror images: (un-)limited losses and a limited and known profit (premium).

6.9 Theories of option pricing

Options are traded on derivatives exchanges at a price (technical term: **premium**) which can be determined mathematically. But before delving into the complex topic of calculating prices, we first need to take a look at the fundamentals of option price determination.

The price of an option can be broken down into two fundamental components: **intrinsic value** and **time value**.

6.9.1 Intrinsic value

Put simply, the **intrinsic value** (= **IV**) of a call is the positive difference between the strike price (**K**) and the price of the underlying (**S**).

$$\text{Intrinsic value}_{\text{Call}} = \max(S - K; 0)$$

Theories of option pricing

A call option has intrinsic value if the price of the underlying exceeds the strike price of the option.

Underlying > strike price

Example:

Underlying: EUR 30
Strike price: EUR 28
Intrinsic value: EUR 2

A put option has intrinsic value if the price of the underlying is less than the strike price of the option.

Underlying < strike price

$$\text{Intrinsic value}_{Put} = \max(K - S; 0)$$

Example:

Underlying: EUR 30
Strike price: EUR 32
Intrinsic value: EUR 2

There are three possibilities for the value of an option. It can be **at-the-money** (= ATM)[8], **in-the-money** (= ITM)[9] or **out-of-the-money** (= OTM)[10] (see Table 6.2).

Table 6.2: Possible values of an option

	In-the-money	At-the-money	Out-of-the-money
Call	Price of underlying > Strike price	Price of underlying = Strike price	Price of underlying < Strike price
Put	Price of underlying < Strike price	Price of underlying = Strike price	Price of underlying > Strike price

---

[8] An investor is indifferent between exercising and not exercising the option.
[9] Time value has served its purpose.
[10] Intrinsic value is zero and the option will not be exercised.

The actual value of an option at expiration can thus be called its intrinsic value.

> The intrinsic value (IV) can never be negative, but it can be zero.

But out-of-the-money options also have value. This is due to the second and highly relevant factor of option price determination: time value.

6.9.2 Time value

If there were no **time value** (= TV), only in-the-money options, which have intrinsic value, would be valuable. In this case, the value would be equal to the intrinsic value.

$$\text{Time value} = (\text{Option price} - \text{Intrinsic value})$$

Time value is the difference between the price of the option and its intrinsic value.

> Time value (TV) is the amount which has to be paid for the opportunity that the option will end up in the money.

Time value is higher, the longer the time to expiration. This follows from the function of the time value. The longer the time to expiration, the greater is the probability that the option will end up in the money and thus provide a positive payoff (intrinsic value) on the last day of trading. Time value declines with decreases in time to expiration. The decline is not linear but accelerates towards the end of the contract period (see Figure 6.7). This behavior can also be explained with reference to the function of the time value. The longer the opportunity exists that the option will end up in the money, the higher the time value. This also means that the time value will decline faster as this opportunity becomes smaller. Put differently: the probability that the option will make money goes down at an accelerating rate due to the approaching last trading day and increases the likelihood of a worthless expiry.

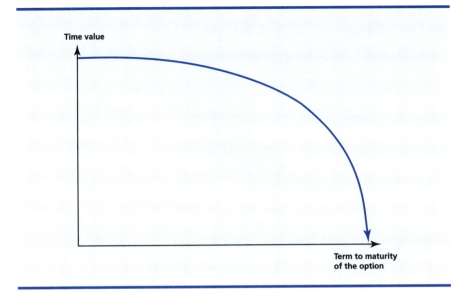

Figure 6.7: The time-value function

Loss of time value

Even in the case where the price of the underlying does not change, the value of the option converges towards its intrinsic value as it approaches its expiration date.

For these reasons, the following rules of thumb apply:

Fundamental teaching insight

As a basic principle, options with a short term to maturity have smaller risk than options with a longer term to maturity. They are therefore suitable for selling, as the decline in time value favors an investor that tends to be more risk averse. The premium can be considered to be risk compensation for the term to maturity and it therefore follows: the higher the premium, the higher the risk implied.

Now that we have clarified that out-of-the-money options have no intrinsic value, we need to add the following: options that are deep in the money have

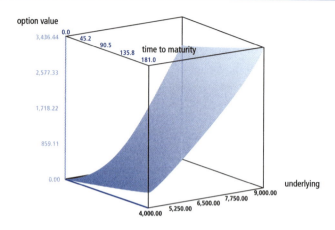

Figure 6.8: Graphical representation of a long call (option price)[11]

almost no time value. The function of the time value – that the option ends up in the money – has already been fulfilled. There is already a higher probability that the option will end up in the money. Figure 6.8 shows the price of a long call in relationship to maturity and price of the underlying. Both variables influence the price of the option.

 Tools for calculation and simulation of option prices can be found in our download area:

---

[11] Source: Interactive Data Managed Solutions AG; Commerzbank AG.

Financial Engineering
The following financial engineering operations can be calculated with the help of this tool:
• Historical volatility
• Monthly volatility
• Implied volatility
• Changes of option prices
• In-the-money or out-of-the-money
• Replication models
• Binomial model (one-period)
• Binomial model (multi-period)
• Black-Scholes (without dividends)
• Black-Scholes (with dividends)
• Quote monitor
• Black-Scholes (including Greeks)
• Put-call parity
• Long call
• Short call
• Long put
• Short put
• Index futures
• Interest rate futures
• Currency futures
• Commodity futures
• Futures on single securities

6.10 Early exercise of options

The pricing mechanism above (see also Figure 6.9) demonstrates that it is often not advisable to exercise an option much before its expiration date, since this means that a large time value has to be forfeited (loss of premium). The following example demonstrates this:

Long 10 call options on x shares
Strike price: EUR 50
Share price: EUR 55
Option price: EUR 7.50
Term to maturity: 3 months

Exercising this option would result in the loss of the time value of EUR 2.50 (EUR 7.50 option price – EUR 5 intrinsic value = EUR 2.50 time value). While the shares could be purchased at EUR 50, a loss of the time value of EUR 2.50 would result.

If the investor fears a decline of the value of the underlying and wants to lock in the profit, it is recommended to sell the option. In this case, he collects both the time value and the intrinsic value of the option.

Figure 6.9: Factors influencing the price of an option

The short speculation in options is always related to the time value, which is often stated explicitly as an agio.

6.11 Which factors influence the price of an option?

6.11.1 The value of the underlying

The price of the underlying is the most important determinant of the option price, since it directly moves the option. A call increases in value if the underlying becomes more expensive and declines if the underlying falls in value. In the case of a put, this relationship is exactly reversed. The put becomes more expensive as the underlying declines and less expensive as it goes up in price.

> The right to purchase an underlying becomes more expensive as it goes up in value. The price declines as the underlying moves lower in price. The right to sell an underlying becomes more expensive as it goes down in value (the insurance function kicks in). The right becomes cheaper as the good goes up in value.

Which factors influence the price of an option?

This also explains why there is a direct relationship between derivative (derived from the underlying structure) and price of the underlying. Any change in price of the underlying results in a price change of the derivative.

6.11.2 Volatility

Volatility σ (Latin volare = to fly) is a statistical measure for the intensity of fluctuations of an underlying within a certain time period (aggregated overall risk[12]) around its mean. Volatility only makes a statement about the intensity of fluctuations but not about their direction. A **historical volatility** of 10 around a mean of 100 implies that an underlying with a normal distribution fluctuates between 90 and 110 with a probability of 68.26%[13]. The calculation of volatility is based on the calculation of the standard deviation (s or σ), which in turn is the square root of the average squared deviations of an underlying from its mean. Standard deviation measures the strength of fluctuations of individual observations (for example returns) around the mean. Squared standard deviations, s^2 or σ^2 are also called variance.

6.11.2.1 Historical volatility

General estimate of volatility:

$$s = \sqrt{\frac{1}{n-1} \sum_{i=1}^{n} (r_i - \bar{\mu})^2}$$

In the above formula, **n** is the number of observations r_i are the individual observations (for example returns) and μ is the mean of the n observations.

As already discussed, volatility is a statistical measure which tracks the strength of variation during a specific time period. Since historical values are not necessarily equal to what is assumed currently or in the future, **implied volatility exists** in addition to **historical volatility** (see Figure 6.10). Implied volatility mirrors the current market expectation concerning **future**

---

[12] Equities normally have a volatility of 15%–60%.
[13] This follows from the density function of the normal distribution.

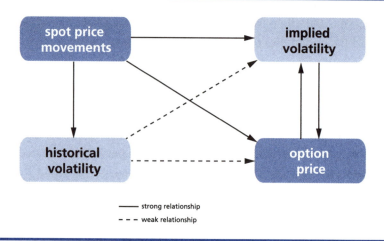

Figure 6.10: Volatility relations[14]

volatility[15]. Depending on the maturity of the option or strike price, it can deviate significantly from historical volatility.

6.11.2.2 Implied volatility

In order to get a measure of **implied volatility**, it must be derived from currently traded at-the-money options[16]. This is done using an iterative procedure[17] from the Black-Scholes formula. Implied volatility is the currently traded volatility and can therefore be interpreted as market consensus on the annualized volatility for a given maturity. In the following, we present the determination of implied volatilities based on the **Newton procedure**. It must be used in cases where it is not possible to solve the Black-Scholes formula analytically for the volatility.

$$0 = S_0 N(d_1) - K e^{-rT} N(d_2) - c =: f(\sigma)$$

---

[14] Source: ZKB Zürich.
[15] Also called perceived volatility, which is present in the market.
[16] In applied work, OTM or ITM options are also used in order to determine the so-called "volatility smile" of the implied volatility for different strike prices (see Chapter 6.16).
[17] Iteration is a mathematical principle in which the solution is approximated step by step. The idea is to repeatedly apply the same procedure.

where
$$d_1 = \frac{\ln(S_0/K) + (r + \sigma^2/2)T}{\sigma\sqrt{T}}$$
and
$$d_2 = d_1 - \sigma\sqrt{T}$$

c = Price of the call option
S_0 = Price of the underlying at time t = 0
K = Strike price of the option
ln = Natural logarithm
e = Base of the natural logarithm = 2.7128 ... [18]
r = Riskless interest rate
N(d) = Cumulative standard normal distribution
σ = Volatility
T = Remaining time to maturity of the option

As can easily be seen, calculation of the zero point of the function **f** is problematic. To solve this problem, a number of numerical iteration procedures exist. At this point, we would like to present the Newton procedure, which is characterized by quick convergence.

6.11.2.3 The Newton procedure

A starting value σ_0 is provided in the Newton procedure. Beginning with this value, the next iterations are determined according to the following rule:

$$\sigma_{i+1} = \sigma_i - \frac{f(\sigma_i)}{f'(\sigma_i)}, \quad i = 0, 1, 2, \ldots$$

The denominator consists of the first derivative of the function **f** with regard to σ. To use the Newton procedure, the derivative $f'(\sigma)$ must be determined. It needs to be kept in mind that the function **f** depends on σ via the factors d_1 and d_2, c is a constant and the derivative of the distribution function of the standard normal distribution N(x) is given by the density function of the

---

[18] logarithmus naturalis = Euler's number =
e = 2,71828182845904523536028747135266249775724709369995
9574366967627724076630353547534571382178525166427427
4663919320030599218174135966290435729003342952605
9563073813232862794349076323382988075319525101901...

standard normal distribution

$$n_x = \frac{1}{\sqrt{2\pi}} e^{-\frac{1}{2}x^2}$$

It holds that:

$$f'(\sigma) = S_0 \sqrt{T} n_{(d_1)}$$

6.11.2.4 The influence of volatility

The time value of an option is the component that reacts to changes in volatility (see Figure 6.11). The following fundamental relationship holds: the higher the volatility, the higher the time value of an option. Option prices increase with increases in volatility and decline with decreases. It also needs to be kept in mind that volatility has a negative correlation with the underlying equities. Figure 6.11 shows the volatility of the DAX® index (30 days and 250 days).

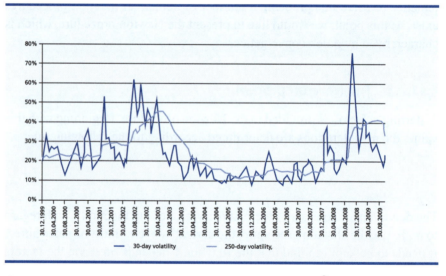

Figure 6.11: Historical 30-day and 250-day volatility of the DAX® index[19]

---

[19] See Bloss, Ernst, Häcker, Haas, Prexl, Röck: Financial Modeling, Stuttgart 2010.

6.11.3 Market interest rates

As **market interest rates** (theoretically: risk-free interest rates) increase, the price of a call goes up and the price of a put declines. This mechanism equates the market interest rate advantage respectively disadvantage of the different types of options. A possible disadvantage of investing in options relative to the direct investment in the underlying is equated. Market interest rates can be derived from AAA-rated bonds of the respective maturity. In applied work, money market interest rates or swap rates from the interbank market are also used as market interest rates.

6.11.4 Dividend payments

Dividend payments can have both a **direct** and an **indirect** effect on the underlying. The direct effect of a dividend payment is a price decline for calls and a price increase for puts. This mechanism only holds for American options. In the case of European options, expected dividends are incorporated in the calculation of the option price. Concerning dividend payments, it is also important to note that the underlying indexes differ in the case of index options. Both performance indexes (the index is adjusted for dividend payments) and price indexes (dividend payments are an outflow and result in a decline of the index) exist. This distinction is relevant and directly affects the determination of option prices (see Table 6.3).

Table 6.3: Dividend payments and their influence on the option price

	Price of a call	Price of a put
Dividend payment	Declines	increases

6.11.5 Term to maturity

As already mentioned, term to maturity is the remaining major influencing factor. The shorter the term to maturity, the larger its negative influence on prices (see Figure 6.12). The time value of an option declines exponentially, as the chances of ending up in the money are going down. Therefore the influence of the time value increases as the time to maturity declines.

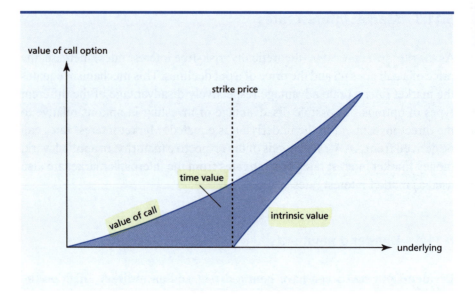

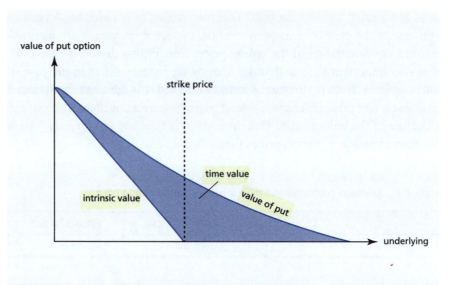

Figure 6.12: Representation of the time value of options (call and put)

6.11.6 The effect of corporate actions

Let us briefly consider the effect of corporate actions on the pricing of options. Changes in ownership structures require an adjustment mechanism which assures that the position of both contracting parties is equivalent to the one before the corporate action. Differences between the situation before and after the corporate action must not arise. A distinction is made between mergers and acquisitions, extraordinary dividends and cash settlement of changes to the capital structure.

6.11.6.1 Mergers and acquisitions

In the case of mergers and acquisitions, pure share offerings, combined offers of shares and cash as well as pure cash offers are possible. For pure cash offerings or mixed offers with an equity share of at least 33%[20], an exchange of the shares of the acquired company for shares of the acquiring company takes place in line with the specified share exchange ratio. Contract specifications are adjusted accordingly.

In the case of a cash offer, the cash component is valued using the **fair value method**. Option prices are thus derived analytically and adjusted.

6.11.6.2 Extraordinary dividends

When extraordinary dividends are paid, their value is included arithmetically and option prices are adjusted accordingly. If necessary, the option series are renamed. The existing series are differentiated[21] from the new ones by adding a serial number (for example DAI1[22]).

6.11.6.3 Cash settlement of corporate actions

In this case, the specifics of the contract are adjusted. It is not unusual that "odd" numbers of shares result (for example 101.654 shares). Differences are settled in cash. In the above case, 101 shares would be delivered and 0.654 shares would be paid in cash when settling the transaction.

Table 6.4 provides an overview of the most important factors that influence option prices:

---

[20] German law and international standards may vary. Specific regulations need to be considered.
[21] Contract XY becomes XY1.
[22] DAI as symbol for Daimler AG + 1 as serial number; in comparison, the "normal" series would only be "DAI."

Table 6.4: An overview of the influencing parameters

Influencing parameter		Option price Call	Option price Put
Underlying	increases	increases	declines
	declines	declines	increases
Volatility	increases	increases	increases
	declines	declines	declines
Time to maturity	declines	declines	declines
Market interest rate	increases	increases	declines
	declines	declines	increases
Dividend payment	American	declines	increases
	European	unchanged	unchanged

6.12 Greeks – sensitivities of option prices

The sensitivity factors, "**Greeks**"[23] in jargon, state the effects of changes of relevant factors on the price of an option. Table 6.5 provides an overview. In the following, we will take a closer look at these relationships and their derivation with the help of the Black-Scholes formula.

Table 6.5: An overview of the Greeks

Delta	Influence of a change in price of the underlying (spot rate) on the option price (premium).
Gamma	Sensitivity measure of Delta. It measures changes of Delta as the underlying changes.
Vega	Influence of volatility on the price of an option.
Theta	Influence of time (reduction of time to maturity) on the price of an option.
Rho	Influence of changes in interest rates on the price of an option.

6.12.1 Delta

The **delta** of an option measures the degree of change of the option price for changes in the price of the underlying. Thus delta can be interpreted as direct sensitivity of the underlying on the option price. It reflects changes of the option price which can be explained by changes in the underlying. It holds

---

[23] Greeks since they are named using the Greek alphabet.

that

$$\text{Delta} = \Delta = \frac{\text{Absolute change in option price}}{\text{Absolute change in underlying price}} = \frac{\delta f(S, T)}{\delta S}$$

For long call options, delta can take on values in the interval [0,1] when using the Black-Scholes model (see Figure 6.13). For long put options, the values are in the interval [−1, 0] (see Figure 6.13). A delta of 0.5, for example, means that the price of an option goes up by 0.5 monetary units as the price of the underlying increases by one monetary unit.

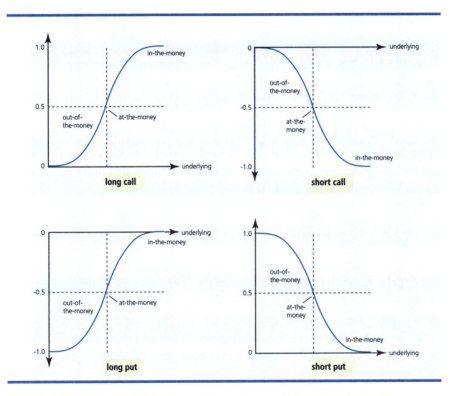

Figure 6.13: Representation of delta (long call, short call, long put, short put)

Table 6.6 reviews the signs of the various delta positions. We see that delta is always positive for a long call position and always negative for a short call position. Why is this? Delta positive is equivalent to a long investment. Therefore a call, which gives the right to buy, is also positive. Hence a short call is negative, since it represents a synthetic negative position. In the case of puts, these considerations are exactly reversed.

Table 6.7 summarizes the value ranges of the delta.

Table 6.6: Signs on call and put delta

	Long	Short
Call	+	–
Put	–	+

Table 6.7: Delta values

Delta of a	Out-of-the-money	At-the-money	In-the-money
Long Call /Short Put	about 0 to 0.5	about 0.5	about 0.5 to 1
Long Put /Short Call	about 0 to –0.5	about –0.5	about –0.5 to –1

Deriving delta from the Black-Scholes formula

From the Black-Scholes model, delta can be derived approximately as follows:

$$\Delta \text{ Call} = N(d_1)$$

$$\Delta \text{ Put} = N(d_1) - 1$$

The arbitrage portfolio which is the foundation of the Black-Scholes model can be interpreted as a delta neutral portfolio. Continuous portfolio restructuring assures that delta is equal to zero at any point in time.

6.12.2 Gamma

While delta measures changes in the option price, **gamma** informs about the change of the delta of an option for a change of the price of the underlying by one unit. Gamma is thus the **"delta of the delta"** and can be interpreted as the second derivative of the option price or the first derivative of the delta (see Figure 6.14). Gamma thus measures changes of the delta for changes of the underlying.

$$\text{Gamma} = \Gamma = \frac{\text{Absolute change of delta}}{\text{Absolute change in underlying price}} = \frac{\delta^2 f(S, T)}{\delta S^2}$$

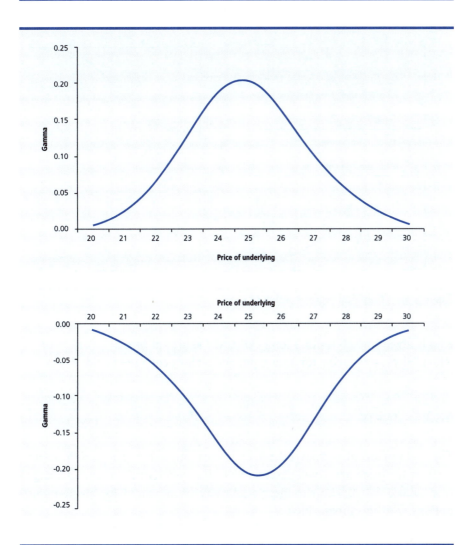

Figure 6.14: Gamma of long option (above) and short option (below)

6.12.3 Rho

Rho provides information about the change in the value of an option for changes in interest rates by one percentage point.

$$\text{Rho} = \rho_{C,P} = \frac{\text{Change in option price}}{\text{Change in financing costs}} = \frac{\delta f(S,T)}{\delta r}$$

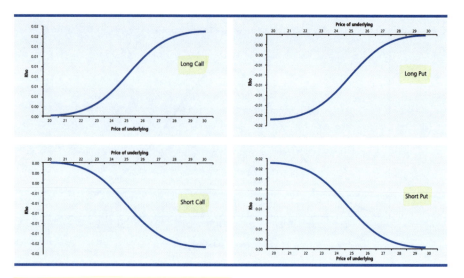

Figure 6.15: Graphical representation of rho

Rho is always **positive** for a long call and a short put (see Figure 6.15). Rho is always **negative** for a long put and a short call (see Figure 6.15).

6.12.4 Theta

The **theta** of an option shows the daily loss of time value of an option, assuming that the price and basic parameters of the underlying remain unchanged (see Figure 6.16). The strongest sensitivity is measured for at-the-money options with short maturities.

$$\text{Theta} = \Theta = \frac{\text{Change in option price}}{\text{Change in time to maturity}} = \frac{\delta f(S, T)}{\delta t}$$

If the theta of an option is 0.25, this means that the option will theoretically lose EUR 0.25 "overnight" (see Figure 6.17).

6.12.5 Vega

The change in **volatility** by one percentage point and its influence on the option price is given by **vega** (see Figure 6.18).

$$\text{Vega} = \Lambda = \frac{\text{Change in option price}}{\text{Change in volatility (implied)}} = \frac{\delta f(S, T)}{\delta \sigma}$$

Greeks – sensitivities of option prices

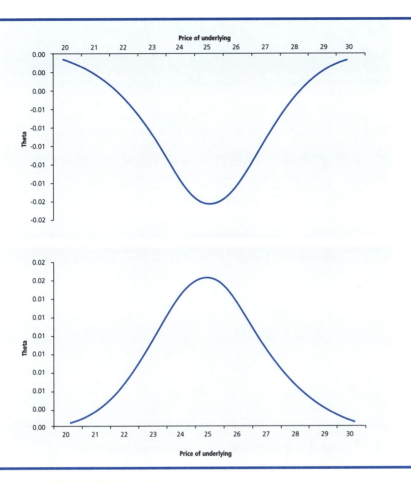

Figure 6.16: Theta for long options (above) and short options (below)

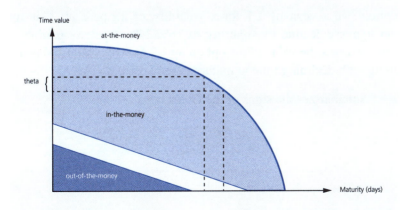

Figure 6.17: Illustration of theta

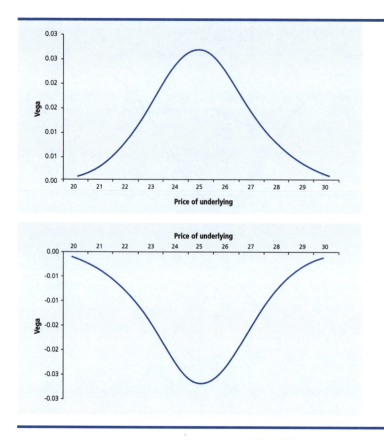

Figure 6.18: Vega of long options (above) and short options (below)

Example:

An option has a vega of 1.7 for a volatility of 25 percent. This means that an increase/decline of volatility to 26%/24% – ceteris paribus – increases/decreases the value of the option by 1.7 monetary units. Vega is also declining with declining time to maturity (see Figure 6.19).

Table 6.8 summarizes the signs of the Greeks.

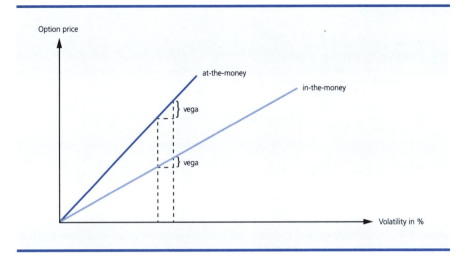

Figure 6.19: Illustration of vega

Table 6.8: Summary of the signs of the Greeks

	Delta	Gamma	Vega	Theta	Rho
Long call	Positive	Positive	Positive	Negative	Positive
Short call	Negative	Negative	Negative	Positive	Negative
Long put	Negative	Positive	Positive	Negative	Negative
Short put	Positive	Negative	Negative	Positive	Positive

6.12.6 Derivation of Greeks from the Black-Scholes formula

For a European option, all of the relationships displayed above can be derived from the Black-Scholes model as follows:

For call options:

$$\text{Delta} = N(d_1)e^{-DT}$$

$$\text{Gamma} = \frac{N(d_1)e^{-DT}}{S_0 \sigma \sqrt{T}}$$

$$\text{Theta} = -S_0 e^{-DT}\left[\frac{N(d_1)\sigma}{2\sqrt{T}} - DN(d_1)\right] + rKe^{-rT}N(d_2)$$

$$\text{Vega} = S_0 e^{-DT} N(d_1)\sqrt{T}$$

$$\text{Rho} = KTe^{-rT}N(d_2)$$

For put options:

$$\text{Delta} = N(d_1)e^{-DT} - 1$$

$$\text{Gamma} = \frac{N(d_1)e^{-DT}}{S_0\sigma\sqrt{T}}$$

$$\text{Theta} = -S_0 e^{-DT}\left[\frac{N(d_1)\sigma}{2\sqrt{T}} - DN(-d_1)\right] - rKe^{-rT}N(-d_2)$$

$$\text{Vega} = S_0 e^{-DT} N(d_1)\sqrt{T}$$

$$\text{Rho} = -KTe^{-rT}N(-d_2)$$

The Excel tool in our download area can be used to derive and reproduce these calculations.

Black-Scholes model including derivation of Greeks	
Assumptions:	
Price of the underlying	61.73
Strike price of the option	61.00
Dividends	0.00%
Term to maturity in years	1.00
Volatility	34.00%
Risk-free interest rate	1.00%
Calculations	
Exp(-rT)	0.9900
Exp(-DT)	1.0000
(r-D+0.5*V²)	0.0678
d1	0.2344
N (d1)	0.5927
N (-d1)	0.4073
d2	(0.1056)
N(d2)	0.4580
N(-d2)	0.5420
Distribution function of the standard normal distribution	0.3881

Results	Call	Put
Price of the option	8.93	7.59
Delta	0.5927	(0.4073)
Gamma	0.0185	0.0185
Theta	(4.3497)	(3.7457)
Rho	27.6570	(32.7360)
Vega	23.9594	23.9594

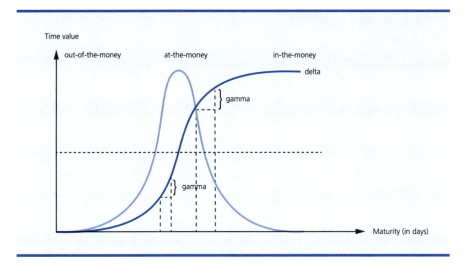

Figure 6.20: The option price and its derivatives

6.13 What is put-call parity?

The option price of a put can be derived from the price of a call (only for European options), since the two are directly related. The relationship was derived by HANS R. STOLL[24] in 1969 and is called **put-call parity**.[25] The required calculations (put-call parity relationship) are as follows.

6.13.1 Put-call parity relationship

$$p + S_0 = c + Ke^{-rT}$$

p = Price of the put option
S_0 = Price of the underlying
c = Price of the call option
K = Strike price of the option

---

[24] Born in 1939, he holds "The Anne Marie and Thomas B. Walker Jr." chair at Vanderbilt University.
[25] The Relationship Between Put and Call-Option Prices in Journal of Finance 24 (December 1969) pp. 801–824.

r = Risk-free rate of interest
T = Maturity

Rewriting yields:
$$p = c + Ke^{-rT} - S_0$$

Including dividends in the above formula leads to the following equation:
$$p + S_0 = c + Ke^{-rT} + D$$

D = Net present value of the dividends expected during the contract period of the option

Expanding S_0 with $S_0 e^{-DT}$, as shown in Chapter 6.14.3, the following expression can be derived. It presents the equation for put-call parity for an option with a dividend yield D.

$$c + Ke^{-rT} = p + S_0 e^{-DT}$$

A tool for the calculation of put-call parity is available in our download area.

Put-call parity	
Assumptions	
Price of the underlying	61.73
Strike price of the option	61.00
Term to maturity of option	1.00
Risk-free interest rate	1.00%
Volatility	34.00%
Price on the call	8.9281
Calculation	
Put-call parity	7.59

6.13.2 Presentation of the put-call relationship using replication

It can also be shown with the help of a replicating portfolio (see Chapter 2.4.3) that the above relationship holds. The two equivalent portfolios are presented below:

First portfolio:
A portfolio is formed which consists of a riskless fixed income investment and call options on an underlying (see Chapter 2.4.3). The fixed income investment constitutes a floor (lower boundary of price). The call options meanwhile allow participation in a possible favorable price development of the underlying. This approach is called synthetic hedge in applied work, since the long position is generated synthetically.

Second portfolio:
A portfolio consisting of equities is hedged with the help of put options. This leads to the same payoff as in the above portfolio. This approach is also called "protective put."

6.14 Determination of option prices using the Black-Scholes model

In 1973, FISCHER S. BLACK and MYRON S. SCHOLES published a relatively simple model for the theoretical calculation of option prices. It quickly became very relevant to practitioners, and today it is an element of every calculation of option prices. The basic idea of the Black-Scholes model is the use of an option and a variable counter-position to construct a portfolio consisting of equities and fixed-income instruments in such a way that the profit or loss from one position is always neutralized by the counter-position. The return of this riskless portfolio is the risk-free rate of return. Today every derivatives exchange prices its options basically with the model developed by Black and Scholes, which is based on a continuous stochastic process and has been refined concerning dividends and other modeling issues.

Fischer S. Black
1938–1995

It should be mentioned that ROBERT C. MERTON also contributed to this work, but aimed for an independent publication[26]. In 1997 Merton and Scholes received the Nobel Prize in Economic Sciences[27] for the model. Since FISCHER BLACK passed away in 1995, the Nobel Prize was not awarded to him. During the awards ceremony, his contribution was honored posthumously.

Myron S. Scholes
born in 1941

Robert C. Merton
born in 1944

---

[26] The Black-Scholes-Merton model includes a constant and known dividend payment of the underlying and is thus an extension of the Black-Scholes formula, which assumes no dividend payments, see Chapters 6.14.2 and 6.14.3.

[27] More formally: The Sveriges Riksbank Prize in Economic Sciences in Memory of Alfred Nobel.

6.14.1 Assumptions of the Black-Scholes model

- Perfect capital markets: information is available to all investors in equal measure and there are no barriers to entry, which might prevent free market access of participants[28].
- Arbitrage profits are ruled out: should an immediate riskless profit materialize due to mispricing, changes in supply and demand will immediately lead to its elimination.
- There are no information or transaction costs.
- There are also no taxes.
- The volatility of the price of the underlying remains constant during the life of the option.
- All options can only be exercised on the last day of trading; they are European options.
- All assets and derivatives are infinitely divisible and their prices do not react to changes in liquidity.
- Both investing and borrowing are possible without limit at the risk-free rate of interest. The risk-free rate of interest remains constant during the life of the option and is known.
- Short sales are possible without limit.

6.14.2 The Black-Scholes formula

Under the influence of the assumptions and approaches listed above, in 1973 BLACK and SCHOLES developed the following model for the determination of the "fair value" of a **European**[29] call option **without dividend payment**:

$$c = S_0 N(d_1) - Ke^{-rT} N(d_2)$$

with

$$d_1 = \frac{\ln(S_0/K) + (r + \sigma^2/2)T}{\sigma\sqrt{T}}$$

$$d_2 = d_1 - \sigma\sqrt{T}$$

and $N(d)$ the standard normal distribution $N(d)$[30].

---

[28] Paradigm of neoclassical finance theory: capital markets are perfect and function smoothly.
[29] For an American option, where the exercise date is unknown, it is recommended to use the Black approximation, an approximation procedure which takes into account the possibility of an early exercise.
[30] The Appendix to this book contains a table for $N(x)$; a calculation in Excel is possible using the formula NORMDIST.

c = Price of the call option
S_0 = Price of the underlying at time t = 0
K = Strike price of the option
ln = Natural logarithm
e = Base of the natural logarithm = 2.7128...[31]
r = Riskless rate of interest
N(d) = Cumulative standard normal distribution
σ = Volatility
T = Remaining time to maturity of the option

The following formula results for the value of a put option **p**:

$$p = Ke^{-rT}N(-d_2) - S_0 N(-d_1)$$

The derivation of the price of the put is also possible using the put-call parity described in Chapter 6.13.1.

6.14.3 The Black-Scholes-Merton model

Expanding the above standard model by Black and Scholes by replacing S_0 with $S_0 e^{-DT}$ gives the price **c** of a European call option and the price **p** of a European put option which takes into account a **dividend yield D**. This expansion was developed by ROBERT MERTON. Therefore the model is frequently called **Black-Scholes-Merton model**.

$$c = S_0 e^{-DT} N(d) - Ke^{-rT} N(d_2)$$

$$p = Ke^{-rT} N(-d_2) - S_0 e^{-DT} N(-d_1)$$

$$\ln \frac{S_0 e^{-DT}}{K} = \ln \frac{S_0}{K} - DT$$

$$d_1 = \frac{\ln(S_0/K) + (r - D + \sigma^2/2)T}{\sigma\sqrt{T}}$$

$$d_2 = d_1 - \sigma\sqrt{T}$$

---

[31] logarithmus naturalis = Euler's number = e =
2,71818182815004523536028747135266 24+775724709369995
9574966967627724076630353547594574 6821785251664274
2746639193200305992181741359662904 3572900334295260
5956307381323286279434907632338298 8075319525101901...

c = Price of the call option
p = Price of the put option
S₀ = Price of the underlying at time t=0
K = Strike price of the option
In = Natural logarithm
e = Base of the natural logarithm = 2.7128...
r = Riskless rate of interest
D = Dividend payment
N(d) = Cumulative standard normal distribution
σ = Volatility
T = Remaining time to maturity of the option

D is the average annual **dividend yield** during the life of the option. Therefore the above model can also be used for a known, but changing dividend yield.

Figure 6.21 displays some sections from the options calculator (Black-Scholes model taking into account dividend payments) which is provided in the download area. In the upper half of the figure, the theoretical option price calculated with the help of the Black-Scholes model is shown. In the lower half of the figure, a live screenshot from Eurex is displayed for the option calculated above.

6.14.4 The Black-Scholes differential equation

An analytical derivation of the Black-Scholes model and the determination of the fair value of an option (following BLACK SCHOLES) are made possible by applying the **Black-Scholes differential equation**. For the equation, the following assumptions hold: a log-normally distributed share price, the use of a perfect hedging strategy, the no-arbitrage condition and the use of ITŌ's lemma[32]. Looked at from a purely mathematical perspective, the Black-

---

[32] Brownian motion; Itō's lemma states: If $h : \mathbb{R}_+ \times \mathbb{R} \to \mathbb{R}$ is a function that is once differentiable in the first component and twice differentiable in the second component, then $Y_t := h(t, X_t)$ is also an Itō process and it holds:

$$dY_t = \left(\frac{\partial h(t, X_t)}{\partial x} f(t, X_t) + \frac{\partial h(t, X_t)}{\partial t} + \frac{1}{2} \frac{\partial^2 h(t, X_t)}{\partial x^2} g^2(t, X_t) \right) dt + \frac{\partial h(t, X_t)}{\partial x} g(t, X_t) dW_t.$$

Determination of option prices using the Black-Scholes model

Assumptions:	
Price of the underlying	61.73
Strike price of the option	60.00
Dividends	2.30%
Term to maturity in years	1.00
Volatility	34.00%
Risk-free interest rate	1.00%

Calculations	
Exp(-rT)	0.9900
Exp(-DT)	0.9773
$(r-D+0.5*V^2)$	0.0448
d1	0.2154
N (d1)	0.5853
N (-d1)	0.4147
d2	(0.1246)
N(d2)	0.4504
N(-d2)	0.5496

Results	
Price of call option	8.55
Price of put option	7.63

Quotenübersichtsmonitor

SIEMENS AG NAMENS-AKTIEN O.N.
61,73 EUR ▼ -0,180 -0,29% | Xetra | 17.12.09 10:14 [R]
ISIN: DE0007236101   WKN: 723610   Geld: 61,69   Brief: 61,73   Tageshoch: 61,76   Tagestief: 61,10   Vortag: 61,91

24 Ergebnisse

		Calls					Puts				
Datum & Zeit	Impl Vola	Volumen	Geld	Brief	Aktuell	Strike/Monat	Aktuell	Geld	Brief	Volumen	Impl Vola	Datum & Zeit
17.12.09 10:08	61,72%	20	1,80	1,89	1,80	60,00 / Dez 09	0,14	0,12	0,15	10	63,66%	17.12.09 09:48
17.12.09 10:11	51,50%	50	0,45	0,50	0,46	62,00 / Dez 09	0,77	0,75	0,79	60	55,79%	17.12.09 10:12
17.12.09 10:09	61,73%	8	0,06	0,09	0,07	64,00 / Dez 09	2,38	2,32	2,41	6	68,52%	17.12.09 10:12
16.12.09 18:51	30,55%	-	2,85	2,93	3,07	60,00 / Jan 10	1,14	1,14	1,20	-	28,36%	16.12.09 18:51
17.12.09 09:42	28,77%	11	1,68	1,74	1,70	62,00 / Jan 10	1,91	1,96	2,02	-	27,42%	16.12.09 18:51
16.12.09 18:51	27,40%	-	0,87	0,92	0,99	64,00 / Jan 10	3,06	3,14	3,23	-	25,89%	16.12.09 18:51
16.12.09 18:51	30,47%	-	3,77	3,85	3,94	60,00 / Feb 10	3,15	3,15	3,23	-	38,98%	16.12.09 18:51
16.12.09 18:51	30,08%	-	2,68	2,74	2,83	62,00 / Feb 10	4,19	4,19	4,27	-	39,14%	16.12.09 18:51
17.12.09 09:13	28,95%	20	1,82	1,87	1,72	64,00 / Feb 10	5,44	5,43	5,51	-	40,14%	16.12.09 18:51
16.12.09 18:51	31,30%	-	4,28	4,37	4,48	60,00 / Mär 10	3,90	3,85	3,93	-	38,38%	16.12.09 18:51
16.12.09 18:51	-	-	3,19	3,32	3,37	62,00 / Mär 10	4,87	4,84	4,94	-	-	16.12.09 18:51
17.12.09 10:05	28,93%	5	2,32	2,41	2,35	64,00 / Mär 10	6,06	6,03	6,11	10	38,07%	17.12.09 09:32
17.12.09 09:56	31,87%	5	5,85	5,95	5,88	60,00 / Jun 10	5,59	5,55	5,64	-	36,76%	16.12.09 18:51
16.12.09 18:51	30,94%	-	3,95	4,05	4,11	64,00 / Jun 10	7,64	7,67	7,78	-	35,86%	16.12.09 18:51
16.12.09 18:51	33,05%	-	7,15	7,32	7,41	60,00 / Sep 10	6,79	6,76	6,92	-	35,57%	16.12.09 18:51
16.12.09 18:51	31,99%	-	5,28	5,42	5,48	64,00 / Sep 10	8,84	8,85	8,99	-	36,11%	16.12.09 18:51
17.12.09 09:01	34,44%	2	8,36	8,57	8,55	60,00 / Dez 10	7,85	7,79	7,99	-	36,45%	16.12.09 18:51
16.12.09 18:51	33,87%	-	7,36	7,57	7,66	62,00 / Dez 10	8,81	8,79	9,01	-	34,44%	16.12.09 18:51
16.12.09 18:51	33,24%	-	6,44	6,65	6,72	64,00 / Dez 10	9,86	9,87	10,10	-	33,84%	16.12.09 18:51
16.12.09 18:51	35,26%	-	9,59	10,00	9,93	60,00 / Jun 11	10,01	9,86	10,27	-	36,42%	16.12.09 18:51
16.12.09 18:51	24,84%	-	-	-	11,51	60,00 / Dez 11	11,19	-	-	-	31,44%	16.12.09 18:51
16.12.09 18:51	-	-	-	-	12,34	60,00 / Jun 12	12,61	-	-	-	27,00%	16.12.09 18:51
16.12.09 18:51	25,03%	-	-	-	13,67	60,00 / Dez 12	13,43	-	-	-	-	16.12.09 18:51
16.12.09 18:51	-	-	-	-	15,24	60,00 / Dez 13	14,99	-	-	-	-	16.12.09 18:51

Figure 6.21: Black-Scholes model and Eurex live trading

Scholes differential equation[33] can be interpreted as a diffusion equation of the following form:

$$\frac{\partial c}{\partial t} + rS\frac{\partial c}{\partial S} + \frac{1}{2}\sigma^2 S^2 \frac{\partial^2 c}{\partial S^2} = rc$$

c = Option price

The Greeks can also be detected in the above formula. The price movement of a call option can thus be interpreted as a function of theta, delta, and gamma.

John C. Cox
Prof. of Finance
MIT Sloan School of Management

6.15 Determination of option prices using the binomial model

In 1979 the American professors JOHN C. COX, STEPHEN ROSS and MARK RUBINSTEIN developed a discrete model (discrete stochastic process as opposed to the Black-Scholes model, which follows a continuous stochastic process) for modeling securities prices and thus also for the derivation of option prices. This model also makes use of replication, which we discussed in Chapter 2.4.3 and which relies on constructing an equivalent portfolio consisting of a share in the underlying and an amount of a riskless security or loan.

Stephen Ross
Prof. of Financial Economics
MIT Sloan School of Management

The option price is determined based on increases or decreases of the underlying, which are simulated in the model (see Figure 6.22). The model starts with a scenario at $t = 0$ and ends with two possibilities in $t = 1$ (in the one-period model). Since only two different situations can arise, this is called a **binomial step**. S is the starting scenario, S_u the scenario for increasing prices and S_d the scenario for declining prices.

Mark Rubinstein
Prof. of Finance
University of California, Berkeley

6.15.1 Basic assumptions of the binomial model

We assume complete markets without transaction costs, taxes and margin requirements. Proceeds from short sales are available immediately and are

---

[33] The statistical initial value problem $dS_t = rS_t dt + \sigma S_t dW_t$, $S_0 = a$ is solved as follows: $X_t = W_t$, therefore $f(t, W_t) = 0$, $g(t, W_t) = 1$. Now the lemma holds (with $h = S$):

$$dS_t = \left[\left(r - 0.5\sigma^2 + \frac{\sigma^2}{2}\right) ae^{rt - 0.5\sigma^2 t + \sigma W_t}\right] dt + \left[\sigma a e^{rt - 0.5\sigma^2 t + \sigma W_t}\right] dW_t$$
$$= rS_t dt + \sigma S_t dW_t.$$

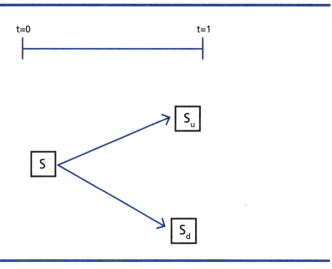

Figure 6.22: Binomial step in the one period model[34]

infinitely divisible. There is only one interest rate which is used for borrowing and lending. For each observation interval, price increases, price decreases and the risk-free interest rate are known. In addition, it is always assumed that these are growth strategies and that arbitrage profits are not possible.

It is the initial model assumption that the price of the underlying can either go up by **x** units (**u** = **up**) or go down (**d** = **down**) (with a probability **q** in either case). Furthermore the model is based on a discrete stochastic process[35]. In this regard it differs from the Black-Scholes model, which assumes a continuous stochastic process.

6.15.2 Setup of a tree

A share is valued today at EUR 50. Therefore $S_0 = 50$. In one period it can either take on the value S_{1u} **51** (price of the option = 1) or S_{1d} **49** (price of the option = 0) (see Figure 6.24).

---

[34] One period model: the process starts at a certain point in time and after one period reaches the endpoint.
[35] A stochastic process in discrete time is a discontinuous process with denumerable steps in time and random events. A stochastic process in continuous time is a smooth process with innumerable steps in time and random events.

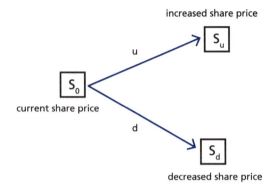

Figure 6.23: Binomial step (basic structure)

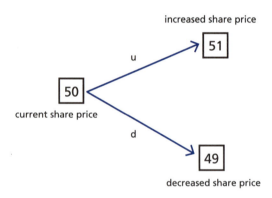

Figure 6.24: First binomial step

6.15.3 Implementation of the binomial model

In each of the discrete periods Δt considered, it holds for the value of the underlying **S** that it changes by the factor **u** with a still to be defined probability q^{36} or by the factor **d** with the converse probability $(1 - q)$. The relationship $d < (1 + r) < u$ must hold.

---

[36] **q** is equal to the probability in a world that is risk neutral. Since this is not usually the case in reality, in most cases a deviation is apparent. A different expression is "pseudo-probability" (see Chapter 2.1).

The volatility σ is used to determine the factor for the up move **u** and the factor for the down move **d**. These factors depend on the length of the time period and the standard deviation (volatility) and can be calculated with the help of the following formula, which is based on "geometric Brownian motion" (see Chapter 2.2.2) and can be used for modeling possible price changes of typical capital market products:

$$u = e^{\sigma\sqrt{\Delta t}}$$
$$d = e^{-\sigma\sqrt{\Delta t}} = \frac{1}{u}^{37}$$

In the binomial model, a call on this underlying at the end of the period has with probability **q** a value of:

$$C_u = \max\{u \cdot S - K; 0\}$$

S is the current value of the underlying and K the strike price. The following value is obtained with a probability of (1 − q):

$$C_d = \max\{d \cdot S - K; 0\}$$

Since the entire life of an option can be described as the sum of a finite number of discrete sub-periods, the one period approach can be extended to multiple periods. Initially a tree for the price development of the underlying S can be derived. The last nodes of this tree display all possible values for the price of the underlying S on the expiration date T of the option.

The price of the option is derived by developing a similar tree for the option prices. In a first step, the option prices at expiration are calculated by subtracting the strike price **K** from the possible values for **S**. The value of the option at the start of the tree is calculated for a European option as the probability-weighted sum of the possible values of the option at expiration T, discounted at the risk-free interest rate **r**. In the one period case, the value of the option at the beginning of the period is calculated as follows:

$$C = \frac{q \cdot C_u + (1-q) \cdot C_d}{1+r}$$

It must be kept in mind that the probability **q** is a so-called pseudo-probability, since it is not estimated, but rather calculated from the known values **u**, **d**

---

[37] The equations were developed by *Cox, Ross* and *Rubinstein*. They show the relationship between the up and down movements in a binomial tree and the current annualized standard deviations of the returns of the underlying.

and **r**. It can be derived from the formula for the option price as follows:

$$C = \frac{q \cdot u \cdot C + (1-q) \cdot d \cdot C}{1+r}$$

$$1 = \frac{q \cdot u + (1-q) \cdot d}{1+r}$$

$$1 + r = q \cdot u + (1-q) \cdot d$$

$$q \cdot (u - d) = 1 + r - d$$

$$q = \frac{(1+r) - d}{(u - d)}$$

As can be seen from the above formula, the determination of the pseudo-probability, and thus of the value of the option, does not depend on the risk-adjusted return of the underlying **S** but rather on the risk-free interest rate **r**.

The one period binomial model can now be extended without restrictions to a two period or multiperiod setting. To do so, the factor for the up movement **u** and the factor for the down movement **d** are calculated for the multiperiod binomial model. If, for example, the life of the option is broken down into twelve months, the monthly factor for the up movement u_M and the monthly factor for the down movement d_M are calculated with the help of the following formula:

$$u = e^{\sigma \sqrt{\frac{T}{12}}}$$

$$d = e^{-\sigma \sqrt{\frac{T}{12}}}$$

In order to develop the tree of the option prices, the pseudo-probabilities need to be derived from the monthly factors for the up movement and the down movement as well as the risk-free interest rate **r**. Taking into account compound interest, the monthly interest rate r_M can be derived according to the following formula:

$$r_M = \sqrt[12]{(1+r)} - 1$$

The pseudo-probability for the up movement is called **q**, and for the down movement $(1 - q)$:

$$q = \frac{1 + r_M - d_M}{u_M - d_M}$$

The inclusion of many periods leads to a refinement of the binomial model. The price of the call is more precisely determined and deviates significantly from that obtained in the one period case. The more nodes are included in the tree, the more precise the approximation becomes (see Figure 6.25). This

Determination of option prices using the binomial model 207

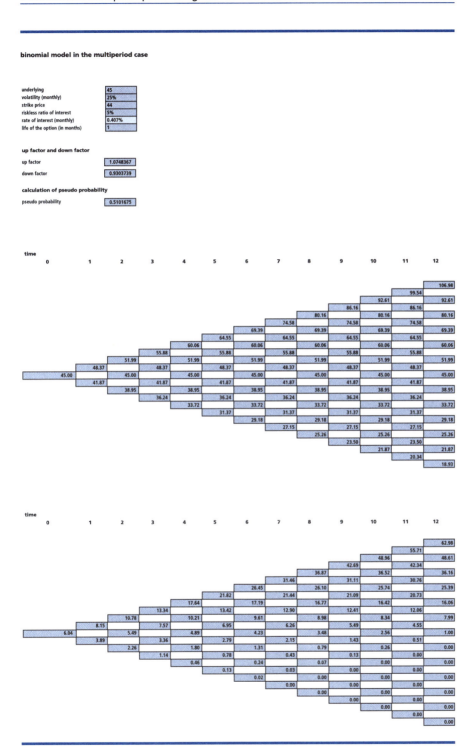

Figure 6.25: Setup of a multiperiod binomial tree including underlying

also implies that the result comes closer to the value derived with the help of the Black-Scholes model. The discrete time solution of the binomial model approaches that of the Black-Scholes model in the limit. The reason for this is the law of large numbers. It states that for a large number of observations (**n** is large), the binomial distribution converges towards the normal distribution.

In the following example, we simulate the development of the option price with these components:

Price of the underlying	EUR 45
Volatility	25%
Strike price of the option	EUR 44
Risk-free rate of interest	5% per annum is equal to 0.407 per month
Time to maturity of the option	1 year = 12 months

6.16 Model critique

Both the Black-Scholes-Merton model and the binomial model derived by COX, ROSS and RUBINSTEIN are not infrequently criticized by practitioners for the deviations of the model assumptions from reality.

The following points are subject to critical review in the Black-Scholes-Merton model:

- Volatility and interest rates are not constant in reality.
- Dividends are assumed to be constant.
- The valuation of American options is not possible.
- Share prices do not follow a log-normal distribution in reality.
- In reality, taxes, arbitrage and transaction costs are relevant.

The biggest conflict between the reality of capital markets and the model assumptions made by BLACK SCHOLES is the premise of constant volatility. But if the option price (for example in the form of binding quotes provided by a market maker) and the other parameters of the Black-Scholes formula are known, the implied volatility can be calculated by inserting all parameters into the pricing formula. When comparing these implied volatilities on the same underlying with identical or similar terms to expiration, but different strike prices, a so called volatility smile[38] can be observed (see Figure 6.26). Options

---

[38] The volatilities are U-shaped with regard to the strike price. Also known are skew and sneer, which are distortions/displacements of the smile.

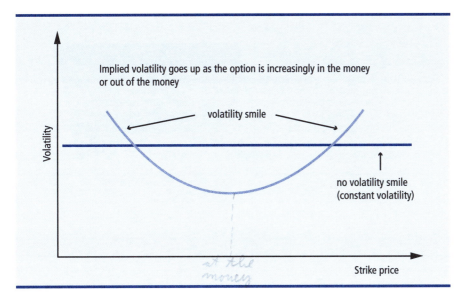

Figure 6.26: Volatility smile versus constant volatility

that are in the money or out of the money have higher implied volatilities (and therefore also higher option prices) than options with a strike price that is at the money. The appearance of a volatility smile or of a volatility skew is founded in the model assumptions of the Black-Scholes model. It is assumed, among others, that the underlying can be modeled with the help of a geometric Brownian motion and that the volatility of the underlying is constant over time. This implies a normal distribution of the returns of the underlying. But as empirical studies have shown, exactly this assumption of a normal distribution of equity returns is open to criticism. The graphical representation of the data obtained shows a volatility surface (see Figure 6.27), which sketches the dependence of strike price, volatility and life of the option in a graph.

Concerning the binomial model of COX, ROSS and RUBINSTEIN, the following issues must be kept in mind:

- Equity prices are quoted continuously.
- Dividends are not considered automatically.
- Investors are not risk-neutral in reality and arbitrage is possible.
- Interest rates are not necessarily constant.
- In reality, taxes, arbitrage and transaction costs exist.

Despite a number of assumptions which are not found in reality, the models can be used to price financial derivatives with little information costs and

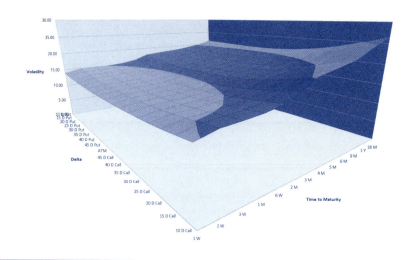

Figure 6.27: Volatility surface of a typical equity[39]

effort. While the weaknesses are acknowledged, both models are broadly accepted by theorists.

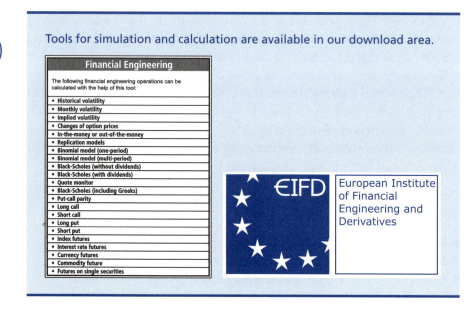

---

[39] Source: Thomson Reuters.

6.17 Monte-Carlo simulation

Approaches based on simulation are used in applied work whenever analytical solutions – for example in the form of differential equations – for the valuation of a financial product are not available. In 1977, **Monte-Carlo simulation** was used for the first time by PHELIM BOYLE. Today these models are an accepted standard. Exotic options and complex structures are regularly valued and studied with the help of Monte-Carlo simulations. Especially path-dependent derivatives can be valued efficiently with the help of simulation models (see Chapter 8.1.6.1 on this issue).

The central element of any Monte-Carlo simulation is the computer-based generation of a large number of random paths, which the financial product can possibly take. These random paths help to capture the uncertainty or risk involved. Possibly the most basic example is a roulette table[40] at the casino of Monte Carlo, which gave its name to this simulation technique. The valuation of a derivative financial product is structured as follows:

- In a first step, the risk-neutral random walk from the time of valuation S_0 to the expiration date S_R is simulated. For each individual time increment μ, a random value of the asset S, depending on drift and volatility is determined. This leads to a path from S_0 to S_T.
- In a next step, payoffs are determined for the path of the asset S which has just been simulated.
- In a third step, steps 1 and 2 are repeated until a certain precision has been reached. Fundamental is the law of large numbers[41].
- Following that, the average payoff from the sum of all simulated paths is calculated.
- Finally, the current value of the option is determined by discounting the expected (average) payments from step 4 using the risk-free interest rate.

In needs to be stressed that the use of Monte-Carlo simulations starts at the point where the Black-Scholes world with its restrictive and partially unrealistic assumptions ends. Monte-Carlo simulations are therefore used regularly for complex derivatives. Problems that are hard or impossible to solve analytically are assessed numerically with the help of probability theory.

---

[40] The name Monte-Carlo simulation is based on the casino in Monaco. For each spin of the roulette wheel, the ball follows a random path until it comes to rest. See Wiedemann, Bernd: Bewertung von Finanzinstrumenten (2007), page 435.

[41] The law states that the result will increase in precision as more and more simulations are conducted (see Chapter 2.2).

Monte-Carlo methods are also used to value derivatives that only have a simulation-based background (see Chapter 14.3.7.2).

6.18 Tradable option prices

Let us again take a look at daily business practices. The quotes[42] that can be used for trading at derivatives exchanges are provided in most cases by market makers. But there are also contracts which are not maintained at all times. It becomes necessary therefore to work with limit orders, especially in the case of contracts that are not maintained. Use of a **market order**[43] can only be recommended in the case of very liquid option series. For series with a narrow market (series that are not very liquid) or contract series that are not maintained, setting a limit is absolutely necessary. Investors also have the possibility to place a quote request[44]. This is absolutely required in cases where no quotes are provided. We explicitly want to warn against "flying blind." Especially when rolling positions[45], this can lead to significant price movements and thus unwanted losses.

The "prices" derived above can be considered to be the fair value of an option. But it must be stressed that they can deviate, if only by small amounts, from the prices actually traded at derivatives exchanges (see Figure 6.28).

6.19 Strategies using options

We now want to turn to individual option strategies. This is the application of the theory presented in the previous chapters. The following needs to be kept in mind: there are four basic strategies on which all combined option strategies are based. No matter how complex the overall strategy is, it can always be decomposed into its components and therefore valued reliably and understood.

---

[42] Tradable bid-ask spread.
[43] Market order: an order without price limit. It is filled at the current "market price".
[44] The quote request is put to the responsible market maker. He is required to answer the query within his guidelines or can decline to answer if he has already fulfilled his obligations (see Chapter 4.9).
[45] Especially if these are "deep-in-the-money" or due to their complexity overstrain the market.

dXETRA DAX PF EUX/EUR GER .GDAXI * LT ↑6267.59147.1710:47 B A H 6339.61 L 6152.62

Time	Vol	Bid IV	Bid	Ask	Ask IV	Calls	Strike/Mth	Puts	Bid IV	Bid	Ask	Ask IV	Vol	Time
:							5150 AUG1							:
:							5200 AUG1							:
:							5250 AUG1	9.30					50	10:53
:							5300 AUG1							:
:							5350 AUG1							:
:				920.00	61.69		5400 AUG1	↑14.00	48.76	15.60	16.70	49.45	120	10:53
:							5450 AUG1	↓16.60	47.72	17.80	19.40	49.08	761	10:49
:							5500 AUG1	↓23.90	46.83	20.80	22.50	47.84	810	10:37
:							5550 AUG1		45.75	23.60	26.20	47.06		:
:							5600 AUG1	↓26.80	45.18	28.10	30.30	46.14	737	10:50
:							5650 AUG1	↑31.30	44.43	33.00	35.10	45.50	402	10:56
:							5700 AUG1	↓36.50	43.74	38.30	40.60	44.67	431	10:52
:							5750 AUG1	↑44.00	43.10	44.50	47.10	44.02	16	10:45
:							5800 AUG1	↓48.50	42.39	52.20	54.60	43.26	1696	10:47
:							5850 AUG1	↓63.80	41.66	60.50	62.80	42.44	175	10:23
:		39.76	403.80	417.10	43.34		5900 AUG1	↓72.00	40.98	70.30	72.40	41.76	374	10:40
:		39.17	365.90	378.40	42.35		5950 AUG1	↓76.20	40.51	81.20	83.50	41.04	21	10:53
09:45	6	38.60	328.50	340.70	41.51	↑331.10	6000 AUG1	↑88.00	39.56	92.60	96.00	40.34	8738	10:55
:		38.25	293.20	302.10	40.26		6050 AUG1	↑107.00	38.95	106.70	109.50	39.63	263	11:01
10:46	2028	37.91	261.60	267.70	39.10	↑275.00	6100 AUG1	↓113.00	38.23	122.30	125.30	38.88	2053	10:49
10:48	30	37.20	229.00	233.30	38.65	↑250.00	6150 AUG1	↑135.90	37.55	139.50	143.30	38.12	699	11:01
10:47	1145	36.62	199.00	203.50	37.53	↑215.00	6200 AUG1	↓150.80	36.79	159.10	162.80	37.58	2737	10:57
10:35	1267	35.78	170.90	174.60	36.71	↓168.00	6250 AUG1	↑173.80	36.08	180.70	184.70	36.92	1065	10:52
10:48	7635	35.53	145.00	149.10	36.25	↑162.00	6300 AUG1	↓195.00	35.10	204.90	209.20	36.01	4852	10:58
10:37	606	34.77	122.10	125.30	35.52	↑126.00	6350 AUG1	↓216.00	34.93	231.30	235.70	35.83	2102	10:53
11:00	3332	34.24	101.40	103.90	34.93	↑111.00	6400 AUG1	↓250.00	33.87	259.30	265.80	35.27	1898	10:52
10:37	277	33.67	82.90	86.20	34.54	↑85.00	6450 AUG1	↓275.00	32.95	289.70	297.80	35.19	113	10:48
10:59	3342	33.05	66.80	70.20	33.97	↓72.00	6500 AUG1	↑327.00	32.03	322.40	334.40	34.94	1030	11:02
10:48	762	32.87	54.00	56.40	33.55	↑62.50	6550 AUG1	↑347.70	26.82	341.60	389.50	39.51	1357	10:51
10:51	2637	32.46	42.30	45.10	33.24	↓48.00	6600 AUG1	↑388.00	25.36	379.90	427.80	39.54	1493	10:57
10:50	153	31.88	33.00	35.40	32.95	↓37.30	6650 AUG1	↓382.20	23.55	405.00			217	10:09
10:52	1474	31.63	25.40	27.90	32.70	↓29.00	6700 AUG1	↓470.00		425.00	620.00	70.02	14374	10:47
10:33	163	31.31	19.20	21.80	32.51	↑20.50	6750 AUG1	↓525.00		470.00			776	10:41
11:02	744	31.76	15.00	16.90	32.31	↓16.50	6800 AUG1	↓550.00	19.64	540.00			695	10:53
10:31	2539	31.32	12.00	13.10	32.38	↑12.90	6850 AUG1	↑635.00		535.00			94	10:32
10:59	783	30.70	7.80	10.30	32.43	↑10.50	6900 AUG1	↓690.00		600.00			175	10:32
10:32	85	30.69	6.00	8.00	32.42	↑7.50	6950 AUG1	↑690.00					50	10:12
10:36	2231	31.43	5.50	5.90	32.38	↑5.00	7000 AUG1	↓725.60		750.00			1562	10:54
10:00	54	30.74	3.50	5.20	33.24	↓3.50	7050 AUG1	↓800.00					55	09:33
11:01	832	30.72	2.30	4.00	33.41	↑3.50	7100 AUG1	↑870.00					187	10:27
11:01	274	32.26	2.00	3.30	33.66	↓2.50	7150 AUG1	↓930.00					6	09:28
10:25	57	32.31	2.00	2.50	33.43	↑2.00	7200 AUG1	↓930.00		800.00			155	10:53
09:33	52			10.00	43.62	↓1.50	7250 AUG1	↓1020.00		950.00			267	09:30
10:25	12	30.07	0.50	2.50	35.73	↑1.60	7300 AUG1	↓1030.00		91.30			469	10:47

Figure 6.28: Quotes of DAX® options at Eurex[46]

6.19.1 What is contained in the four basic strategies in option trading (plain vanilla)?

In option trading there are four basic strategies, on which all other strategies are based. A clear understanding of these four basic approaches is therefore absolutely required.

- **Long call:** in this case the investor (buyer) is convinced that the underlying will go up in value. With the call, he purchases the right to acquire the underlying. If he is correct, the underlying will go up in price. Alternatively, the investor could also acquire the underlying, but he would be required to invest significantly more capital. By using the call, he leverages the capital employed. His loss potential is limited to the premium paid. But at the same time, he has the chance to participate in price increases without limit. He faces no obligation to pay in additional funds and is only exposed to the risk of losing the initial investment (payment of the premium).
- **Short call:** the investor who shorts the call expects a scenario of constant or slightly declining prices of the underlying and intends to generate extra revenue from the option premium. He thus sells calls and makes a max-

[46] Source: Thomson Reuters.

imum profit equal to the premium received. The risk of the short call is that the underlying has to be delivered at the strike price. This risk can be minimized if the underlying is already in the portfolio when the derivatives transaction is closed. These are called covered options, as the obligation to deliver the underlying can me met from "positions held." Therefore no major outflow of liquidity can occur. Nonetheless the investor is suffering an economic loss, since he could have sold the underlying at a higher price without the short call.

- **Long put:** in the case of a long put, the investor expects a (significant) decline in price. With the purchase of the put option, he either intends to protect his portfolio (he holds the underlying) or he wants to actively speculate on declining prices (he does not own the underlying and merely intends to profit from the adverse market environment). Here again, as with all long options, the maximum loss is limited to the option premium paid. The profit is limited, as every investment vehicle can decline at most to zero. This constitutes an effective lower bound.
- **Short put:** an investor who chooses a short put expects markets to increase. He wants to benefit from this development and is willing to actively assume risk. The option premium received is his maximum profit. His theoretical loss is limited to the strike price[47], since he may be required to purchase the underlying at the predetermined strike price. He thus bears the full risk of a complete loss of value of the underlying.

Let us now illustrate the four basic positions in a succinct and detailed manner.

Basic assumptions: it is assumed in all cases that a share is tradable. Possible fees and costs are not taken into account.

6.19.2 The strategy LONG CALL

With a long call, an investor purchases the right, but not the obligation, to acquire the underlying during the life of the option or at expiration. For this right he makes a payment to the counterparty (short call): the option premium. The holder of the short call is required to deliver the underlying upon request to the long call position.

Long call on X shares
Strike price: EUR 50
Expiration date: September
Option premium: EUR 3

---

[47] In case of an insolvency, the share price of a company cannot fall below zero. Therefore the risk is limited to a known amount even in the worst case scenario.

Thus the buyer has the right to purchase the X share during the entire life of the option (until the third Friday in September at the latest) at a price of EUR 50. He has paid a premium of EUR 3 for this right, which the seller received immediately after the closing of the transaction.

If the price of X shares increases above the strike price, in this case EUR 50, the buyer of the option (long) will make use of his right and exercise the option. The seller (short) is required to deliver the underlying at a price of EUR 50 per share.

Breakeven point of this strategy
The breakeven point (see Figure 6.29) is reached at EUR 53. Why is that? The owner of this option has the right to purchase the shares for EUR 50, but he already paid EUR 3 when entering into the derivatives transaction. This payment must be included in the overall assessment.

Scenario analysis:
- **The share is quoted below EUR 50:** the buyer of the calls suffers the maximum loss on the expiration date. The option expires worthless.
- **The share is quoted between EUR 50 and 53:** the buyer of the call suffers a reduced loss. The value of the option at expiration is equal to its intrinsic value, since it is in the money.
- **The share is quoted above EUR 53:** the buyer is making a profit. The value of the option at expiration exceeds the option premium paid at the time of closing.

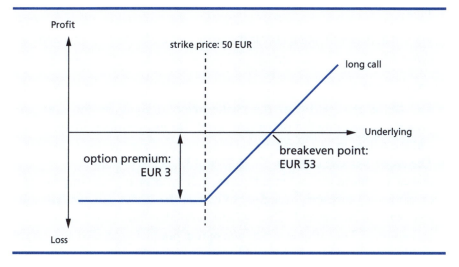

Figure 6.29: Profit and loss scenario for the long call

We see that the underlying must move beyond the breakeven point before the buyer of the option can realize a profit.

6.19.3 The strategy SHORT CALL

A call option was purchased in the above example. Now the investor is selling this call option. We use the same example:

Short call on X shares
Strike price: EUR 50
Expiration date: September
Option premium: EUR 3

As seller of the call on X shares, the investor has received the premium of EUR3. He is the writer of the option, which means that on demand, he has to deliver the underlying.

Two fundamentally different short call positions can be distinguished in this regard. Either an option is written on an underlying which is in the possession of the investor, or it is written without any backing by an underlying (uncovered). **Naked call writing** is the sale of call options for which no underlying is in the possession of the investor. It is clearly more speculative than **covered call writing** (CCW), where the option writer is in possession of the underlying.

Let us initially take a look at the above example for the case of naked call writing.

The profit and loss situation is thus the mirror image of the long position (see Figure 6.30).

Scenario analysis:
- **The share price is below the strike price of EUR 50:** the short call investor is realizing the maximum profit. He has collected the premium and the option expires worthless.
- **The share price is between EUR 50 and EUR 53:** the short call investor makes a reduced profit. Since the long call investor is exercising the call, the short call investor is required to deliver the shares. He purchases the shares in the market and delivers them (reminder: this is the case of naked call writing). The difference between option premium received and cost of purchasing the shares minus strike price is his profit.

Strategies using options

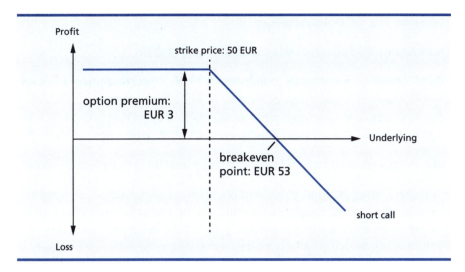

Figure 6.30: Profit and loss scenario for the short call (naked call writing)

- **The share price is above the breakeven point of EUR 53:** the investor is suffering a loss. He is required to deliver the shares at the strike price. His loss is calculated as follows: (purchase price – strike price) – option premium.

Very important: The loss potential of the strategy "short call" is unlimited in markets that are moving higher! The conservative version of a short call is CCW. In this case, calls are sold on existing share holdings. In case of an exercise, delivery by the short call investor can come from these existing positions. CCW is a strategy to increase returns. Especially the return of long-term holdings is increased from collecting premiums. The risk is limited to a foregone profit. If the underlying increases beyond the strike price, the CCW investor is required to deliver the underlying. He no longer participates in additional increases of the underlying. Should the entire holding (spot & derivative) decline below EUR 47 (strike price of EUR 50 – premium of EUR 3), the investor suffers a loss on the combined position: in addition to the option, he also holds the underlying on his books. At the same time, income from the option markets also compensates for price declines in the spot market position.

Example of a CCW investment:

Our investor holds the following shares in his portfolio:

10,000 shares of X company; purchased at EUR 30; current price: EUR 48
10,000 shares of Y company; purchased at EUR 50; current price: EUR 51
 5,000 shares of V company; purchased at USD 35; current price: USD 34
 5,000 shares of C company; purchased at CHF 28; current price: CHF 75

All holdings are long-term. The investor only uses them to collect dividends.

Strategy: During the time period without dividend payments, CCW is applied to the portfolio. One should be careful to write the calls out-of-the-money. The premium income assures a positive cash flow. In the case of an exercise by the counter party (long call), the risk is limited, as the investor is already in possession of the underlying. Due to the collection of the premiums, which are an extraordinary income, the investor is protected against moderate declines in price.

CCW is a perfect introductory strategy and a strategy to increase the return of long-term holdings. The premium collection constitutes an additional source of income and generates additional cash flows.

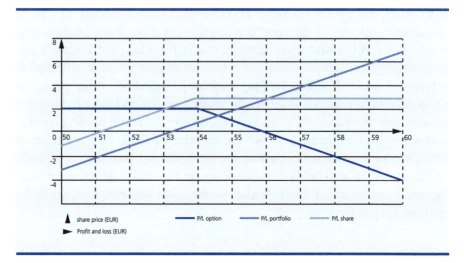

Figure 6.31: CCW payoff including profit and loss statement[48]

---

[48] Source: Eurex.

6.19.4 The strategy LONG PUT

With a long put, an investor purchases the right, but not the obligation, to sell the underlying during the life of the option or at expiration to the seller of the put (short put). He pays the premium to the counterparty for his willingness to actively accept the risk. The long put investor has the right to sell the underlying by exercising the option.

In our example, this looks as follows:

Long put on X shares
Strike price: EUR 50
Expiration date: September
Option premium: EUR 3

The long put investor has the right to sell X shares to the short put investor until September. This right is valued at EUR 3, which is paid to the short put investor when the transaction is closed. At the same time, the strike price of EUR 50 is determined (see Figure 6.32).

The breakeven point of a long put is the market price below which the underlying must fall so that the buyer makes a profit when exercising the option.

Sell at:	50 Euro
Premium:	3 Euro (already paid)
Breakeven point:	47 Euro

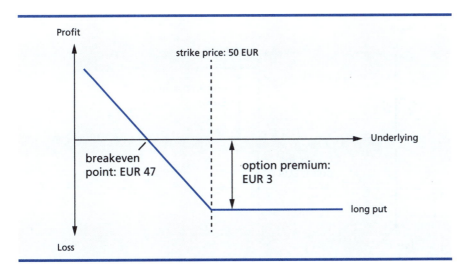

Figure 6.32: Profit and loss scenario for the long put

Scenario analysis:

- **The share price falls below EUR 47:** the long put investor is making the maximum profit.
- **The share price is between EUR 50 and EUR 47:** the investor is suffering a reduced loss, since the option will only have a value equal to the intrinsic value on the last day of trading.
- **The underlying increases in value contrary to the expectation of the investor:** the investor is suffering the maximum loss. While it is limited to the option premium which he already paid, it is nonetheless a complete loss.

This strategy is suitable both for hedging and for speculating on declining share prices. In the case where a long put is used in a hedging strategy, the option premium paid can be interpreted as an insurance premium during the life of the option.

6.19.5 The strategy SHORT PUT

The opposite position to our previous put strategy is the short put (see Figure 6.33). A short put investor agrees to purchase the underlying on a specific date (or during a specific time period) and at a pre-specified price. In exchange, he receives the option premium, which also constitutes his maximum

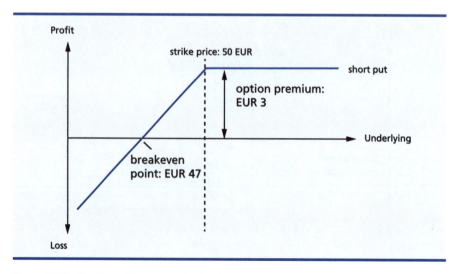

Figure 6.33: Profit and loss scenario for the short put

gain. The loss potential is limited to the strike price since he is required to accept the underlying[49].

In the example already presented, the short put investor would be required to purchase the shares at a price of EUR 50 from the long put investor in case the option is exercised. Since he already received EUR 3, his actual cost base is EUR 47. If the shares decline past EUR 47, the short put investor is suffering a loss.

Scenario analysis:
- **The share price falls below EUR 47:** the short put investor is suffering a loss.
- **The share price is between EUR 50 and EUR 47:** the short put position realizes a reduced profit.
- **The share price is above EUR 50:** the investor keeps the option premium which he already received and achieves the maximum profit.

This strategy is very risky in the case of declining share prices. There is a risk of suffering high losses, while the possible profit is limited to the premium received.

Table 6.9 once again summarizes the four basic strategies. Table 6.10 contains the basic intentions including volatility and time value.

Table 6.9: The four basic option strategies

	Basic intention	Transaction
Long call	Increase of the underlying	Must pay premium, has the right to purchase
Short call	Constant or slightly declining underlying	Receives premium as writer of option and possibly needs to deliver underlying
Long put	Declining underlying	Must pay premium, has the right to sell
Short put	Constant or slightly increasing underlying	Receives premium as writer of option and possibly needs to accept underlying

Table 6.10: The four basic strategies and expectations

Position	Price of underlying	Volatility	Time value
Long call	+	+	−
Short call	+/−	−	+
Long put	−	+	−
Short put	−/+	−	+

---

[49] Since a share can decline at most to zero, this limitation holds for the entire position.

For newcomers to the material, the four basic strategies should initially be sufficient. Only those with enough experience in applying these strategies should deal with combinations and other advanced strategies.

6.20 How to hedge with options

One of the most fundamental ideas in the use of options is the hedging of existing holdings or of holdings[50] which are to be established in the future. The simplest form of protection is the strategy "short underlying"[51]: The part of the portfolio to be hedged or the entire portfolio is sold. While this is simple, it is often not effective. With this strategy, the investor parts with the investment and therefore foregoes all chances for continued income generation. For this reason, a hedge using derivative contracts is preferable.

In order to establish a hedge with options, a "hedge ratio" is always required. As already discussed, the delta of an option measures the degree of change of the option value for price changes of the underlying. It is therefore both necessary and desirable to use this parameter for calculating the specifics of the hedged position. The hedge ratio gives the number of options required to hedge a given exposure.

6.20.1 Delta hedging

$$\text{Number of contracts} = \frac{\text{Number of shares}}{\text{Contract size}} \times \frac{1}{\text{Delta of the option}}$$

Example:

Our investor holds 10,000 shares of company V in his portfolio. He wants to hedge the portfolio at EUR 40. He chooses a put with an strike price of EUR 40 with a delta of -0.5.

---

[50] Elimination of the specific risk of a portfolio position.
[51] Long and short underlying are strategies for the spot market, since the underlying is directly bought or sold. But there is also the possibility to trade the underlying synthetically, for example using a zero-strike option. This is a derivatives transaction and not a spot market transaction.

$$\text{Number of contracts} = \frac{\left(\dfrac{\text{Number of shares}}{\text{Contract size}}\right)}{\text{Delta of the option}}$$

$$-200 = \frac{\left(\dfrac{10{,}000}{100}\right)}{(-0.50)}$$

Thus 200 contracts[52] are required in order to hedge the position. In case of declines in the value of V shares, the hedge position compensates this loss. But an investor is required to constantly adjust this hedge, since the delta of the option changes. For example, if the delta changes to -0.6, he only needs to purchase 167 contracts. This strategy is very expensive, since changes in delta require permanent adjustments.

6.20.2 Protective put

A possible alternative to the delta hedge is the strategy **protective put**[53]. The number of puts to be purchased depends on the number of shares in the portfolio. This would imply a fixed hedge at a ratio of 1:1, which is a strong commitment. In most cases, costs are also higher (but the investor will receive possible dividend payments of the underlying). The protective put is a classical portfolio insurance strategy, with only one aim: to hedge the portfolio. As already stated, protective put is a static strategy, which can be compared to a stop loss on the underlying. In combination with classic **covered call writing** (CCW), premium neutrality or at least a reduction of hedging costs can be accomplished. If an investor chooses this approach, he has simultaneously entered into a static hedging strategy and a static selling strategy. He is bound by the obligation to deliver from the CCW and has also fixed a lower price limit with the help of the protective put. He has fenced in his holding in both directions.

If an investor hedges his portfolio with the help of a put on an index, it must be assured that his portfolio is similar to the index[54]. Otherwise a tracking error would result, which would negatively influence the desired outcome. A second troublesome issue is the term to expiration of the option. Since

---

[52] The sign does not matter.
[53] Protective put: long put on holdings of the same underlying for a 1:1 hedge (static hedge).
[54] See the section on β hedging.

the portfolio usually has a longer maturity than the option, a rolling of the position is usually unavoidable.

6.20.3 Portfolio insurance using calls

If an investor seeks protection against an increasing market, since he plans to invest in the future, he can do this with the help of a long call and a fixed income component (for example zero coupon bond). As in the case of the protective put, the purchase of options is required. The investor profits from increases in the underlying which he plans to acquire at a later date with the help of the call options. It must be kept in mind that a beta hedge is required in case the position is established with the help of calls on an index.

6.20.4 Beta hedge

An additional possibility is the construction of a beta hedge. It makes use of the beta β of a portfolio and is a hedging strategy for a portfolio that is implemented with the help of an index option. This type of hedging is broadly established, since a beta factor can be determined for every portfolio. In contrast to other strategies, the entire portfolio is completely protected and not just isolated components.

Hedge ratio for a beta hedge:

$$\text{Number of contracts} = \frac{\text{Portfolio value}}{(\text{Index value} \times \text{Contract size of index option})} \cdot \beta_{\text{Portfolio}}$$

An investor wants to hedge his portfolio valued at EUR 80,000,000 using ODAX® options. The portfolio beta is 1.2. The contract multiplier for the ODAX® is EUR 5 per point. The index value is 5,000.

$$\text{Number of contracts} = \frac{80{,}000{,}000}{(5{,}000 \cdot 5)} \cdot 1.2$$

Thus the investor is required to trade 3,840 contracts.

In almost all cases, hedging strategies are initially costly. The combination of a long put with CCW, for example, can help to lower these costs.

6.21 Which combinations of options are frequently used?

As stated above, all combinations of options are based on the four fundamental strategies. In the coming sections, we will elaborate on the most frequently used combinations of options.

6.21.1 Straddle

A straddle is the simultaneous purchase or sale of an equivalent number of calls and puts on the same underlying, with the same expiration date and the same strike price. As can be seen, not the direction, but rather the intensity of a price movement is the decisive factor (typical volatility strategy).

6.21.1.1 Long straddle

In the case of a long straddle, the investor expects both a strong movement in prices and an increase in volatility. A long straddle is a typical "long volatility" strategy. This means that the investor is purchasing volatility (long position in the options). The direction of the price movement is not relevant, since the investor has covered both directions. Such a strategy is characterized by an unlimited profit potential and a maximum loss which is limited to the option premium paid.

Constructing a long straddle: the simultaneous purchase of a call (long call) and a put (long put) with the same expiration date and identical strike price leads to a long straddle.

Example:

Long call, X shares, strike price EUR 50, expiration September, option premium EUR 2.
Long put, X shares, strike price EUR 50, expiration September, option premium EUR 1.80.

The total cost of this strategy is EUR 3.80. The breakeven point is either at EUR 53.80 or at EUR 46.20. The entire premium must be recouped before breaking even. If the price of the underlying is between the two breakeven points, the investor realizes a complete or reduced loss (see Figure 6.34). His position starts to be profitable (without limit) once it rises above the upper or

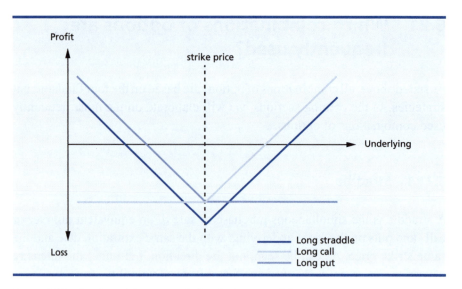

Figure 6.34: Profit and loss scenario for the long straddle

falls below the lower breakeven point. The investor benefits from increases in volatility due to the price increase of long options. Therefore this strategy can also be considered to be a positive volatility strategy.

6.21.1.2 Short straddle

The short straddle is the exact mirror image of the long position: the investor expects only minor movements of the underlying.

Example:

Short call, X shares, strike price EUR 50, expiration September, option premium EUR 2.
Short put, X shares, strike price EUR 50, expiration September, option premium EUR 1.80.

The total premium income for this strategy is EUR 3.80. The strategy starts to lose money outside the range EUR 53.80 to EUR 46.20. The investor will suffer losses for strong movements of the underlying, but he benefits from declining volatility. The loss potential of the strategy is unlimited (see Figure 6.35). It is therefore a risky strategy with only limited premium income received as compensation for bearing risk.

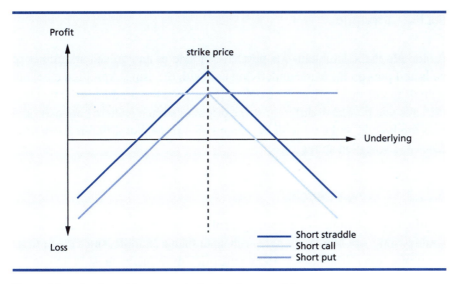

Figure 6.35: Profit and loss scenario for the short straddle

Especially in the beginning, absolute care must be used when using a short straddle. Losses can build very quickly and inexperienced investors are not reacting quickly enough in these situations.

6.21.1.2.1 Straps

Straps are similar to straddles in their construction. Only the volumes are adjusted asymmetrically. In most cases, more calls than puts are traded. A typical relation of calls to puts is 2 : 1. Of course, other ratios are also possible.

6.21.1.2.2 Strips

Strips, just like straps, are set up similar to straddles. But while straps have an overweight of calls relative to puts, this is reversed in the case of strips. More puts are used than calls. Frequently a ratio of 2 : 1 is used as well, but this time we have more puts than calls. As in the case of straps, other ratios are also possible.

6.21.2 Strangle

A strangle is the simultaneous purchase or sale of an equivalent number of calls and puts on the same underlying and with the same expiration date, but with different strike prices. The only difference to the straddle is the fact that the calls and puts have different strike prices (a strategy where both calls and puts are bought and sold with the same strike price, but different expiration dates is also called strangle).

6.21.2.1 Long strangle

In principle, the strategy long strangle follows the same considerations as the strategy long straddle. A strangle is cheaper than a straddle, since the options are further out of the money. Hence the price movements must be larger.

Example:

Long call, X shares, strike price EUR 40, expiration September, option premium EUR 1.

Long put, X shares, strike price EUR 36, expiration September, option premium EUR 0.80.

The breakeven points of this strategy are at EUR 41.80 and EUR 34.20 (see Figure 6.36). In between these two points is a relatively large range where the position loses money: if the underlying stays within that range, the result is a loss for the investor. But once the underlying moves past one of the two breakeven points, the profit potential is unlimited. The maximum loss, meanwhile, is the amount paid to the writer of the option.

6.21.2.2 Short strangle

The short strangle is the mirror image of the long strangle. Compared to the strategy short straddle, it has the advantage of a wider corridor, and thus increased profit opportunities. The maximum profit is equal to the income received from writing the option. At the same time, the loss potential is unlimited.

Example:

Short call, X shares, strike price EUR 40, expiration September, option premium EUR 1.

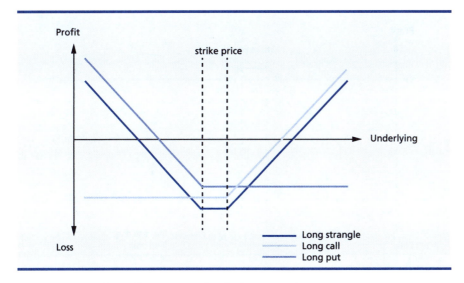

Figure 6.36: Profit and loss scenario for the long strangle

Short put, X shares, strike price EUR 36, expiration September, option premium EUR 0.80.

The breakeven points are EUR 41.80 and EUR 34.20.

It needs to be kept in mind that both for scenarios of strongly increasing and strongly decreasing prices, the strategy can generate significant losses (see Figure 6.37). It is therefore recommended to define in advance, when and how to close a position in a worst case scenario.

> A strangle reacts less strongly than a straddle. Therefore it is more appropriate as "starting strategy" for beginners.

6.21.3 Spreads

A spread is the simultaneous purchase and sale of an option of the same type, with differences in the strike price or the expiration date. In technical terminology[55], spreads constructed from calls are called **bull spreads**. Meanwhile, spreads constructed using puts are called **bear spreads**. As sometimes

---

[55] This is the wording used by the derivatives exchange Eurex. We follow this convention.

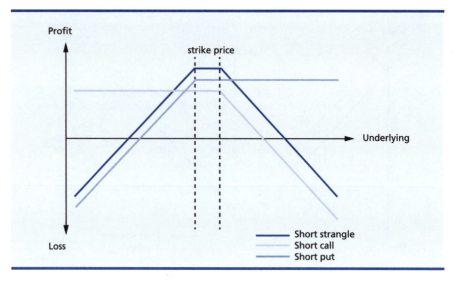

Figure 6.37: Profit and loss scenario for the short strangle

pointed out in the literature, it is also possible to replicate these spreads using the opposite type of option.

A spread is purchased (also called **debit spread**) if the position results in a net expense for the investor. The **credit spread** (also spread sold) provides the investor with net premium income (see Figure 6.38).

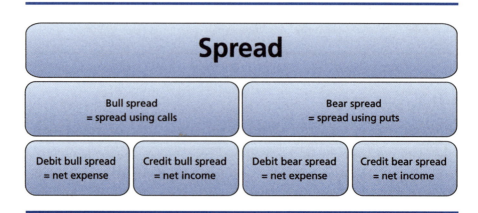

Figure 6.38: Basic versions of spreads

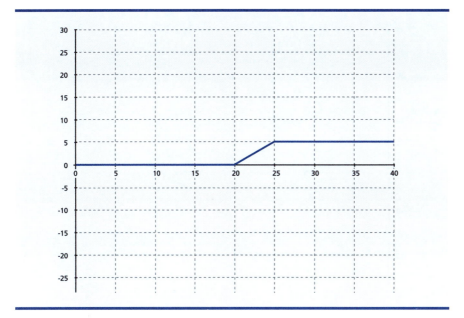

Figure 6.39: Debit bull spread (payoff)

In the following, we want to illustrate the use of spreads with the help of two examples:

Debit bull spread: A call is purchased and a second call with a higher strike price is sold (see Figure 6.39).

Example:

Purchase of a call on X shares
Strike price: EUR 20
Expiration date: September
Option premium: EUR 1.50.

Sale of a call on X shares
Strike price: EUR 25
Expiration date: September
Option premium: EUR 0.50.

Thus the net cost is EUR 1.00.

The maximum profit is realized if the share is priced at or above the upper strike price on the expiration date. It is calculated as the difference between the two strike prices minus the net premium paid. The maximum loss occurs

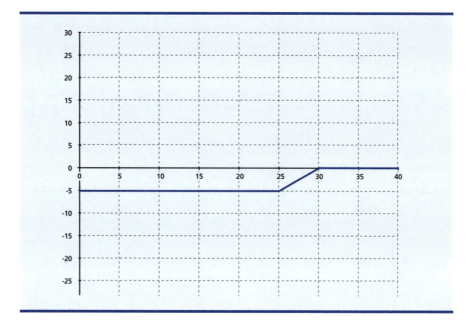

Figure 6.40: Credit bear spread (payoff)

when the share price is below the lower strike price and therefore both options expire worthless.

Credit bear spread: the investor expects markets to move sideways or to increase slightly. But to be prepared for declining markets, a long put position is included. The investor is short a put with a higher strike price and acquires a long put with a lower strike price. By being short a put with a higher strike price, he collects a premium that is higher than the one paid for the long put. On balance he collects a net premium, which constitutes the maximum profit. The maximum loss is the difference between the two strike prices minus the net premium (see Figure 6.40).

Example:

Sale of a put on X shares
Strike price: EUR 30
Expiration date: September
Option premium: EUR 3.00.

Purchase of a put on X shares
Strike price: EUR 25
Expiration date: September
Option premium: EUR 1.00.

Thus the (net) premium income is EUR 2.00. The maximum loss is EUR 3.00[56].

6.22 An overview of plain vanilla option strategies

6.22.1 Strategies for a positive market outlook

+ means long option
− means short option
Number is equal to the strike price of the option

Market expectation	Option position	Potential profit	Loss potential
Strongly increasing	Long call + call 30	Unlimited	At most premium
Moderately increasing	Purchase bull spread + call 30 − call 35	At most difference between strike prices minus net premium	At most net premium paid
Slightly increasing	Short put − put 30	At most premium	Virtually unlimited

6.22.2 Strategies for a neutral market outlook

Market expectation	Option position	Potential profit	Loss potential
Sideways	Sale of bear spread + put 36 − put 40	At most net premium	At most difference between strike prices minus net premium
Sideways	Sale of bull spread + call 40 − call 36	At most net premium	At most difference between strike prices minus net premium

---

[56] Calculated as follows: 30 − 25 = 5; 5 − 2 = 3.

6.22.3 Strategies for a negative market outlook

Market expectation	Option position	Potential profit	Loss potential
Slightly declining	Short call − call 40	At most premium	Unlimited
Moderately declining	Purchase bear spread + put 36 − put 32	At most difference between strike prices minus net premium	At most net premium
Strongly declining	Long put + put 36	Virtually unlimited	At most premium paid

6.22.4 Strategies for a volatile market outlook

Market expectation	Option position	Potential profit	Loss potential
Increasing volatility	Long straddle + call 36 + put 36	Virtually unlimited	Limited to premium paid
Increasing volatility	Long strangle + call 38 + put 34	Virtually unlimited	Limited to premium paid
Declining volatility and constant market price of underlying	Short straddle − call 36 − put 36	At most premium received	Virtually unlimited
Declining volatility and constant market price of underlying	Short strangle − call 38 − put 34	At most premium received	Virtually unlimited

Figure 6.41 displays the classical combinations and the required market environment.

In the next sections, we want to take a look at more complex strategies.

The following strategies should only be used by experienced investors with knowledge in position management of plain vanilla strategies.

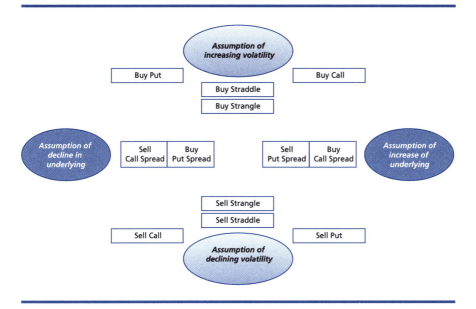

Figure 6.41: Overview of strategies including market and volatility assessments (basic strategies)

6.23 Complex option strategies and their implementation

The complex strategies presented here are directed at experienced clients or financial engineers only. In many cases, individual strategies must be combined. The combined strategies can be used for active portfolio management, in constructing financial engineering products or in proprietary trading.

6.23.1 Butterfly

The long butterfly strategy benefits from the decline in time value and from the intrinsic value at expiration of the two long positions **A** or **C**. The maximum profit is achieved for a price of the underlying equal to the strike price of the short position **B** (see Figure 6.42).

Construction:

Version	Strike price 40 (A)	Strike price 44 (B)	Strike price 48 (C)
1	1 long call	2 short calls	1 long call
2	1 long put	2 short puts	1 long put
3	1 long put	1 short put + 1 short call	1 long call
4	1 long call	1 short call + 1 short put	1 long put

B–A must be equal to **C–B** (see Figure 6.42).

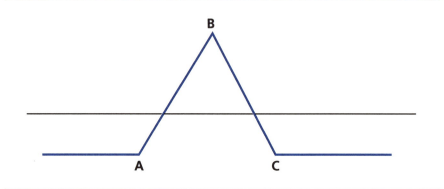

Figure 6.42: Long butterfly

When implementing a short butterfly strategy, which also has both limited upside and downside potential, the investor benefits on balance from the collection of option premiums. The maximum profit is obtained for a strong price movement which at expiration goes beyond point **A** or **C** (see Figure 6.43). The maximum loss is suffered if the underlying at expiration is valued exactly at the strike price **B**. The long positions in the strategy serve to reduce risk.

Version	Strike price 40 (A)	Strike price 44 (B)	Strike price 48 (C)
1	1 short call	2 long calls	1 short call
2	1 short put	2 long puts	1 short put
3	1 short put	1 long put + 1 long call	1 short call
4	1 short call	1 long call + 1 long put	1 short put

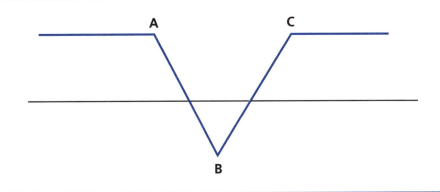

Figure 6.43: Short butterfly

6.23.2 Condor

The strategy condor is very similar to the strategy butterfly. Both profit and loss potential are limited, but the strike prices are further apart.

A long condor is used if low volatility is expected. The price should fall between the strike prices **B** and **C**, in order to obtain the maximum profit (see Figure 6.44).

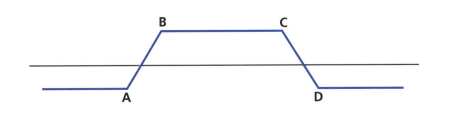

Figure 6.44: Long condor

Version	Strike price 40 (A)	Strike price 42 (B)	Strike price 46 (C)	Strike price 48 (D)
1	1 long call	1 short call	1 short call	1 long call
2	1 long put	1 short put	1 short put	1 long put
3	1 long call	1 short call	1 short put	1 long put
4	1 long put	1 short put	1 short call	1 long call

Figure 6.45: Short condor

Obviously this strategy can also be set up as a short condor. The two long positions between the short positions are characterized by different strike prices. A mirror image appears (see Figure 6.45).

6.23.3 Ratio spread

In a ratio spread, long and short positions with a different number of contracts are established.

6.23.3.1 Ratio call spread

For a ratio call spread, one or several calls with a low strike price are purchased and at the same time a larger number of calls with a higher strike price are sold. The calls all expire on the same date. This combined position of long and short can be both a debit or credit position (see Figure 6.46).

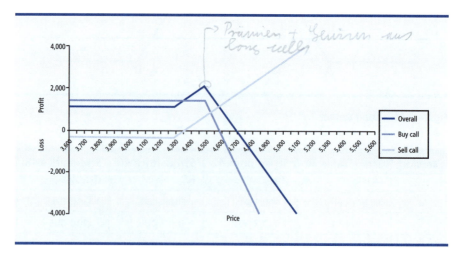

Figure 6.46: Ratio call spread

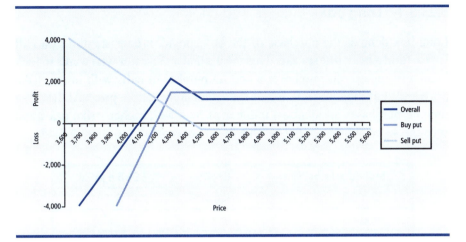

Figure 6.47: Ratio put spread

6.23.3.2 Ratio put spread

For a ratio put spread, one or more puts with a lower strike price are sold and at the same time a smaller number of puts with a higher strike price are purchased. This combined position of long and short can be both a debit or credit position (see Figure 6.47).

6.23.4 Back spread

A back spread is the reverse of a ratio spread.

6.23.4.1 Back spread call

A back spread call is the reverse of a ratio call spread. Long positions exceed short positions.

6.23.4.2 Back spread put

A back spread put is the reverse of a ratio put spread. Long positions exceed short positions.

6.23.5 Box strategies

Box spreads are option strategies which are set up to capture arbitrage opportunities due to imbalances in the valuation of calls and puts.

6.23.5.1 Long box

Long box denotes the purchase of the box spread. It consists of a **bull call spread** and a **bear put spread**. This means that an investor who wants to lock in an arbitrage profit purchases a certain number of calls with lower strike price and sells the same number of calls with higher strike price. At the same time he purchases an identical number of puts with higher strike price and sells the same number of puts with a lower strike price (see Figure 6.48).

Individual position	Expiry	Strike price
Long call	January	5000
Short call	January	5500
Short put	January	5000
Long put	January	5500

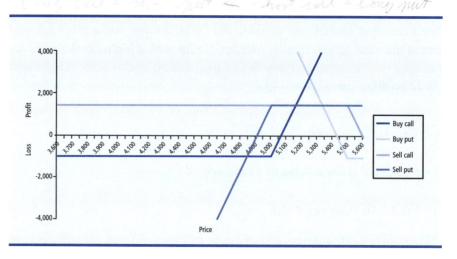

Figure 6.48: Long box

6.23.5.2 Short box

Short box denotes the sale of the box spread. It consists of a **bear call spread** and a **bull put spread**. This means that an investor who wants to lock in an arbitrage profit purchases a certain number of calls with higher strike price and sells the same number of calls with lower strike price. Simultaneously, he purchases an identical number of puts with lower strike price and sells the same number of puts with a higher strike price (see Figure 6.49).

Complex option strategies and their implementation

Individual position	Expiration	Strike price
Long call	January	5500
Short call	January	5000
Short put	January	5500
Long put	January	5000

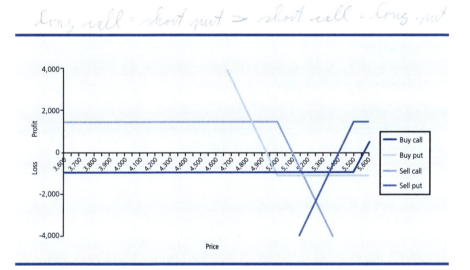

Figure 6.49: Short box

6.23.6 Time spread or calendar spread

In a time spread, also called calendar spread, options with identical strike price are combined in a way that the options with the earlier expiration date are sold and the options with a later expiration date are bought.

6.23.6.1 Bull calendar spread

Long call 5000	March
Short call 5000	January
Long put 5000	March
Short put 5000	January

6.23.6.2 Bear calendar Spread

Long call 5000	January
Short call 5000	March
Long put 5000	January
Short put 5000	March

This strategy can be easily combined with a "ratio."

Ratio call time:
The basic structure of this option position is similar to the **bull time spread**, but consists of a larger number of calls sold.

Ratio put time:
The basic structure of this option position is similar to the **bear time spread**, but consists of a larger number of puts sold.

6.23.7 Long risk reversal

The investor expects prices to increase. He sells puts and purchases calls from the proceeds (see Figure 6.50). He is thus establishing a zero cost strategy.

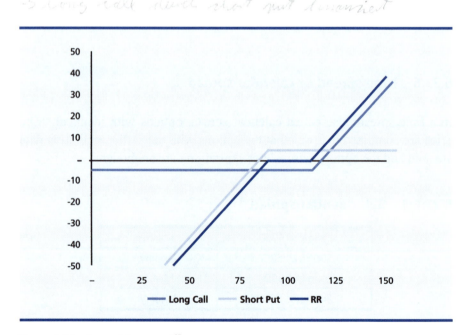

Figure 6.50: Long risk reversal[57]

6.23.8 Short risk reversal

The investor expects prices to decline. He is purchasing puts and finances this with the sale of calls (see Figure 6.51). Again the zero cost strategy is apparent.

As in the long version, both risk and profit potential are unlimited.

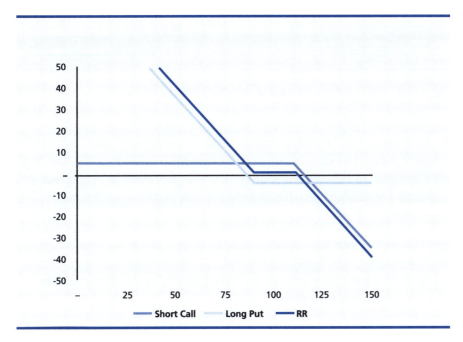

Figure 6.51: Short risk reversal[58]

6.24 How to implement a strategy using options

It is recommended that strategies are built on each other. Before a new position is established, it needs to be assured that sufficient liquidity is reserved

---

[57] Source: UBS.
[58] Source: UBS.

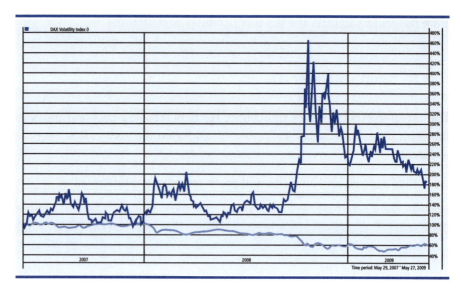

Figure 6.52: DAX® (below) versus DAX® volatility (above)[59]

for later operations. This is a very general and important point: only an investor with enough liquidity is in a position to sufficiently expand and manage the strategies. In this context it holds that it is preferable to open fewer positions and instead manage the already existing positions professionally and consistently.

For option strategies it is also important to keep in mind that external factors such as volatility are important influencing factors which can be exploited. It is possible, for example, to set up strategies that make use of volatility in addition to existing speculative positions.

Volatility can be added to the portfolio either by combining option positions[60] or by trading volatility with the help of volatility futures. Eurex as well as other leading derivatives exchanges are offering volatility futures as independent instruments. Let us take a closer look at the example of Eurex. Volatility futures on VSTOXX®, VDAX®-NEW® and VSMI® are listed. All three are based on the implied volatility of options on the three different equity indexes, the Dow Jones EURO STOXX 50®, DAX® (see Figure 6.52) as well as the Swiss index SMI®. The futures contract is listed in percent. Its payoff can be

---

[59] Source: Interactiv Data Management Solutions.
[60] See option combinations: straddle.

determined as follows:

$$\text{Payoff (Volatility index)} = m \cdot (IV_{REL} - IV_{EXP}) \cdot n$$

m = Index multiplier (EUR 1,000 or CHF 1,000)
IV_{REL} = realized implied 30-day volatility at expiration
IV_{EXP} = expected implied 30-day volatility when closing the transaction
n = number of contracts

While these extensions are only minor additions to the portfolio, they nonetheless contribute to its return or stability and can be traded quickly and inexpensively in most cases. Investors are given a further opportunity to expand the universe and to add one more underlying which can be used to manage the portfolio even more precisely in the context of diversification[61].

Option strategies that reduce risk can also be added at this point, as well as supplemental options, which may only be held for very short time periods (also intra-day).

> In our opinion it is necessary to break down the portfolio into the following three groups:

Group I: long-term strategic transactions. This includes holdings that are established for strategic reasons over a longer time horizon. They are the backbone of the portfolio and can consist of hedging transactions and combined strategies.

Group II: speculative holdings. The typical speculation in the derivatives market targets specific market movements. These holdings are purely speculative in nature.

Group III: extreme short-term speculation. These speculative holdings are frequently conducted intraday[62] only. A maximum of three days is allowed for these holdings, and the boundary to the second group is somewhat fluid. It is up to the individual investor to define an appropriate time horizon. In-

---

[61] Note: volatility is negatively correlated with the equity market.
[62] A transaction is considered to be intraday, if it is opened and closed on the same day. In the evening, there are no open positions.

vestments in group III are established for example ahead of data releases or on days with unusual market movements.

At this juncture, we feel the need to point out that extreme caution is warranted when an investment that started out in group III has migrated to group I. The basic motive, even if it does not materialize, should be remembered!

Examples:

Group I
This includes futures on indexes, futures on interest rate derivatives, options on interest rate futures, hedging transactions, transactions involving related companies and others.

Group II
Investments such as options on indexes, options on equity holdings, short put options and others are examples for members of this group.

Group III
This group consists among others of very short-term futures, currency futures, options on individual securities and commodity futures transactions.

Within the parameters defined above, the investor attempts to utilize as many alternatives as possible. To do so, the following elements are required:

- Sufficient liquidity
- Sufficient information
- Sufficient market perspective

Liquidity and **information** are available in most cases. The weakest link is a sufficient or appropriate market perspective.

What is the relevance of a **market perspective**?
In our opinion, every investor needs to arrive at an independent market perspective, assess that perspective and derive an investment strategy from it. Imposed market opinions or statements taken over from third parties frequently end badly. Every investor needs to form his own opinion and decide independently on the appropriate course of action. For this reason, it is absolutely necessary to slowly introduce a novice option investor to the instruments available. Only if the investor himself is in a position to understand the instruments on his own, can he reach adequate decisions. At the same time, he starts to develop an understanding for opportunities and risks and can relate this to his investments.

In this regard, the two major groups of investors are clearly different. On the one hand, there are institutional and professional investors who are equipped with liquidity and knowledge. On the other hand, there are large numbers of private investors. While they are in a position to also acquire the knowledge, they frequently do not have access to sufficient liquidity or are unwilling to use it. Basically, both groups ought to get the same kind of investment advice. But private investors should get additional information about the risks involved, their magnitude and possible manifestations. In principle, private investors can use the same strategies, but in many cases these cannot be implemented due to the large demands on liquidity. Over the past years, a noticeable trend towards securitized derivatives has become apparent among retail investors. The reasons for this are clear: securitized derivatives can be explained quickly, are understood easily and can be used well in portfolios of different sizes. We point out that securitized derivatives are also available to professional and institutional investors but in many cases are not suitable due to issues related to size and cost[63]. In our experience, it seems to be the case that private investors purchase the securitized derivatives from institutional investors, who in turn prefer to deal predominantly in classical derivatives at exchanges or OTC.

> A strategy tool can be found in our download area. It allows the simulation of the strategies presented above.

6.25 Options on futures, synthetic derivatives transactions & combinations

Options that are written on futures complement the large universe of listed derivatives[64]. They create a direct link between conditional and unconditional derivatives.

---

[63] At the same time, issuer risk needs to be taken into consideration (see the bankruptcy of Lehman Brothers in 2008). Issuer risk can be excluded by posting sufficient collateral with a neutral party (for example the clearing house). These "protected" certificates are also offered, but market demand is not strong.

[64] Also futures options (a term occassionally used in the literature).

This type of option calls for the physical delivery of the futures contract and provides investors with a closed set of opportunities and risks. As a result of the options position, the investor obtains an asymmetric distribution of risk, which suits his needs and provides him with a choice. Once the option is exercised, the choice becomes an obligation, namely the futures position, which is an unconditional derivatives contract.

Especially in the area of interest rate futures, options on futures are quite common. As examples, options on the Euro-Bund future (OGBL) and the 30-year Treasury bond future (T-BOND) are offered.

6.25.1 How are options on futures constructed and structured?

The buyer of an option on the futures contract (such as the Euro-Bund future) obtains the right, but not the obligation, to purchase (call) or sell (put) the futures contract at a price determined at the time the transaction is closed. If the option is exercised, physical delivery of the futures contract results. The option investor becomes a futures investor. This can also be put differently: the option position (conditional transaction) is replaced by the futures position (unconditional transaction).

6.25.2 What is the future-style method?

The payment of the option premium for options on futures is not made when the transaction is closed, but rather over the contract period (analogous to **variation margin accounting**). Thus a daily balancing of profits and losses takes place. An additional important point is the influence of short-term interest rates on option prices. In the case of short-term increases of interest rates, premiums decline both for the call and the put. This relationship can be explained by the fact that the premium is modeled as the net present value of the expected profit at expiration. Therefore, if interest rates increase, the net present value declines and with it option prices.

The option positions are valued every evening with the help of the settlement price and therefore adjusted using the **future-style method**. The procedure used is similar to the one for futures. The buyer of the option benefits from increasing prices of the option, the seller makes a profit in case prices decline.

In most cases, the options are American style. Early exercise is not usually recommended, as time value is lost. The expiration date of the options differs from the "normal" expiration date, so that the owner of a short position can reach adequate decisions and react accordingly. In most cases the corresponding next futures contract is used for delivery and therefore this is also the naming convention used (option on March[65], last trading day in February).

Options on futures are equivalent to the following futures position and delivery is handled as follows:

Table 6.11: Overview of options on futures

Option contract	Futures (following delivery)
Long call	Long futures
Short call	Short futures
Long put	Short futures
Short put	Long futures

6.25.3 How to value options on futures with the Black-76 model?

European options on futures can be described with an extension of the already known valuation methods. In 1976, Fischer Black[66] published first work on the issue. Under the assumption that futures prices follow a log-normal process, European calls and European puts can be determined as follows (S_0 is replaced by F_0, σ is the volatility of the futures price, $q = r$):

$$c = e^{-rT}[F_0 N(d_1) - K N(d_2)]$$

$$p = e^{-rT}[K N(-d_2) - F_0 N(-d_1)]$$

It holds that

$$d_1 = \frac{\ln(F_0/K) + \sigma^2 T/2}{\sigma\sqrt{T}}$$

$$d_2 = d_1 - \sigma\sqrt{T}$$

It must be kept in mind that the model of Black does not require simultaneous expiration of the futures contract and the options contract[67].

---

[65] March, since March futures are used for delivery.
[66] Therefore also known as Black 76 model.
[67] See Hull, page 437 on this point.

The above model is used to value regular options. If instead the value of a future-style option is determined, it follows that

$$F_0 N(d_1) - K N(d_2)$$

and for the put

$$K N(-d_2) - F_0 N(-d_1)$$

It holds that

$$d_1 = \frac{\ln(F_0/K) + \sigma^2 T/2}{\sigma \sqrt{T}}$$

$$d_2 = d_1 - \sigma \sqrt{T}$$

Put-call parity for future-style options is defined as follows:

$$p + F_0 = c + K$$

p = Price of the put option
F_0 = Futures price
c = Price of the call option
K = Strike price of the option

If an American option is exercised prior to the last day of trading, final settlement at the intrinsic value of the option takes place. This is not optimal in many ways, since the futures price is higher than the intrinsic value of the option. But a mathematically equivalent treatment of American and European options is possible in that way.

6.25.4 Which strategies are pursued with options on futures?

It is recommended that option positions also include positions in the corresponding futures in the trading book. The consistent addition of options on futures enables investors to pursue both expansion and hedging strategies. Of course, an isolated strategy is also possible and is often pursued as a derivative strategy (second derivative).

If an investor includes options on futures in his trading book, a short futures investor can open additional positions via short options on futures. He generates an additional cash flow by collecting the premium. Should the options expire worthless, the investor has collected the premium without having established additional futures positions. If, however, the position ends up in the money, additional futures positions are generated and the trading book is actively managed.

Example: A futures investor has sold the Euro–Bund future (FGBL) at 116. His outlook concerning Bund futures is negative; he thinks that interest rates are likely to go up. For this reason, he wants to expand his position. But since he is not quite certain, he decides to expand his position using options and not additional futures.

Current holding:
100 contracts, short FGBL, price 116

He extends this position as follows:
25 contracts, short call, strike price 116
25 contracts, short call, strike price 116.50
25 contracts, short call, strike price 117

The investor generates premium income with these positions and will only become a short futures investor if the underlying reaches the strike price and the counterparty (long call) exercises the option. The investor is thus in the comfortable position to diversify his risk. And in the case of a declining futures price (strike prices are not reached), the investor profits from the premium income and the previously established 100 short futures contracts. The futures positions are expanded via the options if the futures contract, contrary to expectations, should increase in value. The advantage of this strategy lies in the fact that the premium received lowers the acquisition price.

If the expectation of the investor is negative only up to a certain price (maximum lower bound) – for example 114.50 – he can also open offsetting positions. The investor now sells short puts with strike prices 114.50 and 114.00. In case of an exercise, these short puts can be considered to be closing positions, since they are offsetting transactions (admittedly without a closing notice, but with the same effect).

The investor profits from his short futures position until a value of 114.50 or 114.00 is reached in this case. The calls sold expire worthless and the short puts are the offsetting positions. The two short positions and the linked premium income enable the investor to expand his profit. Let us now disassemble the above strategy along an opportunity and risk profile.

Table 6.12 shows an excerpt from a trading book with additional trades.

Trading book: FGBL is valued at 115.50

Table 6.12: Trading book with additional trades

Contract size	Contract type	Strike price	Strategy
100	Short futures	116	Initial position
25	Short call	116	Expansion futures
25	Short call	116.50	Expansion futures
25	Short call	117	Expansion futures
50	Short put	114.50	Cap futures
50	Short put	114	Cap futures

The cap constitutes the offsetting position for the initial futures positions.

The basic profile is simple: the short futures generate a profit if the futures price declines and we get the expected profit. However, we suffer a loss if the futures price increases.

With the first extension, the short calls on the futures, we supplement this strategy only indirectly: we take over the futures contract only if the strike price is reached. At first glance, the premium received appears to add to our profit, but there is also a risk that the existing position is expanded. In order to hedge against this risk, we sell puts with strike prices of 114.50 and 114. This enables us to exit the initial strategy at the strike prices; we have established a cap at 114 and 114.50. The strategy is thus closed. At the same time, we obtain an additional risk buffer in form of the premium income.

Which scenarios can materialize? We expand the short futures position as the calls are exercised (→ **puts expire worthless**) and then possess the position which we wanted to establish initially. Another possibility is the exercise of the puts (→ **calls expire worthless**) and the corresponding closing of the futures position. The third possibility would be a more or less unchanged price of the futures contract, in which case both options expire worthless. We see that the extension of the straightforward futures strategy has resulted in a clearly structured, but also more complex combination strategy. In applied work, linking and combining strategies in such a way is part of the daily routine and quite standard.

Another possibility is the combination of two different futures in order to cover different maturity horizons. In this way, an investor can benefit from changes in the term structure of interest rates. Such strategies are recommended only to investors with strong liquidity: in addition to posting margin, a daily liquidity cushion is needed to pay for the settlement of profits and losses.

In addition, it is advisable to use both profit and loss triggers as well as limit orders for these types of strategies. Setting up a reciprocal limit strategy is appropriate especially for positions that require constant monitoring.

> Options on futures are particularly suitable to extend existing futures positions and for setting up and winding down futures positions.

6.26 What is a synthetic derivatives market position?

The derivatives market positions presented and their profiles of opportunities and risks can also be replicated synthetically (see Table 6.13).

The combination of several individual holdings results in a synthetic position. This overall position should be seen as a new entity and a selective closing of parts cannot be recommended.

Table 6.13 lists possible combinations of synthetic derivative market positions.

Table 6.13: Possible combinations

Synthetic version of:	Combination of:		
	Call option	Put option	Futures
Long call		Long	Long
Short call		Short	Short
Long put	Long		Short
Short put	Short		Long

Synthetic version of:	Combination of:	
	Call option	Put option
Long futures	Long	Short
Short futures	Short	Long

The combination of individual derivatives transactions leads to an expanded profile of opportunities and risks. Investors can create new and more complex profiles of opportunities and risks with these individual components. However, only experienced investors should use these combinations.

6.27 Which combinations and linked strategies are used in practice?

Combinations of options (straddle, strangle and so forth) and securitized derivatives (long call on a discount certificate[68] and so forth) are frequently used in applied work. However: as the complexity of the new structure increases, the profile of opportunities and risks becomes less clear.

It must be assured that the structure remains transparent and can be traded at all times. One of the greatest dangers of these strategies is the lack of clarity. Combinations are not always apparent at first sight and may be missed unless clearly documented. For this reason, strict documentation including trading recommendations is advisable.

Combinations and linked strategies result from the following basic intentions:

- speculation and
- hedging

Speculation means that the investor is trying to obtain an "excess return" by utilizing additional instruments. Especially in markets that trend sideways, this approach can be recommended to generate additional income.

Hedging means that the investor has entered into a position that has developed contrary to his expectations. He now tries to hedge this position by combining it with a derivatives transaction. If he is successful, he can provide a fixed plan value, otherwise he has to accept the resulting loss.

Both forms of combinations are relevant mostly in linked transactions with securitized derivatives (discount certificate and so forth). The basic intention of an investor who expands a securitized derivative is the creation of a profile that provides additional opportunities. To do so, he accepts additional risks that appear manageable to him. He extends the standard features of the securitized derivative (set by the issuer) with the help of a derivatives

---

[68] Securitized derivative on an individual stock or an index, which has a cap on its payoff.

market position that he devises. These strategies taken together give rise to the overall position. These types of positions should only be established by investors who are very familiar with the territory, since not only the classical derivatives transaction, but also the securitized derivative must be evaluated.

Example:

An investor holds a discount certificate on the index X. It has a cap at 7,000 points and the index currently stands at 6,900 points. The discount certificate which is based on the index X is valued at EUR 67.50. The investor expects that the cap of 7,000 points will be reached, but that the index will be quoted below 7,400 points during the term to maturity of the certificate. He therefore also sells call options with a strike price of 7,400 points. The resulting premium income immediately increases his profit.

Scenario 1: the index rises above 7,000 points, but does not exceed 7,400 points. The investor was correct and realizes the maximum profit.

Scenario 2: the index stays below 7,000 points. The investor gets the maximum benefit from selling the call, but only a reduced profit from the discount certificate, since the cap was not reached.

Scenario 3: The index moves beyond 7,400 points. The investor gets the maximum profit from the discount certificate, but suffers a loss from the short call option, which is reduced due to the payment of the premium. Should the index rise further, a timely closing should be considered, as the potential for losses from the short call is unlimited.

As already discussed, the combination created should be viewed as one entity. This is the only perspective that incorporates all opportunities and risks.

Combinations with other securitized derivatives (for example express structures) are also conceivable. But the components of other securitized derivatives are different and must therefore be treated appropriately.

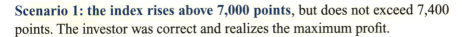

Linked transactions and combinations

Key reasons for a linked transaction are either the minimization of risks or the desire to generate a higher return. In all cases, the logic of the linked transaction and its transparency must be kept in mind. If a combination is no longer understood, the risk of the overall position increases many times over, since active trading and intervention are no longer assured.

Interview with Ralf Burkhardt,
Ralf Burkhardt GmbH Vermögensverwaltung und Finanzkonzepte

Mr. Burkhardt, from the perspective of a wealth manager, what is your current perception of the market for derivatives and financial engineering solutions?
With the eruption of the financial crisis, the market has contracted significantly after several years of continuous growth. While the first half of 2008 was still characterized by solid growth, the speed and breadth of the decline in the second half of 2008 took everybody by surprise. But slowly we can observe stabilization, and I am optimistic about the future.

Which changes will result for you as a wealth manager from the financial crisis?
Our customers are more aware of risks, and are more reluctant with new investments, especially when compared to other past crises. In the previous months, a lot of liquidity was parked in the form of money market accounts, time deposits or money market funds. But owing to the significant decline of short term interest rates, we can observe renewed customer interest in other investment alternatives.

Which derivatives do you actively use in the management of wealthy private clients' portfolios?
Predominantly bonus certificates, discount certificates and equity-linked bonds. We make sure that the structures are simple and can be understood by our customers. Highly structured products are no longer in demand following the experience of the past months.

Which products are not used by you, and why?
From the very beginning, we didn't use alpha certificates and outperformance equity-linked bonds in our wealth management. We prefer products that allow you to benefit from an expected trend, be it increasing, declining or stagnating prices. We only very selectively utilized products with more than one underlying.

Do you prefer products traded at derivatives exchanges over complete financial engineering solutions from the major banks?
Complete structures from issuers have the advantage of easy clearing with the various custodian banks. Direct transactions at derivatives exchanges are not possible with several custodian banks or require an enormous administrative effort, which also affects our customers. But this does not mean that we are not using directly traded products from derivatives exchanges. It must make sense for the individual customer and the custodian banks.

How has the use of derivatives evolved in the area of wealth management?
Derivatives are an integral part of wealth management. Their importance has increased steadily in recent years. Although the market for derivatives and financial engineering products has suffered as a result of the financial crisis, there is no doubt in my mind about the positive long-term development of the sector. Future growth in derivatives was not halted by the financial crisis; it was merely slowed down and the growth trend has flattened.

Which additional products would you like to see in the market?
The market for derivatives currently offers all possibilities to implement strategies for the participation in markets that are growing, declining or trending sideways. Issuers would be hard pressed to introduce new structures in the current market environment. This does not mean, however, that creativity should not be encouraged in the future. But the

issuers must be more in touch with the demands of the investors. This has not always been the case in the past.

Which regulations concerning the use of derivatives are relevant for you?
With the introduction of MiFID, regulations were tightened further. Since we had already introduced the regulations pertaining to investment consulting before they were written into law, we are only facing an increased internal administrative burden. An administrative burden that should not be underestimated, however.

What is your opinion on the future development of derivatives and financial engineering solutions?
The market for derivatives and financial engineering products will continue to develop favorably in the future. I am sure of that. Certainly, both issuers and advisors have learned from the mistakes they made in the recent past. Today's modern investment world with its tight international links is no longer conceivable without derivative investment products.

Literature for this chapter

Hull, John: Options, Futures and Other Derivatives, 7th edition, 2009

Madura, Jeff: International Financial Management, 6th edition, 2004

Rudolph, Bernd, Schäfer, Klaus: Derivative Finanzinstrumente 2005

Rubinstein, Reuven Y.; Kroese Dirk P.: Simulation and the Monte Carlo Method, 2nd edition, 2008

Steinbrenner, Hans-Peter: Optionsrechte in der Praxis, 2002

Wilmott, Paul: Paul Wilmott introduces Quantitative Finance, 2nd edition, 2007

Wiedemann, Arnd: Bewertung von Finanzinstrumenten, 4th edition, 2007

Questions and answers on this chapter

Question 1:
Is the following statement correct?
Options with a short term to maturity should be purchased!

Question 2:
Which variable is affected by implied volatility?

Question 3:
Is the following statement correct?
As interest rates go down, the price of a put increases.

Question 4:
What are straps?

Question 5:
Is the following statement correct?
Short risk reversal is a zero cost strategy.

Answer to question 1:

No, the statement is not correct. Options with a short term to maturity should be sold, since the development of the time value is favorable for the seller.

Answer to question 2:
The option price is affected by implied volatility. But it also affects the implied volatility in turn. Therefore, the two variables are mutually dependent.

Answer to question 3:
Yes, the statement is correct.

Answer to question 4:
This is a type of a straddle, where the ratio of calls to puts is adjusted asymmetrically. In most cases the ratio of calls to puts is 2:1.

Answer to question 5:
Yes, the statement is correct. The purchase of the puts is financed by selling the calls.

7 | Derivatives on currencies and commodities

The following chapter covers these issues:

- What are currency derivatives?
- What are commodity derivatives?
- How are these instruments priced?
- Which types of strategies can be implemented with currency and commodity derivatives?
- Which specific features exist?

7.1 Development of currency trading

When the convertibility of gold was suspended in 1971, currencies began to move freely. At this time, the field of currency derivatives started to expand, as investors realized the chances and risks of the novel currency system. While some market participants saw the necessity to hedge against undesirable depreciations, others took speculative positions concerning these movements.

Two types of **currency derivatives** exist: on the one hand, **OTC transactions**, which are conducted through the currency trading departments of the major banks for their own account and for clients, and on the other hand, **derivatives** which are traded on derivatives exchanges (see Figure 7.1). Today, CME in Chicago holds a leading position in trading. Both kinds of currency derivatives transactions are widely used by practitioners, who tend to use the individual contracts predominantly for hedging of underlying transactions[1]

---

[1] Used mostly by industrial companies and in corporate finance.

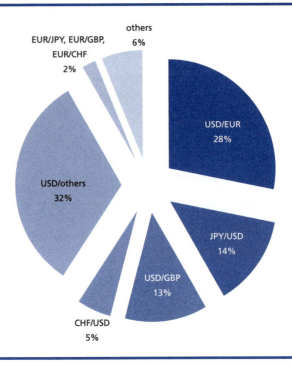

Figure 7.1: Share of currency pairs in trading (as of 2007)[2]

and the currency futures more for speculative purposes[3]. This is due to ample liquidity and tight bid-ask spreads.

7.2 The fundamentals of currency trading

Let us briefly delve into the world of foreign exchange (FX) trading. Foreign currency in the form of book money is called foreign exchange and FX trading involves the exchange of different currencies. From an economic perspective, it serves the important function of regulating business cycle developments of two economies with different currencies.

The exchange rate is defined as the price (stated in home currency) that must be paid for one unit of foreign currency. This is called a **direct quote**. An

---

[3] Used predominantly in investment banking and wealth management.
[2] See Bloss, Eil, Ernst, Fritsche, Häcker: Währungsderivate, Oldenbourg 2009.

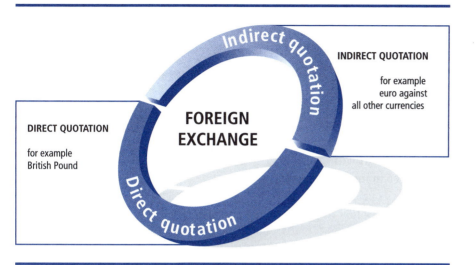

Figure 7.2: Foreign exchange quotations

alternative way of quoting exchange rates is the **indirect quote**. It states the amount of foreign currency required to purchase one unit of domestic currency (see Figure 7.2).

In practice, the indirect notation is used for the euro (EUR) against all other currencies. The sole exception is the British Pound (GBP), for which the direct quotation is used. In principle, both quoting conventions can be used; they merely relate differing perspectives of the observer.

While spot transactions in foreign exchange must be delivered and settled within two working days, there is a time delay in derivatives transactions: settlement does not occur immediately after the contract is closed but rather within a pre-specified time period, which we call the forward period. The international currency market is the world's largest market with a daily volume of USD 3.2 billion. Between 2004 and 2007, the daily currency market volume increased by 71%[4].

---

[4] Source: EUROSTAT, ECB.

7.3 Economic determinants of exchange rate formation

The following factors have an influence on exchange rates:

- Volume of current account and capital account
- Level of interest rates
- Inflation rates
- Economic growth
- Changes in money supply
- Business cycle developments
- Economic policy of governments and central banks
- Crises, unrest, wars
- Political influence, both domestic and international
- Market psychology with regard to resignations, rumors, confirmations, announcements, election results and so forth

7.4 Currency spot transactions

In a spot transaction, the underlying object – in our case foreign exchange – is traded and the transaction is settled within two working days. These types of transactions, where closing and settlement happen without much delay, are conducted routinely in normal business practice (interbank transactions). No specific obligations arise from them and they are treated like any other spot market transaction in securities. Among other things, this also implies that the investor must immediately provide the liquidity required to complete the transaction. The price charged is called spot rate and is equal to the current exchange rate. Trading days are all bank operating days; this excludes Saturdays, Sundays and bank holidays in the different countries. The delivery date is also called the value date.

7.5 Currency derivatives transactions

The price difference between the spot exchange rate and the forward exchange rate depends on the interest rate differential between the two currencies. It is assumed that the investment in two different currencies must yield the same return. Since two interest rates are involved, their difference must be offset by the currency movement. This also implies that riskless investments in foreign

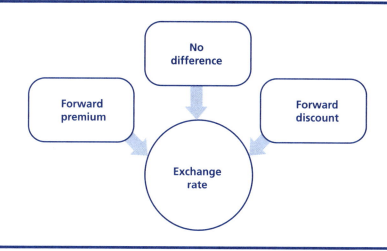

Figure 7.3: Possible interest rate relations between two currencies

currency have the same return as riskless investments in domestic currency. Exchange rate differentials assure the equality of returns.

When the forward exchange rate is above the spot rate, we talk about a **forward premium**. When the forward exchange rate is below the spot rate, we talk about a **forward discount** (see Figure 7.3). According to interest rate parity theory, the interest rate differential between two currencies is called **swap rate** (basis swap).

Interest rate of the other currency > Interest rate of the currency quoted = Forward premium

Interest rate of the other currency < Interest rate of the currency quoted = Forward discount

7.6 Currency derivatives transactions of banks

Let us first take a look at currency trading of banks. A customer can purchase and/or sell currency forward, and the bank acts as counterparty. These kinds of derivatives transactions are mostly related to an underlying transaction and serve as hedge or expansion of a hedging transaction. Most companies hedge their import and export activities (against currency risk) and in this way obtain a reliable calculation basis. Depending on the specification, these transactions are either **OTC options** or **forwards**. Since this is an individual contract between two parties, the transfer of this kind of derivatives contract to a third party is very unlikely and almost never done in practice. The basic intention of the counterparty (frequently a company) is in most cases protection against exchange rate fluctuations with regard to an existing exposure, such as an export or import transaction. While this is possible in theory, these transactions are rarely used for speculation.

Example:

A European company expects to receive USD 1 million in 6 months. Two choices are available:

1. Forward sale of USD 1 million.
2. Immediate sale of USD 1 million in exchange for EUR. The company then needs a loan in the amount of USD 1 million on which it has to pay interest for six months.

Both versions should lead to the same result. This is to be expected; otherwise a riskless arbitrage transaction would be possible.

The vast majority of currency derivatives transactions (about 95%) are OTC transactions conducted by banks. Currency futures, which are listed, are more likely to be used for speculative purposes.

7.7 Calculation of the forward rate

$$\text{Forward rate} = \text{spot rate} \cdot \frac{1 + \left(r_G \cdot \frac{T}{B_G}\right)}{1 + \left(r_Q \cdot \frac{T}{B_Q}\right)}$$

T = Number of days
r_G = Annual interest rate in decimal, currency quoted
r_Q = Annual interest rate in decimal, other currency
B_G = Day-count convention for currency quoted (360 or 365)
B_Q = Day-count convention for other currency (360 or 365)

If it is also taken into consideration that trading actually involves bid and ask prices, the following formulas result:

$$\text{Forward rate}_{bid} = \text{spot rate}_{bid} \cdot \frac{1 + \left(r_{bid,G} \cdot \frac{T}{B_G}\right)}{1 + \left(r_{ask,Q} \cdot \frac{T}{B_Q}\right)}$$

$$\text{Forward rate}_{ask} = \text{spot rate}_{ask} \cdot \frac{1 + \left(r_{ask,G} \cdot \frac{T}{B_G}\right)}{1 + \left(r_{bid,Q} \cdot \frac{T}{B_Q}\right)}$$

T = Number of days
r_G = Annual interest rate in decimal, currency quoted
r_Q = Annual interest rate in decimal, other currency
B_G = Day-count convention for currency quoted (360 or 365)
B_Q = Day-count convention for other currency (360 or 365)

7.8 Currency derivatives transactions at exchanges

An exchange has two important functions which are not limited to the case of currency derivatives: it brings together two parties who can then enter into a transaction, and it also provides liquidity to the market via the market maker system. The exchange is thus an intermediary between two parties with differing intentions.

A distinction is made between currency options and currency futures (see Figure 7.4).

7.9 Cross rates

In some cases, a so-called **cross rate** must be calculated (see Figure 7.5) since a currency pair is not traded directly. This is the case, for example, for the Japanese Yen (JPY) and the Swiss Franc (CHF). Two trades are required: initially JPY for euro and then euro for CHF. The resulting exchange rate is called a cross rate, since trading takes place "across currencies." In applied work, cross rates do not pose any problems since the major exchange rate departments of banks are able to calculate the rates and settle client transactions accordingly.

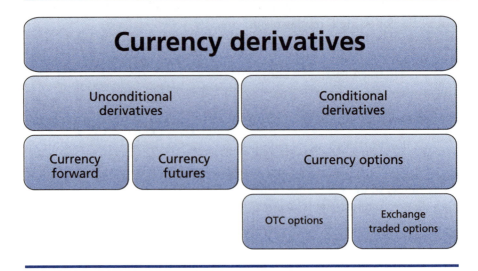

Figure 7.4: Currency derivatives transactions

We are looking for CHF/JPY – calculated via the euro	
Starting values: EUR / CHF = 1.5500 EUR / JPY = 138.00 CHF / JPY = ?	Calculation: Amount of JPY equal to 1 CHF, if 1.5500 CHF = 1 EURO, and 1 EURO = 138.00 JPY
The EUR can be eliminated from these equations and it follows: CHF/JPY = 138.00 / 1.5500 = 89.03 The value of one Swiss Frank is 89.03 Japanese Yen.	

Figure 7.5: Example of a cross rate

7.10 Tobin tax

A much debated issue is the taxation of international currency transactions (financial market transaction tax), which was proposed by JAMES TOBIN[5] in 1972. Tobin proposes to reign in short-term speculation on international financial markets by means of a modest tax on all foreign exchange transactions. But empirical studies refute this proposition. Nonetheless, it is revisited regularly, and the discussions are often initiated by the media. At the moment, the international community is taking up the introduction of a financial mar-

---

[5] 1918-2002: US economist and recipient of the Nobel prize in economics in 1981.

ket transaction tax in the context of the financial market crisis. It is unlikely that such a tax will bring the desired result - a limitation of unfettered speculation – especially since it would require participation of all countries.

7.11 What are currency options?

Here, again, a distinction is made between **OTC options** and **plain vanilla options**. The advantage of OTC options is their flexibility. They can be structured exactly according to the requirements of the investor. A disadvantage is the fact that a resale will be very difficult due to the highly specific nature of the option.

Standardized currency options meanwhile (traded among others at the CME, ISE[6]), just like equity options, are uniformly structured: one EUR/USD contract at CME is standardized at an amount of EUR 125,000. Major advantages of these options are high liquidity and quick trading at the derivatives exchanges.

> The buyer of a currency option, just like the buyer of an equity option, acquires the right, but not the obligation, to purchase or to sell a specific amount of foreign currency during a pre-specified time period and at a predetermined price. To obtain this right, he pays an option premium to the writer of the option (short).

7.12 Pricing of a currency option according to Garman-Kohlhagen

Currency options can be either European or American. To price them, the model of *Mark Garman* and *Steven Kohlhagen* is used. According to this modification of the *Black-Scholes* model from the year 1983 (*Garman-Kohlhagen model*), the price of a currency option is determined as follows:

$$c = S_0 e^{-r_1 \tau} N(d_1) - K_0 e^{-r \tau} N(d_2)$$

---

[6] Settlement of the options involves the corresponding futures contract.

with

$$d_1 = \frac{\ln(S_0/K_0) + \left(r - \Gamma_1 + \frac{\sigma^2}{2}\right)\tau}{\sigma\sqrt{\tau}}$$

$$d_2 = d_1 - \sigma\sqrt{\tau}$$

c = Option price (call)
S_0 = Current spot exchange rate
τ = Term to maturity of the contract
K_0 = Strike price of the option
r = Interest rate in the home country
Γ^1 = Interest rate in the foreign country
N(d) = Cumulative standard normal distribution
σ = Volatility

7.13 What are currency futures?

The CME in Chicago (as an example of an exchange that offers currency futures) offers a large number of currency futures. They are standardized and highly liquid. The typical Euro/USD future (EC) has a contract volume of EUR 125,000 and is among the most frequently traded contracts. The futures are traded around the clock (CME GLOBEX) and can be deployed individually and quickly.

> The market for currency futures and listed options on currencies is relatively small compared to the OTC market. It amounts to about 5% of the global activity in currency derivatives. 95% of all transactions take place in interbank trading[7].

Currency futures function similar to other futures already discussed. The two basic directions – increasing or declining – exist and depending on the outlook, a futures contract is either purchased or sold. Since settlement calls for physical delivery upon exercise, many futures are either closed or rolled forward on the last day of trading. However, if an investor chooses physical settlement, two currencies are involved.

---

[7] Source: Commerzbank AG FX Research.

Example:

An investor expects an increase of the euro relative to the USD. Based on this scenario, he purchases 10 Euro/USD futures (EC) at the CME. If the euro advances relative to the USD, the investor makes a profit. If the euro declines, he suffers a loss.

Even though the 10 contracts are valued at EUR 1,250,000, the investor is only required to make a payment in the amount of the initial margin for this position. This enables him to set up an inexpensive and flexible currency position (see Table 7.1).

Table 7.1: Currency futures and their basic intentions

Currency futures	Expectation	Position
Euro / USD	Euro increases relative to USD USD declines relative to Euro	Long futures
	Euro declines relative to USD USD increases relative to Euro	Short futures
YEN / USD	Yen increases relative to USD USD declines relative to Yen	Long futures
	Yen declines relative to USD USD increases relative to Yen	Short futures
GBP / USD	GBP increases relative to USD USD declines relative to GBP	Long futures
	GBP declines relative to USD USD increases relative to GBP	Short futures
Euro / CHF	Euro increases relative to CHF CHF declines relative to Euro	Long futures
	Euro declines relative to CHF CHF increases relative to EUR	Short futures

7.13.1 Pricing of currency futures

The cost of carry model[8] is also used for the pricing of currency futures. The seller of a futures contract is purchasing foreign currency for later delivery. His costs are a function of the exchange rate of the currency, the domestic and foreign interest rates and the term to maturity of the futures.

---

[8] Financing costs minus revenues foregone.

$$F_0 = S_0 \left(\frac{(1+\Gamma_1)T}{(1+\Gamma_2)T} \right)$$

F = Price of the future
S = Spot price
Γ_1 = Foreign interest rates
Γ_2 = Domestic interest rates
T = Term to maturity

The futures price depends on the interest rates in the two countries and on the difference between these two rates. Included in the price is thus the return[9] differential between the foreign and the domestic currency investment. If the futures price is above the spot rate, this means that interest rates at home are higher than abroad. If the price is below the spot rate, the foreign currency has higher interest rates.

7.13.2 Uses of currency futures

Since currency derivatives transactions are a very quick and inexpensive form of trading, they are not only used for hedging, but frequently also for speculation. Major investors use futures to position themselves for an anticipated currency movement. It is advisable to work with limits, since currencies can move very quickly and also overnight.

In many cases, these instruments are used in addition to existing derivatives positions, for example the Euro-Bund future. But currency futures should also be considered in isolation. Especially in a time of quick and global investments, they are an indispensable tool in the professional management of portfolios and trading lists.

7.13.3 Basic intentions of the investor

Trading in currency derivatives is also grounded in three basic intentions. We want to take a brief look at each:

7.13.3.1 Hedging

The classical protection against currency fluctuations can be justified by several fundamental needs. Examples that can be mentioned are:

---

[9] Interest received.

- Import or export transactions
- Price stability in the case of investment projects
- Hedging of existing holdings (securities, commodities and so forth)
- Hedging of upcoming cash flows

7.13.3.2 Speculation

The investor speculates that exchange rates are changing in a certain direction. These speculations do not depend on an underlying transaction and are exclusively meant to generate additional returns. This also brings with it the risk of losses: if the investor gets the price movement wrong, he has to suffer the loss. No offsetting underlying transaction exists.

Nonetheless, these positions are an optimal addition to the trading books of speculators. In combination with index and interest rate futures, currency futures make an additional investment layer available (see Figure 7.6). This is also true for combinations with commodity derivatives transactions, which can also be used for speculative purposes. At this point we would like to stress again that currency futures can be traded just as easily as index futures.

Expiry	Current	Change absolute	Change relative	Volume	Date Time	Bid	Ask	Open interest	Settlement
Rolling	1.413300	0.001200	+0.08%	126,394	08/05. 11:37 [R]	1.413200	1.413300	186,951	1.412100
Sep 11	1.413300	0.001200	+0.08%	126,392	08/05. 11:37 [R]	1.413200	1.413300	186,951	1.412100
Dec 11	1.412700	0.003300	+0.23%	44	08/05 10:54 [R]	1.410600	1.411200	2,080	1.409400
Mar 12	1.408000	0.000800	+0.06%	2	08/05 09:27 [R]	1.404800	1.410300	392	1.407200

Figure 7.6: Overview EUR/USD future[10]

7.13.3.3 Speculating on spreads or currency pairs

An investor who wants to speculate on changes in the relationship between currency pairs can establish combinations which can partly reduce the risk profile. But there is also the danger that the risk increases exponentially, if the combinations are not offsetting, but cumulative instead.

---

[10] Source: Interactiv Management Data Solution.

7.14 Commodity derivatives transactions versus commodity spot transactions

The difference between commodity derivatives transactions and classical spot transactions is the fact that no delivery takes place upon completion of the transaction – it is moved to a future date. It is therefore possible to enter into a commodity derivatives transaction on a good that has not even been produced or extracted at that moment. These types of derivatives transactions were the origins of today's derivatives markets and provided the impetus for the establishment of modern derivatives exchanges. The main reasons for entering into these transactions were the transfer of risk or the handling of shipments from remote locations. In a very simplified version, these exchanges already existed in antiquity. Today's leading commodity exchanges are located in the Unites States. Most influential are CME in Chicago and NYMEX in New York, which resulted from a merger of smaller milk and butter exchanges. A major part of commodity derivatives transactions takes place at NYMEX, the world's largest commodity derivatives exchange. It is considered to be *"the last bastion of pure capitalism left on earth. Here they trade everything that keeps the world going*[11]*."* Most of these transactions are used for speculative purposes; a large majority is closed prior to expiration. In contrast, delivery close to 100 percent can be assumed for spot transactions (see Figure 7.7).

In most cases, futures are used for commodity derivatives transactions. In principle, however, both futures (standardized and thus easily transferable) and forwards (individually designed, bilateral contract) are available. Thanks

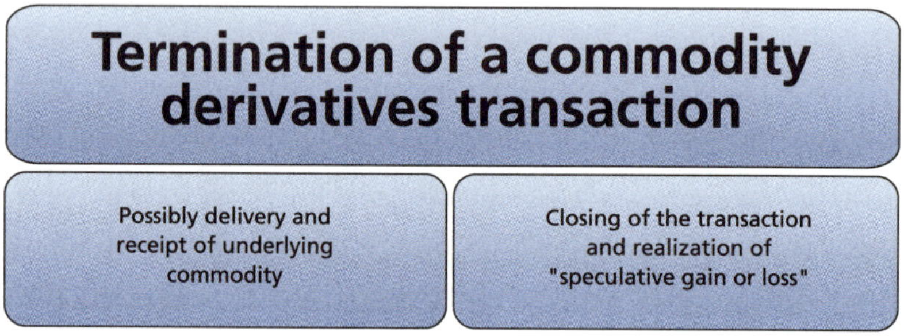

Termination of a commodity derivatives transaction

- Possibly delivery and receipt of underlying commodity
- Closing of the transaction and realization of "speculative gain or loss"

Figure 7.7: Termination of a commodity derivatives transaction

---

[11] Quoted from the movie "Trading Places."

to the standardized contracts, liquid trading is possible and the contracts can easily be transferred to third parties.

We will only consider futures contracts in the following sections, because they are preferred over options in practice.

7.15 Commodity futures

The structure of commodity futures is equivalent to that of index futures or fixed income futures. They are unconditional derivatives transactions; all relevant features have been settled when the contract was formed. As with all other futures, the basic expectation of the long futures investor is that prices of the underlying are increasing, while the short futures investor expects price declines in the underlying. Thanks to fast and inexpensive trading as well as market transparency, commodity futures are the preferred choice of both hedgers and speculators.

7.15.1 Opening, closing and settlement

As already mentioned, the vast majority of all commodity futures is closed prior to expiration and is used mainly for speculation. As in the case of index futures, it is possible to close a position by entering into an offsetting futures transaction, which completely releases the investor from all obligations (see Table 7.2). If futures are not closed prior to expiration, they must be honored.

Table 7.2: Opening and closing transactions

Opening	Closing
Long futures	Short futures
Short futures	Long futures

Due to the large number of investors with different fundamental needs, both commodity futures with physical delivery and with cash settlement do exist.

Let us first take a look at physical delivery: in this case, commodities are changing hands. This – in the normal case – typical and original form of settlement is used, for example by companies that need the underlying in their production process or plan to resell it (this is in line with the original intentions of a commodity derivatives investor).

Especially over the past ten years, there has been a tendency to offer cash settlement in addition to physical delivery, since an increasing number of speculators are active in the area of commodity derivatives transactions. They are not interested in physical delivery and prefer to receive any outstanding amount via cash settlement. The reason for this is very simple: an investor who only speculates on price changes of a commodity chooses a contract with cash settlement, since he has absolutely no interest in physical delivery and merely wants to benefit from market movements.

The early closing is done just as in the case of index futures: any difference is settled in cash. The requirement to deliver or receive the commodity could cause major problems: it would not only require setting up the necessary expensive infrastructure, but also the purchase or sale of the commodity, depending on the type of contract acquired.

Example:

If an investor purchases a Henry Hub Natural Gas futures contract and chooses delivery, he needs to collect the underlying in the United States. This is both impractical and hard to implement in practice by most investors.

7.15.2   Application of the different settlement possibilities

Figure 7.8 displays the different types of settlement.

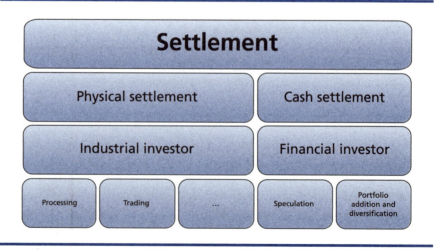

Figure 7.8:   Settlement versions and realizations

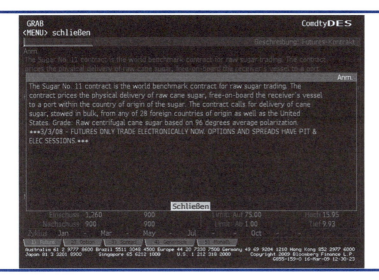

Figure 7.9: Product specifications for physical settlement (here: Sugar No. 11)[12]

Obviously these positions can overlap in practice. Frequently industrial investors also trade a number of cash settlement products as additions to their portfolio. Figure 7.9 uses the example of Sugar No. 11 to show the specifications which are defined individually for every product.

7.15.3 Which commodities serve as underlying for derivatives transactions?

In principle, commodity derivatives transactions are possible for any commodity. In practice, the goods are categorized as shown in Figure 7.10.

The figure is a strongly simplified classification of groups of commodity derivatives transactions. One of the most heavily traded derivatives products is frozen, highly concentrated orange juice[13]. In production, the orange juice is reduced to one seventh; the volatile aromas are previously extracted and added again after the reduction. Then the concentrate is frozen for storage. When the juice is produced, the sirup is melted and water and some sugar are added. Due to strong global demand, contracts on FCOJ are traded very actively.

---

[12] Source: Bloomberg.
[13] Frozen Concentrated Orange Juice = FCOJ.

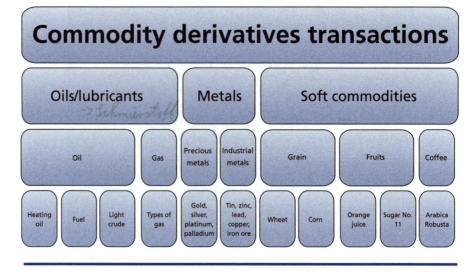

Figure 7.10: Commodities used in commodity derivatives transactions (simplified)

It should be kept in mind that the harvest of coming years is already traded on the commodities exchanges today. Diseases, environmental disasters and crop failures can lead to significant price increases; at the same time, a favorable harvest season or a decline in consumer demand can lead to declining prices. Especially trading in soft commodities has increased strongly over the past years; as an example, the futures on sugar and corn were traded heavily[14] since both raw materials are used when producing ethanol. And even private investors frequently attempt to invest in this area with the help of other derivatives (for example turbo certificates[15]).

Why do futures markets exist?

A standardized underlying (commodity or financial instrument) must be available. Prices must be variable and a sufficient reduction in transaction costs must be achieved. The futures market must provide an opportunity to the investor that is unavailable elsewhere.

---

[14] This is true for 2006-2008 in particular.
[15] Securitized certificates similar to futures.

7.16 Trading in commodity derivatives

In Germany, only the major derivatives brokers and a few banks with relevant competencies are in a position to trade futures at commodity exchanges. Just a few financial institutions have their own trading book for commodities derivatives; in most cases, this business area is still being developed. Only in individual cases will commodity derivatives transactions (especially for corporate clients) be offered for hedging or speculative purposes. One reason for this is the legal situation: it was not until the new "**Principle I**[16]" came into effect that banks were allowed to enter into commodity derivatives transactions.

It is also noteworthy that trading in commodity derivatives is conducted mainly by institutional or professional investors. The market is often closed to private investors due to a lack of liquidity. Instead they utilize classical leveraged products or investment certificates to profit from the commodity derivatives market. These securitized derivatives are backed by major issuers, which securitize the transactions conducted at the derivatives exchange and offer them in quantities that are appropriate for private clients. In principle, the structure of these products is identical to that of the exchange traded derivatives products.

A clear trend is apparent: private investors are making use of securitized derivatives (issued by a major issuer), while professional investors continue to expand the classical derivatives market positions.

7.17 When should investors consider commodity derivatives contracts?

This fundamental question has different answers, depending on the type of investor. But the following requirements must definitely be in place:

- An investor who wants to speculate with commodity derivatives must possess sufficient liquidity to assure that his position can be maintained until maturity.

---

[16] Issued at the beginning of 2004 by the German financial market regulator Bundesanstalt für Finanzdienstleistungsaufsicht (BaFin).

- In addition, qualification and competency are absolutely required, since the derivatives market is no playground and any mistake can become expensive rather quickly (see Chapter 3).
- The third point is absolute market presence. This means that the investor must be willing to deal with his order book daily. The derivatives market is fast moving; therefore not only an absolute market presence, but also the consistent and correct supply of information is crucial. In addition the issue of different time zones must be dealt with, since most derivatives exchanges are located in the US or abroad. Placement, routing and trading of orders must be assured, so does secure clearing.
- A basic transaction or speculative motive must be present. An appropriate strategy should be derived from it.

> **Delivery problems**
>
> What happens if a farmer who has sold all his goods forward is unable to deliver, for example due to a bad harvest or a natural disaster? This question is raised frequently and deserves to be answered. The best way to cover this scenario is through an insurance policy. Of course, it is also possible to close the derivatives position or to purchase the underlying from another source. At any rate, the derivatives transaction exists independent of the "real" commodity and must be honored. In our example, therefore, the farmer must have a backup in the worst case scenario.

7.18 Developments and outlook

In light of quickly changing and developing markets, we see large potential in the area of commodity derivatives transactions. It is quite conceivable that in coming years, commodity derivatives transactions will turn into strategic investment instruments in Germany as well and that trading at derivatives exchanges becomes possible. It is also possible that direct commodity derivatives transactions, also on commodity indexes, will be introduced in the near future. Since demand determines supply, and not the other way around, it is just a matter of time before the first, successful commodity derivatives contracts can be traded as easily in Germany as this is already the case in other parts of the world (such as in the U.S.). First steps in this direction were taken by Eurex with the introduction of options and futures on precious metals (gold and silver). Since July 20, 2009 trading at Eurex is now also possible for agricultural futures, and since November 2009, clients can trade electrical power derivatives[17] (also a commodity) at Eurex. With these initiatives, markets are developing significantly in Europe as well.

7.19 Price determination of commodity derivatives futures

As already outlined for index futures, the fair price of the futures instrument depends on the spot rate and the cost of carry (financing costs). But for commodities contracts, storage and insurance costs must also be considered in addition to financing costs. Storage costs can only be ignored in the case where goods or living commodities cannot be stored. Financing costs are higher if additional costs (such as storage costs) arise, and they go down if positive cash flows can be realized. However, this is not straightforward in the case of commodities. Equities pay dividends, which constitute a positive cash flow, but things are more complicated for commodities. Here the so called **convenience yield** of holding the commodity is assessed. This additional non-monetary benefit can either increase or decrease the cost of carry: if the convenience yield rises above the calculated cost of carry, the futures contract will be traded below the current spot price. This is called "the futures contract is trading in **backwardation**." If, however, the cost of carry exceeds the convenience yield, the futures price exceeds the spot price: the situation is called **contango** (see Figure 7.11 and Figure 7.12).

7.20 Prices of commodity futures

In Table 7.3, we once again focus on the issue of different quotations and display them graphically in Figure 7.11.

Table 7.3: Relation between spot and futures price

Commodity futures			
Spot price	<	Futures price	Contango
Spot price	>	Futures price	Backwardation

---

[17] Phelix® derivative.

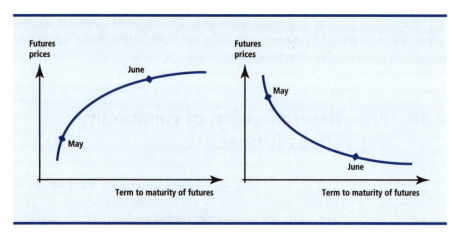

Figure 7.11: Contango and backwardation

Figure 7.12 presents a numerical example of the principles displayed graphically in Figure 7.11.

It needs to be determined whether the convenience yield calculated leads to an increase or a reduction of financing costs. Why this is of primary importance will be discussed in the coming sections.

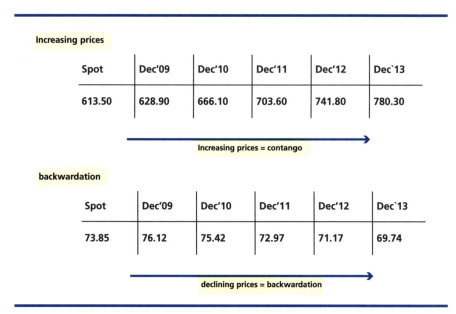

Figure 7.12: Contango (above) and backwardation (below)

The convenience yield is the return to the investor, which is derived from physically holding the underlying instead of a derivative. For consumption goods, this is not a variable that can be measured directly, but instead must be derived from the maturity structure.

The futures price can be determined according to the following formula:

$$F_0 = S_0 \cdot \frac{(1+r+L)^T}{(1+y)^T}$$

F_0 = Futures price
S_0 = Spot price
L = Storage cost (net)
r = Risk-free rate of interest
y = Convenience yield
T = Term to maturity in years

For y (convenience yield), the following expression can be derived:

$$F_0 \cdot (1+y)^T = (S_0 + L) \cdot (1+r)^T$$

Storage costs can also be expressed as a proportional storage factor L. This leads to:

$$F_0 \cdot (1+y)^T = S_0 \cdot (1+r+L)^T$$

In order to give a non-mathematical explanation for the above equations, one could say that y represents the market uncertainty expected by investors, which could be caused, for example, by the possibility of a bad harvest. Put simply, it in fact expresses a shortage of the commodity. As long as strong supply is expected, y will be small or non-existent. In the case of an excess supply, $-y$ leads to a price-reducing discount.

As already stated, calculating the price of a commodity futures contract is similar to the case of index futures:

futures price =
  spot price + ((financing cost + storage cost) – convenience yield)

This simplified formula reflects the complex material just presented.

7.21 What is problematic about contango?

The answer to this question is derived from the topic itself. An investor who has purchased contango futures has also paid the premium relative to the base. Due to the contango, he is suffering losses if the spot price remains unchanged or changes only slightly. If this contract is rolled over in coming months, and the contango continues, the loss potential is increased further. This mechanism is illustrated in Figures 7.13 and 7.14.

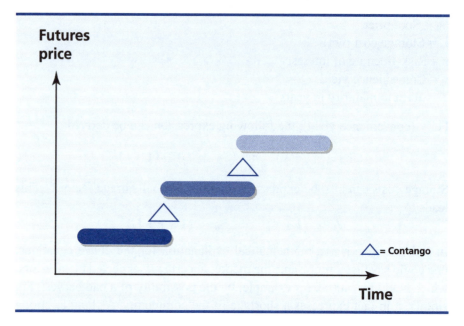

Figure 7.13: The problem of contango in futures positions

Expiry	Current	Change absolute	Change relative	Volume	Date Time	Bid	Ask	Open Interest	Settlement
Rolling	86.65	+0.03	+0.03%	51,075	08/05 11:28 [D]	86.65	86.67	356,689	86.63
Sep 11	86.66	+0.03	+0.03%	51,066	08/05 11:28 [D]	86.65	86.69	356,689	86.63
Oct 11	87.27	+0.23	+0.26%	4,501	08/05 11:28 [D]	87.05	87.10	123,858	87.04
Nov 11	87.80	+0.31	+0.35%	1,692	08/05 11:28 [D]	87.52	87.57	98,127	87.49
Dec 11	88.25	+0.29	+0.33%	3,977	08/05 11:27 [D]	88.02	88.07	205,534	87.96
Jan 12	88.94	+0.51	+0.58%	216	08/05 11:27 [D]	88.50	88.57	54,984	88.43

Figure 7.14: Light sweet crude futures with noticeable contango[18]

---

[18] Source: Interactive Data.

In practice, contango can reach from 15 to 20 percent annually. An investor must be aware of this. In order to make a profit, contango must first be exceeded. Of course it is possible that due to specific market situations, profits are realized quicker and more efficiently, but the basic relationship must be considered when assessing an investment opportunity. Of course, the same holds in the opposite case of backwardation.

7.22 Futures trading

When trading commodity futures, a number of things must be considered which are not relevant for index futures. The trading calendar for index futures in most cases only includes the next three end-of-quarter months while commodity futures frequently have monthly expiration dates for each contract (often many years ahead). This makes steady and liquid trading possible[19]. The quality of the underlying is defined in the contract data. As an example, the futures on light sweet crude oil call for delivery of an oil with at most 0.42 percent sulfur content and a relative density of 37° to 42° API. These detailed contract specifications are important to uniquely define the underlying. Especially in the case of oil, where many differences exist, this is crucial. But the same principle applies to other commodities as well. A precise specification of the underlying is needed for each futures contract. As an example, a distinction is made between sugar of the type No. 11 and type No. 14 (see Figure 7.9).

7.23 Storage

Another unique feature of commodity futures is the question of storage. Precious metals and oil can be stored with relative ease, while soft commodities and livestock (such as cattle) can cause significantly bigger problems. It is always advisable to take a look at the storage volume and the storage situation before reaching an investment decision. Especially under specific circumstances (for example following natural disasters[20]), it may also be hard to identify alternative storage spaces.

---

[19] The liquidity of each contract should be studied individually prior to trading.
[20] For example, the disaster in New Orleans.

7.24 Which factors can influence pricing?

It is obvious that commodity derivatives markets are subject to large fluctuations and external influences. The most important influencing factors are:

- Supply and demand figures
- Production numbers (real)
- Weather situation and climatic change, natural disasters
- Bad harvests and pests
- Subsidies and grants
- Wars, embargos and disasters
- Import taxes, storage costs
- Economic growth

These potential influencing factors hold both risks and opportunities. Therefore investors must be familiar with the major themes and be able to assess the influencing factors and their effects on the respective futures contracts. At the same time, the availability of relevant information is crucial: an investor with an exposure to coffee futures needs to have access to timely and precise information about the investment. In this regard, institutional and private investors are different: institutional investors possess profound and always current knowledge (due to their access to technology), while most private investors are forced to painstakingly collect relevant information from different sources. This will change over the next years: wealthy private investors will increasingly focus on this sector and will become an additional source of demand.

As already discussed above, soft commodities have witnessed a large increase in demand over the past years. This can partially be explained by changes in our society. The world is experiencing a coffee boom. "Coffee to go" is the latest rage. Even in the land of smiles, where tea used to be the exclusive beverage of choice, coffee is quite popular these days. This means that a large and still "dormant" new source of demand is waiting in the wings. Let us point out a second example: sugar. What used to be a sweetener is now one of the most important sources of energy. As they are used in the production of ethanol, both sugar and corn can be expected to be in high demand.

At the moment, there are still more young people than older ones in our society. But due to demographic change, this structure will change drastically in the coming years and will affect our behavior as consumers as well. The increase in the personal standard of living will also contribute to changes in consumption patterns. This means that the prices of some goods will rise as our priorities change. While coffee or orange juice futures used to be somewhat of an oddity until recently, they constitute important markets today. What makes futures markets interesting is the fact that one can profit both from increasing and declining prices. Therefore it is always possible to be active as an investor. The key is to identify current trends and to invest accordingly. As straightforward as it sounds, implementation is rather difficult. Especially the simplicity and transparency of commodity futures means that successful strategies can be developed, in some cases even intraday.

As discussed, the availability of information is very important when using commodity futures. At the same time, this is one of the fundamental problems of many investors: it is not possible to set up a coherent long-term strategy without access to a consistent and reliable supply of information. And the adequate assessment of information is also of paramount importance – especially in the area of commodity derivatives, solid and above all realistic expert analysis in indispensable. Only very few derivatives experts are really able to correctly interpret a coffee harvest report.

Investors without a strategy rarely get lucky. A consistent analysis from a fundamental and technical perspective is the first step in a successful strategy. Instruments with reliable trading and clearing processes must be chosen. At the same time, a strategy for the case of delivery of the underlying must be in place and a net cost-benefit analysis must exist. If a commodity derivatives transaction is too expensive due to its complexity and specifics of settlement, it should not be undertaken. As a matter of principle, the profit potential must increase in line with the risk.

Access to necessary information is the one consideration; the other is herd behavior and group thinking. We discussed these topics in Chapters 2.9.3.1 and 2.9.3.2 of this book. The frequency and relevance of these behavioral patterns in financial markets can be studied during every bubble, crash or market disequilibrium.

7.25 Strategies in the area of commodity derivatives transactions

As for all other type of derivatives transactions, the following basic intentions are also relevant for derivatives transactions in commodities:

- Hedging
- Arbitrage
- Speculation

In the following we will look at each of these basic intentions and explain the required strategies.

7.25.1 Hedging with commodity derivatives

The basic idea behind hedging is the existence of an underlying commodity transaction. We either purchase or sell commodities. In order to hedge these underlying transactions, we establish derivatives positions. The most straightforward position can be established using futures: if, for example, we want to hedge against rising prices in the industrial metals segment, we will choose to purchase a futures contract. If prices go up as expected, the purchase of the futures contract compensates for the price gap which has opened up. However, if prices do not increase, we suffer a loss with the futures position, which must be limited. Quick decisions may be required. An additional possibility is the purchase of options, which are a valid hedging instrument, since increases in raw materials can make it rather difficult to estimate costs and profits. The hedge provides a certain reliability of the planning process. A distinction must be made between hedging an existing transaction and fixing the price of an upcoming transaction ahead of time. Either transaction mainly serves to make planning more dependable, as discussed above.

With the help of classic strategies such as long put or short futures, hedging of an existing transaction can be accomplished. Strategies such as long call and long futures are necessary to protect against an expected upcoming increase in prices. Profits from these strategies compensate price increases of the underlying. This should be considered in case an investment is planned, but the financial means are not yet available.

7.25.2 Speculating with commodity derivatives

A completely different basic intention explains speculation on changes in commodity prices: it is not tied to an underlying transaction, but is conducted in order to generate additional income. We can speculate both on positive and negative price changes without any other basic intention with the help of futures. Our investment strategy is based only on the expectation that the price of the underlying commodity will change.

Example:

The price of orange juice (FCOJ) appears too low to an investor who expects a poor harvest as a consequence of unfavorable weather changes. This will lead to a decline in supply and thus to higher prices. Consequently, he purchases futures contracts on FCOJ. If prices develop as expected (in our case an increase in prices), he generates a profit. Meanwhile, he will suffer a loss if prices fall due to other influences.

As already stated, the investor actively positions himself for a change in prices and thus actively seeks risk, since there is no underlying transaction. He engages in pure speculation, which should be based on solid analysis.

A majority of commodity derivatives contracts traded today are used to speculate. Most of these derivatives transactions are cash settled and do not involve delivery.

7.25.3 Arbitrage with commodity derivatives

The third possibility is commodity arbitrage: an investor purchases a good on exchange X and resells it at the same moment on exchange Y. The resulting difference is his profit or loss. Due to the simultaneity of the two transactions, the transaction is riskless for the investor.

7.25.4 Spreads with commodity derivatives

An investor establishes a spread in order to benefit from price differences. He sells the contract that appears expensive and purchases the seemingly inexpensive one. The difference between the two transactions is, as with every spread, his limited profit. The only source of profit is the relative price movement of the two contracts.

These strategies supplement larger strategies and are used for expansion. One could also say that in some sense, they are used for market management. Active derivatives investors establish new strategies daily and close out previous ones.

7.26 What are combinations between currency and commodity derivatives?

Combinations between currency and commodity contracts are found frequently in trades that are related to an underlying transaction: in this way, investors can hedge against changes in both commodity prices and the currency used (mostly USD).

Example:

In six months, an investor plans to purchase copper in an amount of USD 10 million. Since he expects increasing prices, the investor enters into a copper future (long copper future) today. At the same time, the investor expects a significant strengthening of the USD relative to the euro. Since he needs USD to pay for the copper, he also wants to hedge against such an USD appreciation over the next six months. To do so, he sells EUR/USD futures[21] in the amount of the underlying transaction. If the expected development in the currency markets does in fact materialize, the futures contract assures that the investor is protected against the weakening of the euro relative to the USD. Additionally, he is hedged against copper price increases due to the long copper future. As the price of both uncertain components of the contract has now been locked in, a sound basis for decision making exists.

Of course, attempting to hedge every euro does not make sense. There must be a reasonable tradeoff between possible losses and hedging costs. At the same time, it must be carefully assessed whether the basic intention is consistent and in line with fundamentals. Otherwise the entire hedging transaction makes little sense.

---

[21] Selling EUR relative to USD is a synthetic purchase of USD for EUR.

7.27 What strategies for currency derivatives exist?

7.27.1 Hedging strategies

An investor wants to hedge against the depreciation of his home currency. He thus sells forward his home currency against a foreign currency. He makes a profit if the expected development materializes.

Example:

An investor will receive a payment of EUR 10 million in three months. Since his home currency is the US dollar, he wants to hedge against declines in the value of the euro and therefore sells EUR futures. This transaction is equivalent to a sale of euro and a simultaneous purchase of US dollar; it enables the investor to cover any difference that may arise.

Hedging strategies in the currency area are used mostly by investors with large underlying transactions. They provide a clearly defined basis for planning and cost calculation.

This is different in the case of currency speculation: changes in the relative value of two currencies are the object of speculation. These kinds of transactions are independent of any underlying contractual obligation and are used purely to generate additional income.

Example:

An investor expects a depreciation of the euro relative to the US dollar and therefore sells euro futures. This is a synthetic purchase of the US dollar. If the euro does in fact lose in value, the investor profits; in the opposite case he suffers a loss.

Among other things, this example also shows that it is possible to compensate losses from a spot transaction (for example a bond portfolio) with the help of such a transaction.

7.27.2 Speculative strategies

In this strategy, the investor speculates on a change in the relative value of a currency pair, preferably using exchange traded currency futures. If the investor expects increasing prices, he buys a futures contract; if he expects a depreciation of the currency, he sells a futures contract. Currency futures, due to quick and inexpensive implementation, are the best instrument for foreign exchange speculation.

Example:

An investor expects an appreciation of the US dollar relative to the euro and takes a short position in euro futures (this is equivalent to the purchase of USD futures). If the euro loses value relative to the US dollar, the expectation of the investor is fulfilled, and he makes a profit. If, instead, the euro gains in value against the US dollar, the investor suffers a loss. He participates in every movement of the underlying at a rate of 1:1, since a futures contract is a delta-1 instrument.

Interview with Marc Bachhuber, quirin bank AG

Mr. Bachhuber, what is your view on the development of the derivatives market in the years ahead?
I expect continued growth of the derivatives market, albeit not at the rates seen in the past years. In my opinion, products with a clearer structure will dominate.

Which fundamental changes are ahead in your opinion?
At the moment, only clearly structured products with little complexity are in demand. I expect this trend to continue for the time being.

Which products (securitized financial engineering solutions) do you consider to be relevant in the years to come?
I assume that commodity products will continue to play a major role. And of course, plain vanilla equity/index products will continue to be useful and in demand.

In your opinion, which products will disappear from the market, and why?
Everything that is intransparent, expensive and obscure. Investors are no longer willing to bear unnecessary costs.

Do you think the financial crisis, which started out as a sub-prime crisis, has had a lasting effect on the market for securitized products and financial engineering solutions, or will things continue as before, once the crisis is overcome?
Yes, I think that the process of reorientation is already under way. This can be felt particularly in the area of private banking. Investors are more cautious and start to do more of their own research. I very much welcome that trend.

How about the developments in the segment of high net worth individuals?
I think that the separation from the retail segment lies ahead. Private banking and the selling of products – that is not a good match. In my opinion, fee based advice will lead to a path-breaking renewal of private banking.

Where do you expect to see the biggest growth potential for financial engineering solutions?
In private banking/wealth management. In this segment tailor-made solutions can be fully utilized. This is often not possible in the retail sector due to size limitations.

As a wealth manager, do you have favorite products? And if yes, which are these and why?
Discount certificates are an example of clearly structured and inexpensive products that can be used flexibly. They are also suitable for large portfolios (that do not trade options and futures directly) in order to accomplish structural aims. The big plus of these certificates is the fact that clients can easily evaluate them and thus utilize them in a straightforward manner.

Can you briefly sum up the developments in the market for securitized derivatives and financial engineering solutions over the past years?
We needed the previous years of fast growth. Many ideas were turned into good and targeted products. It is regrettable that a lot of this is condemned by today's media (frequently based on little knowledge). The financial engineering industry also needed time to grow and to develop. But I think that the child has grown up by now. We will discover much that is good and new in the coming years. But we must also learn from our mistakes. Not everything that can be realized must be realized. The courage to speak out against a structure is more valuable than the unquestioning placement of such a product.

Literature for this chapter

Bloss, Michael; Eil, Nadine; Ernst, Dietmar; Fritsche, Harald, Häcker, Joachim: Währungsderivate, 2009

Choudhry, Moorad: The Bond & Money Markets, 2001

Eilenberger, Guido: Währungsrisiken, Währungsrisikomanagement und Devisenkurssicherung von Unternehmen; 4th edition, 2004

Hull, John: Options, Futures and Other Derivatives, 7th edition, 2009

Steiner, Bob: Foreign Exchange and Money Markets, 2002

Wiedemann, Arnd: Bewertung von Finanzinstrumenten, 4th edition, 2007

Questions and answers on this chapter

Question 1:
What is the term used for the positive difference between a currency forward rate and a spot rate?

Question 2:
A company based in the euro-zone will receive in 3 months an amount of x monetary units in foreign currency. Which option strategy should be used in order to protect against a decline in value?

Question 3:
You are trading a futures contract on EUR/CHF.
BUY 5 EUR/CHF DEC10
Did you purchase EUR or CHF? Which volume did you trade?

Question 4
What are the different types of settlement for commodity derivatives? What are they used for?

Question 5:
What is problematic about a futures contract trading in contango?

Answer to question 1:
This is called forward premium.

Answer to question 2:
A long put position with a term to maturity of three months. It assures that the company can exchange foreign currency for EUR.

Answer to question 3:
You purchased the euro against the Swiss Franc. The volume traded is equal to 5 × EUR 125,000 = EUR 625,000.

Answer to question 4:
Possible are physical settlement and cash settlement. Speculators and financial market participants without the intention to use the underlying for production will normally prefer cash settlement and are not interested in physical delivery.

Answer to question 5:

The problem is the increasing cost of coming contracts. Every time the investor rolls the position, he incurs a loss, since the current futures contract is sold at a price of X and the following contract must be purchased at a price X + y. y = loss from rolling the position.

→ convenience yield

Module III – Structured derivatives

8 | Exotic and non-listed derivatives

The following chapter covers these issues:

- What are derivatives that are not exchange traded?
- In what way do they differ from plain vanilla derivatives?
- What are exotic derivatives?
- What are swaps and swaptions?
- What types of swaps exist?
- How are exotic options used?
- What are caps and floors?

8.1 Derivatives that are not exchange traded

At this point, we want to take a look at derivatives that are not traded at an exchange[1]. They are negotiated individually between two parties and are thus not standardized (individual bilateral financial contracts). As shown in previous chapters, only standardized derivatives can be easily transferred at an exchange. The derivatives which we will discuss now are used either to speculate (medium to long term) or to hedge an underlying transaction. Investors who hold derivatives that are not exchange traded are mostly professional or institutional market participants. The flexible contracts discussed in the following section are considered OTC derivatives, even though they can be cleared via the Eurex system.

---

[1] OTC – over the counter.

8.1.1 OTC derivatives as "flexible options/futures" at Eurex

There are several possibilities for entering into OTC derivatives contracts. Typically they are negotiated between two parties and processing is taken over by banks or brokers. The possibility to trade individually negotiated options and forwards at a special platform provided by Eurex[2] has been available for some time now. These **OTC Flexible Options and Futures** are cleared via the Eurex system, but like all other OTC derivatives, are completely flexible concerning specifications.

The following parameters can be set individually in the case of options:

OTC Flexible Options

- The chosen strike price can either exceed the highest strike price of the corresponding regular option series or be the lowest strike price of an option (for example LEPOs) that can be supported in the Eurex system. Or it can lie in between these two values. Maximum strike prices for OTC Flexible Options are limited to 2.5 times the highest available strike price of the respective product.
- Every trading day (with a few exceptions as defined by Eurex) can be used as expiration day. The range starts at the next trading day and extends to the longest currently traded standard expiration date of the product.
- Both American and European options are supported.
- Settlement of OTC flexible options can be chosen freely. Participants can choose either cash settlement or physical delivery of the underlying.

Futures can be structured individually by setting the following parameters:

- **Flexible term to maturity:** the market participants can choose the maturity of the contract. Possible expiration dates begin with the next trading day and extend to the last expiration date of standard futures contracts traded at Eurex.
- **Choice of settlement:** similar to OTC flexible options on single stocks, market participants can choose how to settle the transaction. Both cash settlement and physical delivery are possible.

Should market participant decide not to use this platform for their OTC transactions, they can ask their bank or broker to use their own processing systems.

---

[2] Other derivatives exchanges also offer this possibility (for example CBOE).

8.1.2 Caps, floors and collars

8.1.2.1 Caps

The buyer of a cap (**long cap**) acquires the right, against payment of a premium, to receive a balancing payment from the seller (**short cap**), if, at a pre-specified point in the future, an agreed reference interest rate lies above a predetermined upper interest rate limit. The long cap thus has locked in a guaranteed upper limit on interest rates (see Figure 8.1). Investors can obtain protection against rising interest rates and hedge their interest expenses. The short cap investor receives an option premium for his willingness to guarantee the balancing payment to the long cap investor in case the negotiated upper interest rate limit is breached (see Figure 8.2).

8.1.2.2 Caplets

In contrast to typical options on bonds, which only entail one option right, a cap consists of a series of options. At each predetermined point of time, it is assessed whether the reference rate is above the contract rate. It is quite possible that the option is exercised at some points in time and not exercised at others[3]. A cap is thus a series of interest rate options. Its value is derived by adding up all individual option prices (see Figure 8.3). The individual interest

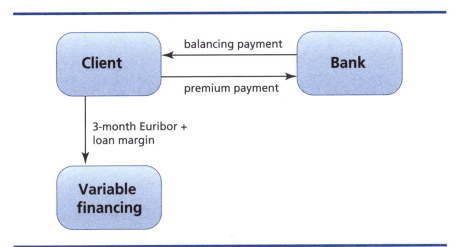

Figure 8.1: Cash flows of a long cap including underlying transaction (variable rate loan)

---

[3] In case of a positive difference between forward rates and the contract rate, the option is exercised (it has intrinsic value). An option expires worthless if it is not exercised.

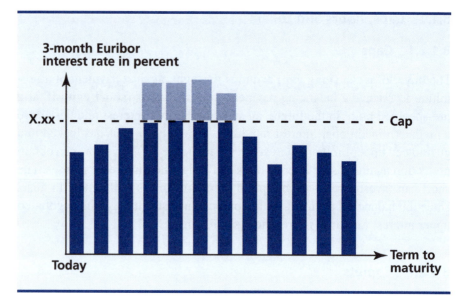

Figure 8.2: Upper interest rate limit of a cap[4]

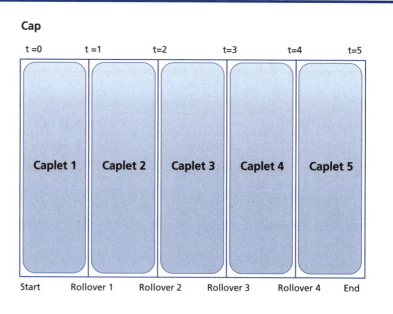

Figure 8.3: The cap is broken down into individual caplets

---

[4] Source: Commerzbank AG ICLM.

rate options are called caplets. The sum of all caplets (and their individual prices) makes up the total price of the cap.

8.1.2.3 Floor

A floor is the counterpart of a cap. It is also a conditional derivatives contract. The buyer (**long floor**) acquires the right, against payment of a premium, to receive a balancing payment from the seller (**short floor**), if an agreed reference interest rate falls below a predetermined lower interest rate level.

The seller of the floor receives the premium payment from the buyer. He is required to make the balancing payment to the long floor investor.

8.1.2.4 Floorlets

Just like a cap, a floor consists of several interest rate options, called floorlets. The prices of the individual interest rate options are calculated and added up to get the price of the floor (see Figure 8.4). The sum of the floorlet prices is thus equal to the price of the floor[5].

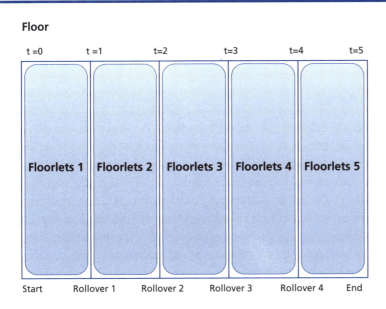

Figure 8.4: Floor is broken down into individual floorlets

---

[5] Valuation with the help of the Black model.

8.1.2.5 Valuation of caplets and floorlets

As already mentioned, the overall price of the caps and floors can be determined by adding up all the individual caplets and floorlets. The individual caplets and floorlets are valued with the help of the **Black-76 model**.

$$C_i = NB \cdot \delta \cdot e^{-rT} \cdot [Fw \cdot N(d_1) - K \cdot N(d_2)]$$

$$F_i = NB \cdot \delta \cdot e^{-rT} \cdot [K \cdot N(-d_2) - Fw \cdot N(-d_1)]$$

$$d_1 = \frac{\ln(Fw/K) + \sigma^2 \, t/2}{\sigma\sqrt{t}}$$

$$d_2 = d_1 - \sigma\sqrt{t}$$

C = Caplet
F = Floorlet
σ = Volatility
NB = Nominal value
r = Congruent interest rate for maturity
K = Strike price
T = Term to maturity
Fw = Forward
δ = Term to maturity of option
t = Time until option starts

8.1.2.6 Collar

A **collar** is a combination of a **cap** and a **floor**. A long collar consists of a long cap and a short floor. A long collar guarantees that the interest rate expense does not exceed a certain value, but also does not fall below a certain level. The opposite position is the short collar, consisting of a short cap and a long floor. Collars are constructed synthetically and are always a combination of basic positions required to form the overall position. Valuation of the individual basic positions enters into the overall valuation of the collar. It follows that the price of the collar is equal to the sum of the individual components contained in the collar which are valued as discussed above. Table 8.1 shows an example of individual components.

Table 8.1: Data sheet on the collar (individual components)

Interest rate option	Cap	Floor
Reference rate	4%	2.5%
Volatility	25% p.a.	45% p.a.
Contract volume	2 million	2 million
Term to maturity	3 years	3 years
Reference rate	12 month Euribor	12 month Euribor

8.1.3 What is a forward?

A forward is an individually negotiated and unconditional derivatives transaction, similar to a futures contract. It is "only" similar, since the individuality prevents exchange trading. The contract specifications are negotiated by the parties (financial intermediary and client). In practice this kind of transaction is done between banks and their clients. It is used predominantly to hedge an existing transaction. Unlike futures (exchange traded), forwards entail counterparty risk. This issue should not be ignored, especially if the contract parties are unequal (for example a small or medium-sized enterprise and a major bank). Risk transfer via the secondary market is not possible. While an additional hedging transaction can be established, this must be considered a new holding (with new risks and additional demands on capital). Due to the unique nature of the transactions, the pricing of forwards is also individualized. For the valuation of forward contracts with a known yield, we consider the following approach:

$$F_0 = S_0 \cdot e^{(r-f) \cdot T}$$

F_0 = Forward rate
S_0 = Spot rate
r = Risk-free rate of interest
f = Known return
T = Term to maturity

It is usually assumed that forward and futures prices are identical. However, if interest rates are uncertain, there is a theoretical difference in prices.

In case of a high positive correlation between interest rates and the price of the underlying (S), the futures price is above the forward price. It follows that the opposite is true in case of a strongly negative correlation[6].

---

[6] See Murawski 2007a University of Zurich.

Table 8.2: Comparison between forwards and futures[7]

	Forwards	Futures
Market	OTC	Derivatives exchange
Contract structure	Individually structured in all regards	Standardized with regard to quantity, quality, delivery date and delivery location, individual features not possible
Liquidity	Almost no fungibility	High liquidity due to continuous exchange trading
Counterparty risk	Yes, as in any other contract	No, the clearinghouse acts as counterparty
Settlement	Only one final settlement at expiration	Daily variation margin accounting and final settlement at expiration
Exercise	Exercised in most cases, cash settlement or delivery takes place	Majority of positions are closed prior to expiration
Transaction costs	Possibly lawyer's fees, structuring fees of the banks involved, and so forth	Brokerage fees

8.1.4 What is a swap?

Formally, a swap is a bilateral financial contract, which defines payment streams between two parties. An exchange of payments is agreed, which is based on a nominal value and conditions that are specified when the contract is closed. Swaps help to realize a comparative advantage.

Since only payment streams are exchanged in a swap (see Figure 8.5) in most cases, the creditworthiness of the parties involved must be considered, because it constitutes part of the risk (counterparty risk).

Figure 8.5: Swap

---

[7] See Rieger, Marc Oliver: Optionen, Derivate und strukturierte Produkte, Stuttgart 2009, p. 44.

Derivatives that are not exchange traded

Four basic types[8] of swaps can be distinguished:

- Interest rate swaps
- Currency swaps
- Equity index swaps
- Commodity swaps

8.1.4.1 What are the terms of a swap?

The following terms of the swap need to be defined in advance:

- Term to maturity
- Starting date
- Nominal value
- Fixed payer/fixed receiver
- Swap rate
- Reference rate
- Payment frequency
- Interest rate convention
- Short/long first and last stubs

8.1.4.2 Types of swaps and their setup

The exchange of payment streams in a swap can take the following forms, independent of the type of swap.

From	To
Fixed	Fixed
Fixed	Variable
Variable	Variable

Example of a swap:

A swap is independent of any underlying transaction but can be used to hedge other payment streams, such as liabilities from a loan. It enables the "payer" to fix interest rates or to pass along interest rate risk.

---

[8] Other asset classes are possible, but less frequently used.

Figure 8.6: Example of a swap

In the example presented in Figure 8.6, the investor is exchanging the risk of fixed interest rates against a variable risk in the form of the 3-month CHF-Libor[9]. He generates a profit if the fixed rate, which he receives, exceeds the variable rate, which he is required to pay. Otherwise, he is suffering a loss. The investor is thus betting that the variable interest rate does not move higher and exceed the upper interest rate boundary of 5 percent. He can use such a position for example to hedge a loan (guarantee a certain interest rate) and add it to the underlying transaction (loan contract).

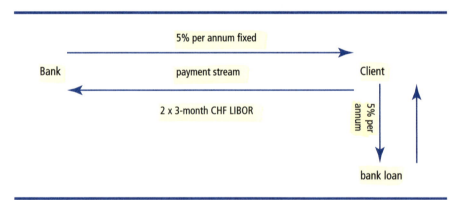

Figure 8.7: Swap example with a loan as underlying transaction

8.1.4.2.1 Interest rate swap

In the case of an interest rate swap, the parties agree on the exchange of interest payments, which are made on a specified nominal value. For example, variable interest rate payments can be exchanged for fixed interest rate payments. If the

---

[9] London Interbank Offered Rate on the basis of CHF.

client pays the fixed rate, this swap is called a **payer swap**. If, instead, the client receives the fixed rate, it is called a **receiver swap** (see Figure 8.8). A basis swap involves the exchange of two variable rates. As measured by trading volume (approximately EUR 50 trillion[10]), the swap market is larger than the bond market. This magnitude clarifies the relevance of these instruments for hedging and speculation.

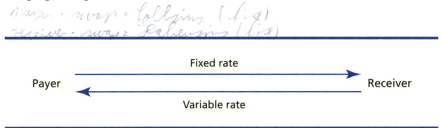

Figure 8.8: Payer and receiver in a swap

Put simply, an interest rate swap is the equivalent of the exchange of a bond with a fixed coupon for a bond with a variable coupon (floater). In an interest rate swap, however, the principal is not exchanged, and interest payments are netted. At the beginning of the transaction, the value of the interest rate swap is zero; otherwise a compensation payment by one party would be required. The payer either assumes that interest rates are rising faster than expected by the markets or that the decline is slower than anticipated. Based on this reasoning, he pays the fixed rate. His counterpart is the receiver. If the market expectation of the payer materializes, he is making a profit; otherwise he is suffering a loss, which is the profit of the receiver. A swap, just like other derivatives, is a typical zero sum game.

8.1.4.2.2 Constant Maturity Swap (CMS)

In a Constant Maturity Swap (CMS), also called a **yield curve swap,** a capital market interest rate (for example the ten year swap rate) is exchanged for another rate (mostly a money market rate) (see Figure 8.9). Two things are noteworthy about this instrument. First, the CMS swap rate is newly determined for every fixing and is equal to the swap rate on a specific maturity. Therefore the CMS rate is a floating rate. Second, the market risk (interest rate risk) is much larger than that of a "plain vanilla" interest rate swap. If, for example, an investor enters into a CMS with a maturity of ten years and

---

[10] Source: ISDA.

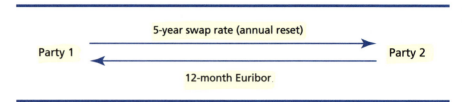

Figure 8.9: Swap, fixed versus variable rate

the ten-year swap rate as CMS rate, his interest rate risk extends over the zero coupon rates of the next twenty years, even though the swap only has a maturity of ten years. Since a CMS reacts very strongly to changes in the term structure of interest rates, it can be used to benefit from such changes. The interest payments are adjusted in line with the contract specifications (in most cases quarterly, semi-annually or annually).

8.1.4.2.3 Currency swap

In a currency swap, the exchange of two different currencies is agreed. The differences in the currency values at the payment dates as well as the nominal values at the beginning and the end of the transaction are normally exchanged.

8.1.4.2.4 Equity index swap

The exchange is tied to the development of two index values. The exchange of payments is determined by the changes in the index values.

8.1.4.2.5 Forward swap

The forward swap is a variation of the "standard swap." Unlike the standard swap, it does not commence immediately, but rather after a lead period (start date). At the starting date, the forward swap is binding, regardless of the level of interest rates at that moment.

The interest rate of the forward swap is a forward rate, which is calculated from spot rates. No exchange of interest payments takes places prior to the start date. This assures the separation in time of the liquidity agreement and the interest rate component. The regular exchange of interest payments begins on the agreed date in the future at the rate already agreed (forward swap rate). As an example, the investor might receive the money market rate (to cover a variable rate loan) from the bank and make payments at the forward swap rate.

In this case, the basic intention of the investor is to lock in the current interest rate level to finance specific projects in the future. The investor expects rates to increase and thus fixes them already today with the help of a forward swap rate.

8.1.4.2.6 Commodity swap

In a commodity swap, the exchange of payments depends on the development of commodity prices. No physical exchange is required; it is also possible to simply make cash payments in line with relative price changes.

Example for a commodity swap on diesel fuel
Starting situation for the investor
A company regularly requires large quantities of diesel fuel. Changes in the purchase price for diesel fuel can be traced predominantly to changes in the price of the commodity itself. The investor wants to hedge against increases in the price of diesel fuel, since he expects a continuous increase in prices. This will provide him with a fixed cost base. In addition, the hedge needs to be in euro, the investor's domestic currency, which he uses in most of his business transactions. No liquidity should be tied up in the hedging transaction.

Entering into a diesel fuel swap
The investor enters into a diesel fuel swap in line with his basic intention and demand (see Figure 8.10).

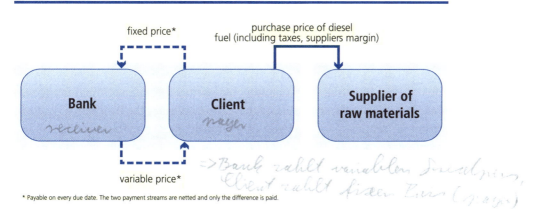

* Payable on every due date. The two payment streams are netted and only the difference is paid.

Figure 8.10: Payment streams of the diesel fuel swap[11]

---

[11] Source: Commerzbank AG.

Functioning of the diesel fuel swap

- The periodic exchange of payments takes place in EUR and is based on a notional amount of diesel fuel (in metric tons) per period.
- For each period, the investor pays the fixed amount on each due date, while the bank pays the variable amount.
- The fixed amount/variable amount is calculated by multiplying the agreed amount of diesel fuel with the fixed price/variable price.
- The fixed price is agreed when entering into the derivatives transaction.
- The variable price is determined by the bank each period and depends on the current price of the underlying.
- If it is agreed to use more than one price for the fixing of the variable price, the arithmetic mean of all the relevant prices of the underlying is used.
- The USD price which is determined at a specific date is translated into EUR on the basis of the current EUR/USD exchange rate.

The diesel fuel swap thus protects the investor against rising fuel prices. He can plan and is not dependent on physical delivery. The separation of the currency derivative from the physical delivery increases his flexibility. Both components can be dealt with separately. However, the hedge is for the underlying only. If, for example, increases in taxes drive product prices, the hedge does not protect the investor.

8.1.4.3 Swap trading

Trading existing swaps enables banks, for example, to pass on certain risks. Swaps are continually valued in line with market developments. If a client wants to close out a swap position (offsetting transaction), he needs to pay the market price.

Theoretically and in a perfect market, the value of a receiver swap is always equal to the value of a fixed coupon bond minus the value of the floating rate note. Put differently, the value of the swap expresses the difference between the net present value of the fixed coupon instrument and the variable coupon instrument at t = 0. The value of the payer swap is the mirror image of the value of the receiver swap.

8.1.4.4 Valuation of swaps

Replication methods are used for the valuation of swaps[12]. For both sides of the swaps, a bond with the corresponding payment stream is analyzed. An interest rate swap, for example, can be valued using a bond with a fixed coupon and a bond with a variable coupon. A credit default swap can be valued with the help of a default free bond and a bond with default risk.

Normally, the principal is not exchanged at the beginning and end of the investment period. In an ordinary swap, both instruments have the same nominal value and the same market value initially. The payment obligations of both parties must be equivalent in order to assure that the market value is identical initially.

8.1.4.5 Swaps with variable interest rates

The variable interest rates used for swaps are mostly based on the reference rates of Euribor and Libor[13]. Payment conditions can be set in line with the wishes of the investors. In practice, payments are not only due once a year, but can also be paid on a semi-annual or quarterly schedule. The contract parties are free to set this schedule without restrictions. In practice, payments are often made in line with the reference rate; for example quarterly in the case of the 3-month LIBOR.

Market expectation	Realization	Payer	Receiver
Interest rates will increase ...	... increase is quicker or more pronounced than anticipated	Wins	Loses
	... increase is slower or less pronounced than anticipated	Loses	Wins
Interest rates will decline ...	... decrease is quicker or more pronounced than anticipated	Loses	Wins
	.... increase is slower or less pronounced than anticipated	Wins	Loses

---

[12] This refers to the synthetic construction of portfolios (replication or duplication), which generate the same cash flows as the investment to be valued. See chapter 2.4.3 on this issue.
[13] For euro or the foreign currencies from the perspective of a euro investor.

8.1.4.6 Uses of swaps

Typically, swaps are tied to an underlying transaction and serve as a hedge or as speculation to obtain an additional profit margin.

The following motives usually prevail:

- Hedging of interest rates
- Credit management
- Balance sheet adjustments
- Currency and interest rate hedges
- Speculation on differences
- Financing opportunities
- Utilization of global currency and interest rate differences
- Locking in profits
- Utilization of supplier loans while eliminating currency risk
- Diversification of bond portfolios and hedging against currency fluctuations

Before entering into a swap transaction, a solid assessment of the market must be conducted. It is the basis for a successful conclusion of the transaction.

8.1.4.7 Examples of swaps

A large number of classic and exotic swaps exist. Exotic swaps are significantly more complex in most cases and are therefore used only by major investors.

8.1.4.7.1 Inflation swaps

Inflation is always an important topic when hedging payment streams. Inflation swaps can provide a solid calculation basis for underlying transactions.

An inflation swap can be either an **inflation payer swap** or an **inflation receiver swap**. Depending on inflation expectations, the investor needs to choose the appropriate instrument.

8.1.4.7.1.1 Inflation payer swap

An inflation payer swap serves to protect payments received against fluctuations in inflation. An example is the future payment stream received from a solar power plant.

With the swap, the investor exchanges the payments received, which depend on inflation, for fixed interest rate payments. He obtains a fixed calculation basis for future cash flows. He is protected against declines in inflation, but does not benefit from increases.

8.1.4.7.1.1.1 How does the inflation payer swap work?

In an inflation payer swap, the investor receives a fixed interest payment from the bank at predetermined payment dates. He makes a variable payment in exchange, which depends on the actual inflation rate.

If the actual inflation rate is below the agreed fixed rate, the investor receives net payments from the counterparty. If actual inflation exceeds the agreed fixed rate, the investor is required to make net payments to the counterparty. In order to guarantee the best possible hedge against inflation risks from the underlying transaction, the reference inflation rate as well as payment and determination dates should be aligned as closely as possible between the underlying transaction and the inflation payer swap (see Figure 8.11).

In an inflation payer swap, the following parameters are usually determined:

- Term to maturity
- Nominal value
- Reference index for the calculation of the relevant inflation rate (for example Eurostat HICP excluding tobacco)
- Dates on which the reference rate is fixed (usually the index values 15 and 3 months prior to the date on which the values are determined)
- Fixed interest rate
- Payment dates
- Interest rate conventions

8.1.4.7.1.1.2 Payment streams of the inflation payer swap

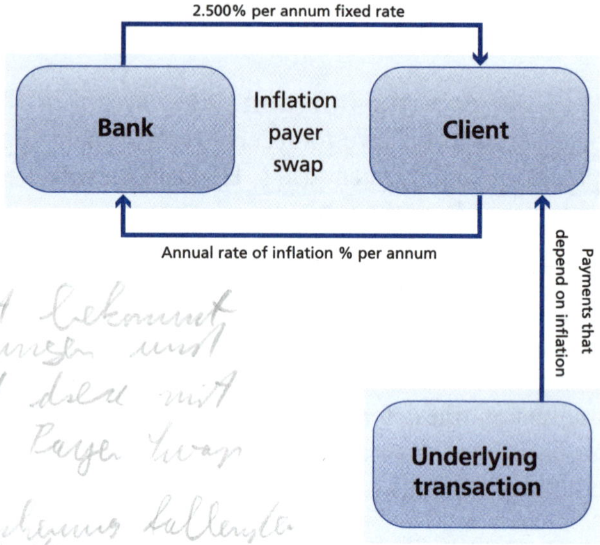

Figure 8.11: Payment streams inflation payer swap[14]

8.1.4.7.1.2 Inflation receiver swap

An inflation receiver swap serves to hedge future payments that must be made in an underlying transaction against changes in inflation.

With the inflation receiver swap, the investor exchanges payment obligations that are subject to changes in inflation against a fixed interest payment. He is thus independent of future developments in inflation and can make known payments in the future. An inflation receiver swap thus protects against increases in inflation but does not allow participation in declining or low rates of inflation.

8.1.4.7.1.2.1 How does the inflation receiver swap work?

In an inflation receiver swap, an investor pays the predetermined fixed interest rate on the agreed payment dates to the bank. In exchange, he receives a variable interest payment, which depends on the measured inflation rate. If the inflation rate on the relevant date is above the agreed fixed rate, the investor receives net payments from the inflation receiver swap.

---

[14] From the perspective of the bank. Payer here = Bank = Bank pays the fixed rate. Source: Commerzbank AG.

Derivatives that are not exchange traded

If the inflation rate is below the agreed fixed rate on the relevant date, the investor is required to make net interest payments to the counterparty in the inflation receiver swap.

In order to guarantee the best possible hedge against inflation risks from the underlying transaction, the reference inflation rate as well as payment and determination dates should be aligned as closely as possible between the underlying transaction and the inflation receiver swap.

In an inflation receiver swap, the following parameters are usually determined:

- Term to maturity
- Nominal value
- Reference index for the calculation of the relevant inflation rate
- Dates on which the reference rate is fixed
- Fixed interest rate
- Payment dates
- Interest rate conventions

8.1.4.7.1.2.2 Payment streams of the inflation receiver swap

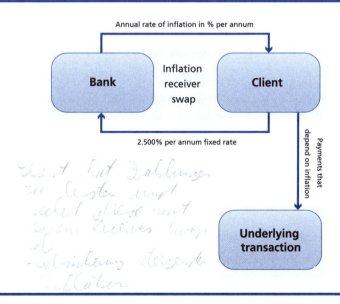

Figure 8.12: Payment streams inflation receiver swap[15]

---

[15] Receiver here = Bank perspective = Bank receives fixed rate of interest. Source: Commerzbank AG.

What is inflation?

Inflation is the broad based increase in prices, which in most cases is related to prior increases in the money supply. Statistical agencies such as Eurostat measure inflation and publish inflation indexes. In the following we will explain the HICP ex tobacco.

HICPexT = Harmonised Index of Consumer Prices excluding Tobacco
The HICP is a consumer price index that measures the price development of services and goods. It is based on a representative basket of goods and services offered domestically (in this case in the European Union) to private households. The HICP is calculated by Eurostat, the statistical office of the European Commission, in a harmonized fashion. It is called harmonized because the same rules and identical baskets of goods are used in all the European member countries when determining the index. Deviations from national indexes (for example the German inflation index) are therefore possible. The HICPexT includes all goods and services excluding tobacco products. It is considered to be the standard instrument for use in financial contracts on European inflation. The HICPexT is published monthly by Eurostat.

Computation:
In order to determine the inflation payment in the swap, the inflation rate published three months ago is usually used (3 months gap). The first published value is used and later revisions are not considered.

8.1.4.7.2 Express swap EUR/TRY

Initial situation:
- The investor holds a loan denominated in euro.
- The investor expects at most a modest appreciation of the EUR/TRY exchange rate.
- The investor intends to optimize his loan portfolio (Euro financing).

Aims of the investor:
- He wants to reduce the interest charge on his EUR loan.
- Should his market expectation fail to materialize, he is willing to make additional interest payments as a result of the swap.
- He is aware of the fact that the loss potential is theoretically unlimited.
- All payments are denominated in euro.

Setup of the swap:
- At the end of the maturity, the swap investor makes an interest payment which is related to the EUR/TRY exchange rate.

- The counterparty (bank) makes interest payments which depend on the EUR/TRY exchange rate.

Perspective of the investor:

- The investor receives a one-time payment of the following interest rates:
- 5.00% / 10.00% / 15.00% / 20.00% / 25.00% / 30.00% of the nominal value if the EUR/TRY exchange rate is below or at the strike price of 2.4000 TRY/EUR.
- Once a payment has been made, the swap is terminated.
- In exchange, he pays 0.00% of the nominal value.
- If the EUR/TRY exchange rate is quoted at or below the strike price of 2.4000 on the payment date, he receives a payment from the swap.
- However: if the EUR/TRY exchange rate is above the agreed strike price on the payment day (for example after 6, 12, 18, 24, 30 and 36 months), he does not receive a payment and the swap continues to exist.
- If the EUR/TRY exchange rate continues to be quoted above the strike price of 2.4000, he is required to make a payment based on the following formula:
nominal value × (EUR/TRY exchange rate at the maturity date − 2.4000)/ 2.4000.
- He is thus required to make a swap payment if the EUR/TRY exchange rate is quoted above 2.4000 on all payment dates.
- In the case of a EUR/TRY exchange rate that is quoted above the strike price, the interest rate risk is theoretically unlimited.

Figure 8.13 once again summarizes the entire swap transaction.

Exchange of payments

As we can see from the above example, it is crucial to arrive at an adequate assessment of the current and future development of the exchange rate. The historical development of the EUR/TRY exchange rate is displayed in Figure 8.14. However, for the valuation and therefore the structuring of the derivative, we need to look into the future and not the past. What matters is the coming development of the EUR/TRY exchange rate. The above structure is a typical case of increasing EUR/TRY forwards in the market. To expect a profit from this transaction, investors must think that the forwards are increasing less quickly or are even declining. From an economic perspective, the riskiness of the transaction is best expressed by the forward rates[16] at the time of closing.

---

[16] Including implied EUR/TRY volatilities.

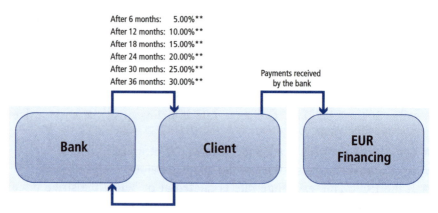

Figure 8.13: EUR/TRY swap[17]

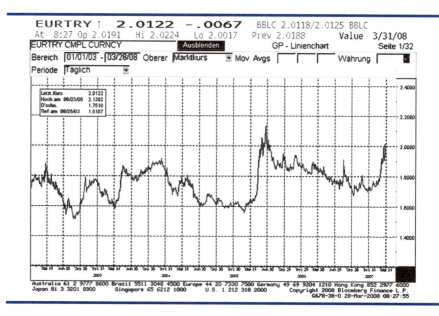

Figure 8.14: EUR/TRY exchange rate[18]

---

[17] Source: Commerzbank AG ICLM.
[18] Source: Bloomberg.

Derivatives that are not exchange traded

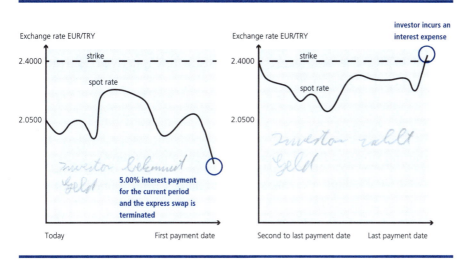

Figure 8.15: Possible interest payments[19]

Exchange rate analysis

Before such a swap transaction is conducted, an exchange rate analysis including stress tests is always required (see Figure 8.15). Currencies in particular can be subject to massive fluctuations that are hard to interpret at times.

In order to make the above chart more concrete, we also provide figures on possible exchange rate developments.

We use a nominal value of the swap of EUR 1 million.

Strike EUR/TRY:	2.4000				
Nominal in EUR:	1,000,000				
Investor receives % of nominal value:	30.00				
Payment[20] (formula)	National × ((EUR/TRY exchange rate − strike)/strike)				
Scenario	1	2	3	4	5
EUR/TRY exchange rate:	2.0000	2.3900	2.4000	2.5000	2.9000
Investor receives % of nominal value:	30.00	30.00	30.00	0.00	0.00
Investor pays % of nominal value:	0.00	0.00	0.00	4.17	20.83
Advantage/disadvantage in %	30.00	30.00	30.00	−4.17	−20.83
Sum in EUR	300,000	300,000	300,000	−41,667	−208,333

---

[19] Source: Commerzbank AG ICLM.
[20] Assuming that the EUR/TRY exchange rate was not quoted below/exactly at 2.4000 on the payment date of previous periods.

The above example nicely demonstrates the interest rate advantage which the investor gets for exchange rates below 2.40 EUR/TRY, but it also makes clear that an additional interest charge must be paid at exchange rates above 2.40 EUR/TRY. The term "express" for this structure is derived from the path dependency of the payments.

8.1.4.7.3 Second chance swap

The starting situation for this type of exotic swap is as follows:

- The investor intends to reduce interest charges from a number of loans denominated in euro.
- He wants to profit from his assessment that the 12 month Euribor will move within a predefined corridor until the maturity date of the product.
- In a worst case scenario, he is willing to make additional interest payments.

Structure of a second chance swap

- The investor pays either a best chance, second chance or worst case interest rate. Whether the 12 month Euribor is quoted inside or outside a predetermined corridor determines which of these rates must be paid.
- The counterparty (bank) pays a fixed interest rate over the entire life of the swap.

Functioning

- The investor receives a fixed payment on all payment dates.
- In exchange, he is required to pay the "best case" interest rate of 3.20% p.a. if the reference interest rate (for example 12 month Euribor) stayed within the agreed corridor I (see Figure 8.16) on all bank working days during the interest rate period.
- If the reference interest rate was quoted outside corridor I for at least one day during the interest rate period, but inside corridor II (see Figure 8.17), he pays the "second chance" interest rate of 3.70 % p.a.
- If the reference interest rate was quoted outside corridor II for at least one day during the interest rate period, he pays the "worst case" interest rate of 6.70 % p.a.

He thus benefits from the swap during an interest rate period if the 12 month Euribor never breaches the boundaries of the corridor in either direction.

---

[21] Source: Commerzbank AG ICLM.

Derivatives that are not exchange traded

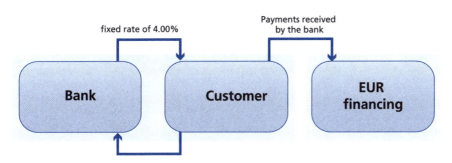

- "Best case" interest rate of 3.20% p.a. if the reference interest rate has stayed within corridor I (3.60% -5.00%) on every day of the interest rate period
- "Second chance" interest rate of 3.70% p.a. if the reference interest rate has moved outside of corridor I at least for one day of the interest rate period, but has stayed within corridor II (3.10% -5.00%) on every day
- "Worst case" interest rate of 6.70% p.a. if the reference interest rate has moved outside of corridor II at least for one day of the interest rate period

Figure 8.16: Swap including reference rate and corridors[21]

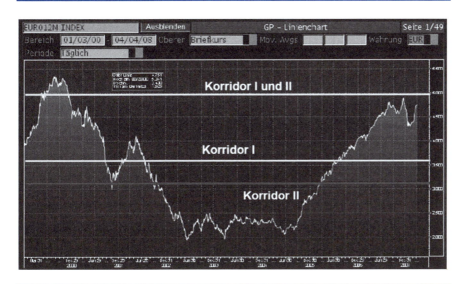

Figure 8.17: 12 month Euribor from 2000 to 2008 including corridors[22]

---

[22] Source: Bloomberg.

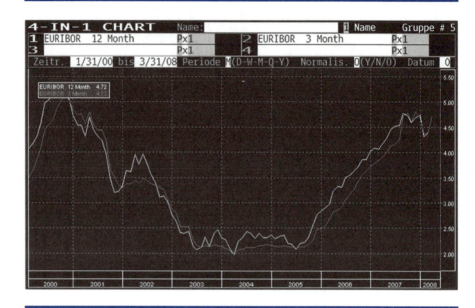

Figure 8.18: 3 and 12 month Euribor[23]

Payment streams of the swaps

Scenario analysis

Best Case*:	3.20	Nominal:		2,500,000	
Second Chance*:	3.70	12-M-EURIBOR*:		4.75	
Worst Case*:	6.70	3-M-EURIBOR*:		4.74	
Corridor I in %:	3.60	5.00			
Corridor II in %:	3.10	5.00	* in % p.a.		
	3.10	5.00			
12-M-EURIBOR*	5.15	4.85	3.75	3.50	3.00
You receive*	4.00	4.00	4.00	4.00	4.00
Investor pays per payment date	6.70	3.20	3.20	3.70	6.70
Advantage/ disadvantage*	−2.70	0.80	0.80	0.30	−2.70
In EUR per fixing	−16,875	5,000	5,000	1,875	−16,875

---

[23] Source: Bloomberg.

8.1.4.7.4 Callable range accrual swap

In an accrual swap, interest payments for one party are due only if the variable reference interest rate is quoted inside a certain range. This range remains constant during the entire life of the swap or is adjusted in regular intervals.

A callable swap can be terminated by one of the parties. In our example, only the bank has the right to terminate the swap.

Starting situation for the investor in our example:

- He wants to optimize interest payments on his loan portfolio.
- He is willing to accept limited risks as a consequence.
- He is of the opinion that the 10 year swap rate will not change too much over the next three years.

Structure of a callable range accrual swap

The investor makes payments at a fixed rate. On the days during which the reference interest rate is within a certain range, the bank (counterparty) pays a higher fixed interest rate. The bank has the right to terminate the agreement (after 3 months, quarterly) (see Figure 8.19).

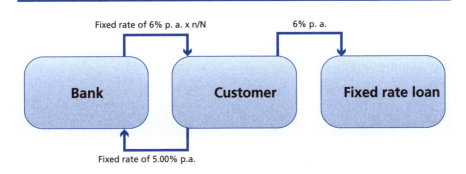

Range: 3.50% p.a. – 5.15% p.a.
Current 10-year swap rate: 4.43% p.a.
n = number of days during which the 10-year swap rate is within the range
N = total number of days of the transaction
The bank has a unilateral termination right, for the first time after three months

Figure 8.19: Payment streams of the swap transaction[24]

---

[24] Source: Commerzbank AG ICLM.

Payment streams of the swap

Scenario analysis

Number of days within the range or on the boundary	360	180	60
Reference rate of the range	10 year swap rate		
Underlying transaction ./. Fixed rate (% p.a.)	6.00%	6.00%	6.00%
Investor pays fixed rate (% p.a)	5.00%	5.00%	5.00%
Variable rate of the bank, depending on the number of days inside the range (6.00% p.a. × n/N)	6.00%	3.00%	1.00%
Rate of the investor including the underlying transaction	5.00%	8.00%	10.00%

Chances:

- Maximum interest rate provides basis for planning.
- Strong participation in sideways movement of the reference interest rate.
- Great flexibility thanks to the separation of liquidity and interest rate derivative.
- If closed prematurely, a profit may result.
- Possibility to reduce interest payments.

Risks:

- Possibility of higher interest costs.
- Bank can terminate every quarter after three months.
- If the underlying loan ceases to exist, the swap will not be terminated automatically.
- If closed prematurely, a loss may result.

8.1.4.7.5 FX linked knockout swap

An FX linked knockout swap provides investors with the opportunity to optimize their cash flow.

The investor bases his considerations on the following starting scenario:

- He expects that the US dollar moves sideways or weakens (euro appreciates) and will continue to be quoted above 1.40 with regard to the euro.
- The investor wants to optimize his investment portfolio.

Structure of the swap

The investor makes payments which depend on the exchange rate between USD and EUR. In a "best case," this interest rate is 0% p.a.

The bank (counterparty) pays a fixed interest rate of 1% p.a.

Detailed functioning

- The investor receives 1.0% p.a.
- In exchange, he makes a payment which depends on the EUR/USD exchange rate.
- The following is agreed: if the EUR/USD exchange rate is quoted above the agreed strike price (1.36 EUR/USD), he does not pay a premium and receives the "best case," a return of 1.0% p.a. from the swap (see Figure 8.20).
- If the upper knockout barrier (1.50 EUR/USD) is reached or exceeded during the knockout period, this "best case" is valid for the entire term to maturity of the swap.
- If the EUR/USD exchange rate is quoted between the strike price of 1.3600 and the break even of 1.3465 (break even) he still makes a profit from the swap.
- If the EUR/USD exchange rate does not breach the knockout barrier and is quoted below the breakeven rate on the payment dates, a loss results for the investor.

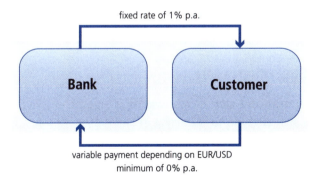

Figure 8.20: The swap parameters[25]

---

[25] Source: Commerzbank AG.

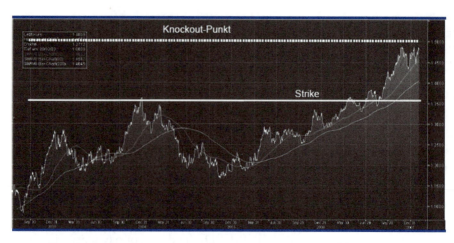

Figure 8.21: Analysis of the historical exchange rate development[26]

The payment streams of this swap can be seen in Figure 8.20[27].

Scenario analysis

Strike rate:	1.3600
Knockout limit:	1.5000
Bank pays:	1.00% p.a.
Bank receives:	((1.3600 − EUR/USD)/EUR/USD); min.0% p.a.

EUR/USD exchange rate:	1.1000	1.3000	1.3465	1.3700	1.6000
Investor pays	23.64%	4.62%	1.00%	0.00%	0.00%
Investor receives fixed rate	1.00%	1.00%	1.00%	1.00%	1.00%
Advantage/disadvantage	−22.64%	−3.62%	0.00%	1.00%	1.00%

8.1.4.7.6 Step down swap

The starting point for a step down swap is a significant decline in market interest rates which leads to attractive financing conditions. The financial market outlook is unclear and therefore investors are looking for ways to reduce planning uncertainties. At the same time, chances to participate in further market declines are to be maintained.

---

[26] Source: Bloomberg.
[27] Source: Commerzbank AG ICLM.

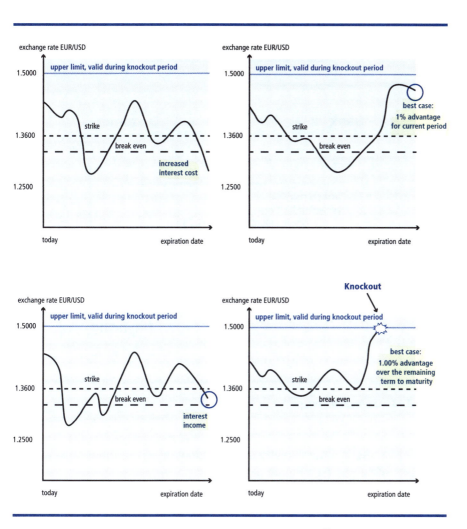

Figure 8.22: Graphical scenario analysis of the swap over time[28]

Functioning of a step down swap

In a step down swap, both contract parties agree to make regular interest payments. The bank regularly pays the current 3 month Euribor to the counterparty. The client, meanwhile, pays the step down swap rate to the bank.

The interest rate to be paid is locked in at **2.50% p.a.** in the first year. For the coming years, it increases to **3.85% p.a.** if the 3 month Euribor is quoted above 2.75% p.a. But if the 3 month Euribor should continue to decline,

[28] Source: Commerzbank ICLM.

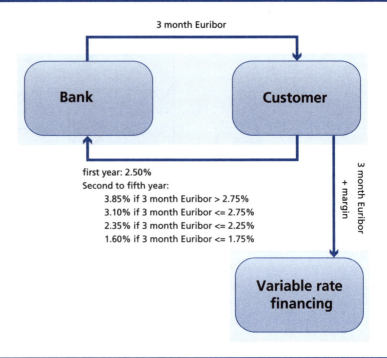

Figure 8.23: Step down swap[29]

the interest rate is automatically adjusted downwards in three steps until it reaches **1.60% p.a.** (see Figure 8.23):

3 month Euribor $>$ 2.75% p.a. = 3.85% p.a.
3 month Euribor $\leq$ 2.75% p.a. = 3.10% p.a.
3 month Euribor $\leq$ 2.25% p.a. = 2.35% p.a.
3 month Euribor $\leq$ 1.75% p.a. = 1.60% p.a.

Scenario analysis

In the above example, the interest cost amounts to 1.60% p.a. in a best case scenario or to 3.80% p.a. in a worst case scenario. The swap investor can thus protect himself against rising interest rates, or at least limit them to the worst case scenario of 3.80% p.a. If money market rates continue to decline, the investor also continues to participate due to the step-wise adjustment of interest rate payments. There is a risk that money market rates decline below

---

[29] Source: Commerzbank AG.

Table 8.3: Scenario analysis[30]

2 month Euribor (in % p.a.)	1.70%	current (1.88%)	3.00%
Underlying transaction ./. variable rate on the loan*	1.70%	1.86%	3.00%
Swap + variable rate (reference rate)	1.70%	1.88%	3.00%
./. step down swap rate	1.60%	2.35%	3.85%
interest rate charge	1.60%	2.35%	3.85%

* Not considering the loan margin of the bank providing the financing. Depending on the specifics of the underlying contract, this margin can change during the life of the swap and thus lead to changes in overall interest charges.

the lowest step down rate. In this case, his interest costs will no longer decline (see Table 8.3).

8.1.4.8 Swap confirmation

A confirmation is a legally binding agreement which underlies a swap transaction. The signature of both contract parties is required. **International Swaps and Derivatives Association** (ISDA) in New York has simplified the writing of these confirmations by developing a number of master agreements, which normally contain all relevant data. What needs to be established are general guidelines and standards for the documentation of an OTC transaction, but not specifics, for example with regard to the structure. This serves to increase efficiency in post-trade clearing and handling of OTC transactions. The following is an example of a typical swap confirmation:

Closing date	May 2, 2009
Effective date	May 5, 2009
Business day convention	Next business day
Holiday calendar	US
End date	May 5, 2010
Swap payer	Sample Company, Sampletown
Nominal value for the fixed interest rate	1,000,000 EUR in words: one million euro
Fixed interest rate	5.000% p.a.
Fixed rate day count convention	actual / 365

[30] Source: Commerzbank.

Payment dates[31]	March 5, September 5, starting on September 5, 2009
Payer variable interest rate	XY Bank AG, Frankfurt
Variable interest rate	6 month USD Libor
Day count convention for the variable interest rate	actual / 360

8.1.5 What are swaptions and interest rate guarantees?

8.1.5.1 Swaptions

A swaption (swap option) is an options contract on a swap. Against the payment of a premium, the buyer acquires the right, but not the obligation to enter into a predetermined swap transaction with the seller (see Figure 8.24). The conditions are already determined when entering into the swaption. Thanks to the options structure, a swaption includes an asymmetric risk profile, which is known from our previous treatment of options, namely the right of the buyer to choose during a limited time period and the obligation of the buyer to make a premium payment to the seller in exchange for the asymmetric risk profile.

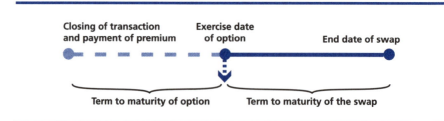

Figure 8.24: Timeline of a swaption

The option thus enables investors to secure access to a swap ahead of time. This kind of transaction is used in case a definite underlying transaction does not yet exist, but is likely to materialize, and there is a fear that the terms of the swap could worsen. In this case the long is willing to pay a premium to

---

[31] If one of the dates is a Sunday or holiday, the next bank working day is considered to be the settlement date.

the short. If the long does not exercise the option, he suffers a loss equal to the option premium (see plain vanilla options on this point). The writer of the option (short) collects the premium and is thus obliged to take the other side in the swap contract (see Table 8.5).

Table 8.5: The two positions in a swaption

Position	Counter position
Long payer swaption (similar to a long call)	Short payer swaption
Short payer Swaption (similar to a short call)	Long payer swaption
Long receiver swaption (similar to a long put)	Short receiver swaption
Short receiver swaption (similar to a short put)	Long receiver swaption

Concerning the exercise of swaptions, three possibilities exist:

- **American:** exercise is possible on any date during the term to maturity.
- **European:** exercise is possible only at expiration.
- **Bermuda:** exercise is possible during a predetermined period or on pre-specified points in time.

Especially for structured products, swaptions play a key role. They are first of all suitable as building blocks that can be used to adjust the entire risk profile of a product. Especially termination rights or rights to extend contracts are modeled using swaptions. This makes it possible to generate additional "pick-up" (additional value for the investor)[32]. In addition, swaptions make the active management of **delta and gamma risks** (convexity) possible, for example of a portfolio or trading book.

8.1.5.2 Receiver or payer swaption

In a **receiver** or **call swaption**, the buyer has the right to receive the fixed interest rate in the swap (once the swaption has been exercised). In a **payer swaption** or **put swaption**, the buyer of the swaption will receive the variable payment and make fixed interest rate payments once the swaption has been exercised (see Table 8.6).

---

[32] Usually this also entails an increase of risk or investment costs.

Table 8.6: Swaption and the swap position that exists once the option is exercised

Swaption	Following exercise of the swap
Receiver swaption	Buyer of the option receives the fixed rate and pays the variable rate
Payer swaption	Buyer of the option receives the variable rate and pays the fixed rate

8.1.5.3 Valuation of swaptions

The valuation of swaptions relies on the Black76 model for swaptions. In principle, a receiver swaption can be considered a put and a payer swaption a call on a swap rate.

$$\text{Payer} = K \cdot S \cdot [FR \cdot N(d_1) - X \cdot N(d_2)]$$

$$\text{Receiver} = K \cdot S \cdot [FR \cdot N(-d_2) - X \cdot N(-d_1)]$$

where

$$S = \frac{1}{m} \sum_{i=1}^{mn} Z(0, t)$$

$$d_1 = \frac{\ln\left(\frac{FWP}{X}\right) + \frac{\sigma^2 \cdot T}{2}}{\sigma \sqrt{T}}$$

$$d_2 = d_1 - \sigma \sqrt{T}$$

K = Contract volume
S = Discount factor for the sums
FR = Forward rate
m = Periodicity of the payment
n = Term to maturity of the swaption
Z = Swap payments
T = Term to maturity of the option
X = Strike for the swap rate
σ = Volatility

Table 8.7 once again summarizes expectations and contract specifications of the two swaptions.

Table 8.7: Attributes of swaptions

	Buyer payer swaption	Seller payer swaption
Agreement	Right, but not the obligation to enter into the predefined swap and to pay a fixed interest rate	
Interest rate expectation	Increasing interest rates	Declining or constant interest rates
Risk	Limited to the premium paid	Full market risk (unlimited)
Cash flows at closing	Pays swaption premium	Receives payment of swaption premium
Swap rate with same maturity above swap strike	Option is exercised	Must fulfill obligation from swaption and will receive fixed rate in the swap
Swap rate with same maturity below swap strike	Option is not exercised	No obligation

	Buyer receiver swaption	Seller receiver swaption
Agreement	Right, but not the obligation to enter into the predefined swap and to receive a fixed interest rate	
Interest rate expectation	Declining interest rates	Increasing or constant interest rates
Risk	Limited to the premium paid	Full market risk (unlimited)
Cash flows at closing	Pays swaption premium	Receives payment of swaption premium
Swap rate with same maturity above swap strike	Option is not exercised	No obligation
Swap rate with same maturity below swap strike	Option is exercised and will receive fixed rate in the swap	Must fulfill obligation from swaption and will pay fixed rate in the swap

8.1.5.4 Settlement of a swaption

Both physical settlement and cash settlement exist for swaptions. In the case of cash settlement, payment depends on the market value of the swap. In the case of physical settlement, the two parties enter into the swap (see Figure 8.25).

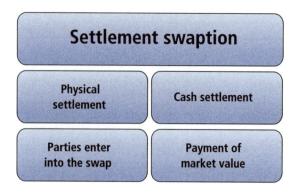

Figure 8.25: Possibilities for settling swaptions and their implications

8.1.6 What are exotic options?

Exotic options[33] are not exchange-traded, but individually agreed bilateral financial contracts. They are negotiated individually among the two contracting parties and are thus not standardized. This opens up the possibility for the two parties to include additional features in the contract specifications. In contrast to classical options, where the pattern of payoffs is determined mainly by the price of the underlying, things can be quite different in the case of exotic options – as an example, several strike prices can be involved (**rainbow option**).

Exotic options can either be call options (right to buy) or put options (right to sell). They are OTC options, which are not traded at derivatives exchanges, but instead are bilaterally agreed between different trading departments or other contract parties.

Exotic options are of particular importance for issuers of securitized derivatives: they are used when structuring certificates for both retail[34] and institutional investors[35]. The fast growing market for securitized derivatives implies

---

[33] The development of exotic options goes back to 1967, when the first down-and-out calls were traded. The term exotic options, meanwhile, is rather new and was introduced by Mark Rubinstein in his monograph "Exotic Options" in 1990. Previously, these products were referred to as boutique or designer options.

[34] Retail investors in this case include all private investors who are invested in securitized products.

[35] This is done in the context of financial engineering.

a rising demand for exotic derivatives. In most cases, structured products are constructed by combining a derivative (swap) with a zero coupon bond or with reference to a single derivative (swap). Zero bonds are used mostly for **products with a capital guarantee** and assure the repayment of the structured bond (or a structured certificate) at par. An additional value driver for the bond is the refinancing rate of the issuer. It depends both on the default risk of the issuer as well as on the interest rate level. This is called the **funding** of the bond, since the issuer has access to the liquidity (nominal value) until maturity. The funding can be used to finance embedded options and/or to accrue a minimum return. Examples of the often overlooked default risk of the issuer are the certificates of the insolvent investment bank Lehman Brothers, which recently were at the center of popular debate.

8.1.6.1 What kinds of exotic options do exist?

As already discussed, exotic options are characterized by individual features, the addition of option rights, variations of the option rights or exclusion of option rights. In the following we want to list the most frequently used types of exotic options and explain their functioning as well as the rights involved (see Figure 8.26).

There are numerous types of exotic options. Among them are path dependent options, time dependent options and correlation dependent options, but also multivariate[36] options. A distinction is also made between one time payments and specific payment patterns. Examples are **leveraged options**, which produce a multiple or an exponential value of the intrinsic value at expiration.

For the valuation of different types of options, a derivatives calculator is provided in the Download Area.

8.1.6.2 Types of exotic options

In the following, we present the most widespread exotic options with a stress on the option features most frequently used in financial engineering.

---

[36] Linked to a number of different underlying securities (for example rainbow options, basket options).

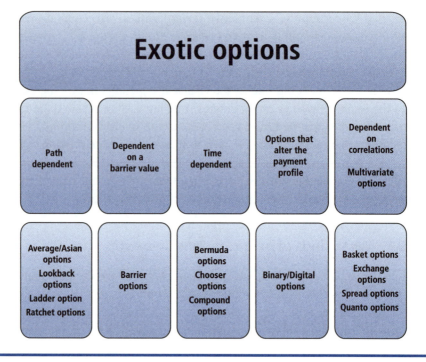

Figure 8.26: Exotic options

8.1.6.2.1 Barrier options

Barrier options come into existence or cease to exist if a barrier price is reached, touched, exceeded or undercut. Since this barrier can be above (up) or below (down) the current price of the underlying, there are eight possible types of barrier options. These options can be either European or American (see Table 8.8).

Table 8.8: Knock-in/-out options

Event	Activation (knock-in)	Expiry (knock-out)
Underlying up	Up-and-in call/put	Up-and-out call/put
Underlying down	Down-and-in call/put	Down-and-out call/ put

The intrinsic value of a barrier option is identical to that of a standard option, assuming that the option still exists or was activated. Principally, **knock-out** and **knock-in** options are less expensive than standard options and therefore

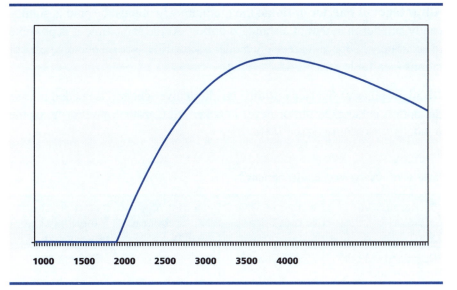

Figure 8.27: Example of the price development of a down-and-out put[37]

offer a higher profit potential (see Figure 8.27 as an example). These options were introduced in response to the large demand for inexpensive hedging instruments. It is an additional advantage that some barrier options have a money back element. It is also possible to define the barrier dynamically ("dynamic barrier option"). As an example, the knock-out or knock-in level can increase from EUR 100 in the first year to EUR 110 in the second year. If the knock-out level also has a time dimension, the product is called a "Parisian option." An example would be the requirement that the price be below the knock-out level for four weeks in a row. Such a feature is truly exotic, even for an exotic option.

Knock-out barrier: if the barrier is touched during the term to maturity of the option, the option immediately expires worthless.

Knock-in barrier: the option is initially not active, even though it was already paid. It is activated once the barrier is touched during the term to maturity. After that, the option reacts just like a standard option.

Reverse-knock option: with a reverse-knock option, a movement of the underlying makes it more likely that the barrier will be touched and at the same time the option gains in value. The barrier is always in the money for these types of options.

---

[37] Source: Commerzbank AG.

Advantages of barrier options: the premium which must be paid is significantly smaller than that of a standard option. At the same time it is possible to accurately hedge and precisely model a scenario based on personal expectations (see Table 8.9).

Disadvantages of barrier options: an alternative scenario is needed in case the option is knocked out or never knocked in. Constant monitoring of the option is thus required (see Table 8.9).

Table 8.9: Overview of Barrier options[38]

Barrier option	Trigger relative to spot price	Payoff profile if the trigger is reached	Payoff profile if the trigger is not reached
Down-and-out call (regular knock-out)	below	0	Standard call
Up-and-out call (reverse knock-out)	above	0	Standard call
Up-and-in call (reverse knock-out)	above	Standard call	0
Down-and-out put (reverse knock-out)	below	0	Standard put
Down-and-in put (reverse knock-in)	below	Standard put	0
Up-and-out put (regular knock-out)	above	0	Standard put
Up-and-in put (regular knock-in)	above	Standard put	0

8.1.6.2.2 Digital options

Digital options (sometimes also referred to as binary options) are characterized by the payment of a predetermined amount if the price of the underlying is above or below the strike price agreed. These contracts also exist both as European and American options. They are called digital, because in the digital system they can be either "0" (not exercised and no payment) or "1" (exercised and fixed payment). This type of option is generally used jointly with other options and generates a specific payoff pattern (see Figure 8.28).

---

[38] Source: DZ Bank.

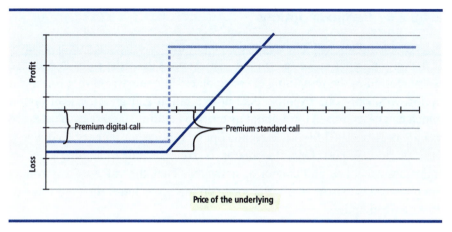

Figure 8.28: Digital versus standard call: payoff at maturity (long call)[39]

One-touch and **double-touch** as well as **no-touch** and **double-no-touch** options are normally held until the expiration date and paid back on the delivery date. **Instant-one-touch** and **Instant-double-touch** options are paid out immediately in the event of a hit.

European digital calls and **European digital puts** are special in the sense that the option trigger is relevant only on the expiration date. Meanwhile, a European digital option with a fixed payout can be valued like a leveraged long-short position in a plain vanilla call option (case of the digital call) or a plain vanilla put option (case of the digital put).

8.1.6.2.3 Range options

The price development of range options depends on the development of one or more underlying securities within predetermined boundaries.

The following distinctions can be made:

- Bottom up/top down
- Single range
- Dual range
- Knock-out range

---

[39] Source: DZ Bank.

8.1.6.2.4 Bermuda options

A Bermuda option can be exercised on a number of different exercise dates. If the option is not exercised on the first exercise date, the right to exercise is transferred to the remaining exercise dates. In comparison to a European option with only one exercise date at expiration and an American option which can be exercised throughout its term to maturity, the exercise dates are exactly pre-specified for the Bermuda option (always on January 15 of every year as an example). Once the option is exercised, all remaining exercise rights are cancelled and cannot be activated. Thus the value of a Bermuda option exceeds the value of a European option but is lower than the value of an American option.

8.1.6.2.5 Chooser options

Chooser options provide the owner of the option with the opportunity to choose whether the option should be a call or a put at a specified point in time. The price of a chooser option increases with increases in volatility, while the direction of the price movement of the underlying does not play a major role. Chooser options are well suited to implement volatility strategies. It is possible to profit from increases in volatility, without being too dependent on the price of the underlying.

Chooser options are basically more expensive than comparable calls or puts; however they are still cheaper than trading a combination (such as a straddle). The earlier the decision point, the cheaper the chooser option.

8.1.6.2.6 Compound options

Compound options are options on options. The option thus secures the right to another option (the right to obtain a right, see Figure 8.29). The advantage of compound options is the comparably low price relative to a normal option. The low price is justified by the fact that "only" a right to obtain a right, and not the right to obtain the underlying, is purchased.

8.1.6.2.7 Window options

As the name implies, a window is assigned with the help of a window option. Consequently, a trigger or price limit is not active during the entire term to maturity, but only during a predetermined window of opportunity. The window during which the option is active can be placed either at the beginning or the end and can be of differing duration.

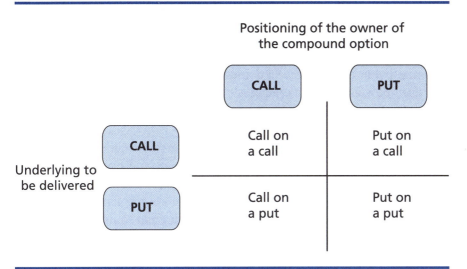

Figure 8.29: Compound options

8.1.6.2.8 Quanto options

Quanto options play an important role for banks, fund managers and issuers of certificates. The exchange rate risk in options on foreign indexes can be eliminated with the help of a quanto option[40]. The quanto option can be written, for example, on an index quoted in foreign currency, which will be translated into domestic currency at an exchange rate that is already set in advance. Thus the investor does not have any currency risk. Quanto products thus cover all payment streams in domestic currency (for example euro) even though the underlying is quoted in foreign currency (the Nikkei index, for example, is quoted in JPY).

With regard to equities and commodities, three different basic types of quanto options can be distinguished. There is the possibility to trade a call (or put) with a strike price in foreign currency while all payments are made in domestic currency. We assume an investment in the Dow Jones Index with a strike price of 9,000. If the index is quoted below the strike price at expiration, the option expires worthless. If the index is above the strike price, a gain in US dollars results, which is translated into domestic currency at the exchange rate which is in effect on that day and paid out in euro. In this case, payment depends

---

[40] Also called a cross-currency derivative.

on the development of the index in US dollar as well as on the exchange rate development.

In the second version, the strike price of the option is not quoted in foreign currency, but at the spot rate in domestic currency. In this version, the call may even be valuable if the index actually declined, since the foreign currency may have depreciated. In the third version, the strike price is quoted in foreign currency, but on the maturity date, it is translated into domestic currency at a predetermined rate. In addition, many variations of this idea are possible. One could think about an investor who purchases a call on equities/commodities and in addition a currency option, which is only triggered if the domestic currency appreciates. Quanto structures are also correlation instruments, since the relationship between currency and equity developments for example, or the relationship between two interest rates or term structures is a factor that determines the value of the options. For interest rate instruments, the standard instrument is a **quanto swap** or **index differential swap**. In the most basic version, two interest rates are exchanged for each other, for example 6M Euribor for 6M US Libor and all payments are made in euro. In this fundamental application, a EUR investor could tie his variable EUR loan to the development in the Yen money market in order to participate from comparably low interest rates. If this is done with the help of an index differential swap, no additional exchange rate risk arises.

8.1.6.2.9 Rainbow options

Rainbow options are classical multivariate options[41]. They are written not only on one underlying, but on several (at a minimum two). Thus price determination becomes significantly more complex, since not one, but several underlying securities and their volatilities influence prices. Rainbow options are used for example in "**best of**" or "**worst of**" products. The option payoff is determined by the best value (best of) or most negative value (worst of) in the basket.

The investor thus expects the performance of the underlying assets to develop differently. Strategically, these products can be constructed with standard options. In the case of two different shares, for example, it would be possible to acquire a call on share A and a put on share B. In the case of the two standard options, the payoff would be determined by the intrinsic value of the options.

---

[41] Multivariate options, also called correlation options, depend on several underlying securities.

In the case of an outperformance option, the buyer will only receive a payment if the relative price increase of share **A** is stronger than that of share **B**. As a consequence, however, the premium is also considerably lower and depends on the correlation of the underlying assets. The more synchronous the price movement, the lower is the probability of major performance differences. This means that the expected payoff is smaller and the difference in premium larger compared to the purchase of two standard options. The versions presented all make use of correlations as a factor to lower costs for purchasing the option. The buyer of these options fundamentally expects that the underlying securities will develop differently. Both the buyer and the seller are thus assuming a correlation position. The buyer of an outperformance option positions himself for a future correlation of the two underlying securities that is lower than the one which is currently priced into the contract. Valuation and hedging of these options is considerably more complex, as these options have more than one delta and show different price sensitivities with regard to each of the underlying securities. In addition to gamma, so called "**cross gammas**," changes in delta with regard to share **A** if share **B** fluctuates in price. With regard to volatility, price fluctuations of all underlying securities must be considered. In addition, an increase or decrease of the correlation changes all relevant values of delta and gamma. The relationship between volatility and correlation also must be taken into consideration, since the two variables are somewhat interdependent. If, for example, the volatility of one of the two underlying securities increases, while the second remains unchanged, this also results in a decline in correlations. Since volatility and correlation affect the valuation in a multiplicative fashion, the price effect is magnified as the two variables change.

8.1.6.2.10 Basket options

As the name implies, a basket of securities serves as underlying for these options. This means that instead of one underlying, several securities, which are combined in a basket, determine prices and price changes of the option (see Table 8.10). This type of option is used frequently when generating retail products. Basket options are also a preferred tool of portfolio managers who need to hedge currency and equity risks. All the underlying securities are used when valuing the option.

Table 8.10: Basket option: Prices at closing and at expiration[42]

	Price at closing	Price at expiration
Share A	10	9
Share B	20	10
Share C	30	29
Share D	40	35
Sum	100	93
Percent	100%	93%

8.1.6.2.11 Lookback options

In a lookback option the market value of the underlying is determined over a specific time period. The strike price of a **strike lookback option** is determined by the lowest value (call option) or the highest value (put option) of the underlying during that time period. While the strike price remains fixed in a **price lookback option,** the option value is determined with reference to the highest price of the underlying in the case of a call option and the lowest price in the case of a put option.

8.1.6.2.12 Cliquet options and ladder options

The strike price of a **cliquet option**[43] is regularly adjusted for the upcoming period in line with the development of the underlying. A possible intrinsic value of the option is captured (**lock-in**). All lock-ins that accrue during the entire term to maturity are added up. For a **ladder option,** adjustment does not take place periodically, but when specific prices of the underlying are reached. Normally, only the highest intrinsic value is captured (lock-in). In exceptional cases, all captured intrinsic values are added up (see Figure 8.30).

8.1.6.2.13 Spread options and outperformance options

Both option types are related to two different underlying securities. The value of the **spread option** is determined by the absolute difference in the development of the two underlying securities. In contrast, the relative difference, in

---

[42] Source: DZ Bank.
[43] Also called a ratchet option.

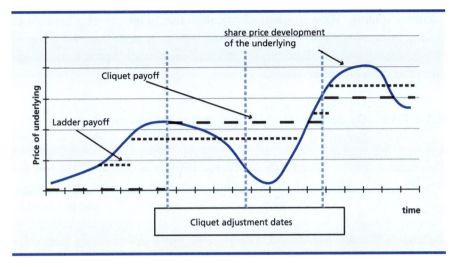

Figure 8.30: Schematic representation of the payout structure of a cliquet option[44]

other words the percentage difference in the performance of the two underlying securities is the determining factor for the value of an **outperformance option**.

8.1.6.2.14 Shout options

A **shout option** combines features of the **lookback** and **ladder/cliquet option**. The value of the option increases as the price of the underlying is headed in the appropriate direction. While no activity on the part of the buyer of the option is required in the cases of lookback and ladder options, he must become active in the case of a shout option. While the reset levels are predetermined in the case of a ladder option, they can be chosen by the buyer of the option in the case of shout options. Once a price level has been reached that is considered to be attractive by the buyer, he informs the seller and the current price is fixed (**shout**). Compared to a standard option, a shout option in all likelihood will be more expensive since it provides the possibility to lock in a profit. The shout option should also be more expensive than a ladder option because the lock-in levels are determined by the buyer. One key determinant of the value of the shout option is the number of "**shouts**" allowed (the more shouts, the closer the shout option resembles a lookback option and the more expensive it will become). Shout options are mostly popular in

---

[44] Source: DZ Bank.

currency trading. They are particularly attractive to buyers who are able to predict price movements of the underlying with great precision or are able to detect turning points. These buyers can realize significant premium savings compared to a lookback option.

8.1.6.2.15 Options with delayed premium payment – Boston options

This type of option, called either **deferred premium option** or **Boston option** is characterized by the fact that no premium payment at closing takes place. This type of option was developed for companies that did not want to miss out on possible favorable exchange rate developments after entering into a currency forward transaction. Therefore currency options were frequently traded in addition to the futures transaction. But the companies were often unable to make the required upfront premium payment. This type of option was introduced for the first time by the Bank of Boston in 1985 in order to alleviate this kind of liquidity problem. Boston options combine a currency forward with a currency option and can be bought by the investor as one combined product. The premium of the option is paid via an adjustment of the forward rate. As a result, the forward rate is less favorable, but the liquidity problem has been solved. Thus Boston options are combined strategies consisting of a currency forward and a currency option.

8.1.6.2.16 Multifactor options

As an example, currency risks and commodity risks can be jointly covered with one option. The prices are interlinked and the individual components that form the underlying are interwoven.

8.1.6.2.17 Exchange options

Exchange options grant the right to exchange one predefined asset against another asset, which is also determined ahead of time.

8.1.6.2.18 Asian options (average options)

Asian options are a specific type of exotic option: the buyer will receive payment of an average value of the underlying during the term to maturity of the option. A distinction is made between arithmetic and geometric Asian options. As implied by the names, different procedures for forming the averages are used. Concerning the exercise of Asian options, they can be both American and European in nature.

- **Geometric mean:**

$$(P_1 \cdot P_2 \cdot \ldots \cdot P_n)^{(1/n)}$$

- **Arithmetic mean:**

$$\frac{(P_1 + P_2 + \ldots + P_n)}{n}$$

General observations on exotic options

In this chapter, we have provided only a brief overview of the most frequently used exotic options. Thanks to combinations, variety and possibilities are very large. It must be stressed that exotic options cannot be traded on derivatives exchanges, but only as OTC (over the counter) transactions. The specifications are – or can be – complex and classical option pricing models will not always be able to provide solutions. Complex approaches such as **Monte-Carlo simulations** may be required instead.

Interview with Dr. Axel Vischer, Eurex and ISE

What future developments do you foresee for the derivatives markets?
We are currently emerging from a financial crisis and while we foresee a slow recovery, we still face many challenges and opportunities. The main challenges and opportunities facing the derivatives markets in the near future are:

- **De-leveraging:** by institutional investors, the professional trading community and private individuals.
- **Exchange Consolidation:** A continued consolidation of the exchange industry into global exchange groups, and on the other hand the proliferation of new exchange start-ups specializing in product or regulatory niches. One prime example of this trend is the U.S. equity options market, where we recently saw a consolidation of the American Stock Exchange (AMEX) into NYSE-Euronext Group, but also expect new entrants into the market within this year, for example the BATS options exchange. Thus far, new entrants have "grown the pie" by creating different types of trading opportunities through the introduction of different fee structures or a different market structure, creating new opportunities for arbitrage, additional opportunities for moving order flow and overall a larger pool of liquidity.
- **A New Emphasis on Exchange Trading and Clearing:** The financial crisis has reinforced the value of exchange trading and central clearing. Both regulators as well as politicians now recognize the importance of a regulated financial market place ensuring transparency and liquidity through clearing via Central Counterparties (CCPs).

This new appreciation of the values we bring to the market will ultimately create new business opportunities for all market participants in terms of transparency, neutrality and efficiency.

We expect that the fundamental factors which drove our market growth in the past will still exist and will continue to drive our business in the long run. Specifically, a steady increase in the use of derivatives by institutional players, including hedge funds, and an expansion into new markets and asset classes. We expect strong demand for new products enabling the market to hedge particular risks and, especially in the U.S., new equity options products resulting from an increased number of IPOs.

What major changes to you expect for the next couple of years?

The regulatory agenda will dominate the derivatives landscape on both sides of the Atlantic. Specifically, regulation of OTC derivatives will have a major impact on all aspects of the financial industry.

In Europe, for example, the EU Commission is in a consultation process with the member states to introduce a European Market Infrastructure legislation later this year. You can expect a stronger emphasis on expanded use of CCPs for OTC derivatives transactions to reduce or eliminate counterparty risk.

In the U.S., the focus has shifted partially away from a pure focus on the OTC markets. Instead, there is an increased regulatory scrutiny of securities exchanges and their trading practices. Although they performed the function they were designed for during the financial crisis, the exchanges turned out to be easier targets for some lawmakers and since they are so highly regulated. While these markets did not cause the financial crisis, this scrutiny does shift the focus away from the OTC derivatives market, which was one of the major causes of the crisis.

Another major driver of change will be regulatory reform and harmonization in the U.S. The regulatory structure of the U.S. markets is currently divided by instrument or product – the SEC regulates securities markets and the CFTC regulates commodities and futures markets. This division has resulted in regulatory gaps, jurisdictional stalemates, and inconsistent regulation of financial products and industry participants.

On October 16th 2009, the SEC and CFTC published their Joint Report on the Harmonization of Regulation. The report put forth recommendations for harmonization in four categories – markets, enforcement, financial intermediaries and operational coordination. It does not address the regulation of the OTC derivatives market or fungibility in the futures markets. We expect that the harmonization process will have a strong impact on the U.S. derivatives market in the short-term. Eventually the two regulatory bodies will diverge again as new products and participants enter the markets. Only a broader reform effort to reorganize and consolidate the agencies under a risk-based regulatory framework can lead to a long lasting solution.

While the next couple of years will certainly be dominated by regulatory issues and regulatory changes we still will see and feel the continued technological arms race. The quest for the lowest possible latency and highest possible throughput will continue unabated. New technologies will actually drive the market into a race for ever faster speed.

What type of product innovation do you expect to reach the market in the coming years? Do you expect new futures based on underlyings which seem to be rather exotic today? Like, for example garbage, water or similar underlyings?

We will see a drive for standardization of OTC derivatives to ensure that they can be cleared via CCPs. In the long run this will facilitate the transition of standardized products to become successful exchange traded products. For example, one of the new Eurex products with the fastest growth rates are dividend derivatives. They are designed to provide very similar exposure as OTC derivatives to various types of dividend swaps.

Another area with a strong demand for product innovation is the commodity sector. Commodities were one of the strongest growth segments in recent years. Globalization in combination with a steadily increasing demand for natural resources has driven strong demand for derivatives on commodities and will continue to do so in the foreseeable future. Eurex has responded to this trend by offering agricultural, commodities as well as commodity indices derivatives. Scarce resources like water will become a major topic if a standardized underlying can be found and be defined.

Within the commodity space we see additional strong demand for derivatives linked to environmental factors and to climate change. Here Eurex has engaged in the European Emission reduction scheme through cooperation with EEX, the European Energy Exchange. We currently offer trading in European emission reduction futures (EUA, CER) and hope to participate in similar programs if and when the US joins the Kyoto protocol or its successor.

Which products do you expect to disappear from the market and why?

It is likely that regulators will either strongly regulate or even ban products showing large and unsustainable risks. This should affect some of the products trading in the OTC markets and highlighted during the financial crisis. During the financial crisis we observed that OTC products with their associated bilateral risk distribution can be the cause of chain reactions resulting in broad and systemic risks. However, CCPs mitigate these types of risks for many of the OTC products, especially if they show a certain level of standardization.

Other OTC products which are highly standardised might even migrate onto the exchange. A typical example is the ISE FX options. The FX market is one of the largest OTC markets. The ISE FX options correspond to the FX options traded OTC but they allow investors to hedge their exposure to foreign currencies by trading an exchange-listed, centrally cleared, cash-settled options product.

In general marginal costs for listing new products on any exchange are relatively low. Exchanges will continue to explore new product opportunities by speaking with its participants, analyzing customer demand, and finally listing new derivatives to test new product ideas or product categories. At the same time we will also see the delisting of unsuccessful ones.

The Financial Crisis greatly affected the markets last year. What challenge does the Financial Crisis pose for exchanges today and how do you meet them?

The financial crisis as well as the Lehmann Brothers default showed that in general, exchange-traded and centrally cleared markets worked as designed. They provided systemic advantages, in particular liquidity and transparency. Clearinghouses eliminated counterparty risk and the CCP mutualised the risk. All members have equal access to the market and pay the same fees.

While our market design proved successful we still did see some significant reduction of our trading volumes, driven by the de-leveraging process and a consolidation process within our membership. In recent months we have seen that customer flows and interest is returning and our volumes have stabilized and are growing again.

Especially the default of Lehman Brothers has created an astute awareness of the effects of counterparty risk emphasizing the benefits of our CCP offering. In addition, regulators strive to implement measures to assure market stability and reduce systemic risks inherent in the financial markets. Customers want to react to the now easily observable risk exposures and ask for enhanced risk services from exchanges.

Eurex Clearing has reacted by offering its Enhanced Risk Solution which as of spring 2010 provides real-time risk assessment for both users and a stop button to halt trading for a client whose exposure due to technical or market reason is going haywire.

What is your view about the future of Financial Engineering?

I foresee that investment banking will drift from rapid growth towards a steady state. This will result in fewer entry opportunities for first time job seekers. It could also result in a consolidation of financial engineering programs. Overall there will be a stronger trend for graduates to find employment within proprietary trading firms and hedge funds.

Hands-on experience will become ever more important, i.e. practical trainings or work experience is a must. Finally there will be a stronger focus on higher quality instead of quantity. I expect that all these trends will actually balance each other and result in graduates being placed more easily again.

What aspects and developments within financial engineering do you see in demand for the next couple of years?

The financial crisis has resulted in an enormous emphasis on risk management in all areas of the financial industry. Financial engineering programs will react to this emphasis by streamlining their courses and offering more in depth training. Another related area with higher demand is valuation, especially valuation of OTC products.

Finally we see a tremendous interest from the financial engineering community with regards to our high-frequency, full order book data. Both the Eurex Historical Order book as well as the ISE HOT data are unique and in high demand. Financial engineering programs will have to refocus part of their courses on the challenges such massive and complex data sets pose.

Do you believe that further consolidation within the exchange industry will occur in the next few years?

We believe that consolidation does need to create value for shareholders, customers and all other stakeholders. Based on such values, inorganic growth, i.e. mergers and acquisitions can be valuable. In addition, exchanges and their members operate both as partners and sometimes as competitors. When over-consolidation occurs, new consortiums of members and exchanges will create new trading platforms.

We are actively participating in this cycle of consolidation and creation: through mergers or acquisitions, partnerships or through the formation of strategic alliances and exchange networks. Exchange networks have the advantage of sharing liquidity through cross-listing, direct market access and order routing agreements

How will the exchange industry assure further growth?

We always strive to expand and improve services. Some of our main focus currently is on new data offerings (e.g. HOT or Eurex Historical Order book), access to new flow (e.g. Eurex/ISE Link), access to new types of customers (e.g. buy-side), strategic alliances (e.g. link with the Korean Exchange KRX), new and improved products (e.g. new ETFs on ISE), new services (e.g. GC Pooling by Eurex Repo), expansion into new asset classes (e.g. commodities) and new geographies (e.g. Asia).

One example to explain here more in detail is the Eurex/ISE Link. It will provide Eurex customers with more efficient access to the ISE options product range, and will bring new liquidity to ISE's market. Regulatory approval is pending.

Literature for this chapter

Hull, John: Options, Futures and Other Derivatives, 7th edition, 2009

Fabozzi, Frank J.: The Handbook of Financial Instruments, 2002

Lyuu, Yuh-Dauh: Financial Engineering and Computation-Principles, Mathematics, Algorithms, 2002

Madura, Jeff: International Financial Management, 6th edition, 2004

Nelken, Israel: The Handbook of Exotic Options-Instruments, Analysis and Applications, 1996

Questions and answers on this chapter

Question 1:
What is meant by the term swap?

Question 2:
What does CMS mean?

Question 3:
Do options on swaps exist?

Question 4:
How are swaps valued?

Question 5:
What is a quanto option?

Answer to question 1:
A swap is a bilateral financial contract in which the exchange of payment streams is arranged.

Answer to question 2:
CMS means Constant Maturity Swap and relates to the exchange of two variable payment streams.

Answer to question 3:
Yes, they are called swaptions. They lock in a swap at a future point in time.

Answer to question 4:
This is done using the replication/duplication approach. A portfolio which has the same profile of payments is formed to value the swap.

Answer to question 5:
This is an option which excludes the currency risk. An example is the purchase of an option on a foreign index without the currency risk.

9 | Credit derivatives

The following chapter covers these issues:

- What are credit instruments?
- What are credit derivatives?
- What capital structures exist?
- What kinds of credit derivatives can be traded in what way?
- What problems developed following the financial market crisis?

9.1 Fundamentals of credit derivatives

Credit derivatives are used to transfer credit risk from one party to another. The party which assumes the risk receives a premium payment. In that way, a financial intermediary can partly or completely eliminate the credit default risk (standard loans and bonds). In addition, an investor can seek protection against a price decline of company bonds, which could be the result of a decline in creditworthiness or a default.

9.2 What is credit?

Initially, the term credit derivative needs to be defined. The word credit is derived from the Latin "credo" and "creditum" which means "faith" and "trust in good faith." A credit transaction thus implies the faith that the liquidity lent will find its way back to the lender. The relationship between creditor and debtor is characterized by mutual trust, which is reflected in the transaction. Unfortunately, however, not every borrower has a credit standing that allows to "trust him in good faith" with the money. Therefore a lender attempts to obtain protection against a possible default (non-payment of interest, delay in interest payment, failure to repay the loan). Credit derivatives were developed to serve this function of protection: they can be used for hedging and enable the lender to eliminate the default risk of his credit portfolio.

> **Credit risk**
>
> Credit risk is the risk or probability that a **default**[1] occurs and the provider of the loan suffers a loss. This loss can be either partial or complete. Changes in the credit standing of the debtor can also affect the lender (for example by requiring valuation adjustments).

9.3 Which capital structures exist?

Let us take a brief look at this point at the different capital structures and their balance sheet positions. This enables us to focus on credit derivatives as well as on refinancing opportunities called **hybrid** or **mezzanine structures**[2].

The adequate capital structure of banks in Germany is regulated in Section 10(1) of the German Banking Act (KWG=Kreditwesengesetz). It defines the amount of equity capital that a banking institution is required to hold in order to be able to fulfill its obligations to creditors. These funds must be formally shown as equity capital on the balance sheet.

The own funds of a banking institution consist of liable capital and tier 3 capital according to Section 10 (2), sentences 1 and 2, KWG. Liable capital in turn is broken down as follows

- **Core capital (tier I**[3]**):** paid-up capital, which is permanently available to the company, published reserves and retained earnings, special items for general banking risks (funds for general banking risks). The core capital quota can theoretically be between 0% and 100%, in practice the values are in a range of 4-20%.

---

[1] Default = inability of the debtor to repay.
[2] Complex financing structures which fall in between equity and debt capital. See Spremann, Finance 3rd edition, Oldenbourg 2007.
[3] Tier refers to the rank in the case of insolvency.

- **Supplementary capital (tier II):** positions with lower quality concerning liability
  - Supplementary capital class I
  - Supplementary capital class II
- The following are considered **tier III** according to Section 10 (2c), KWG:
  - The pro rata profit that would arise from the notional closing of all trading book positions
  - Short-term subordinated liabilities within the meaning of Section 10 (7), KWG (examples are short-term liabilities with subordination clause).

Supplementary capital and tier III capital can only be used in a limited way when calculating eligible own funds.

A complete list of all balance sheet items that are considered to be core capital can be found in Section 10 (2a, first sentence, KWG, which are paid-up and which are permanently available to the company. A minimum of 4% of the own funds must thus be core capital (in general 50 funds).

Figure 9.1 once again lists the three possibilities.

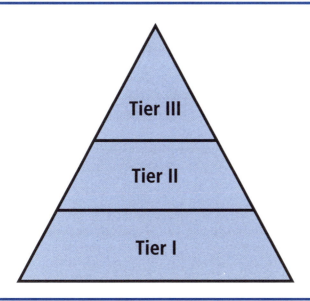

Figure 9.1: Tier capital on the bank balance sheet

Components of the core capital quota
Paid-up capital (business capital, capital stock, common capital stock)
− Own shares and partnership assets
− Cumulative preferred share
− Withdrawals by the general partners and loans granted to them
− Net debt in the proprietor's unencumbered personal assets
− Capital from profit participation rights
+ Open reserve
+ Retained earnings plus unrealized profit
+ Assets contributed by silent partners
+ Special items for general banking risks
− Losses including losses not yet reported
− Intangible assets
− Loans not customary in the market
= **Core capital**

Supplementary capital class I consists among others of **participation rights**, **valuation reserves** and **special items** with reserve elements related to real estate. Supplementary capital class II consists among others of long-term subordinated liabilities that are to be repaid only after the claims of other creditors have been met and the surcharge on the liability amount. **Tier III capital** includes all items that have a lower quality concerning liability than **core** and **supplementary capital**. An example of this is a **hybrid bond**.

As we can see, there are many possibilities to refinance or structure credit risks. In the following, we want to take a brief look at credit derivatives which are used to reduce and structure risk in this context.

Credit ratings

Rating agencies such as **Mood's**, **S&P** and **Fitch** provide ratings which describe the credit standing of companies, and thus of debtors. Individual companies are rated and thus made comparable. Default probabilities are studied and visualized with the help of this approach. In the appendix to this volume, you find a table which lists the different rating categories and the average cumulative default probabilities in percent.

9.4 Which types of credit derivatives exist?

9.4.1 Classical credit derivatives

Classical credit derivatives are bilateral contracts between the buyer and the seller of protection (see Figure 9.2). The seller of protection transfers the loan protection to the buyer of protection, who in turn passes along the risks. The premium to be paid is determined by the rating, and thus the risk of a credit event. The premium is normally calculated as the product of probability and expected loss in the case of default.

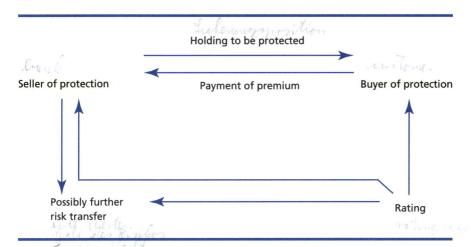

Figure 9.2: Credit derivative

The premium for credit derivatives which is calculated using ratings is usually stated as a spread. The market for these derivatives is internationally standardized, since not the interest rate risk, but rather the credit risk is priced and ratings are used in the same way globally. This homogeneity allows a quick comparison of credit risks globally, which favors the development of an active market. The market was broadened with the possibility of transferring risk. At several levels, it is developing into an effective and consistent market. This was made easier by the transfer of the classical risks by the classical banks. Otherwise they would remain on the balance sheet as risky assets.

The role of **rating agencies** can be considered a pertinent issue for credit derivatives. The existence of a rating, which can be used for pricing, is crucial. The sub-prime crisis which began in 2007 and turned into a financial crisis exemplifies possible repercussions of an imprudent use of these instruments.

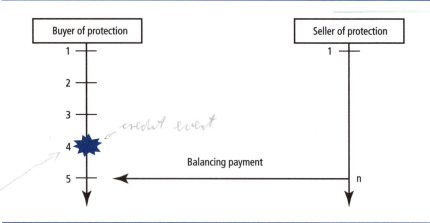

Figure 9.3: Payment streams for the buyer and seller of protection

It is important to clearly define the default. This is called a credit event (see Figure 9.3). It is important to clearly and consistently define the event so that both contract parties can easily verify whether it has occurred.

The following are examples of credit events[4]:

- Delayed payment by the debtor
- Restructuring of the liabilities

The amount covered as well as the nominal value of the contract must also be determined.

9.4.2 Modern credit derivatives

In earlier times, credit derivatives only existed in the form of Credit Default Swap (CDS[5]). Since 2007 they can also be traded via Eurex.

In principle, a CDS (see Figure 9.4) works just like a put option: in case the **credit event**[6] takes place, the option is triggered and the credit risk is sold. The term **swap** can be understood historically: a company bond was

---

[4] Complete listing of all credit events in: "2003 ISDA Credit Derivatives Definitions. Article IV – Credit Events."
[5] To this day, CDS are considered to be the most important credit derivatives.
[6] The underlying credit event is specified in the contract in advance.

exchanged for a government bond. Unlike a classical swap, this exchange only happens in the case of a credit event. Delivery can be either **physical** or via **cash settlement**[7]. The premium always consists of an upfront payment at the time the CDS is closed and an optional annual payment. The days when only banks were active in CDSs are over: in the past years, aggressive hedge funds have also been active in this area.

The CDS premium depends on the risky credit position and its credit standing[8]. The larger the probability of default, the higher is the premium to be paid[9]. For a number of years now, it has been possible to draw on standardized contract components for CDS, which make a quick and uncomplicated closing of the contract possible. ISDA[10], which is headquartered in New York, developed comprehensive guidelines in 1999. With the ISDA Master Agreement, a standardized contract was drawn up, which can be used as a neutral basis by the contract parties.

In a CDS, the following items must be covered:

- Reference entity
- Credit event covered by the CDS
- Assets used to identify the credit event
- Starting date
- Term to maturity
- Nominal value
- Premium (mostly stated in basis points of the nominal value)
- Obligation of the protection seller in case the credit event materializes
- Physical delivery or cash settlement

Figure 9.4 lists the payment streams of a CDS.

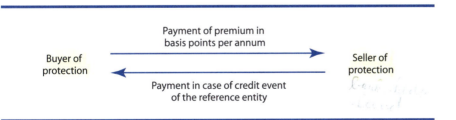

Figure 9.4: Credit Default Swap

---

[7] Also called difference payment.
[8] Good credit standing is less frequent than not so solid credit standing.
[9] In the wake of the financial market crisis which began in 1997, new pricing systems were introduced and used.
[10] International Swap and Derivatives Association.

Classical forms of credit

Among the classical forms of credit are for example bank loans, bonds and promissory note bonds. Depending on the specification, these can be advantageous for the investor or not. Especially bonds and promissory notes (deposit insurance for the provider of the loan[11]) give medium to long term access to liquidity for an investor and are traded on the market or OTC. The bank loan is among the oldest financing instruments[12].

9.5 Valuation of credit derivatives (CDS)

The market standard for the valuation of credit default swaps (CDS) is the **reduced form model** (see Figure 9.5). Valuation is based on the net present values of two payment streams: one cash flow characterizes the premium payment, a second one payments in case of a credit event.

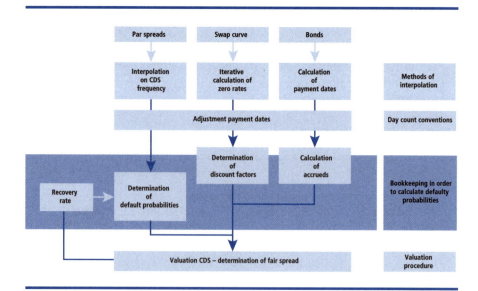

Figure 9.5: CDS valuation following DVFA[13]

---

[12] Only in the case of non-banks. There is no protection for banks and insurance companies.
[12] For more detail, see: Wöhe, Bilstein, Ernst, Häcker: Grundzüge der Unternehmensfinanzierung, Vahlen 2009.
[13] Source: DVFA, Issue 06/07 "Standards zur Bewertung von Kreditderivaten."

$$S_T = \frac{(1-R)\sum_{j=1}^{m}[P(0,t_j) - P(0,t_{j-1})] \cdot DF(0,t_j)}{\sum_{j=1}^{m} \Delta(t_{j-1},t_j) \cdot DF(0,t_j) \cdot (t - P(0,t_j))}$$

An additional possibility to value credit risks is the use of data from the equity markets. Two arguments support the use of these so-called **structural models**:

- A **credit default** needs to be determined for a reference entity which has not issued any company bonds.
- Valuation of the inherent risk which is implied by the market in the form of a probability of default for the reference company. Intensity models make use of CDS spreads to determine default probabilities. If this source of information is not available, **structural models** are used.

In applied work, the **reduced form model** is used most frequently. For that reason, it is also discussed more prominently in the literature.

Credit options or options on credit default risks are valued using the valuation approaches of LONGSTAFF and SCHWARTZ[14], DAS[15] or with the models of JARROW[16], LANDO and TURNBULL.

9.6 What are iTraxx® futures at Eurex?

Since March 2007, it is possible to trade credit futures on the three "iTraxx Europe®" indexes[17] at Eurex, which are based on the closing of a forward agreement (classical forward). These are standardized credit indexes, where measured changes in the net present value of a portfolio of reference issuers lead to index adjustments. The index increases in the case of a positive development. It declines in case of a negative development. The premium is based on the index value; contracts have a nominal value of EUR 100,000 and are

---

[14] See Longstaff/Schwartz 1995a.
[15] See Das 1995 "Credit Risk Derivatives."
[16] Jarrow and Turnbull value options on risky bonds with the help of martingale assumptions and explicitly refer to credit derivatives (see Jarrow/Turnbull 1995).
[17] iTraxx Europe Crossover 5-year Index Future, iTraxx Europe 5-year Index Future, iTraxx Europe HiVol 5-year Index Future.

cash settled. The last day of trading is the fifth working day prior to the 20th calendar day of the contract month.

9.7 What are securitized credit derivatives?

Securitzed credit risks are called Credit Linked Notes (CLN)[18]. They are based on Credit Default Swaps (CDS) and in addition have issuer risk[19]. CLN are issued as securities and also sold to retail clients[20] (see Figure 9.6). In case of a credit event, repayment of the CLN falls below the nominal value. Normally, any recovery proceeds are paid out. Since CLN are securities, they are also subject to the credit risk of the issuer. The overall risk is thus the sum of the risk of the CDS plus the credit risk of the issuer.

Scenario 1: the securitized loan is repaid by the debtor on schedule and no credit events are recorded. The CLN thus also witnesses regular payments and the investor receives regular interest payments (on every payment date $t_1 - t_7$) and the nominal value at maturity (t_7) (see Figure 9.7).

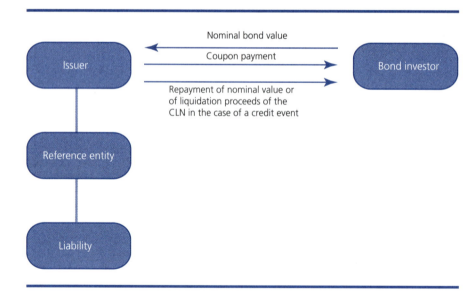

Figure 9.6: Structure of a CLN with cash settlement

---

[18] This is the structure used by banks. Should the issuer be a special purpose vehicle, which was set up purely for this reason, implementation takes place via this vehicle.
[19] See the insolvency of Lehman Brothers in 2008 as a result of the financial crisis.
[20] Addition to the portfolios of private clients.

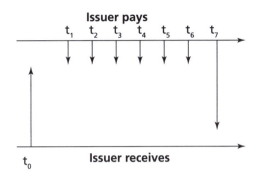

Figure 9.7:   CLN without credit event

Scenario 2: Not all payments are made on the securitized loan by the debtor; a credit event occurs (for example insolvency or restructuring of the loan). No more payments are made on the CLN. Instead it is settled in line with the conditions for liquidation (stated in the prospectus). As can be seen in Figure 9.8, a credit event occurs after t_3. As a consequence, the interest payments in t_{4-7} and the repayment in t_7 are affected and are no longer made. The CLN is liquidated.

An alternative to a CLN is the so-called CDO (Collateralized Debt Obligation). A CDO is a security which is backed by bonds held in the portfolio of the issuing institution. In the case of a synthetic CDO, the portfolio does not contain bonds, but credit derivatives (for example CDS) instead.

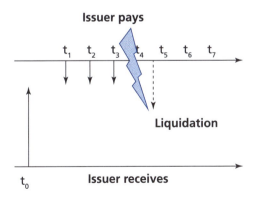

Figure 9.8:   CLN with credit event

Our brief summary shows that credit derivatives have the basic function of transferring risk; they were developed with this idea in mind. Today the market for credit risks has become diverse and large. Credit derivatives are traded by professional investors and companies. Private investors are active in the market for credit derivatives via CLN. However, private investors must be aware of the risks involved and must be able to absorb them in their liquidity plan. In a worst case scenario – a credit event – a complete loss usually results.

9.8 Problems in the securitization market following the financial market crisis in 2007

Drastic problems became apparent in the securitization market in the wake of the financial market crisis beginning in 2007. Eventually, the market came to a complete standstill. The spreads (see Figures 9.9 and 9.10) increased drastically and rapidly following the bankruptcy of Lehman Brothers. It was practically impossible to resell existing securitization structures or to issue new ones. Large value adjustments on existing holdings became necessary.

This development shows the problems of credit securitization. Trading can only be successful in functioning markets that are willing to bear risk. In

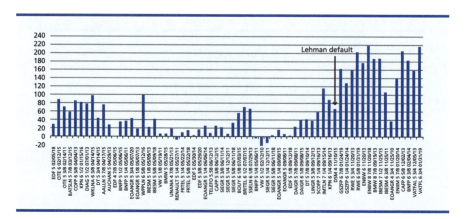

Figure 9.9:   New issues in Euro (classical) including spreads over CDS[21]

---

[21] Source: LBBW and Bloomberg.

CDS 5 years in basis points:

Issuer	16 Sept. 2009	2 Sept. 2009
Commerzbank	69.6	92.5
Deutsche Bank	83.5	109.5
BNP Paribas	48.5	57.0
Societé Générale	77.3	86.0
ING	64.7	75.5
Rabobank	52.2	60.0
RBS	110.3	128.4
HSBC	54.7	60.6

Issuer	16 Sept. 2009	2 Sept. 2009
Barclays	74.3	84.9
UBS	97.7	118.9
Crédit Suisse	70.6	86.4
Goldman Sachs	87.3	143.2
Morgan Stanley	130.6	175.1
Citigroup	167.9	266.6
JPMorgan Chase	57.5	72.7
Bank of America	110.1	165.7

Figure 9.10: CDS spreads of the individual banks in basis points[22]

times of crisis (recession, depression), it is virtually impossible to transfer credit risk. The likelihood that a transfer of the credit products may become impossible in times of crisis must be considered by every investor before entering into such a transaction. This is a conclusion reached by many as a result of the financial crisis which began in 2007.

9.9 Complexity of the instruments

The complexity of the instruments has contributed significantly to the severity of the financial crisis of 2007. Numerous products were only incompletely understood by buyers and sellers alike. In some cases, the complexity of the instruments was abused. The risk attributes were presented only schematically when the investment case was made. This highlights the dangers inherent in products with a high degree of complexity. If the products are poorly understood and not fully analyzed, unwanted and hard to assess risks may materialize, which in turn can even cause severe systemic problems (for example the necessity to rescue banks in the 2007 financial crisis[23]). The complexity of such products cripples an otherwise solid investment process and leads to increased risk which is not in line with return expectations.

---

[22] Source: Bloomberg.
[23] See Bloss, Ernst, Häcker, Eil: Von der Subprime-Krise zur Finanzkrise Oldenbourg, 2008.

9.10 Which problems arose during the financial crisis with respect to credit derivatives?

We want to close the chapter with this question, for which no complete answer can be provided at this point. It is true that credit derivatives contributed to the outbreak and acceleration of the financial crisis of 2007. However, it would be even more appropriate to say that credit derivatives were instruments that played an important role during the crisis. Complex instruments are problematic only if they are poorly understood and thus used inappropriately. This was one of the problems that ultimately led to the financial market crisis. While the instruments cannot be blamed, their inappropriate use caused the crisis. This more subtle way of describing the problem is necessary, especially when it comes to the various "rescue operations" which were conducted during the financial market crisis[24].

> As the financial market crisis unfolded, the possibility to trade CDS via a clearing system of ICE Clear Europe and via Eurex Credit Clear (as central counterpart) was created. This system has the advantage of being transparent and clear. Even though only a small fraction of trades are done via these systems at the moment, they are the wave of the future.

---

[24] See Bloss, Ernst, Häcker, Eil: Von der Wall Street zur Main Street Oldenbourg, 2009.

Literature for this chapter

Bloss, Ernst, Häcker, Eil: Von der Subprime-Krise zur Finanzkrise, 2008

Bloss, Ernst, Häcker, Eil: Von der Wall Street zur Main Street, 2009

Hull, John: Options, Futures and Other Derivatives, 7th edition, 2009

Madura, Jeff: International Financial Management, 6th edition, 2004

Spremann, Klaus: Finance, 3rd edition, 2007

Wiedemann, Arnd: Bewertung von Finanzinstrumenten, 4th edition, 2007

Questions and answers on this chapter

Question 1:
What does tier I mean?

Question 2:
How are credit derivatives valued?

Question 3:
What is a CLN?

Question 4:
Are credit derivatives traded only OTC?

Question 5:
Is the following statement correct? The market for credit derivatives remained liquid during the financial crisis.

Answer to question 1:
Tier I capital is core capital and thus equity capital of a company which was paid in.

Answer to question 2:
Valuation is done with the help of the reduced form model or the structural model. The first one is used more frequently in applied work.

Answer to question 3:
A CLN (= Credit Linked Note) is a securitized credit derivative.

Answer to question 4:
No. For example iTRAXX indexes are traded at Eurex.

Answer to question 5:
No, the statement is not correct. In the course of the financial market crisis of 2007, the market for credit derivatives factually collapsed. The lack of prices and credit defaults forced massive write-offs.

10 Weather derivatives

The following chapter covers these issues:

- What are weather derivatives?
- What are their uses?
- How are these derivatives priced?
- What strategies exist?
- Which markets exist?

10.1 Fundamentals of weather derivatives

Weather derivatives are innovative financial products which are based on parameters such as precipitation amounts (rain and snow), rainy days, hours of sunshine, air temperature or wind speeds. The following groups can be distinguished in practice for this kind of derivative:

- **Conditional weather derivatives** (options), **unconditional weather derivatives** (futures and swaps), **combinations** (collar, straddle and strangle).
- **Exotic products** (hybrid weather derivatives such as weather indexed bonds, weather indexed loans or weather indexed interest rate forwards (swaps)).

The main reason for the use of a weather derivative is the transfer of risk. Unlike other derivatives on equities, interest rates, commodities and so forth, weather derivatives cannot easily be used for hedging or speculation. Weather can strongly influence the quantity and thus the market risk of a commodity (see Figure 10.1). This implies a financial risk, which can be partially or completely transferred to the counterparty with the help of weather deriva-

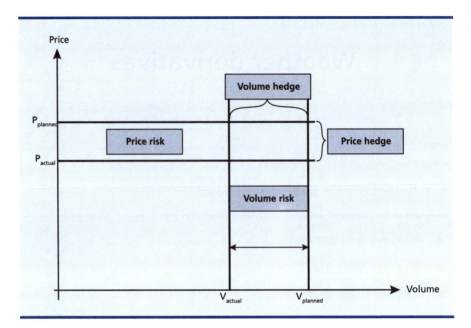

Figure 10.1: Volume and price risk

tives. In order to hedge against both price risks and volume risks, weather derivatives must be combined with classical energy derivatives. This is called **cross hedging**.

10.2 Information on the underlying in weather derivatives

The biggest difference between a weather derivative and the other derivatives discussed in this book concerns the underlying, which is not tradable or tangible. It is instead represented with the help of weather parameters, usually stated in the form of a suitably constructed index.

Several interesting consequences follow from this fact:

1. Since it is impossible to physically store or transfer weather, the underlying cannot be manipulated.

2. In contrast to all previously discussed derivatives, cash settlement is the only possibility. Delivery is ruled out.

3. The price fluctuations of the typical underlying (equities, indexes, bonds and so forth) are stated using historical and implied volatility. The volatility of the weather can only be captured with reference to its past development.

An additional fundamental difference between weather derivatives and other derivatives relates to the fact that the derivatives presented so far are used to hedge prices. This is not the case for weather derivatives, which aim to eliminate the volume risk discussed.

The following sections show the standard underlying objects used for weather derivatives in applied work. As already discussed, there are several possibilities to describe the weather. According to Weather Risk Management Association (WRMA), the temperature, which is represented in the United States with the help of so called degree day indexes, is the most widespread measure and most frequently used underlying in exchange trading and OTC transactions. The calculation and the concept of this index, the average temperature indexes and the temperature index *Gradtageszahlenindex* (GTZ, degree day figures index) used in Germany, as well as other underlying variables related to weather are presented in detail on the following pages. Various possibilities to develop derivatives on these variables are presented next (see Figure 10.2).

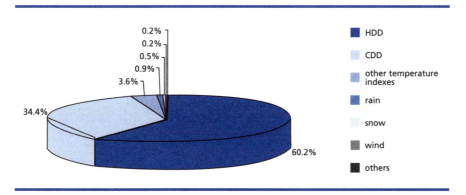

Figure 10.2: Distribution of contracts among different possibilities to measure weather[1]

---

[1] Source: Weather Risk Management Association.

10.2.1 Degree day indexes

The use of degree day indexes as underlying for weather derivatives started in the United States, when utilities realized the need for hedging during the liberalization of energy markets. The idea for this index was developed from the experiences of American energy companies and postulates a relationship between daily temperature and energy use or consumption. A large number of utilities in the U.S. had discovered that energy use is correlated with the difference between the current average daily temperature and a fixed reference temperature. This leads to the following relationship, which can be better understood by looking at Figure 10.3: the larger the difference, the stronger is demand.

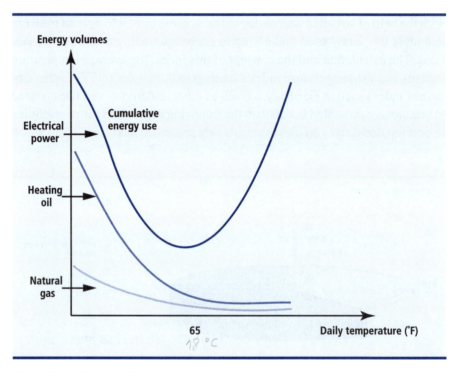

Figure 10.3: Relationship between temperature and energy consumption

As can be seen from this figure, the low point in electrical power consumption is reached at a temperature of about 65°F or 18.3°C. This value is appropriate for large parts of the United States. One reason is the fact that people in the United States consider a temperature of about 18°C as pleasant. Electrical power consumption increases as the temperature falls below or rises above that value, since heating or cooling systems are activated.

10.2.2 Heating Degree Days (HDD) & Cooling Degree Days (CDD)

To calculate degree day indexes, so called energy degree days for the individual days are needed. Such a day is defined as the difference of one degree between the average daily temperature and a reference value. The average daily temperature is calculated as the arithmetic mean of the lowest and highest values at certain meteorological stations. The reference temperature in the United States is 65°F (18.3°C) and in Europe 18°C. The average daily temperature can be either below or above the reference temperature. If the average daily temperature is below the reference value, the energy degree days are Heating Degree Days (HDD). If the reference temperature is below the average daily temperature, the energy degree days are called Cooling Degree Days (CDD). For the calculation of HDD and CDD, the following formulas are used.

$$\text{HDD (i)} = \text{Max} (0; 18°C - \emptyset \text{ Temperature (i)})$$
$$\text{CDD (i)} = \text{Max} (0; \emptyset \text{ Temperature (i)} - 18°C)$$

with $\emptyset$ Temperature (i) =

$$\left(\frac{\text{Maximum temperature (i)} - \text{Minimum temperature (i)}}{2} \right)$$

Example:

With an average daily temperature of 1°C in winter, we get 17 HDDs and 0 CDD. In contrast, average daily temperatures of 28°C in summer imply 10 CDDs and 0 HDDs.

Over a specified period of time, individual values of the HDDs and CDDs are added to form Degree Day Indexes, which are available on a daily, monthly and seasonally adjusted base and which can be used as underlying for weather derivatives. The values of a CDD index, which is used in summer or of an HDD index, which is used in winter, are calculated as follows:

$$\text{HDD (Interval)} = \sum \text{HDD (i)} \quad \forall i \in \text{Interval}$$
$$\text{CDD (Interval)} = \sum \text{CDD (i)} \quad \forall i \in \text{Interval}$$

One feature of the degree day indexes should be kept in mind: use of a certain temperature as reference value implies that an HDD or CDD value of zero is possible. This means that such an index does not fully reflect all the information concerning temperature.

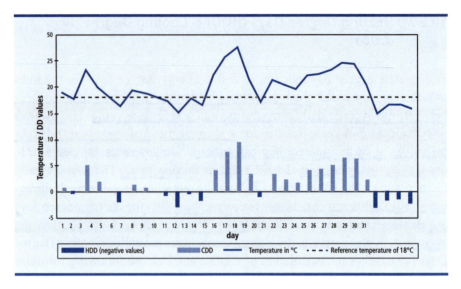

Figure 10.4: Temperatures and DD values in Berlin, August 2001

This concept, especially the CDD indexes, does not fully reflect the situation in Europe, especially since the European summers are relatively mild compared to those in the United States and temperatures fluctuate around a reference temperature of 18°C. This relationship is illustrated with reference to the temperature development in Berlin, as displayed in Figure 10.4.

In order to avoid this problem, **Average Temperature Indexes** (AVT) are issued, which capture the average value of measured daily average temperatures in a time interval of i days.

$$\mathbf{AVT} = (1/i) \cdot \sum (\emptyset \, \mathbf{Temp} \, (i)) \qquad \forall \, i \in \mathbf{Interval}$$

Compared to DD indexes, more users can be reached with these constructions. According to WRMA, the importance of alternative temperature indexes is growing.

10.2.3 Gradtageszahlenindex (GTZ)

An additional alternative, which is frequently used in the winter season in Germany, is the *Gradtageszahlenindex* (GTZ, degree day figures index). Its structure is similar to that of the HDD index. It is published regularly by the German weather service *Deutscher Wetterdienst* and represents the cumulative difference of the average daily outside temperature (below 15°C) and the average room temperature (20°C).

Since temperature is the most frequently used underlying according to a study by the WRMA, it is understandable that most concepts presented so far are related to it. But there are additional underlying variables besides temperature, which gain in importance in the area of weather derivatives and which are briefly presented in the coming section.

In second place is precipitation in the form of rain or snow. At measurement stations, the 24-hour volumes of precipitation in millimeters are measured daily. As in the case of temperature, these can be cumulated over certain time intervals and then used as underlying for weather derivatives. But due to regional differences, it is hard to measure representative volumes of precipitation. This leads to the necessity that companies in need of a hedge against this type of weather risk must pick a specific weather station which is representative of the relevant site. If no such weather station exists, the company has two choices: it can either hedge over a longer period of time or use a basket index. The latter is, figuratively, a portfolio which combines a number of weather stations into one index.

Other underlying variables and combinations of variables, such as hours of sunshine, wind speeds, water levels, cloud coverage, short-term weather forecasts, basket indexes and others are used in exotic or tailor-made contracts.

10.3 Structuring of weather derivatives

The types of derivatives discussed so far (futures, forwards, puts and calls) can also be used for weather derivatives with little alterations and in line with customer demand. In addition to standardized products such as options or futures, swaps and collars deserve mention at this point and will be studied more closely in later sections. All products share the following contract specifications:

1. The **weather station** which provides the values for the index or basket and which can be specified precisely with the help of the WBAN or WMO identification number.
2. Underlying: in most cases one of the indexes presented such as the degree day index for example.
3. Term to maturity: the term to maturity of a weather derivative is limited. It is stated either in months or seasons.

4. Exercise level: beginning with this value, one party is making a balancing payment to the other party. It depends on the development of the underlying and is given by the tick size.
5. The **cap** states the maximum amount that must be paid. It is stated in monetary amounts or index points.
6. Premium: the buyer of an option needs to make a premium payment to the seller, since he has acquired a right and the seller is actively taking on risk. No premium payment is required in the case of swaps as the profile of risks and opportunities is symmetric.

The weather derivatives presented are used in particular for the transfer of weather risks (hedging). Two different hedging possibilities exist:

1. One party can hedge against weather risks by making a premium payment and acquiring an **option**. These types of contracts provide independence from the counterparty. The option can be exercised if the weather becomes a risk factor for one party. This becomes meaningful once the option is in the money. It must be kept in mind that only American options can be exercised prior to the expiration date.

2. The second possibility is provided by **swaps or collars**. They also allow to hedge against weather risks, but only by relinquishing the upside potential. The differences between swaps and collars relate to the required premium payment on the one hand and to the degree of surrender on the other hand. Swaps do not require the payment of a premium, but the counterparty fully participates in the profit potential. The premium which is paid in the case of the collar is lower, since the counterparty only participates in the profit potential up to a certain point.

10.4 Conditional weather derivatives

As was shown before, options are conditional derivatives contracts, where the buyer acquires a right in exchange for a premium payment. At a certain point in time and starting at a specific strike price, the buyer can either exercise the option or let it expire worthless. For weather options, which account for an estimated 75% of all weather derivatives, the basic structure is expanded with the help of a cap, which assures that the payments cannot exceed a certain level and therefore protects the providers of these derivatives from extreme volatility.

10.4.1 Hedging with call options

Once a premium payment is made to the seller, the buyer of a standardized call option can benefit from increasing prices. This premium payment is also required in the case of weather derivatives. In the case of a call option, the payment is triggered if the underlying variable (temperature, rain, snow and so forth) is measured above a certain level during the term to maturity or at expiration. These payments are necessary compensation for the company using the hedge, since the increase in the underlying causes a decline in the operative result.

The selection of the underlying value is dependent on the industry: HDD indexes are used in the winter season. The corresponding calls (HDD calls) are used to hedge against extreme cold in winter and can be used in particular by the construction industry. In contrast, CDD indexes and CDD calls are used more frequently in summer. They can be used for example by companies that offer travel abroad, to protect against extremely hot summers. The situation is different for utilities: the volume and distribution risks that result from temperature changes cannot be hedged with the help of DD indexes, since the operative result of these utilities goes up as HDD or CDD values increase.

The following, extremely simplified example shows the use of a call option by a utility company:

A utility company that is active in the state of Baden-Wuerttemberg is specialized in providing electrical power for agricultural uses and makes 50% of its annual profits in summer. A thorough analysis has revealed that revenues depend on the use of electrical power, which in turn depends on the average amount of precipitation in Baden-Wuerttemberg (see Table 10.1).

For every 10 mm of additional precipitation, the use of electrical power by agricultural producers is reduced by 150,000 kWh. This in turn reduces the profit by € 1,500,000 (assumption: 1kWh = € 10). The utility company needs a minimum profit of € 8,500,000 from this line of business in order to maintain overall profitability and to cover current expenses for its plant and staff. In other words: should precipitation in Baden-Wuerttemberg exceed an average of 40 mm, the utility company faces a financial risk, which is directly related to the weather.

In order to get out of this dependency and to eliminate this risk, the utility company decides to purchase a call option. It is written on the average precipitation in Baden-Wuerttemberg and has the following features:

Table 10.1: Relationship between precipitation and electrical power use

Precipitation (in mm)	Use of electrical power (kWh)	Profit (€)
0	1,450,000	14,500,000
10	1,300,000	13,000,000
20	1,150,000	11,500,000
30	1,000,000	10,000,000
40	850,000	8,500,000
50	700,000	7,000,000
60	550,000	5,500,000
70	400,000	4,000,000
80	250,000	2,500,000
90	100,000	1,000,000

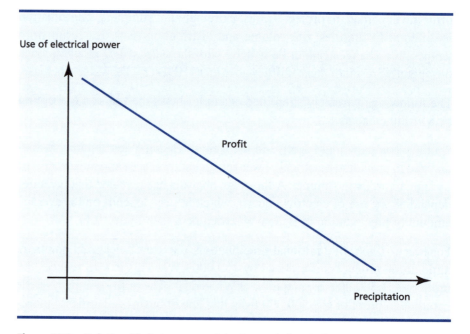

Figure 10.5: Relationship between precipitation and electrical power use

- Term to maturity: April 1, 2008 until August 31, 2008
- Strike level: 40 mm
- Tick size: € 150,000 per mm
- Limit: 100 mm
- Premium: € 500,000

Four possible scenarios help to illustrate the effects of this option:

First scenario: average precipitation of 20 mm
In this situation, the utility company makes a profit of € 11,500,000. The option is not exercised. The utility company was required to pay the option premium of € 500,000. This reduces the total profit to € 11,000,000.

Second scenario: average precipitation of 40 mm
The utility company makes a profit of € 11,500,000. Again it does not make sense to exercise the option, since no compensation payment is due for a precipitation level of exactly 40 mm. Since the premium of € 500,000 must also be paid in this case, profits decline to € 8,000,000 and the company faces a liquidity shortage.

The features of the option are therefore not sufficient to eliminate all risks for the utility company. It must be amended by changing the strike level in such a way that the premium is also covered. A reduction of the strike level from 40 mm to 36.67 mm (40 − (500,000/150,000)) means that the utility company will exactly make a profit of € 8,500,000 (€ 9,000,000 − € 500,000) for an average amount of precipitation of 36.67 mm. If the utility company owns this new option, it will be exercised at an average precipitation level of 40 mm. Without the option, the utility company receives € 8,500,000 from daily operations. The payoff from the option is € 500,000, which can be used to pay the option premium.

Third scenario: average precipitation of 50 mm
In case average precipitation reaches 50 mm, the utility company will exercise the option. This results in an operating profit of € 7,000,000 plus an option payment of € 2,000,000. The profit is at € 8,500,000, since the option premium of € 500,000 must be deducted.

Fourth scenario: average precipitation of 120 mm
In this case the utility company does not have an operating profit and it would exercise the option. The compensation from the option is not € 12,000,000 (120 − (Strike = 40) x € 150,000), since a cap at 100 mm was agreed. The maximum payoff of this option, which is reached in this scenario, is € 9,000,000, from which the option premium must be subtracted for a total profit of € 8,500,000.

The payoff profile is summarized in Figure 10.6.

For call options, two points of reference are available and they are suitable for different situations: an HDD call can be used in order to hedge against cold winters. Meanwhile, a CDD call is used to protect against the effects of a warm summer.

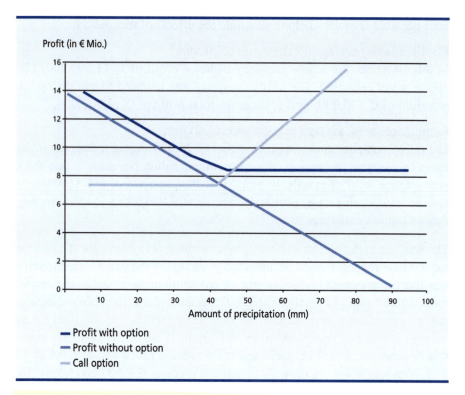

Figure 10.6: Payoff profile of a call on precipitation

As was shown with the help of a simple example, companies can use call options to hedge against severe precipitation (or other extreme weather events). This allows them to offset operative declines. The next section shows how to hedge with the help of put options.

10.4.2 Hedging with put options

As already demonstrated, put options are used mainly as protection against price declines. If the buyer of the option is correct, he has the right to sell a predefined quantity of the specified underlying at a predetermined price. To obtain this right, he needs to make a premium payment to the seller. With regard to weather derivatives, the basic idea of a put option is similar. Since the underlying varies, implementation is somewhat different. We will show this with the help of a simple example.

The utility company presented above does not only provide electrical power to agricultural companies in summer, but also sells heating oil to private homes in Baden-Wuerttemberg in winter. This line of business accounts for the remaining 50% of annual profits. The income from the heating oil business has decreased substantially over the past years as a result of the milder winters which can be attributed to climate change. An analysis of past data has revealed the following relationship:

An increase of the temperature by 1°C leads to a daily reduction of heating oil sales by 400 barrel at a price of USD20/barrel. This means that the utility company loses USD 8,000 per day if temperatures go up by 1°C. This translates into a monthly (30 days) loss of USD 240,000.

Now the utility company wants to purchase protection against the effects of mild temperatures. They turn to weather derivatives and invest in an HDD put offered by their bank.

The individual attributes of the put are determined with reference to the temperature in Baden-Wuerttemberg over the past years. They are as follows:

The option has a term to maturity of one month. (January 01, 2009 until January 31, 2009) and is written on the cumulative HDD index, which provides the average temperature of all weather stations in Baden-Wuerttemberg. The option has the following specifics: it can be exercised at expiration starting at a level of 600 HDD or below. The tick size is 1 DD = USD 8,000 (daily loss of the utility company) and the maximum payment that the seller is required to make is capped at 300 HDD or 300 HDD x USD 8,000 / HDD = USD 2,400,000. As compensation for the risk, the bank is asking for an option premium of USD 300,000.

Figure 10.7 presents the situation with and without the use of the put option.

Again different scenarios are possible:

Scenario 1: At expiration, the value of the cumulative HDD is above the strike level of 600: the option expires worthless and no compensation payment is due. Since the operative result benefits from the colder temperatures, this is not required. If the average temperature is −10°C, the HDD reaches 840 ((18°C − (−10°C)) × 30 days), and the option is not exercised. A loss from the option of USD 300,000 results (− option premium). The profit of the utility company amounts to 10°C × 30 days × 400 barrel × USD 20/barrel = USD 2,400,000; the net result is USD 2,100,000.

Scenario 2: The losses of the utility company from the operative business in the range between 300 to 600 HDD are compensated by the payment from the bank. The option is exercised.

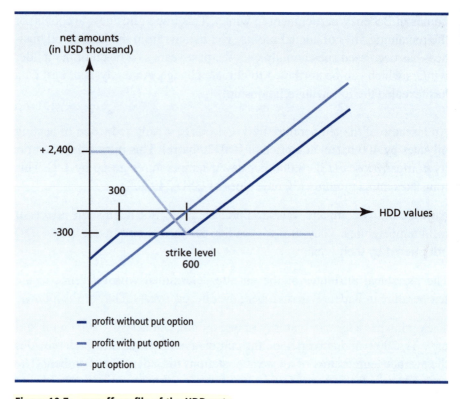

Figure 10.7: payoff profile of the HDD put

Example:

At an average temperature of 4°C during the relevant time period, the HDD takes on a value of 420 ((18°C − 4°C) x 30 days). The difference to the strike level is 180 HDD and thus the option is exercised. The utility company receives compensation in the amount of 180 x USD 8,000 = USD 1,440,000. The net payment (minus the option premium) is equal to USD 1,140,000 (see Table 10.2).

Table 10.2: Calculation of the net amount

Sales decline: 30 days × 400 barrel × USD 20/barrel × 4°C	− USD 960,000
Option payment	+ USD 1,440,000
Option premium	− USD 300,000
Net amount	= + USD 180,000

Scenario 3: if the cumulative HDD value is below 300, the option will be exercised. Due to the cap, a net amount of USD 2,300,000 will be paid out, which reduces the loss of the utility company. At an average temperature of 10°C, the value of the HDD is 240 and the option will be exercised. Since the cap is in place, the compensating payment is limited to USD 2,400,000. The loss of the utility company at this temperature level amounts to 30 days × 400 barrel × USD 20/barrel × 10°C = − USD 2,400,000. This loss is covered by the option payment. Once the option premium is deducted, a net loss of USD 100,000 results.

As is the case for call options, put options can be used both on the HDD and on the CDD. An HDD put can be used to seek protection against a mild winter. Meanwhile, a CDD put is used to hedge against adverse effects of a cool summer.

For the case of the call it was already demonstrated which features of the contract can be amended in order to achieve a complete hedge. If the premium payment appears too high to the company, there are several ways to reduce the premium:

1. Reduction of the strike level and the cap: if the strike level is reduced, the company is only hedged against high temperatures. If the cap is reduced, the company no longer holds protection against less extreme temperatures. No matter which feature is amended, the risk borne by the company has gone up.
2. In case the tick size is reduced, profits are hedged only partially and not completely.

Now that call and put options have been presented and illustrated with the help of simple examples, the next section deals with the advantages and disadvantages of these important representatives of conditional weather derivatives.

The biggest advantage of options related to weather is the possibility to completely hedge against weather-related risks without abandoning potential gains. This not only reduces risk, but also increases the ability to plan on the part of the buyer or company.

A further advantage for the buyer is the payoff profile, which is asymmetric, as was demonstrated with the help of the examples. Risks and opportunities are not locked in at a rate of 1:1. This is due to the fact that a buyer purchases an option and not an obligation. In the worst case, the buyer can exercise the option and is protected in that way. In the best case, the buyer benefits from favorable weather developments and does not exercise the option. Thus the maximum loss is already known ahead of time and limited to the option premium. The only disadvantage relates to the payment of the option premium, which is due already at the beginning of the conditional derivatives transaction. It is also possible that the standardized options which are available at the derivatives exchanges are not suitable for certain companies. In this case, the companies must resort to individually structured contracts, which are more expensive (see Table 10.3).

Table 10.3: Uses of CDD/HDD Call/Put

HDD Call	CDD Call
Protection against cold winters	Protection against warm summers
HDD Put	CDD Put
Protection against mild winters	Protection against cool summers

10.5 Unconditional weather derivatives: swaps and futures

Swaps and futures are unconditional or fixed derivatives transactions, which are characterized by predetermined obligations of both parties and symmetrical payoff structures. For the most part, weather derivatives are, as already mentioned, dominated by options. Nonetheless, swaps and futures hold a combined share of 25% of all weather derivatives traded and are therefore also relevant. This chapter mainly deals with the functioning of these instruments in the area of weather derivatives. Fictional examples are presented which illustrate possible uses of these instruments.

10.5.1 Example of a swap between an ice cream parlor and a travel agency

A swap transaction leads to an exchange of weather-related risks. The payoff profile is symmetrical and no premium payment is required. Swaps are appropriate for companies that seek protection against weather-related risks. Since no premium is paid, upside potential in the form of sales increases is also abandoned. The compensation payments of the swap are made by one of the two parties in line with the contract specifications and the weather development. For this type of weather derivative, the maximum payment can also be limited with the help of caps (upper limit) and floors (lower limit).

The following fictitious and strongly simplified example serves to demonstrate how swaps are constructed and how these constructions can help companies to hedge against weather-related risks and sales declines.

An ice cream parlor which is active in Stuttgart with several branch locations has most of its sales in August. Sales depend strongly on the temperature. The managers of the ice cream parlor have discovered that the company loses € 5,000 per day in August if the temperature falls by 1°C below the long-term average temperature. The opposite is true for the travel agency which is also located in Stuttgart.

The travel agency is specialized on travel abroad and due to the vacation schedule of the schools also has the highest sales volume in August. But sales depend in the temperature in Stuttgart: if the temperature is high, more travelers prefer to stay in Germany. This leads to the following relationship: sales decline by € 5.000 per day if the temperature exceeds the long-term average temperature by 1°C. As can be seen, both the ice cream parlor and the travel agency are subject to weather fluctuations and the possibly adverse effects on sales. In this situation, a swap between the two companies can be used. No premium payment is required and the risks (cool or warm August) are exchanged between the two parties. The swap has the following features: the long-term average temperature in August in Stuttgart, as recorded by a measuring station is 80 CDDs. The maximum is at 160 CDDs and the minimum at 15 CDDs. The average temperature of 80 CDDs is used as the strike level or reference value by both parties. In addition a floor of 30 CDDs and a cap of 130 CDDs are agreed. The payoff profile of such a swap transaction is shown in Figure 10.8.

As in the case of the options, three different scenarios for the swap can be described. Fees and other costs are not considered.

Scenario 1: At the end of August, the average temperature is equivalent to 80 CDDs. In this case, the two companies are not suffering any weather-related declines in sales. No compensatory swap payments are made. Since no premium payments are due, the companies are better off in this scenario compared to the option purchase.

Scenario 2: Should the average temperature fall between 30 und 80 CDDs, for example 50CDDs, the travel agency is required to pay € 5,000 for every CDD below the strike level to the ice cream parlor. The travel agency passes along parts of the increased sales to the ice cream parlor. In the example, the ice cream parlor would receive 30 × € 5,000 = € 150,000 from the travel

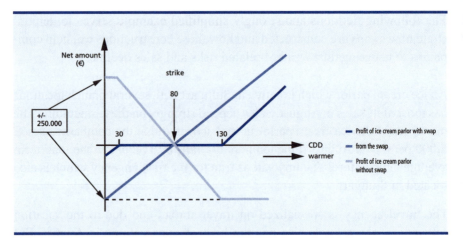

Figure 10.8: graphical representation of a CDD swap

agency. This would completely cover all losses of the ice cream parlor. If the CDD value is below 30 at expiration, the ice cream parlor will receive the maximum payment of € 250,000 from the travel agency as specified by the floor. This payment may not be sufficient to cover all losses of the ice cream parlor.

Scenario 3: Should the average temperature fall between 80 and 130 CDDs, the ice cream parlor must make payments to the travel agency. In the example of 100 CDDs, this would imply compensation in the amount of € 150,000 for the travel agency. In this case, the ice cream parlor passes along parts of its increased sales instead of paying a premium. The cap defines the maximum compensation payment of the ice cream parlor, in this example € 250,000.

The example clearly shows the advantages of such a structure: both companies can hedge against weather risks and at the same time reduce the volatility of their sales in August. Furthermore, no premium payment, which is required for options, must be made in such an arrangement. Still, the disadvantages of such a setup must be pointed out as well: in reality it is rather difficult to find two companies for a swap which matches as well as in our example. Companies must be identified that are active in the same region, are affected in opposite ways by the weather and have a low risk of default. In addition, every company must decide independently whether it prefers to make a small option payment or is willing to forego parts of the increased sales in order to obtain protection against weather-related risks.

Further members of the family of unconditional derivatives transactions are futures, respectively **weather futures**. They are the exchange-traded counterpart to the bilaterally agreed **weather swaps**, and also have a symmetrical payoff profile. They are offered today at the Chicago Mercantile Exchange (CME). The fact that futures are standardized and can thus be traded at an exchange leads to the elimination of a significant disadvantage: it is not necessary to find a suitable partner when purchasing such an instrument. In addition, futures can be used flexibly: the counterparty can either hedge certain weather-related risks or speculate with regard to specific weather situations.

10.5.2 Futures on the HDD for a railroad company

The following hypothetical example demonstrates how to use weather futures and how to eliminate potential weather-related risks.

A railroad company in London was suffering declines in revenues during particularly cold winter months, since the formation of ice blocked some routes for several days and trains did not run or could operate only at low speeds. This kind of weather not only results in the reimbursement of fares to the customers affected, but also to a decline in users of the railway system. They switch to other alternatives such as buses or cars. In the coming year, especially in January, the railroad company again expects very low temperatures, which are likely to have an adverse effect on revenues. Normally, the railroad company has one million passengers during a winter month. At an average price of £ 50/passenger this translates into revenues of £ 50 million. In addition, an analysis has revealed that the revenues of the railroad company have a negative correlation with the HDD index of LIFFE (London International Financial Futures and Options Exchange) of − 0.9. This means that revenues will decline by 0.9% (£ 450,000), for an increase of the index by 1% due to colder temperatures. For that reason, the railroad company decides to hedge against the potential decline in revenues and enters into a long (buyer) position on futures written on the HDD index of LIFFE. On the purchase date, the index is listed at 2,000 points and this value is used as the strike level. Due to the tick size (£ 100 = 1 HDD), an increase of the index by one percent is valued at £ 2,000. Since the company needs more than one futures contract, a so-called hedge ratio (change in revenues for 1°C / change of the value of the futures contract for 1°C) must be determined. It states the number of contracts needed. In this example: 450,000/2,000 = 225 contracts (see Figure 10.9).

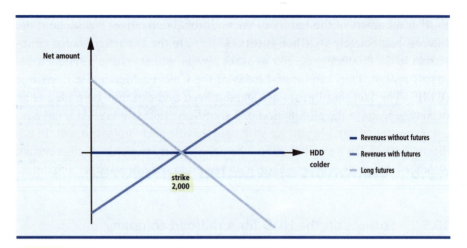

Figure 10.9: Payoff profile of an HDD futures contract

As can be seen in Figure 10.9, the payoff profile for the futures contract is symmetrical and the company is fully protected from revenue declines which are caused by its dependency on the weather.

Again several outcomes are possible for this weather derivative. They can be characterized as follows:

Scenario 1: The index is quoted at expiration at a level of 2,100 points. This implies that the forecast of the railroad company was accurate and the winter turned out to be rather cold. Revenues will have declined by £ 50 million × 0.9 × ((2,000 − 2,100)/2,000)) = £ 2.25 million. Since a long position was established, a payment of 100 × (2,100 − 2,000) × 225 contracts = £ 2.25 million results from the futures position. In this example, which does not consider fees and other costs, the revenue decline is fully compensated with the help of the futures position.

Scenario 2: At expiration, the index is quoted at 1,800 points. This implies that, contrary to the expectations of the railroad company, the winter was mild and revenues did not suffer. The long futures position must be closed which leads to a loss of 100 × (2,000 − 1,800) × 225 = £ 4.5 million. Normally, increases in revenue of the railroad company should serve as compensation for the cost of this futures transaction.

Due to their standardization, weather futures can be traded continuously on derivatives exchanges. This fact implies two advantages: thanks to the backing of the exchange as central counterpart, the default risk of such products can be minimized. Furthermore standardization implies a cost efficient way of hedging against weather-related risks. But there are disadvantages as well: standardization means that the geographical location of a company determines whether it can use futures. The protection, as in the case of swaps, comes at the cost of abandoning revenues. If a company is not willing to accept this, it needs to employ options, which were presented earlier. These are also not without costs, since payment of an option premium is required.

10.6 Valuation of weather derivatives

In our discussions so far, the price of the weather derivatives was always assumed. But in reality, determination of this price is not easy, as no generally accepted valuation method such as the Black-Scholes model is available. This lack of an accepted method and the fact that market participants use different valuation methods has implications for the market: at current it is very difficult to arrive at a price which is acceptable to both buyers and sellers.

10.7 Reasons for the failure of the Black-Scholes model in pricing weather derivatives

Attempts to use the model of Black and Scholes to value weather derivatives fail for a number of reasons, which were listed by ZIMMERMANN, JÄGER and JOVIC in 2001:

1. The Black-Scholes model can only be used for underlying assets that can be stored and traded physically. The model furthermore assumes the formation of a riskless portfolio consisting of a share and an option, which is completely hedged against any change in the underlying. Due to their attributes, such a combination is not possible for the underlying of weather derivatives (temperature, precipitation, wind speeds and so forth). This feature rules out use of the Black-Scholes model.

2. The percentage changes of the underlying objects of weather derivatives cannot be captured with the help of a normal distribution due to their complex features at expiration. They can be represented using other stochastic processes, but this leads to models that are very different from the one presented by Black and Scholes.

3. An additional difference between the valuation of weather derivatives and derivatives on financial assets is the assumption of a stochastic development in value: the valuation of options on equities assumes a random walk. This essentially means that the price of a share follows a random course and is not path dependent (attribute of a Markov process), while volatility and probability remain unchanged. The valuation of weather derivatives requires a conditional process, since weather patterns during a day or month reveal certain regularities (autocorrelation), which are not captured adequately by a random walk.

4. The final reason why the Black-Scholes model is not suitable for weather derivatives is the data situation: the valuation of derivatives requires current and past price data. Weather derivatives in contrast draw on measured and aggregated basis values, which in turn depend on the region and the method of measurement.

For these reasons, alternative valuation models were developed. The most important approaches are briefly presented in the coming sections. At current, these approaches are no match for the Black-Scholes model concerning broad acceptance and the corresponding breakthrough in application.

10.8 Burn analysis or burning cost method

The **burn analysis** or **burning cost method**[2] is a simple and widely used valuation model for the determination of weather derivatives and insurance contracts. The model is based on scenario analysis, which is generated using historical weather data. It shows the payments that would have been due in case the derivative had been in place. The arithmetic mean of these payments is equal to the value of the option. The expected value which has been determined in this way is equal to the expected payment from the derivative $E(D_T)$, which must be discounted at the rate e^{-rt} in order to obtain the fair price F_0, which also incorporates a risk premium π. The following formula represents this relationship:

$$F_0 = e^{-rt} \cdot E(D_T) + \pi$$

The determination of a price with the help of the burn analysis is simple and also does not require much effort. But there are significant disadvantages as

---

[2] The burning cost method is used to determine the costs which a reinsurance company would have incurred under the assumption that the quoted contract already existed in the past.

well: First, the model assumes that the future will look exactly like the past. This assumption implies that current climate changes or anomalies with their global repercussions are not taken into consideration. In addition, DISCHEL demonstrates that historical scenario analysis cannot be used without limits: on the one hand, large amounts of data are required in order to determine an appropriate estimate of volatility. On the other hand, only current data points, which capture climatic change, can be used in order to obtain meaningful projections of future developments. In addition, the option premiums derived with the burn method are too high, since all past weather events receive equal weights. Despite these shortcomings, this model is used by the majority of market participants due to the limited expenditure of time, the low costs and the simplicity. In order to eliminate the above mentioned disadvantages of the burn analysis, DISCHEL has developed an alternative approach, which is based on Monte-Carlo simulation.

The historical data is used only to obtain volatilities and other statistical values to describe the weather pattern. Based on the generated values, several development paths are derived with the help of numerous simulations, which can be used to set prices. An advantage of this approach is the ability to provide a comprehensive analysis and interpretations, since both current developments of the climate as well as historical data can be included. But this model also does not provide the base for the determination of a precise price of a weather derivative.

The following two models are particularly well suited for degree day contracts respectively options which are written on temperature. Both methods focus on describing and capturing the fundamental statistical process with the help of a model. In the context of these models, the specific attributes of temperature must also be recognized. Examples are:

- Daily temperatures have an autocorrelation of 1 for short intervals. This means that tomorrow's temperature depends on today's values.
- Due to differences in the volatilities of daily temperatures over the year, the time series of temperatures is heteroscedastic (unequal variance of two random samples). The volatility of temperatures is much higher in the winter months than in the summer months.

10.9 Index Value Simulation Method (IVSM)

This approach values weather derivatives with the help of payment streams of other securities. It assumes that market participants are risk neutral and that the no arbitrage condition holds in the complete market for weather derivatives. Therefore riskless profits are not possible. These assumptions imply that only exchange-traded weather derivatives can be valued with the help of this model. OTC weather derivatives do not meet these assumptions, especially with regard to the completeness of markets and the no arbitrage condition. Therefore they cannot be valued using the IVSM.

A characteristic feature of this approach is the statistical modeling of the temperature development within an index at expiration. Due to the assumption that the index follows a normal distribution, its mean and standard deviation can be derived from historical weather data.

But use of the IVSM also has some drawbacks. The most important ones are listed at this point:

- Due to the poor quality of the data, a normal distribution cannot be verified. It is merely an assumption.
- The index is constructed in such a way that temperatures which are below a certain reference value are assigned a value of zero. The true temperature development is therefore not reflected by the index.

Despite these drawbacks, it is possible in principle to obtain precise prices for weather derivatives with the help of the model presented. But what is needed is a highly developed, complete and transparent market such as an exchange. Furthermore, a simulation must be conducted for each transaction, since both the interval and the expiration date vary.

10.10 Daily Simulation Method (DSM)

This model was developed initially by CAO and WEI and can be used for the valuation of those weather derivatives that are related to temperature. This model accomplishes the daily modeling of temperature developments which are broken down into a deterministic and a stochastic part. In addition, an equilibrium model with external assumptions is used, which relates to the economy as well as the risk attitude and behavior of market participants. This approach is suitable for the calculation of an equilibrium price of the weather derivative and can also determine its expected value with the help of Monte-

Carlo simulations. The advantages of such a simulation are the very high precision and the inclusion of specific and current temperature developments which result from the daily modeling. In addition the DSM, unlike the IVSM, does not require fixed prices, is better able to represent reality due to the larger amounts of data and is not subject to assumptions. This implies that weather derivatives in the OTC market can also be valued.

10.11 Trading in weather derivatives

When American power companies were faced with the repercussions of the El Niño effect[3] and the deregulation of the energy sector, they looked for opportunities to escape the dependency on weather developments and began to use weather derivatives in the year 1997.

10.11.1 The first weather derivatives transactions

There is no agreement in the existing literature concerning the first transaction involving weather derivatives.

According to HEE and HOFMANN the first transaction was conducted in September 1997 by Enron, which attempted to hedge against existing weather-related risks with the help of an insurance contract and Koch Industries. Since the insurance premium amounted to about 60% of the nominal value, Enron was looking for ways to hedge with the help of derivatives. While most transactions were conducted on the OTC market initially, exchanges also showed an interest as volumes and the number of transactions increased. But as we will show later, the anticipated deepening of the market did not materialize.

10.11.2 The markets for weather derivatives

In addition to the OTC markets, classical derivatives exchanges are also offering weather derivatives. But the market for weather derivatives remains rather manageable and can be considered a marginal offering for the major derivatives exchanges.

---

[3] Spanish for "boy" or "child." It refers to a non-cyclical change in the currents of the oceanographic and meteorological system of the Equatorial Pacific. The name also means "Christ child" and is used in reference to the season when the effect occurs.

10.11.2.1 Chicago Mercantile Exchange (CME)

Trading in weather derivatives commenced on September 22, 1999 at CME. Initially only futures and options on futures for degree day indexes of 10 American cities could be traded. European companies that were looking for protection against weather-related risks could not use CME, since instruments to deal with their company-specific weather risks were not offered. This changed in the years 2003 and 2004, when CME included five European and two Asian cities in its product offering (see Figures 10.10 and 10.11).

10.11.2.2 London International Financial Futures and Options Exchange (LIFFE)

Due to the problems which European companies encountered early on with their attempts to hedge against weather-related risks at CME, LIFFE initiated trading in weather derivatives on December 10, 2001. Unfortunately, the expected growth rates in this segment did not materialize and only five futures contracts were traded in 2001. Since no orders were placed in 2002 and 2003, LIFFE was forced to abandon this line of activity.

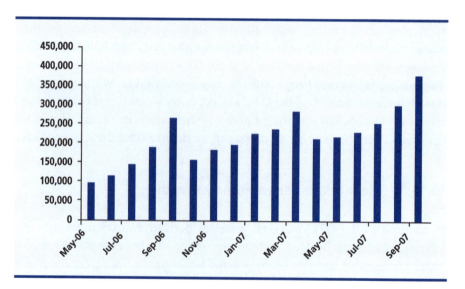

Figure 10.10: Monthly open interest at CME[4]

---

[4] Source: CME.

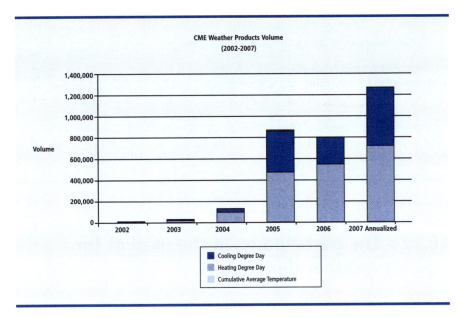

Figure 10.11: Contract volume at CME between 2002 and 2007[5]

10.11.2.3 Deutsche Börse AG

In December 2000, Deutsche Börse AG introduced weather indexes for 30 European cities under the name "**Xelsius**". But according to current market sentiment, the demand for exchange traded derivatives transactions on weather risks does not exist. Therefore Deutsche Börse AG has discontinued activities in this area.

10.11.2.4 Eurex

Eurex was the first European exchange to start trading in hurricane futures on June 29, 2009. Three possibilities are available with regard to the regional coverage: USA, Florida and the states along the Gulf Coast (Alabama, Louisiana, Mississippi and Texas). The various regions have different trigger levels.

---

[5] Source: CME.

> **The functioning of hurricane futures at Eurex:**
>
> If the estimated amount of the insured losses is above a certain trigger level (USD 10 – 50 billion), the contracts are settled at USD 10,000 due to their binary nature. If the amount is below that threshold, the value of the contract is only USD 0.10. To calculate the insured losses, Eurex uses data from the Property Claim Service of ISO (Insurance Services Office), the only internationally recognized estimation agent for catastrophe insurance claims in the U.S.

10.12 The participants in the market for weather derivatives

10.12.1 End user

The initial demand of the energy sector for protection against weather-related risks is the starting point for weather derivatives and the market. These market participants can be considered to be hedgers and for the most part come from the following industries: energy, agriculture, construction, tourism, leisure, foods and others. The negative effects of the weather and the various possibilities of the sectors to hedge against these risks were discussed with the help of examples in previous sections. But the end user is faced with a number of problems when using weather derivatives, which are briefly listed at this point:

- Standardized contracts are often not suitable as complete hedges of individual, complex and company-specific weather risks.
- A thorough analysis by the end user is required in order to determine the appropriate underlying, specific contract details and number of derivatives needed for an effective hedge.
- For an end user, the search for a suitable counterparty can be very difficult, especially if the weather-related risk is relatively small.

10.12.2 Trader

This group is similar to the speculators, which were already introduced. The main task of the traders is to actively take over (weather-related) risks from the end users in exchange for a premium. Additional tasks include acquisition of new end users as well as assistance and advice to these users. Over time, three major groups have evolved:

- Energy companies,
- (Re-)insurance companies and
- Banks (70% of the risks which are transferred by insurance companies with the help of weather derivatives are assumed).

These groups have the following attributes, which are necessary in order to fulfill the role of trader:

- excellent access to information,
- low management costs,
- strong credit standing and capital,
- willingness to assume risk and ability to value risks,
- strong client base.

Other participants include market makers, brokers and investors (private & institutional). They all have different aims and motives.

10.12.3 Market maker

Market makers are institutions which continually or on request provide binding quotes for the products which they maintain. This guarantees continuous and frictionless trading. Market makers provide the liquidity which is required for trading, even in unattractive series.

10.12.4 Broker

The main task of brokers in the market for weather derivatives is the matching of the first two groups so that risks can be transferred. They receive fees and premiums for this service. In addition, a broker can also identify weather risks and develop suitable hedging instruments. But it is not the function of the broker to assume risks. The process of matching works as follows: a party which wants to purchase protection against certain weather-related risks contacts a broker and puts him in charge of finding an appropriate counterparty at favorable conditions. Following a successful search, a transaction between the two parties takes place, which is beneficial to both contract parties and the broker.

10.12.5 Investor

Weather derivatives are an attractive investment opportunity both for private and for institutional investors (see Figure 10.12). From what we have pointed out so far, it follows that weather derivatives and the underlying indexes are independent of other assets in the financial world. It can thus be assumed that they are not correlated with these investments and that the portfolio risk can be reduced as a result of diversification. The influence of this investor group on the market is still small, since liquidity is still limited and therefore flexibility is reduced. In addition, a generally accepted valuation model which is a prerequisite for a fair product valuation is still missing.

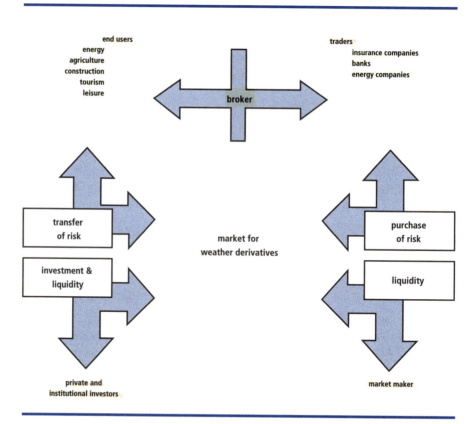

Figure 10.12: Overview of participants in the market for weather derivatives

Climate change

People's awareness of climate change has increased steadily over the past years. It is clearly observable that we are currently confronted with climate change which was caused by human action, such as global industrialization. Especially against this backdrop, the importance of weather derivatives, insurance derivatives and similar instruments will continue to gain in importance.

Literature for this chapter

Hee, Christian, Hoffmann, Lutz: Wetterderivate Grundlagen, Exposure, Anwendung und Bewertung, 2006

Werner, E.: Wetter als Börsenprodukt, Versicherungswirtschaft 55; Nr. 22

Zimmermann, H.; Jäger, S.; Jovic, D.: Bedeutung, Bewertung und Einsatz von Wetterderivaten, 2001

Questions and answers on this chapter

Question 1:
Is the following statement correct?
Weather derivatives are the world's most liquid type of derivative.

Question 2:
Are weather derivatives valued with the help of the Black-Scholes model?

Question 3:
Who is trading weather derivatives?

Question 4:
Is it true that no weather derivatives can be traded at Eurex?

Question 5:
What alternatives to weather derivatives are available?

Answer to question 1:
No, the statement is not correct. The market is small and very illiquid.

Answer to question 2:
No, the burn analysis or the burning cost method can be used instead.

Answer to question 3:
Mostly institutional investors or insurance companies who want to hedge their portfolios.

Answer to question 4:
No, the statement is not correct. For example the trading of hurricane futures is possible at Eurex.

Answer to question 5:
Examples of alternatives to weather derivatives are insurance contracts, insurance derivatives or commodity derivatives transactions.

11 Insurance derivatives

The following chapter covers these issues:

- What are insurance derivatives?
- Why are they traded and who does the trading?

11.1 What are insurance derivatives?

This market has grown significantly over the past years as a result of an increased incidence of risks and the possibility to trade these in financial markets. In the past, the insurance industry covered risks arising from natural disasters[1] with the help of reinsurance policies. Derivatives that are tied to insurance claims were used for the first time in so-called **contingent capital programs**. They provide capital support in the form of profit participation rights or preferred shares to insurance companies which have suffered losses in equity capital as a result of massive insurance claims, caused for example by natural disasters.

11.2 Why are they traded and who does the trading?

In this context, one investor is purchasing, against payment of a premium, the right to sell preferred shares or profit participation rights to another investor in case of occurrence of a clearly specified natural disaster, which leads to the loss of equity capital. The option can only be exercised once a clearly de-

---

[1] Hurricane, flooding, hailstorms and so forth.

fined natural disaster has occurred. The new investor receives shares or profit participation rights[2] and in exchange provides the company with fresh equity capital. A comparison to catastrophe bonds makes clear that the investor provides capital only after the catastrophic event has occurred. In the case of catastrophe bonds, the capital is provided in advance and can be completely lost in the worst case.

Standardized derivatives which are based on indexes of regional losses for 9 regions of the U.S. have been available at CBOT for a number of years now. Coverage is available for up to one year. The cost of these derivatives is equal to the reinsurance premium.

An alternative form of insurance derivative is an OTC insurance swap. The investor who makes a fixed premium payment receives a variable payment from the swap in the case of an insurance claim. It is also possible to swap the respective portfolio risks in the context of a portfolio swap or exposure swap. No variable payment is due in this case.

The contracts can be considered to be bilateral financial contracts. Standardized sample agreements are used, which have been developed by the International Swap and Derivatives Association (ISDA).

As with all bilateral financial contracts, counterparty risk exists in the case of insurance derivatives. What happens if the counterparty is unable to pay once a contract is exercised? Before entering into the derivatives transaction, it should be assured that the counterparty possesses good credit standing and ample liquidity. Due to the existence of a collateral trust and prepayment, this risk is not as dramatic for catastrophe bonds. But the structure is significantly more complex and involves a larger administrative burden.

---

[2] Mezzanine capital structures.

Literature for this chapter

Hull, John: Options, Futures and Other Derivatives, 7th edition, 2009

Questions and answers on this chapter

Question 1:
Which disasters triggered the creation of insurance derivatives?

Question 2:
Who invests in insurance derivatives?

Question 3:
Are these derivatives traded at an exchange?

Question 4:
Which is the most active market for insurance derivatives?

Question 5:
Which risk must be considered when entering into an insurance derivatives transaction?

Answer to question 1:
The product development was triggered by natural disasters.

Answer to question 2:
Mostly insurance and reinsurance companies are active in the market.

Answer to question 3:
Yes, CBOT in Chicago.

Answer to question 4:
Most derivatives are traded OTC.

Answer to question 5:
The credit standing of the counterparty must be considered. In case of a default, the derivative is worthless.

12 | Real options

The following chapter covers these issues:

- What are real options?
- What is the real options approach?
- How are real options classified?
- What is the difference between financial options and real options?
- How are real options valued?

The real options approach is an innovative management and valuation method, which can be used in capital budgeting, company valuation and as a management concept. In modern research, this model has been discussed for about 30 years. The term real option was coined by PROF. STEWART C. MYERS of the Massachusetts Institute of Technology (MIT) in 1977. In applied work, this approach is not without its critics. It became apparent rather quickly that the real options approach requires a lot of time and data and that its predominant use is restricted to the commodities industry[1]. Exxon Mobile and Texaco used the real options approach in practice to value new investments in extraction capacities for crude oil and other industries as well made use of it. As an example, the pharmaceutical company Merck valued its research and development investments in the mid-nineties. Startup companies use the approach to get access to venture capitalists and to obtain liquidity for their activities. Providers of risk capital use the approach to evaluate extensive research and development projects which have to pass several milestones.

---

[1] This is also due in part to the existence of commodity derivatives which are known and used in the industry.

12.1 What are real options?

Real options provide management with flexibility concerning their activities by reaching decisions about future investments and disinvestments on the basis of information that becomes available in the future[2]. The possibility to wait with an investment decision and to make it dependent on the development of relevant states of the world at a later point in time must be provided with the help of an earlier initial investment. This means that real options have a price or a specific value. The goal of the real options approach is to quantify the value which is generated via investments in entrepreneurial flexibility.

The real options approach is complementary to the well respected methods of valuing investments and companies – such as the **discounted cash flow method**[3]. It focuses on the value of strategic flexibility, an issue that is not given adequate weight by traditional methods of company valuation. Strategic flexibility is the result of management accomplishments and allows alternative reactions to differing scenarios. The aim is to develop successful areas of business and eliminate loss-making ones. Real options that create value can result from opportunities to increase production if demand picks up, possibilities to delay investments up to a certain point, to tie additional project steps to the achievement of predefined milestones, to discontinue projects or to produce with different input factors.

Not every course of action is also a valuable option. Real options are defined with reference to the following features:

- **Value**: real options must be created deliberately. This means that they are usually tied to an initial investment. As a result of the initial investment, the option and the accompanying valuable rights are created.
- **Goal orientation**: the creation of a real option is always connected to a concrete reason for investing or divesting that goes beyond the initial investment. Consequently, different types of real options can be distinguished.
- **Flexibility**: an option describes the right, but not the obligation to implement a certain investment or divestment. Flexibility is created if the investment decision can be postponed to a certain degree and/or the investment expenses can be spread out over a number of periods.
- **Uncertainty**: the application and valuation of options only makes sense in an uncertain market environment with highly uncertain investments. Oth-

---
[2] See Ernst, Häcker: Realoptionen im Investment Banking, Schäffer-Poeschel, Stuttgart.
[3] For more detail see Ernst, Schneider, Thielen: Unternehmensbewertungen erstellen und verstehen – Ein Praxisleitfaden 4. Auflage, Vahlen.

erwise the strategic flexibility of management and thus the option features of the investments will lose their relevance.
- **Irreversibility:** once it is exercised, the option right is used up. The following investment decision has become irreversible in that case and **sunk costs** in the amount of the initial investment plus the follow-up investment are created. If the option is not exercised, sunk costs only amount to the initial investment.

The features of real options are summarized again in Figure 12.1.

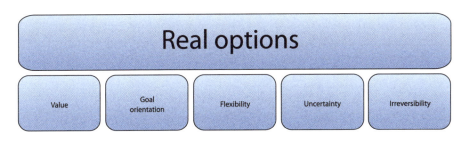

Figure 12.1:   Features of real options

12.2   How to classify real options

Real options can be classified in line with Figure 12.2. In the following, we provide an explanation for this classification.

- An **entry option** covers the situation of a completely new strategic alternative. This can be the case, for example, for a single stage investment decision, which can be postponed.
- A **continuation option** typically relates to the decision whether to continue a multi-level investment project which was already initiated earlier by paying for the next tranche.
- An **expansion option** allows the owner to expand the success of an investment that was already undertaken. This is the case, for example, if a machine, which produces a good that is selling well, can be purchased once more in order to increase sales.
- Similar to a continuation and expansion option, a **growth option** provides its owner with the opportunity to secure the possibility for follow-up invest-

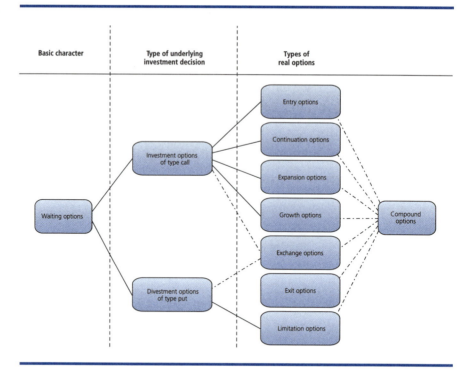

Figure 12.2: Classification of real options following Ernst/Thümmel (2000)[4]

ments and expansion with the help of an (initial) investment. In that sense, the growth option can also be considered to be a concept which includes the previous two types of real options. But they are related mostly to the short-term operative flexibility in a concrete investment project, while growth options are mostly discussed in the context of strategic decisions. The entry of a foreign company into the national market as part of a buy-and-build strategy is one example.

- An **exit option** entails the possibility to terminate an unsuccessful project or to sell it at its liquidating value in order to reduce current losses.
- A **limitation option** meanwhile concerns the liquidation of parts of the project or capacity reductions.
- An **exchange option** is characterized by the possibility to use capacities which were created or are to be created within a project not only exclusively for that project, but for other uses as well. With regard to the expected revenues from the original project, this can be considered a put option; with

---

[4] Source: Ernst, Schneider, Thielen 2008.

regard to possible additional revenues from an alternative capacity use, it can be considered a call option. An exchange option becomes available with a manufacturing unit that is suitable for the production of different goods.
- A **compound option** is obtained when several real options are combined or when the underlying of a real option again has the character of an option. Most of the option types described above can also be interpreted as compound options. This is the case, for example, if the next tranche in a multi-step investment problem is not the last one, but again can be considered an option to continue the project by investing in the following tranche.

12.3 Real options and financial options

Entrepreneurial scope of action is frequently very similar in character to a financial option. As was already the case with previous financial options, asymmetric payment or risk profiles also exist in investment projects in the real economy. But one requirement is the existence of a multi-step project. This is always the case when the anticipated investment volume is invested in several tranches or if, in the case of a one-step project, the time of payment of the entire investment amount can be delayed by paying an option premium.

Table 12.1 shows the relationship between real options and classical financial options.

12.4 Valuation of real options

For the valuation of real options, the procedures developed by *BLACK-SCHOLES* and *COX, ROSS* and *RUBINSTEIN* are used, which we already discussed. Figure 12.3 summarizes the steps needed when valuing real options.

12.5 Valuation of real options in practice

Compound options are used in the following to demonstrate the use of the real options approach in practice[5]. It is the aim of the compound real options approach to value these options in a methodologically closed model.

---

[5] The example is taken from Ernst, Schneider, Thielen: Unternehmensbewertung erstellen und verstehen, 4. Auflage, Vahlen.

Table 12.1: Comparison of the value drivers of financial options and real options[6]

Call option/put option on equities	Real call option	Real put option
Value of the underlying (current share price)	Present value of the expected future positive cash flow (gross, meaning without outflows for investments)	Present value of the expected future positive cash flow (gross, meaning without inflows for divestments)
Strike price	Present value of future payments for investments (due on the exercise date)	Present value of future payments resulting from divestments (accrue on the exercise date)
Term to maturity of the option	Time period during which a decision to invest (or to pay an additional tranche) can be postponed	Time period during which a decision to divest can be postponed
Volatility of the share price	Volatility of the present value of the expected cash flows	Volatility of the present value of the expected cash flows
Riskless rate of interest	Riskless rate of interest	Riskless rate of interest
Dividend payments	Current revenues from the underlying that are foregone prior to exercising the option	Current revenues from the underlying that are foregone prior to exercising the option

The valuation of compound options usually follows the model of Geske, which is based on the valuation assumptions of Black and Scholes. Due to the demonstrated advantages of the binomial model for an applied valuation of companies and the desired comparability of the compound real options approach with the real options models already presented, the presentation of the Geske model will in the following be based on the binomial model. Real options valuation in turn is conducted in four steps:

1. Modeling of the starting situation
2. Determination of input parameters
3. Implementation of valuation
4. Fine tuning

---

[6] Source: Ernst, Schneider, Thielen 2008.

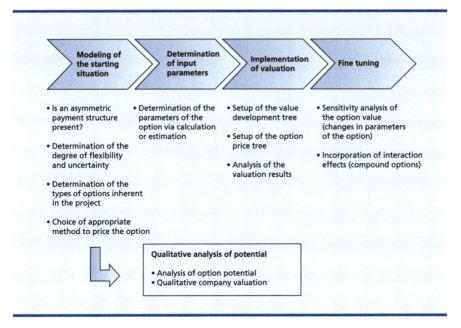

Figure 12.3: Steps in the valuation of real options[7]

Modeling of the starting situation

For the applied example (we choose the fictitious Automotive Vision AG), the existing real options (exit and continuation options), due to their interrelations, are defined and valued as a series of call options. Since inflows and outflows do not occur at the same points in time in this applied example, the basic premises of the model must be modified. It is assumed that the project payments which are made can be valued as calls on the expected value of sales already during the development phase. The riskiness of the market prices which can be obtained is reflected in the fact that both upward and downward movements are possible. These fluctuations around the expected value can be captured with the help of one risk measure, namely volatility.

Determination of input parameters

The value of the basic instrument is determined by discounting the payments at a required rate of return on equity of 20%. It amounts to 176,782 €thousand (see Table 12.2).

In our discussion of option price models so far, the exercise price was determined as the present value of the payments made during the investment

---

[7] Source: following Hommel/Pritsch, 1999, p. 122.

Table 12.2: Value of the basic instrument and period-specific strike prices

Year in €thousand	0	1	2	3	4	Residual value beginning 5
payment receipt		0	400	30,000	55,000	275,000
discount factor (interest rate 20%)		0.83	0.69	0.58	0.48	0.48
present value		0	277	17,361	26,254	132,620
Sum = value of the basic instrument	176,782					
payout = periodic specific strike prices			−6,900	−10,600	−16,000	−31,800	−159,000
free cash flow			−6,900	−10,200	14,000	23,200	116,000

period on the exercise date. Meanwhile, the approach to calculate compound options is a stage model, where project payments are made during the development phase, which can be interpreted as period-specific exercise prices. A particularity arises with regard to the determination of the residual value (final value). It amounts to 159,000 €thousand. Since this value refers to the valuation date December 31 of period $t(4)$ and thus has the same time dimension as the value 31,800 €thousand of period $t(4)$, while the residual value of period $t(5)$ is relevant for the valuation, the residual value at the beginning of $t(5)$ is compounded for one period to the end of $t(5)$. It thus amounts to 190,800 €thousand.

Table 12.2 shows the calculation of the value of the basic instrument and the period-specific strike prices. The determination of the free cash flow serves as a control.

Dividend payments or revenues foregone are captured in this model via technological risk. Revenues foregone can arise if a project is discontinued during the development phase and no marketable product is created. The technological risk is included in the model by weighting the options value which is derived from the compound options approach with the probability of a successful realization of the project. This value is 3.28%.

For the determination of a riskless rate of interest, a long term government bond is used. It has a yield of 5%.

The term to maturity of the option is 5 years.

There are basically two possible approaches to determine volatility: either a peer group analysis or a Monte-Carlo simulation. For a start-up company, the derivation of volatility via peer group analysis is not possible, since publicly listed companies cannot be compared to start-up companies. A meaningful peer group analysis would require that the companies considered deal with the development of the same product, are at the same development stage and have identical financial structures.

These demands, coupled with the difficulties of generating the data, require a different approach for the determination of volatility. One obvious choice is Monte-Carlo simulation. It allows modeling of those project or company risks that are considered to be of prime importance. Overall volatility is determined by simulating the interaction of the relevant uncertainty factors.

For the valuation of the compound options in our fictitious example of the Automotive Vision AG, the volatility must be determined with the help of a Monte-Carlo simulation. It is equal to 50%.

Implementation of the valuation

The valuation of compound options, in analogy to European and American options is done in two steps:

- Determination of the binomial tree for the underlying project
- Determination of the binomial tree for the option

In order to calculate the compound options, an initial determination of the **binomial tree for the underlying project** is required. Starting point is the present value of all cash inflows in **t(0)**, which amounts to 176,782 €thousand. For the project development, a constant uncertainty of the market development is assumed, which is reflected in an annual volatility of the expected value of the free cash flow. This volatility σ amounts to 50%.

Given the volatility, the factors for the up-movement u and the down-movement d can be calculated:

$$u = e^{\sigma\sqrt{\Delta t}}$$
$$d = e^{-\sigma\sqrt{\Delta t}}$$

The annual standard deviation is adjusted with the help of the term $\sqrt{\Delta t}$ to reflect the time interval under consideration. In the current example, the overall project time is five years and five time periods are considered. This means that Δt can be set equal to 1. For a volatility which was determined at 50%, the following values for the up-movement and down-movement can be calculated:

$$u = e^{0.50\sqrt{1}} = 1.649$$
$$d = e^{-0.50\sqrt{1}} = 0.607$$

Starting from the present value at market introduction in $t(0)$, a binomial tree for all possible outcomes of the underlying project until its completion can be determined by multiplication with the factors for the up-movement and down-movement. In this way, all possible states of the world ($n = 1$ to 6) for the project value in $t(5)$ [$S_1(5)$ to $S_6(5)$] can be calculated (see Figure 12.4).

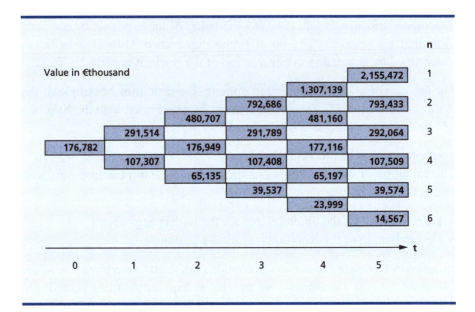

Figure 12.4: Possible states of the project values

In the next step, the pseudo-probabilities for the certainty equivalent are determined. With the derivation of **u** and **d** from the volatility, a model in discrete time is generated. Therefore, the probability of an up-movement **q** is determined with the help of the following formula:

$$q = \frac{1 + r_f - d}{u - d} = \frac{1 + 0.05 - 0.607}{1.649 - 0.607} = 0.4255 = 42.55\%$$

The probability of a down-movement $(1 - q)$ can thus be determined as follows:

$$1 - q = 1 - 0.4255 = 0.5745 = 57.45\%$$

In the second step, the **binomial tree for the option** is set up. Since compound options are considered specifically in each period, several binomial trees for the option are determined.

Valuation of real options in practice

Beginning from the possible values of the project in $t(5)$, the option is calculated with the help of a roll back analysis. The cash flows in each specific period, which can be considered to be the investments in each round of financing, are the period-specific exercise prices. The cash flows in the previous period thus represent payment of the option premium. It is the goal of the roll back analysis to calculate the option value of the venture capital project in period $t(0)$ via the calculation of the period-specific option values.

In a first step, the strategic flexibilities (**calls(5)**) which exist in $t(5)$ are valued. This requires a determination of the values on the due date. The strike price $X(5)$ is equal to 190,800 €thousand.

Using
$$c_n(5) = \max\{S_n(5) - X(5); 0\}$$
$$\text{for } n = 1 \text{ to } 6$$

the values of these calls are determined. For example, the value of $c_1(5)$ is equal to:

$$c_1(5) = \max\{S_1(5) - X(5); 0\}$$
$$= \max\{2{,}155{,}472 \text{ €thousand} - 190.800 \text{ €thousand}; 0\}$$
$$= \max\{1{,}964{,}672 \text{ €thousand}; 0\}$$
$$= 1{,}964{,}672 \text{ €thousand}$$

Figure 12.5 presents all possible outcomes for the call in $t(5)$, which are the starting values for the determination of S in $t(4)$. The relevant figures are shown in bold letters.

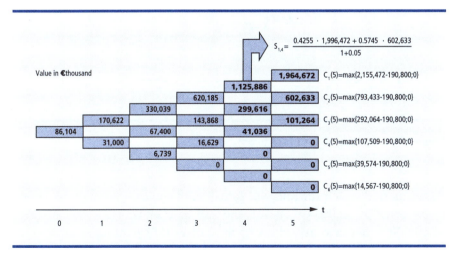

Figure 12.5: Possible values of call in t(5)

To calculate the values in $t(4)$, the following formula is used:

$$S_n(t) = \frac{q \cdot c_n(t+1) + (1-q) \cdot c_{n+1}(t+1)}{1 + r_f}$$

$S_1(4)$ for example can be determined as follows:

$$S_1(4) = \frac{q \cdot c_1(5) + (1-q) \cdot c_2(5)}{1 + r_f}$$

$$= \frac{0.4255 \cdot 1{,}996{,}472 \,\text{€thousand} + 0.5745 \cdot 602{,}633 \,\text{€thousand}}{1.05}$$

$$= 1{,}125{,}886 \,\text{€thousand}$$

The values of the investment opportunities that were determined in this way constitute the underlying for the calls in period $t(4)$. The strike price of these options is equal to 31,800 €thousand. The values of the calls in $t(3)$ are calculated based on the scheme used previously. The results are provided in Figure 12.6.

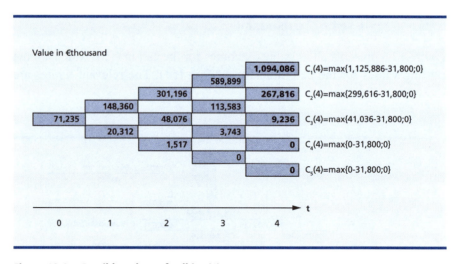

Figure 12.6: Possible values of call in t(4)

Based on this same principle, the valuation of the call in $t(3)$ with an exercise price of 16,000 €thousand, the call in $t(2)$ with an exercise price of 10,600 €thousand as well as of the call in $t(1)$ with an exercise price of 6,900 €thousand is conducted. Figure 12.7 provides an overview of the period-specific option values.

Valuation of real options in practice

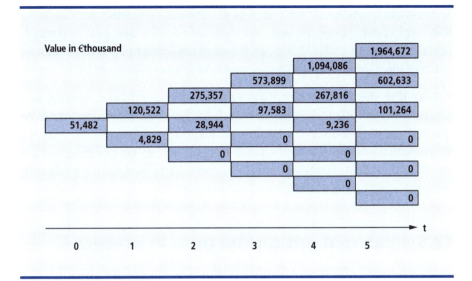

Figure 12.7: Option values for Automotive Vision AG

The approach presented provides a possibility to assess development projects with a special focus on market risks. In advance of every payment that must be made, it can be assessed whether it is still possible to obtain a positive free cash flow after making the required payments. The uncertainty about the sales potential is transferred to the development stage. But it must be mentioned that technological risk is not captured. The risk that it is not possible to produce a marketable product will always reduce the cash flow. Therefore it cannot be captured in the risk measure volatility, which also causes positive changes in the expected value. In order to incorporate technological risk, the project value is weighted with the expected probability of project success of 3.28%. A value of 1,688 €thousand is the result.

$$\text{Project value} = 51{,}482 \text{ €thousand} \cdot 3.28\% = 1{,}688 \text{ €thousand}$$

The value of the entire investment project is composed of two parts: the passive project value from the decision tree procedure of –5,489 € thousand and the active project value in the amount of 7,177 € thousand. The expanded project value is equal to 1,688 €thousand.

Fine tuning

A comparison of the results from the real options approach and the classical investment analysis (for example a decision tree) reveals significant differences, which are due to the value provided by strategic flexibility. The use of compound options shows that a project which previously was unfavorable can become beneficial once the value of added scope is incorporated. This underlines the relevance of an active management of participations by utilizing managerial flexibility.

Results that suggest a positive outcome using one valuation method and a negative result using another approach suggest that the project must be checked carefully before continuing. In addition to a sensitivity analysis, an assessment of the relevant value drivers as well as an evaluation of the project and product chances by industry experts in the context of a qualitative company valuation is needed.

12.6 Can real options be used in practice?

Academic researchers and practitioners alike frequently ask about the use and value added of the real options approach compared to other, established capital budgeting and company valuation methods. The use of the real options approach is meaningful in cases where the capital value is near zero and no clear decision can be reached. If, in contrast, the capital value is high, most options have a relatively low value, since it is unlikely that the added flexibility which they provide will be heavily used. The same also holds for the opposite case of a clearly negative capital value: the options approach will not overturn such an assessment. So what are the advantages of the real options approach compared to the classical procedures? In the following we want to elaborate on a few issues.

- Before conducting a company valuation with the real options approach, it must be ascertained whether the company is in the possession of real options. This demands an intensive engagement by the valuation expert both at a qualitative and quantitative level. In addition to a company analysis and an analysis of past performance, it is particularly important to identify those company divisions that have an options character and to decide how this can be incorporated in the enterprise planning and which methods are suitable to arrive at an adequate company valuation.
- Risk is treated in the real options approach not only as exposure to dangers that reduce the value of the company, but also as potential market uncertainty, which can open up strategic flexibility and market opportunities if management reacts appropriately. The transparency of the company value is increased by demonstrating which of its components are more certain and which components can only be achieved if the option is used optimally, but at a higher risk.

- The real options approach also makes a contribution as a management philosophy, which goes beyond the mere facts of company valuation. It stresses the ability to act flexibly and combines the topic of investment and company valuation with the topic of flexible and rolling planning. This provides an operative, tactical and strategic foundation for the decision making processes of the stakeholders and for the importance of active process management in uncertain markets. The real options approach can provide a more differentiated view of uncertainty and its concrete manifestations as well as the process of dissolving and influencing uncertainty.
- Thus the advantages of the real options approach are
  1. identification,
  2. valuation and
  3. management

  of uncertainty and options in a company. They form a three-step management cycle, which is a useful instrument in value-based management.

Despite its uses in company valuation, which we demonstrated with the help of applied examples, the real options approach was subject to criticism. The crucial issues can be summarized as follows.

The most fundamental criticism starts with the foundations and premises. Option price theory assumes the existence of a complete capital market. But this does not hold in the specific case of real options. Therefore the use of the real options approach – especially when valuing companies that are not publicly listed – must be viewed with reservations.

This criticism is valid from a theoretical perspective. But it must be kept in mind that the **DCF method**[8] utilizes **CAPM** and therefore also assumes a complete capital market. Due to the broad acceptance of the DCF method by valuation practitioners as the standard for company valuations, the model assumptions are no longer questioned. In that regard, the real options approach does not suffer from any shortcomings in methodology compared to the DCF approach. Furthermore, it must be added that the combined use of the DCF method and the real options approach requires identical model premises. Otherwise the valuation results would be flawed.

---

[8] Discounted cash flow method: company valuation model which uses cash flows that are discounted to arrive at a capital value. See on this: Ernst, Schneider, Thielen: Unternehmensbewertung erstellen und verstehen, 4. Auflage, Vahlen.

In addition to this fundamental objection, the individual value drivers are also subject to criticism. The following disadvantages of the real options approach are mentioned.

The first line of criticism refers to the adequate valuation of the underlying instrument. As we demonstrated, the value of the real option depends to a large degree on the value of the underlying instrument. If no underlying instrument exists, a DCF analysis must be conducted before the option can be valued. Such an approach does not simplify matters, since the problems of finding an adequate discount factor and forecasting the cash flows continue to exist. If it is determined that the DCF analysis is not suitable for the derivation of a potential market value, it will also not be meaningful to use the DCF value in an option valuation.

While this criticism can be easily understood, it is a fundamental attack against the possibility to determine market values and the required attempt to define objective factors. Since it is impossible to conduct a company valuation that does not use any subjective assessment, no disadvantage for the real options theory compared to other valuation methods can be identified if this line of reasoning is pursued.

Additional criticism is directed at the assumption that the future strike price can be determined with sufficient precision. Given the degree of uncertainty that is actually present in markets, this assumption is not realistic and casts doubt on the information value of the calculations.

One solution would be to model the strike price as a random development – similar to the approach taken for the underlying instrument – and to calculate the value of the strike price with the help of simulation procedures. While this better represents uncertainty, it still does not rule it out – as is the case in any valuation exercise which has a planning horizon that extends into the future.

A further reason for criticism is the treatment of risk in the real options approach. While volatility is considered to be a risk parameter in the DCF method, which from the perspective of a risk averse investor only captures the possibility of losses (and not the opportunity to make a profit), volatility is interpreted as a parameter that provides opportunities for future income in the real options approach. This perspective follows from the character of options, which have asymmetric payoff profiles and limit the risk of losses to the option premium, while on the other hand the profit potential remains unlimited.

This criticism is fully justified from the perspective of classical company valuation and its risk definition. The solution to this dilemma is to only use data for the DCF valuation of the underlying instrument that is not in doubt and of almost certain nature. In this case it makes sense to add to the DCF value that amount that is derived from uncertain strategic flexibility (option value). In any case, double-counting must be avoided.

If viewed critically, the DCF value and the option value should not be considered to be an absolute total value, as is often assumed, but rather a range which is delineated by the minimum value from the DCF valuation and the maximum value from the expanded analysis (DCF value plus option value). The precise company value lies within this range and depends on the actual substance of the real options included. The breakdown of the company value into a rather certain and an uncertain component also responds to the criticism that the real options approach always generates higher company values than the DCF method and therefore tends to be used especially during boom periods in support of high transaction prices. This is precisely not the case, since the real options approach, used properly, will increase the transparency of the company value. This reduces the uncertainty surrounding any investment decision, especially during economically difficult times and supports the determination of realistic prices.

It may be worthwhile to contemplate whether volatility estimates, which measure opportunities, need to be reduced in the presence of unsystematic risk. As a similar procedure is used in the case of the DCF method, academic researchers and valuation practitioners still have the task of deriving a methodologically sound and understandable relationship between risks and opportunities. This would be an important contribution towards broader acceptance of the real options approach in applied valuation work.

From the perspective of a practitioner in the field of company valuation, the biggest weakness of the real options approach is its practical implementation. As was also apparent in the valuation examples, use of the real options approach – especially if a **number of strategic real options** exist – requires not only considerable effort in identification and collection of the data, but also mastery of complex option pricing models for the valuation of compound options. Furthermore, standard models, which allow the valuation of different real options and their interactions with manageable effort are still lacking.

The effort required in using real options as a valuation tool is a major obstacle in applied work. Even the decision tree procedure, which is a stringent refinement of the DCF model in situations of uncertainty, is applied in practice only in exceptional cases. The reason for this restraint can be traced to the demanding data requirements. Similarly large – if not larger – is the effort required to conduct an option price valuation. The mere fact that the determination of volatility, the most important value driver, almost always requires the use of complex Monte-Carlo simulation approaches, which in turn are based on specialized programs, shows the complexity of the methodology and the data requirements of the real options approach.

It is an additional major problem for the application of the real options approach that real options often play only a minor role when valuing companies on a **stand-alone basis**. This follows from the fact that companies would use their real options as part of their business model – and therefore valuation with the help of the DCF method would become possible – if they could. Real options often become available to external investors in the context of a company transaction. This raises the question why a company should have to pay for options which it has to make valuable by contributing own funds and accepting related risks. One exception is a sellers' market, in which the seller holds a favorable negotiating position and investors are willing to share parts of the option premium with him.

The reservations of valuation practitioners, who are afraid that the real options approach, due to its conception and complexity, can be abused to give academic support for exaggerated price demands is related to this idea. While this danger is also present for other valuation approaches, the real options procedure can be abused more easily due to the difficulties in tracing the valuation process. And it can be assumed that the valuation of some new economy companies, which are occasionally mentioned in connection with the real options approach, has heightened these concerns.

These points of criticism reveal where improvements in methodology, aimed at the acceptance and dissemination of the real options approach, are required. Despite this criticism, it must be stressed that the real options approach can frequently make a substantial contribution to the determination of company value. This is due to the fact that strategic opportunities are analyzed explicitly and justifiable reasons for inclusion in the analysis are provided. Once it has been determined that an application of the real options theory is practicable, there is no reason to ignore this approach when valuing a company.

Literature for this chapter

Black, F., Scholes, M. (1973): The Pricing of Options and Corporate Liabilities, in: Journal of Political Economy, Vol. 81, pp. 637–659.

Copeland, T., Antikarov, V. (2002): Realoptionen: Das Handbuch für Finanzpraktiker, Weinheim.

Copeland, T., Koller, T., Murrin, J. (1998): Unternehmenswert: Methoden und Strategien für eine wertorientierte Unternehmensführung, 2nd edition, Frankfurt/Main, New York.

Cox, J. C., Ross, S. A., Rubinstein, M. (1979): Option Pricing: A Simplified Approach, in: Journal of Financial Economics, No. 7, pp. 229–263.

Ernst, D., Schneider, S., Thielen, B. (2006): Unternehmensbewertungen erstellen und verstehen, 2nd edition, München.

Ernst, D., Häcker, J. (2002): Realoptionen im Investment Banking: Mergers & Acquisitions, Initial Public Offering, Venture Capital, Stuttgart.

Geske, R. (1979): The Valuation of Compound Options, in: Journal of Financial Economics, No. 7, pp. 63–81.

Hommel, U., Pritsch, G. (1999): Marktorientierte Investitionsbewertung mit dem Realoptionsansatz, in: Achleitner, A., Thoma, G. (eds.): Handbuch Corporate Finance, Supplement September, pp. 1–67.

Hommel, U., Scholich, M., Vollrath, R. (eds., 2001): Realoptionen in der Unternehmenspraxis: Wert schaffen durch Flexibilität, Berlin.

Hull, John: Options, Futures and Other Derivatives, 7th edition, 2009

Kilka, M. (1995): Realoptionen: Optionstheoretische Ansätze bei Investitionsentscheidungen unter Unsicherheit, Frankfurt/Main.

Koch, Ch. (1999): Optionsbasierte Unternehmensbewertung, Wiesbaden.

Liebler, H. (1996): Strategische Optionen: Eine kapitalmarktorientierte Bewertung von Investitionen unter Unsicherheit, St. Gallen.

Müller, J. (2000): Real Option Valuation in Service Industries, Wiesbaden.

Rams, A. (1998): Strategisch-dynamische Unternehmensbewertung mittels Realoptionen, in: Die Bank, Nr. 11, pp. 676–680.

Rams, A. (1999): Realoptionsbasierte Unternehmensbewertung, in: FINANZ BETRIEB, Jg. 1, Nr. 11, pp. 349–364.

Rams, A. (2001): Die Bewertung von Kraftwerksinvestitionen als Realoption, in: Hommel, U., Scholich, M., Vollrath, R. (eds., 2001): Realoptionen in der Unternehmenspraxis: Wert schaffen durch Flexibilität, Berlin, pp. 156–178.

Sandmann, K. (1999): Einführung in die Stochastik der Finanzmärkte, Heidelberg u.a.O.

Schäfer, H. (1999): Unternehmensinvestitionen: Grundzüge in Theorie und Management, Heidelberg.

Questions and answers on this chapter

Question 1:
What are real options?

Question 2:
What are the attributes of real options? Name three!

Question 3:
What is an expansion option?

Question 4:
What is a compound option?

Question 5:
What valuation methods are used for real options?

Answer to question 1:

Real options are strategic flexibilities of management.

Answer to question 2:
Examples include value, goal orientation, flexibility, uncertainty and irreversibility.

Answer to question 3:
In an expansion option, the owner has the possibility to expand the success of a past investment.

Answer to question 4:
Compound options are combinations of several real options.

Answer to question 5:
The classical approaches for valuing options such as Cox, Ross and Rubinstein as well as Black-Scholes-Merton are used.

Module IV – Application of derivatives

13 | Structuring complex portfolios with the help of derivatives

The following chapter covers these issues:

- How are derivatives used when structuring complex portfolios?
- How are positions managed?
- Which extension strategies are available?
- How are exit strategies established?
- Which rollover operations exist?

13.1 Averaging and pyramiding

Basically two approaches are possible when setting up derivatives market positions.

Averaging (see Figure 13.1) refers to the addition of an identical number of contracts to the position by an investor. If this strategy works out, it is a good source of income. But if it fails, the investor is significantly increasing his risk with every new position. That is why this approach to implementing a position should not be encouraged. It should be reserved to experienced derivatives specialists and only be applied after careful consideration.

The opposite approach is called **pyramiding** (see Figure 13.2): a smaller number of new positions are added to the existing holding in the form of a pyramid. This approach is to be recommended since it represents a classical risk-weighted strategy.

Pyramiding absolutely requires an appropriate construction of the pyramid (see figure): if a lot of positions are added to a small base, the risk increases

Figure 13.1: Schematic representation of averaging

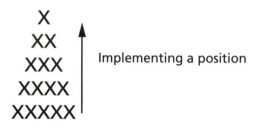

Figure 13.2: Schematic representation of pyramiding

exponentially. In this case exactly the opposite of the intended result happens. The Egyptian pyramids also would not have lasted upside down!

Third increase	Purchase of 1 put	EUR 2.00	X
Second increase	Purchase of 3 puts	EUR 1.60	XXX
First increase	Purchase of 5 puts	EUR 1.30	XXXXX
Initial position	Purchase of 7 puts	EUR 1.00	XXXXXXX

In the above example, the average purchase price has gone up by 27% to 1.27 compared to the initial position. Following the third adjustment, the overall position shows a profit of 57%.

If instead we had set up the pyramid the other way around, the average purchase price would be higher by 68% at EUR 1.68 and the profit of the overall position would only amount to 19%. An adverse market movement would mean quicker and more severe losses.

As we can see from the above examples, for any extension of a position, the risk of the original position must be related to the risk of the new position. Especially during unclear market phases, many investors are not acting purely rational, but are rather driven by emotions. This can quickly lead to major losses. It is often advisable to get a second (**consultatory**) opinion from another expert or a group of derivatives specialists.

13.2 Why should positions be extended?

Fundamentally, there are two possible basic intentions: extension of gains or position management for positions that are not successful. In both market situations a derivatives specialist is required to make decisions. Even though daily operations are guided by a certain experience, the following basic rules should be considered:

13.2.1 Extending gains

A position develops as expected and the investor wants to further extend his gain. He decides to expand the position and enters into additional contracts. He expects to also make a profit with these additional positions. But it must be kept in mind that the possibility of losses is increased as the number of contracts goes up.

The reason for a strategy of extending gains is not an adverse market development, but rather the success of the chosen strategy. Furthermore, his risk can be limited due to the profit already obtained. Nonetheless, this strategy requires caution, since the risk exposure of the investor in a worst case scenario is increased due to the higher volume.

Example of a strategy to extend gains

Initial position:
5 contracts on X index

Expansion of the position in three steps (layered):
3 contracts on X index
2 contracts on X index
1 contract on X index

With this strategy, the investor more than doubled his initial investment and therefore his trading book shows a correspondingly higher risk. Since he has a profit on the initial position, this risk is somewhat reduced.

13.2.2 Position management if investments develop unfavorably

The investment does not develop as anticipated by the investor. He reduces the average price by making additional investments and thus increases the potential for losses. At the same time, the profit potential is also expanded if the investment develops as expected by the investor. But it must be carefully assessed whether the expansion makes sense. Such strategies of reducing the average purchase price should be considered a last resort, since it rarely makes sense to increase the risk of the initial position. Often, the main problem is the fact that an expectation was disappointed. But this does not necessarily change with the expansion. Therefore it may be better to close, rather than expand, the position. If the investor, based on a careful analysis, decides to expand the position after all, he should act with due caution.

At this point we would like to stress that every investor should already consider possible extensions when entering into a position. He should already define entry and exit points, both with regard to time and value.

In the following case we take a closer look at such a situation:

An investor holds a position of long futures contracts. Unfortunately, the underlying has declined in value and the investor is suffering a loss. But he wants to maintain the position, since he is convinced that the underlying will increase in value, both from a fundamental and chart-technical[1] perspective. He decides to add to his holding in order to reduce the average purchase price.

What does he need to keep in mind?

- There is a risk that he does not assess the market appropriately.
- When adding to his holding, he multiplies the risk of suffering losses.
- The quantitative risk of losses is larger than the initial loss potential which he was willing to assume.

---

[1] A comprehensive technical analysis has been conducted.

In the best case, the investor lowers the average price of his position by adding to his holding. In a negative case he only "leverages" his losses with the new position.

We therefore recommend that only investors with strong liquidity make use of these strategies.

Example of an extension strategy:

The investor already holds 5 long contracts on index futures in his portfolio. He decides to expand his holding by pyramiding and purchases 3 additional contracts. If the expected price movement materializes, he will benefit from 8 contracts. But if his market assessment is not correct, he will suffer a leveraged loss on 8 contracts, which exceeds the loss on his initial position (see Figure 13.3).

Figure 13.3: Schematic representation of the extension strategy used in the example (pyramiding)

If the index develops favorably, he can also purchase additional contracts. But unlike the previous example, he is establishing these in a positive market environment and thus profits from the market development. He can add 3 new contracts to his 5 contracts which already show a profit. The loss potential of the initial position is reduced due to the profit made. Only if this profit is used up will the investor have the same risk profile as in the first example.

We see that setting up positions in line with the market is clearly preferred. A positioning against the market with the help of derivatives can quickly lead to large financial losses.

13.3 What is a rollover?

In a rollover, an investor extends his position beyond an initial expiration date by closing the original position and opening a new one. He may have the following basic intentions:

- Losses in the initial position (since his market expectation did not materialize)
- Preventing a premature assignment
- Extending a favorable position

> Many derivatives exchanges offer the possibility of trading only the spread between the two rollover contracts in a rollover transaction. For the investor, this means that he does not have to pay the bid-ask spread in addition.

13.3.1 Rollover in case of an adverse market development

An investor has sold calls on the X index (short call) at a strike price of 5,000 points and collected a premium of 50 points. One day prior to expiration, the index is trading at 5,100 points. It had been the basic assumption of the investor that the index would not rise above 5,050 points (premium + strike price). But he continues to believe that the index is too expensive. Therefore he closes the old position (by purchasing back the options), again sells calls on the index X with a strike price of 5,100 points and collects another premium. If the premium received covers the amount required to purchase back the old options, the rollover is called premium neutral, since no net payment is required. If the investor is of the opinion instead that the index can move somewhat higher, he is rolling to a higher strike price (for example 5,200 points). It is very likely that he will not be able to generate a premium neutral rollover at this level. He either faces an expense or has to increase the number of contracts. This results in increased risk, since he has expanded the initial position, which was not planned at the beginning.

Closing call 5 contracts
Opening call 10 contracts
= Increase of the risk of the position by 100%

This type of rollover is most frequently used. Since it occurred as the result of an incorrect market assessment, it could also be called a forced rollover. Practical experience does show, however, that this type of rollover can frequently be used to get positions back into the profit zone.

Every rollover requires an analysis of the current and expected market situation. Only if both are consistent, a rollover should be implemented. If one no longer expects that the initial market assessment will be realized, the position should be closed and a different position established.

13.3.2 Preventing an early exercise

A short investor fears an early assignment of his position (the option is exercised by the long investor). He decides to roll the position to a later expiration date, despite the fact that he will only receive little time value for this. His main motive is to prevent the possible exercise (see Figure 13.4). Not the premium, but rather the possible exercise is his motive for rolling the position.

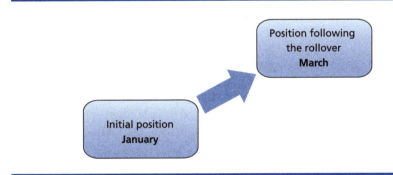

Figure 13.4: Preventing an early exercise by rolling

13.3.3 Extension of positions that are favorable to the investor

Initial situation: an investor has taken the long position in a futures transaction and he has made a profit. On the last day of trading, he sells his futures position and purchases the following contract. With this he profits from the current strategy and prolongs his position. We see that the derivatives position is extended in time when rolled over. Should the quantity also be adjusted during the rollover, the considerable increase in risk compared to the original position must be taken into account.

A rollover enables an investor to extend his derivatives position into the future. Theoretically, this possibility is unlimited, assuming that there is a liquid market. But it must be assured that the transaction makes sense.

Let us summarize: it is foolish to establish risks without accompanying positive results. When entering into a derivatives transaction, possibilities for closing of the position should already be considered. Should an investment fail to deliver the expected profit, it needs to be closed. The strategy needs to be reconsidered or an alternative investment must be established. An investment should definitely not be rolled by opening additional positions (possibly even in a different investment) just to achieve neutrality of premiums. An initial position in X shares should definitely not be transformed into a position in X and Y shares as well as in the index Z, since this investment would not have been established without the initial position. In order to prevent the losses which can result from such an increase in risk, an exit strategy in case of an emergency should always be in place. It should already be contemplated when opening the initial position.

13.3.4 Cross rollover

If an investor is in the possession of a call on share X, which does not develop as planned, he can also close this transaction and open a different one. Even though this cross rollover is not a rollover in the classical sense, since the underlying is exchanged, it can still be advisable for certain investments (see Figures 13.5 and 13.6).

The investor is financing the closing of the initial position X by opening a position Y. With this, he separates himself from the old and unsuccessful

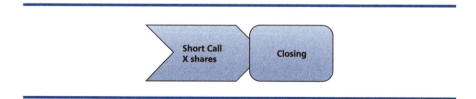

Figure 13.5: Closing of the original transaction

Figure 13.6: Opening of a new transaction to continue the original transaction with a different underlying

investment. While the two underlying transactions are different, they are combined for financing purposes.

13.4 Combinations

Clarity is the key to managing combinations. Effective action requires a clear view. The partial closing of combinations should be avoided. Positions which were established jointly, as combinations, should also be closed jointly. Only in very specific stock market situations such as insolvencies does this rule not apply.

13.5 Position management of swaps and other OTC derivatives

The possibilities discussed above are relevant for classical exchange traded derivatives and for OTC options and forwards. But at this point we also want to take a look at other OTC derivatives such as swaps and so forth. Especially in the case of swaps that are generating losses, it is advisable to think about an early closing. In this case, a balancing payment, called repurchase value, will be due. In some cases it is rather advisable to close out swaps with a negative repurchase value and to enter into a different swap. The negative repurchase values can possibly be charged to the new swap.

In practice, this strategy is frequently implemented with the help of so called "back to back" swaps. In this case, the existing swap is not terminated in order to prevent the realization of a possibly negative market value. Instead, the negative market value becomes part of the new swap, which is structured in a way that the same (negative) market value as in the original transaction is maintained. In this procedure, the investor has entered into two swap transactions. Economically, they can be considered as one swap, since one leg remains identical[2].

The above approach can be recommended especially in cases where the success of the original swap can no longer be expected and active position management is required. This is also true for the provision of collateral (use of credit lines) for swaps and other instruments. Both investor and derivatives expert must remain alert to this possibility.

OTC options and exotic options can also be rolled. In the case of exotic options which were established to back a financial engineering product, this is often not necessary. The reason is the structure of the certificate, which explicitly links the option to the product. It will more likely be the case for OTC options which are used in internal management or in proprietary trading, since no underlying transaction (which can also be used to account for a loss) exists in this case.

> When dealing with complex trading books, such as the ones maintained by hedge funds (see Chapter 15.7 for their strategies), the strict adherence to profit and loss limits is absolutely required. This is especially true for OTC derivatives, as opposed to listed derivatives, where no regulated market exists.

13.6 The key to success is liquidity!

It is important to hold sufficient liquidity so that positions can be maintained even if markets are developing unfavorably. Major problems arise if investors are unable to provide required collateral. Following a margin call, they are threatened with the forced liquidation of their holdings. Investors are required to react to a margin call. The ability to cover all the positions in the portfolio is therefore of the utmost importance. The same holds true for the knowledge coverage: once the overview is lost, "the devil has entered the temple of God[3]." Therefore it is sound advice to only maintain that number of positions

---
[2] Albeit with different sign.
[3] See Paul PP VI 1897–1978.

which can be controlled and managed. One thing is clear: an investor must be able to analyze and assess the underlying in order to act on the insight in a timely and qualified manner!

Emergency plans should always be available for extreme scenarios. An example is the plan to sell 50 index futures in case of a stock market crash. In this way, the investor is prepared for possible emergency situations. This is important especially when large spot market positions are present: if a quick directional change materializes as a result of extreme developments, only futures instruments allow the quick and efficient hedging of the spot market portfolio. Important: the decisions for such a case must always be reached ahead of time. On the day things are happening, only minor adjustments should be required; otherwise valuable time is lost.

At the same time, the technical clearing facilities must be in place. Frictionless trading can only be maintained if these facilities are available in extreme situations. Communication with the trading departments must be established and open. This is relevant especially for major private investors who do not run their own trading platforms.

It is recommended to put the emergency plan in writing. A simple algorithm should be used, which can be followed in an emergency. This algorithm should contain trading recommendations, orders of magnitude, contacts, communication devices as well as recommendations for an intra-day reversal[4].

13.7 Portfolio structure[5]

In principle, the portfolio structure should adhere to the aspect of diversification. The risk attitude of the investor must be taken into consideration. Many major investors have considerably less risk than smaller retail clients. This is frequently linked to the basic attitude. Major investors put a greater focus on value preservation and the possibility to maintain wealth for future generations than classical retail clients. Major institutional clients also pursue individual goals. It must be considered which current market trends can be adopted. Spot market investments can then be augmented with the help of derivatives positions. It is possible, for example, to write calls on holdings which are only expected to move sideways or to finance a long put

---

[4] Complete price change within one day, for example from negative to positive.
[5] Here the structure of derivative portfolios, for example in wealth management.

with the help of covered call writing. Additional purchases can be realized via aggressive short put strategies. If a prolonged downturn becomes evident, protective measures such as CCW and long put, an isolated long put or short futures can be implemented.

These examples support the notion that derivatives positions can expand or complement the portfolio and provide stability and additional returns. An investor who actively structures his portfolio with derivatives is in a position to direct spot holdings with the help of derivatives. He uses derivatives to actively extend or reduce spot holdings. In addition he is in a position to generate extra income and to eliminate potential risks. Not only is portfolio planning enhanced, since expected effects can be determined, the portfolio is also more stable. The investor is partly able to transfer decisions (in the case of short transactions). A final decision is reached only if he actively intervenes (closing). Otherwise, the decision which was reached when entering into the derivatives transaction is still valid.

The following is an example for derivatives instruments used to expand an existing portfolio:

Table 13.1: Sample portfolio and expansion with the help of derivatives transactions

Existing portfolio (excerpt)				Expansion
Underlying	Holding	Purchase price	Price today	Derivatives transaction
X shares	10,000	34.50	39.00	Short call strike 41
Y shares	15,000	43.10	41.90	Short put strike 41
M shares	7,000	89.45	91.23	Short call strike 92
Index certificate L index	15,000	54.40	67.10	Index futures as additional component

The investor expands his strategies by writing covered calls and derives premium income from this. He applies a return strategy. The short puts are intended for the acquisition of additional holdings in Y shares. As he continues to have a positive outlook on his investment, the investor is lowering the effective purchase price. The index certificate is extended using similar index futures. This creates an identical profile of opportunities and risks suitable for trading while the certificate is considered to be a long-term investment (see Table 13.1).

> The above considerations and expositions are also relevant for the design of financial engineering products, which will be discussed in Chapter 14.

This simple example illustrates the use of derivatives positions as additions and as elements to manage the position. It can also be seen clearly that a combination between a securitized derivative and a derivatives contract can be advantageous. In applied work, such constructions are used frequently. As an example, calls are written on **discount** and **bonus certificates** or liquidity is enhanced with the help of short **options** and in turn the premiums are invested in futures or securitized **leveraged products**.

By combining different profiles of risks and chances, new investment opportunities arise. The same is also true for combinations of commodity and currency derivatives transactions and/or the establishment of swap positions.

> **Accounting of derivatives**
>
> **Accounting of options according to HGB**
> Long options are shown on the balance sheet with the premium paid (other assets) and then valued on the balance sheet date. Options sold are recognized as liabilities and valued in the same way. In the case of clearly defined valuation units according to HGB (for example cap on Euribor as a hedge against increases in short term interest rates), the premium can also be written off over the term to maturity.
>
> **Accounting of swaps, other derivatives and futures according to HGB**
> If valuation units can be defined (combination of the derivative with an underlying transaction as hedge), valuation on the balance sheet date is not required (but this must not necessarily be the case) and the derivative is explained in the appendix. This holds for HGB. Things are more complex on the case of IFRS. But the result is similar to the procedure explained above.
> If no valuation units can be defined, for example in the case of a speculative transaction, the market value on the balance sheet date must be determined. According to HGB, negative market values require provisions for contingent losses (P&L); positive market values are only mentioned in the appendix (lowest value principle/prudence principle). IFRS usually requires that both positive and negative market values appear in the P&L statement.

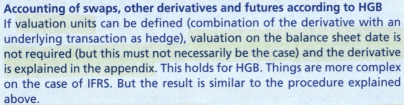

Interview with Michael Streich, managing partner, BambooVentures GmbH

Mister Streich, what is your outlook on the development of the derivatives market in the coming years?
In my opinion, the industry is poised for additional growth. It is possible that we will witness a slowdown, but especially against the background of an increasing interest in hedging transactions, further growth is likely.

Did the financial market crisis which began in 2007 lead to significant changes in the derivatives market?
Certainly the main point is an increase in risk awareness. Today there is more demand for stress tests, risk figures and so forth than five years ago.

Which products (listed options & futures) are important in your opinion in the years to come?
I think that simple, plain vanilla products will gain in importance. Complex products will continue to exist, for example for revenue reasons.

What role will be played by commodity derivatives in the years to come?
A rather big one. I expect an additional increase in volume. Hedging will be the main motivation for the transactions.

What role will credit derivatives play in the future?
Credit derivatives will always remain a legitimate instrument. Here as well, hedging will be the primary motivation.

What is your view on the future development of an integrated clearing system, like the one offered by Eurex?
Eurex has a very strong system which provides a lot of security and transparency.

Do you think that retail clients will continue to access the market for listed options & futures or will they turn to securitized derivatives as more appropriate instruments?
Not really. Most retail clients do not possess the adequate financial strength or subject knowledge. They are better off with securitized derivatives and I expect that is what they will use.

Recently Eurex even launched derivatives on real estate. What other products would make sense in your mind?
I can imagine that futures on water or waste are interesting. And in the area of the commodities mentioned, more products can still be listed.

Can you briefly summarize the developments on the derivatives markets over the past years?
The derivatives market is and will continue to be a growth market. The main driver in the past years may have been speculation. I think that the derivatives market will return to its original purpose and hedging transactions will dominate. But as you know, effective hedging requires a speculator who is willing to take the risk. This is where the loop closes. I am fully convinced that the derivatives market will continue to grow in the years to come. As in the past decades, new and innovative products will be made available.

Literature for this chapter

Hull, John: Options, Futures and Other Derivatives, 7th edition, 2009

Maier, Kurt M. Risikomanagement im Immobilien- und Finanzwesen, 2nd edition, 2004

Rudolph, Bernd; Schäfer, Klaus: Derivative Finanzmarktinstrumente, 2005

Seetaler, Peter; Steitz, Markus: Praxishandbuch Treasury-Management, 2007

Steinbrenner, Hans-Peter: Professionelle Optionsgeschäfte, 2001

Questions and answers on this chapter

Question 1:
What is a speculation plan?

Question 2:
What is pyramiding?

Question 3:
Is it true that averaging is a better strategy than pyramiding?

Question 4:
What is a rollover?

Question 5:
Is it true that according to HGB, long options principally must be activated with the premium paid and valued at the balance sheet date?

Answer to question 1:
It is a plan which discusses the speculation either in the context of a portfolio or as an individual transaction. It specifies entry and exit scenarios as well as risk planning.

Answer to question 2:
The successive establishment of a derivatives position in the form of a pyramid.

Answer to question 3:
No! Averaging involves significantly more risk than pyramiding.

Answer to question 4:
A rollover is the extension of a derivatives market position past the original expiration date. The initial transaction is closed with the help of an offsetting transaction and an additional transaction with a later expiration date is opened up.

Answer to question 5:
Yes, the statement is correct.

14 | Use of derivatives in financial engineering and fund management

The following chapter covers these issues:

- How are derivatives used in financial engineering?
- Why is there a need for product engineering?
- How are commonly used certificates constructed and valued?
- What specifics must be considered?

The instruments which are discussed in this book are of great relevance in financial engineering[1]. Especially concerning structured products, they are indispensable. In the past years the market for structured and securitized products (certificates) has been growing strongly (see Figure 14.1). One of the reasons is that certificates make derivative financial instruments and their pay-off structures available to retail investors. Otherwise, many investors would not have access to these instruments. With reference to the most frequently used structures, we want to briefly demonstrate how these certificates are constructed.

> "The task is not to see what nobody has seen before, but rather to think what nobody has thought about what everybody sees!" This insight by Arthur Schopenhauer is an appropriate description of financial engineering and the responsibilities of a financial engineer.

---

[1] Especially when structuring new asset and liability products.

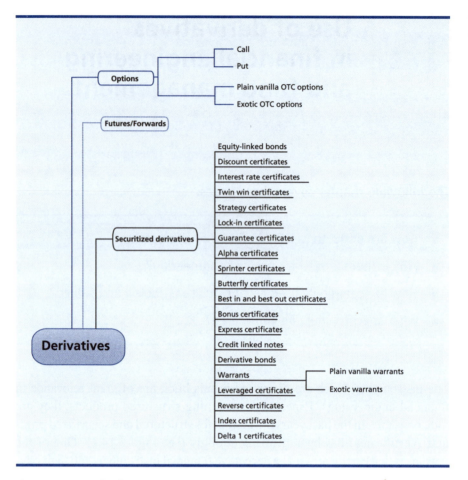

Figure 14.1: Derivatives tree

14.1 Considerations when designing new products

Every new product starts with an idea. But which considerations of the financial engineer come after that first idea?

- What is the demand of the investor?
- What is his market expectation?
- How is the financing done?
- Which instruments are required to construct the product?
- How can the price for the structure be influenced?

- Which costs and/or returns (structuring fees, funding[2] and so forth) do I have in the structure and which additional costs or profits can arise?

Only after these questions have been asked, should the structuring of a new certificate begin.

Basically, almost all kinds of certificates can be issued. It is important that the financial engineer can represent and value the payoff profile and assess its riskiness. An important role in this regard is played by the **counterparts**. They also need to be analyzed and assessed. Counterparts with high default risk are not usually the first choice for inclusion in a transaction. Credit risk is frequently not the primary value driver. It must also be determined whether a **flow product**[3] or a **buy and hold product**[4] is being discussed. Conditions can be more or less favorable as a result. Once these basic considerations are clearly defined, even the most exotic underlying (for example an index of freight rates or housing prices in the U.S.) can be issued as a securitized derivative in the form of a certificate.

14.2 Basic component zero bond

A zero bond is frequently used as basis component when constructing certificates (and structured bonds/promissory notes). For that reason, we want to briefly discuss the instrument here. A zero bond is issued below par and repaid at maturity at 100%. It is also possible to issue the bond at 100% and to accrue interest over time. The repayment value is higher in that case. The basic function of the zero coupon bond is to protect the invested capital, independent of the chosen structure of coupon payments. It is determined, in turn, by the derivatives used in the structure.

Zero bonds are used regularly in products with a capital guarantee such as guaranteed bonds or guaranteed funds. Valuation always requires calculation of the present value:

---

[2] Cost of raising the capital, revenues from investing the amounts; funding is an important aspect, since the internal allocation of interest payments with treasury is included. This strongly determines the conditions and the credit risk of the certificate.
[3] Product which is traded regularly (purchased and sold).
[4] Product which is purchased once and held to maturity (at least the majority of the issue).

$$\text{Present value} = \frac{\text{Nominal value}}{(1+i)^n}$$

i = Market interest rate for every period
n = Term to maturity in years

14.3 Financial engineering products and their construction

In the following we want to discuss those financial engineering products that are most frequently used at current. We want to highlight both the individual components as well as their interactions in the new financial engineering product.

14.3.1 Discount certificates

Discount certificates are products with a fixed term to maturity. They are issued at a discount compared to the price of the underlying and have a maximum payout (cap).

There are two different ways to construct these certificates (see Figure 14.2):

First alternative:
The issuer purchases a **zero strike call**[5] and sells a call on it. The zero strike call covers the underlying in this construction, while the call sold represents the cap.

Second alternative:
It is also possible to purchase a **zero coupon bond** and to sell puts. The zero coupon[6] bond is used to cover the position and the sold put makes the payoff profile possible. Both constructions yield the same result (see Figure 14.2).

---

[5] Zero strike options: zero strike options always have a strike price of zero. Therefore the option is always deep in the money. It covers the underlying. A different expression is LEPO (Low Exercise Price Option). See chapter 6.5.
[6] Discounted zero coupon bond.

Financial engineering products and their construction

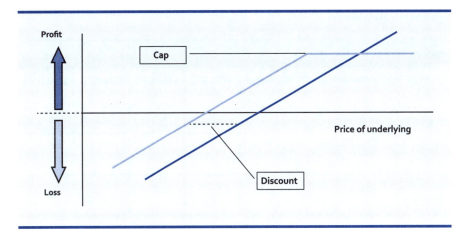

Figure 14.2: Payoff of a discount certificate[7]

Portfolio positions	Alternative 1	Alternative 2
Nominal value zero bond	50.00 Euro	
– (Short put + discount)	–14.12 Euro	
Zero strike call		39.22 Euro
– Short call		–3.34 Euro
Portfolio value	35.88 Euro	35.88 Euro

To make a qualitative statement about the pros and cons of an investment in discount certificates, a scenario analysis must be used. In the following, a simple example is used as illustration.

Comparison of a direct investment in shares versus investment in discount certificates

Share price (at time of purchase)	EUR 400
Cap (of the discount certificate)	EUR 450
Exchange ratio	1:1
Price of discount certificate	350 EUR

---

[7] Source: UBS.

Scenario analysis

Scenario	1	2	3	4	5
Price of the underlying at maturity	EUR 350	EUR 400	EUR 450	EUR 500	EUR 550
Repayment/Value of shares	EUR 350	EUR 400	EUR 450	EUR 450	EUR 450
Profit/loss of direct investment	−12.5%	0%	12.5%	25%	37.5%
Profit/loss of discount certificate	0%	14.3%	28.6%	28.6%	28.6%

14.3.2 Reverse Convertibles

Reverse convertibles (for example equity linked bonds) are constructed and function just like the discount certificates already discussed. The only difference is that the investor receives an interest payment (which is always paid) instead of a discount. For the investor a reverse convertible bond is a bearer debenture with a choice of repayment. The issuer decides (has the agreed barrier been breached or not) whether he delivers the underlying (theoretically there is no limit to the choice of underlying: equity, commodity, and so forth) or pays back the nominal value. Thus the issuer holds a put option on the underlying which the investor has written. The profit and loss potential (see Figure 14.3) of an equity linked bond for example is shifted, just as in the case of the discount certificate. An investor has only limited participation in positive movements of the underlying (the coupon in the case of the equity linked bond and the cap in the case of the discount certificate).

An investor in a reverse convertible bond has a price cushion compared to the direct investment, while the investor who directly purchases the underlying has a different profile of opportunities and risks. The same can be said for the option strategy "short put," if it is implemented directly and not securitized.

The main risk in both reverse convertible bond and discount certificate is a price decline of the underlying. Such a price decline is negative for the investor, just as in the case of a short put. The maximum return is the agreed interest payment or the cap, which is equivalent to the option premium in the corresponding option strategy (see Figure 14.3)[8].

---

[8] In practice, differences can arise due to hidden fees and other factors.

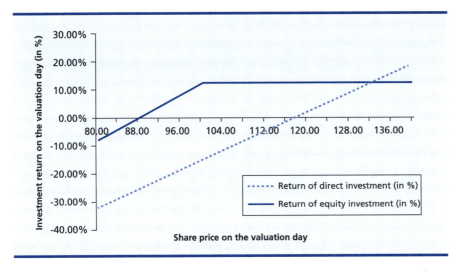

Figure 14.3: Payoff of a reverse convertible bond (here: equity linked bond) versus direct investment in shares[9]

Valuation of these instruments

The derivatives discussed above, as well as those which follow, are structured financial products. They are constructed from several basis instruments, which can be valued individually and summed up. The basic elements are replicated synthetically and valued for that purpose (replication method, see chapter 2.4.3 on this). The usual replication method for reverse convertibles is the combination of a classical bond (for example zero coupon bond) with a short put (European) on the underlying. It is also possible to value the equity and a short call.

14.3.3 Bonus certificates

Bonus certificates are characterized by bonus payments to the investor in case certain predetermined price levels are not crossed. These certificates are very popular and several types of bonus structures exist. These are classical structures which do not feature a cap and have only one threshold value (see Figure 14.4). From the perspective of the investor, these structures are combinations of a zero strike call purchased plus a down and out put purchased. Capped versions include the sale of an additional call, which constitutes the cap (see Figure 14.5).

---

[9] Source: Commerzbank AG.

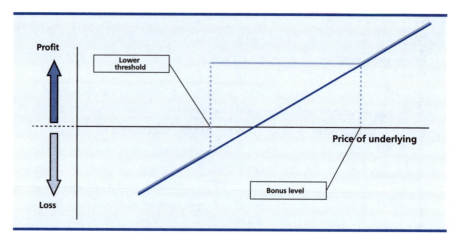

Figure 14.4: Pay-off classical bonus certificate [10]

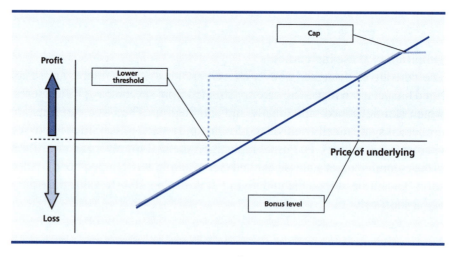

Figure 14.5: Pay-off capped bonus certificate [11]

For reverse bonus versions, which work as mirror images, a 200% strike put is combined with an up and out call.

Bonus structures are particularly popular in markets that trend sideways or, in the version without a cap, in markets that move higher. For a manageable level of risk, speculation on the bonus payment is made possible.

---

[10] Source: UBS.
[11] Source: UBS.

14.3.4 Leveraged products

Leveraged products involve the purchase or sale of the underlying. It must be kept in mind that not every underlying can be sold (short selling). Reasons are legal restrictions or the lack of security lending facilities[12]. The position which is generated with the purchase or the sale is securitized in form of the leveraged product and can thus be traded by the end user.

Functioning

The functioning of leveraged products is most easily explained against the backdrop of a classical direct investment in the underlying. While the direct investment requires full payment of the underlying in order to participate in price movements, a leveraged investor only has to put up a fraction of the capital. The leverage effect is a result of the reduced capital expenditure. The lower the level of capital used, the higher the leverage effect and the higher the risk. In other words, the payoff diagram resembles the credit financed purchase of the underlying[13]. Intraday, every movement of the underlying will be traced exactly by the leveraged product within the bid/ask spread. In that regard, the leveraged products are identical to a classical futures transaction. That is why they are occasionally called mini futures. In contrast to a classical futures contract, no need to make margin payments can arise. If such a margin payment should become necessary for market reasons, the leveraged product can be knocked out with the help of a knock out mechanism. In this case it expires worthless or a small payment of the residual value takes place. For the investor, the loss is therefore limited to the invested capital.

Example

Type	Index	Financing level	KO-threshold	Index level	Capital required	Leverage
Long	DAX®	3000 points	3060 points	4000 points	EUR 10	4
Type	Index	Financing level	KO-threshold	Index level	Capital required	Price development of the certificate
Long	DAX®	3000 points	3060 points	4200 points	EUR 12	+20%

---

[12] Securities lending involves the borrowing of securities which are then used and returned at the end of the lending period. A fee is paid by the borrower to the lender for securities lending. Normally a bank acts as intermediary and clearing house for securities lending.
[13] With a knockout mechanism.

Type	Index	Financing level	KO-threshold	Index level	Capital required	Leverage
Short	DAX®	5000 points	4900 points	4000 points	EUR 10	4

Type	Index	Financing level	KO-threshold	Index level	Capital required	Price development of the certificate
Short	DAX®	5000 points	4900 points	3800 points	EUR 12	+20%

14.3.5 Warrants

Let us briefly visit the issue of warrants at this point. They are issued either as option bonds[14] or as covered warrants[15] mostly by banks. Warrants always represent the long position of an option. The valuation of a warrant thus resembles that of a classical "plain vanilla" long option. In contrast to classical options, which we discuss in this book, warrants are not typically considered to be derivatives transactions and are not traded on derivatives exchanges but rather on spot exchanges[16]. Still, the mechanism of loss of time value is the same as in classical options. In the eighties and early nineties, warrants were rather popular, but they only play a marginal role today.

14.3.6 Structured financial products with interest rate options

Obviously structured products are also possible for fixed income products. They can be tied either to the price of a bond or to an interest rate. A distinction is made between callable bonds and putable bonds. Callable bonds give the issuer the right to repurchase the bond at a specified point in time (he has a termination right). The investor is short vol in this type of bond (has sold the option) and therefore is faced with negative convexity as market interest rates decline. Putable bonds involve the right of the purchaser of the bond to return the bond at a specified point in time. The investor is long vol (has purchased the option). An additional distinction is made between **single** and **multi callable** or **multi putable**. In the single version, there is only one date on which the securities can be returned; in the multi version, a number of

---

[14] Traditional warrants.
[15] Are issued by banks which hold the respective amount of shares of other companies on their books.
[16] Euwax in Stuttgart for example.

dates are possible. The repurchase prices (usually at par) are already set when the bond is issued.

Multi callable bonds, for example in the form of side step certificates[17] are rather popular especially when dealing with retail clients. Investors lock in a fixed coupon in a sideways market which accumulates if a termination date is not utilized. However, these certificates will show a significantly negative outperformance if markets decline.

14.3.6.1 Single putable bonds

A single putable bond gives the investor the right to return a bond to the issuer at a predetermined price and at a point in time that was determined on the issue date. Thus the investor is long the bond and the issuer is short the bond. Since the present value is calculated in each case, the bond investor is suffering a loss if market interest rates increase, while the issuer benefits. This relationship is of course reversed in case of lower rates. But all this changes as the investor is given the right to terminate the contract. When interest rates go up, the investor will simply exercise the put.

The payoff of such a single putable bond can be replicated synthetically with the help of a coupon bond and an option on the bond. We need a position long bond and a position long put. The potential loss in the present value is compensated by the profit of the put option. The position of the issuer is opposite to that of the investor. It follows that the risk profile is asymmetric, a feature which is already known from classical option transactions.

The following equation can be used for valuation purposes:

$$\text{Present value}_{cum} = \text{Present value}_{ex} + p$$

Present value$_{cum}$ = Present value of the bond with termination right
Present value$_{ex}$ = Present value of the bond without termination right
p = Price of the put option

This formula can be used both for the issuer and the investor; merely the sign need to be reversed. For the investor the termination right implies an addition to the present value, which must be paid. For the issuer, this represents a discount.

---

[17] Side step certificates, an invention of Commerzbank, use multi callable options; the maximum profit momentum is obtained in markets that trend sideways.

Two factors frequently complicate issuing putable bonds in practice. First, the investor must pay a premium for the termination right. Second, most issuers have lower spreads on putable bonds, since the availability of the nominal value (the liquidity) is not guaranteed. For a "5yrNC1" bond (5-year bond with one termination right after one year), the issuer normally shows lower funding levels for the first year (up to the time of the termination right) and higher spreads for the remaining four years.

14.3.6.2 Single callable bonds

A single callable bond provides the issuer with a termination right. The date on which this right can be exercised is predetermined. The investor is long the bond, but the issuer is given the right to repurchase it at a specified point in time. For this purpose, the investor is selling a call option on the bond to the issuer. He is long the bond and short the option. Thus, the investor collects an option premium. In exchange he receives no compensating payment if the present value of the bond changes. The issuer again holds the opposite position. For him, any change in the value of the bond is compensated by a change in the call option.

Both parties can value a single callable bond with the help of the following formula:
$$\text{Present value}_{cum} = \text{Present value}_{ex} - c$$

Present value$_{cum}$ = Present value of the bond with termination right
Present value$_{ex}$ = Present value of the bond without termination right
c = Price of the call option

The termination right is a disadvantage for the investor, which is equalized by a discount on the issue price. He thus pays less for this bond compared to a bond without termination right by the same issuer. For the issuer, the termination right is an advantage.

14.3.6.3 Bonds with several termination rights

In addition to the bonds discussed above, it is also possible to issue bonds with multiple termination rights. They can be structured with the help of **Bermuda options**. A Bermuda option can be exercised at multiple points in time. Not always, as in the case of American options, but only on clearly defined and pre-specified points in time. Such bonds with multiple termination rights are often issued as perpetuities with annual coupons. The face value is repaid on the maturity date. Normally, the issuer holds the termination right.

14.3.6.3.1 Multi callable bonds

A multi callable bond gives a termination right to the issuer. This is the normal case. He acquires the right to pay back the bond at different points in the future. The investor thus holds a long position in the bond and a short position in the option. The valuation of the **Bermuda option,** which is part of the structure, requires a numerical procedure or a **Monte-Carlo simulation**.

14.3.6.3.2 Multi putable bonds

The investor holds the termination right in the case of a multi putable bond. He acquires the right to return the bond to the issuer at different upcoming points in time. As in the multi callable product, a Bermuda option is used. Valuation is again done with the help of a numerical procedure or a Monte-Carlo simulation.

14.3.6.4 Reverse floater

A reverse floater is a bond with a variable interest rate. The coupon changes and is determined by subtracting a money market interest rate from a fixed base rate. Reverse floaters are purchased in expectation of declining market interest rates.

The payoff profile of a reverse floater can be created synthetically with the help of symmetric and asymmetric individual components. The symmetrical components of the reverse floater are a classical floater, where interest payments are continually adjusted to the current market environment, as well as two receiver swaps. The receiver swap generates constant interest income. The floater and the variable side of the swap make payments at the reference interest rate[18]. Each fixed income component of the swap receives an interest payment equal to one half of the basic interest payment. The asymmetric component, the option, is a cap in the case of a reverse floater. The basic interest rate is equal to the fixed component of the swap. The cap is purchased to prevent the possibility of negative interest rates. If the variable rate increases above the fixed basic rate, the interest rate option equalizes any losses. This mechanism guarantees a zero return of the reverse floater in case the fixed base rate is exceeded and prevents negative returns (see Figure 14.6).

---

[18] Euribor, Libor.

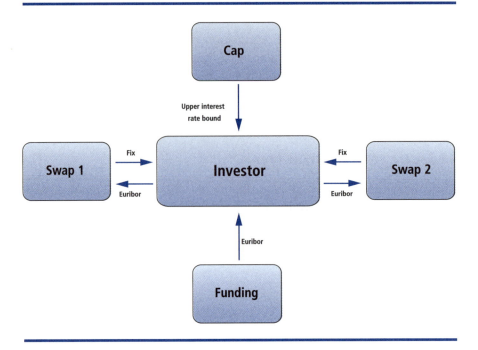

Figure 14.6: Construction of a reverse floater[19]

An active valuation of the reverse floater requires the valuation of the individual components. These valuations are then summed up. We thus value the two swaps, the floater as well as the cap and bring these valuations together. The overall value is always equal to the sum of the individual components.

14.3.6.5 Leveraged floater

A leveraged floater is a bond with variable interest payment, where the coupon is calculated as a leveraged money market return (for example 2 times 3-month Euribor) minus a fixed base rate. Again, the return can never be negative. Such a floater is constructed by combining a floater and a payer swap (symmetrical component) with two floors (asymmetric component). The basis interest rate of the two options is equal to the fixed base rate from the payer swap divided by the leverage factor. In this way, negative interest rates on the leveraged floater are prevented. The payer swap amplifies the variable interest side of the floater (see Figure 14.7).

---

[19] See: Wiedemann.

Financial engineering products and their construction

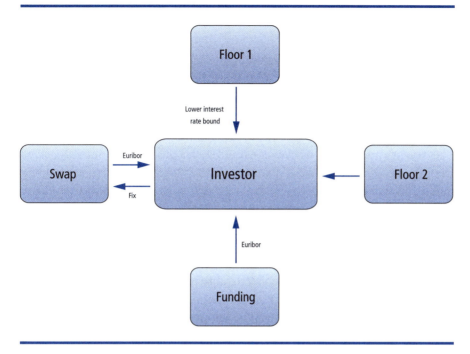

Figure 14.7: Construction of a leveraged floater[20]

Again the individual components are valued and the valuations are combined. The overall valuation of the leveraged floater is derived from the various components.

14.3.7 Highly structured financial products

Frequently, products are offered that cannot simply be decomposed into options and futures. They are called complex or highly structured products. They usually contain many individual components or are constructed with the help of a synthetic payoff profile (based on a Monte-Carlo simulation, see Chapter 6.17).

14.3.7.1 Inflation bond

When purchasing such a bond, an investor expects a positive inflation development. The task of the financial engineer is to develop a product, which (1) can be easily understood (since retail investors are also a possible customer

---

[20] See: Wiedemann.

segment) and (2) comes as close as possible to the basic intention of the investor.

We develop the following product:

Inflation bond with a term to maturity of 5 years. In the first two years, the investor will receive a fixed coupon. In years 3 to 5, he will receive a coupon which depends on the actual inflation rate at this point.

The treasury approach is used to construct such a product. The funds received from the customer are invested with the issuer. The issuer pays the funding rate, in most cases a floating rate[21]. For two years, the financial engineer makes a payment at a fixed rate to the investor. The funding received and the payment of a fixed rate can be modeled as a two year payer swap with the identical fixed rate and the funding rate as the floating leg. In order to cover the inflation component in years three to five, the financial engineer enters into a three year inflation swap which starts in two years (see Chapter 8.1.4.7.1). From this, he receives the realized inflation rate in years three to five while he pays the fixed rate. From the inflation swap, the financial engineer will receive positive payments on balance if the actual inflation rate is above the fixed rate. The opposite is true if the actual inflation rate does not exceed the fixed rate. The financial engineer passes along the realized inflation rate to the investor within the framework of the inflation bond. Since the financial engineer is exposed to the risk of negative inflation rates (deflation) in the context of the inflation swap, he also purchases a floor on actual inflation at 0%. He has thus eliminated this risk.

The valuation of such a product again relies on the individual valuation of the product components and the aggregation of the component values.

14.3.7.2 Simulation based certificates

In contrast to the certificates presented above, purely simulation based certificates can also be issued without the backing of additional instruments. The payoff profile is modeled with the help of a Monte-Carlo simulation and securitized. Main representatives of this product group are path-dependent[22] structures.

---

[21] Optional: plus/minus a fixed "spread" (premium/discount), which depends on the refinancing rate of the issuer and possible termination rights.

[22] They depend on the exact development of the underlying during a specific period.

14.4 Use of derivatives in fund management

Funds have significantly gained in importance in the past years. And fund management also increasingly relies on the use of derivatives. According to a statement by "Europan Fund Management Industry," which was published in May 2006 in Financial News, the volume of derivatives in fund management has increased from 48% to 62% in the year 2004. According to a new study (from the year 2009) more than 70% of all European fund managers use derivative structures in the portfolio allocation process. First, active hedging strategies are implemented with the use of derivatives and second, derivatives are used directly in investments (speculation or strategic focus). Both linear (for example swaps) and nonlinear derivatives (for example swaptions) are utilized. The largest share of derivatives is found in the asset classes equity, fixed income (interest rates) and foreign exchange. But especially over the past years, commodities have increasingly gained popularity.

14.4.1 Strategies for the use of derivatives in the portfolio management of a fund

In the following we want to present some of the classical strategies for portfolio managers. We are focusing on the five most frequently used strategies which are traded at Eurex[23].

14.4.1.1 Call volatility trade

In a call volatility trade, the underlying is sold (also synthetically with the help of futures) and call options on the underlying are purchased in exchange. This leads to a positioning which depends on the volatility of the underlying (see Figure 14.8).

Short	Underlying
Long	Call

---

[23] Measured by volume; source: Eurex.

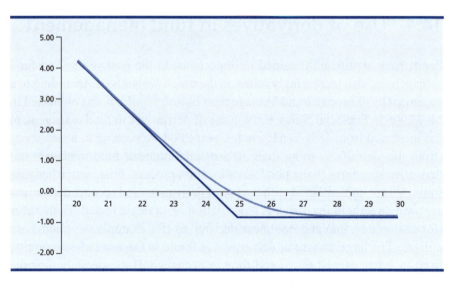

Figure 14.8: Payoff call volatility trade

14.4.1.2 Put volatility trade

In a put volatility trade, the underlying is purchased (also synthetically with the help of futures) and in addition, put options on the underlying are acquired. The fund manager can thus establish a put strategy which depends on volatility (see Figure 14.9).

Long	Underlying
Long	Put

14.4.1.3 Combo versus long underlying

A combo versus long underlying strategy is established with the help of short calls, long puts (with low strike price) and a long underlying (see Figure 14.10).

Short	Call
Long	Put
Long	Underlying

Use of derivatives in fund management 475

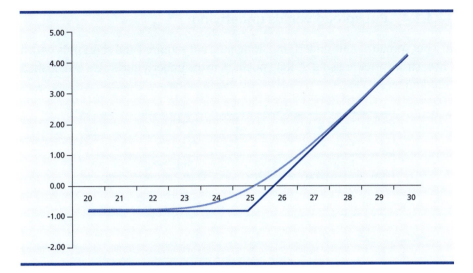

Figure 14.9: Payoff put volatility trade

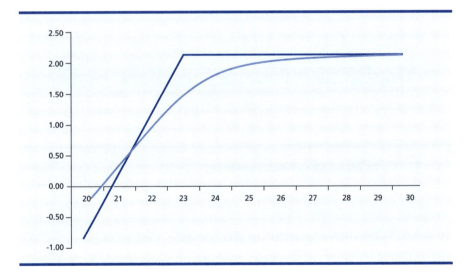

Figure 14.10: Payoff combo versus long underlying

14.4.1.4 Put spread versus underlying

In a put spread versus underlying, long puts are acquired and short puts with a lower strike price are sold. A long position in the underlying is also established (see Figure 14.11).

Long	Put
Short	Put
Long	Underlying

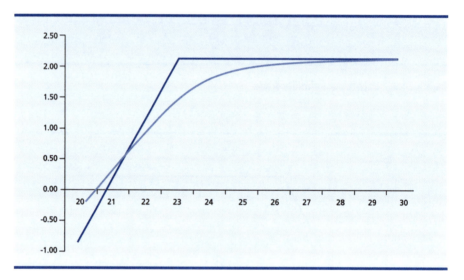

Figure 14.11: Payoff put spread versus underlying

14.4.1.5 Conversion versus underlying

In conversion versus underlying, long calls are acquired and short puts are sold (both with the same strike price). The underlying is also sold (see Figure 14.12).

Long	Call
Short	Put
Short	Underlying

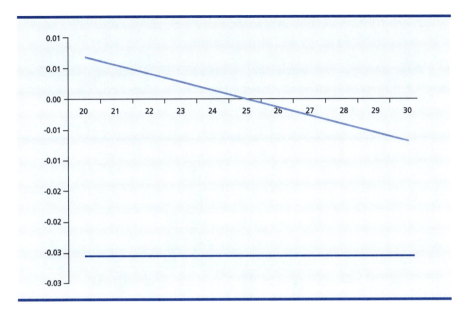

Figure 14.12: Payoff conversion versus underlying

14.4.2 Why are these strategies used in fund portfolio management?

With the combinations presented in the previous section, the portfolio manager can either obtain a return which exceeds that of the underlying used as reference or hedge the portfolio (for example a protective put, see Chapter 6.20.2). The strategies listed are all among the volatility strategies[24]. Why is that the case? The answer is simple: a portfolio manager wants to achieve "alpha," an outperformance relative to the benchmark, which differentiates him from the competition. Since alpha can best be obtained by making use of volatility, a lot of volatility strategies are established. But of course, fund managers also employ many of the other strategies presented in this book (see Chapter 6.19). This can be seen with the help of the following examples.

Figure 14.13 displays the outperformance of the strategy protective put versus the DAX® index using the example of a publicly listed fund. As can be seen,

---

[24] On this issue please also see options and futures on volatility. For example FVS (Volatility on the EuroStoxx50 Index) can be traded separately at Eurex. Volatility thus becomes a trading product and can be used for example to generate cash flows or to hedge.

an outperformance was obtained in the years 1998, 2001 und 2002. The plus was considerable in the years 2001 and 2002.

If a fund manager had established a classical CCW strategy (see Chapter 6.19.1.2), an outperformance would have resulted as well. This is shown in Figure 14.14 for the period 1992 until 2005.

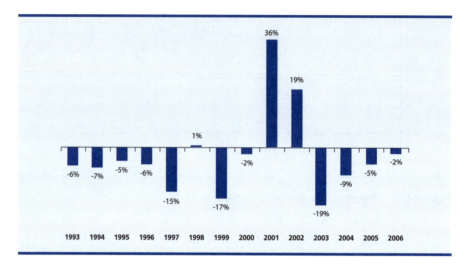

Figure 14.13:   Outperformance protective put versus DAX®[25]

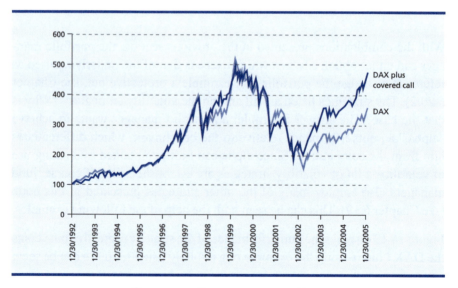

Figure 14.14:   Long DAX® versus DAX® with CCW strategy[26]

---

[25] Source: Dr. Axel Vischer, Eurex, ISE New York.
[26] Source: Dr. Axel Vischer, Eurex, ISE New York.

Literature for this chapter

Rudolph, Bernd, Schäfer, Klaus: Derivative Finanzinstrumente 2005

Wiedemann, Arnd: Bewertung von Finanzinstrumenten, 4th edition, 2007

Questions and answers on this chapter

Question 1:
Which component is most widely used to guarantee the repayment of the nominal value in guarantee products?

Question 2:
Which synthetic component is used to replicate the underlying in a discount certificate?

Question 3:
In a short leverage product, the knock out threshold was touched. What will happen with the certificate?

Question 4:
Which type of option is used to construct and value multi callable bonds?

Question 5:
Which components are used to construct a leveraged floater?

Answer to question 1:
The zero bond. The discounted security guarantees the repayment of the nominal value of the financial engineering product at maturity.

Answer to question 2:
If a discount certificate is constructed without a direct underlying, a zero strike call is used in its place.

Answer to question 3:
The underlying has gone up in value and the certificate was knocked out. It has expired worthless, unless a minimum repayment amount was specified.

Answer to question 4:
Bermuda options are used. They can be valued with the help of a binomial tree.

Answer to question 5:
2 floors, a floater, a swap.

15 What is a hedge fund?

The following chapter covers these issues:

- What is a hedge fund?
- What is the structure of a hedge fund?
- What are the strategies that can be used?
- What is the difference between single hedge funds and funds of hedge funds?

What exactly is a hedge fund? The answer to this question is highly complex, but we want to deal with this topic because of the strong reliance of hedge funds on derivatives. The term hedge fund was used for the first time by Carol Loomis in an article in Fortune Magazine in April 1966. It described the first hedge fund, which was founded by Alfred Winslow Jones in 1949. While hedging was still the predominant aim of the first hedge fund, numerous different investment strategies exist today. Due to the globalization of financial markets, technological progress, the multitude of financial instruments that can be traded and the development of innovative financial instruments, hedge fund managers today can choose from a multitude of possible investment opportunities and often move away from the original hedging motive. A precise definition of the term does not exist. The literature provides a number of attempts at defining the funds, which all stress different attributes. Some characteristics are found more frequently, and the following definition can be used: hedge funds are investment companies that are subject to few regulations and are characterized by their high flexibility, specific return profile and profit-based remuneration. In the following, we want to take a look at the setup of hedge funds, their strategies and structural peculiarities.

15.1 What is the aim of a hedge fund?

A hedge fund aims to achieve absolute returns. This means that a positive return is targeted regardless of the market environment. Returns of a hedge fund, unlike returns of traditional investments, are not judged relative to a benchmark[1]. Especially the separation from classical benchmarks gives special relevance to the use of derivatives by hedge funds.

15.2 Use of leverage

Hedge funds use debt in order to leverage their return on equity. Especially for investments with a somewhat small profit margin, the return of the fund can be enhanced in that fashion. But the leverage effect is positive only as long as the total return of capital, respectively the internal rate of return of the investment, exceeds the interest rate paid on the debt. An increase of the portion of debt capital raises both return expectations and risk. Fundamentally, two different types of leverage exist: "balance sheet leverage" involves debt financing in the form of loans, while "instrumental leverage" describes the establishment of positions that require relatively little capital, for example with the help of derivatives.

15.3 Legal transparency

Hedge funds are not subject to any legal or investment restrictions. For that reason, the value of the holdings, the structure of the portfolio and completed transactions are made public only irregularly or in many cases not at all. Hedge funds utilize pricing inefficiencies in various markets. If they were required to publish their holdings and transactions, other market participants could copy their strategies and thus reduce the profits of the funds or even turn them into losses. Low transparency is therefore an important prerequisite for the functioning of hedge funds.

---

[1] There are, however, a few hedge fund indexes which can be used as "benchmark."

15.4 Offshore companies

A majority of the hedge funds is operated out of financial centers such as New York or London, but has their place of business (hedge fund companies) in **offshore jurisdictions**. Among these offshore regions are among others the Cayman Islands, British Virgin Islands, Bermuda, Bahamas, Luxemburg or Ireland. Especially hedge funds can benefit from the major advantages offered by these locations:

- No taxes, or only very low levels of taxation concerning the following: income tax, corporation tax, capital gains tax, withholding tax.
- Lack of supervisory control or weak supervisory regimes.
- Stable economic and political environment.
- Competitive and mature market environment for suppliers of hedge fund services.
- No requirement for the physical presence of the hedge fund management and routine failure to ratify mutual extradition agreements or legal assistance agreements.
- Most important for hedge funds are the freedom from supervisory oversight and the tax advantages.

15.5 Risk attributes of hedge funds

The non-traditional asset allocation of a hedge fund compared to standard investments does of course entail additional risks. In the following, we highlight the major risks, which in some cases are inherent to the system.

15.5.1 Market risks

Hedge funds can apply virtually all financial instruments and techniques for their investment strategies. With these wide-ranging business activities and the not insignificant use of leverage, the risk of an unfavorable development of the holdings increases. The instruments used to assess, monitor and minimize market price risks are constantly advanced and refined. Especially Value at Risk (VaR) has been established in this area as a relevant metric to avoid the concentration of risk.

15.5.2 Address non-payment risk

A hedge fund is exposed to address non-payment risk if contract partners are not at all or only partially able to fulfill their obligations or if their credit standing suffers. This can be the source of potentially large losses for hedge funds. In the following we will consider issuer, counterparty, credit and country risk:

15.5.2.1 Issuer risk

Issuer risk[2] relates to the possibility that the issuer, for example of structured products such as certificates and so forth, is unable to meet his payment obligations, since he has become insolvent. Thus an investor not only needs to consider possible losses from a decline in value of the underlying securities, but also the possibility of a complete loss of the invested capital due to the default of an issuer.

15.5.2.2 Counterparty risk

Counterparty risk exists in transactions that are not conducted at an exchange or a regulated market, but OTC instead. Losses result if the counterparty is unable to pay (risk of having to purchase the securities again) or pays late (transaction risk). In addition, many hedge funds are depositing their fund assets with the issuer in the framework of a prime brokerage agreement. In the case of an insolvent counterparty, access to these assets may be limited.

15.5.2.3 Credit risk

Credit risk describes the possibility that a borrower does not meet all his payment obligations. Hedge funds are particularly exposed to this risk, due to the massive use of leverage. This entails the risk of heavy over-indebtedness if the return on the invested capital falls below the cost of debt for an extended period of time.

15.5.2.4 Country risk

For the most part, hedge funds are domiciled in offshore centers and invest globally. Therefore they are heavily exposed to country risk. It describes the possibility that clients in other countries are unable to fully meet their payment obligations due to government regulations such as the freezing of assets or

---

[2] On this point see the insolvency of Lehman Brothers in 2008.

the limitation of currency transfers. In addition, country-specific economic factors such as a lack of foreign reserves or devaluations can also affect the liquidity of clients. In order to assess these risks, hedge funds, among other information sources make use of country ratings, which are issued by the international rating agencies Moody's, Standard & Poor's and Fitch.

15.5.3 Liquidity risk

Hedge funds are interrelated in many ways with other providers of financial services. A particularly close relationship exists with their prime broker. He manages the margin account, where deposits for credit financed transactions or derivative investments are made. If the value of this account turns negative as a result of adverse price developments, fresh funds must be deposited immediately[3]. If the hedge fund has run out of liquid assets, it is forced to sell other holdings, which may lead to massive losses in some cases. In the worst case, it is not even possible to liquidate positions and the hedge fund is threatened with a complete loss.

15.5.4 Manager risk

The hedge fund and the investment strategy are directed by management. This means that the success of the hedge fund depends on its reliability and individual abilities. Losses can be the result of human error and related operational weaknesses, sudden changes in strategy or fraudulent behavior. In order to minimize this risk, decision competencies are distributed among a larger number of managers, who are carefully selected and whose investment decisions are constantly monitored. This is true in particular for multi manager hedge funds. An additional protective measure is the requirement that mangers must invest part of their personal wealth in the hedge fund.

15.5.5 Operational risk

Operational risks are the result of shortcomings in the daily operations of the organizational structure, among personnel or in the technical infrastructure or of external factors. Among the sources of risk are:

---

[3] See Chapter 16.

- Employee risk (see manager risk): fluctuations, key personnel
- Fraud, individual mistakes
- Technological risk: programming or modeling mistakes
- Capital asset risk: catastrophes, security risks
- External risks: fraud, legal and tax risks, war/terrorism

15.5.6 Strategic risk

Hedge funds have return targets which are specified by management. In order to meet these targets, hedge funds invest in a large spectrum of financial market instruments. Strategic risk arises when the business environment changes abruptly. A successful business strategy always requires the ability to react to such changing framework conditions. It is important for that reason to carefully monitor discontinuities in the market and its competitive environment and to continually adjust investment strategies.

15.6 Organizational setup of a hedge fund

Figure 15.1 once again provides a graphical summary of the organizational structure of a hedge fund and its individual components.

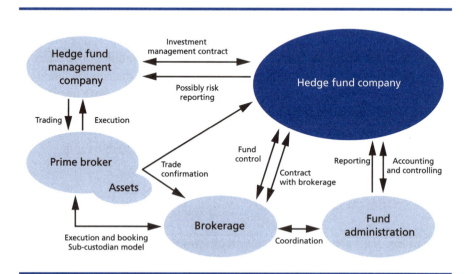

Figure 15.1: Organizational setup of a hedge fund[4]

---

[4] Source: Graef 2008, p. 58.

15.6.1 Hedge fund company

When deciding on a legal form, predominantly tax considerations in offshore domiciles play a role. The domicile of the company determines the regulatory environment. The majority of hedge funds globally are structured as limited partnerships. Limited partners contribute a fixed amount to the hedge fund company and their liability is limited to that amount. They are not part of the management team, but hold financial claims such as a participation in the assets of the fund, the right to receive profit distributions and the right to receive a portion of the fund assets in the case of liquidation. General partners have a personal and unlimited liability. They are responsible for daily operations and legal representation of the hedge fund company. Frequently the general partners are identical to the management team, but in some cases, external managers support the hedge fund company in the decision making process.

15.6.2 Hedge fund management company

The hedge fund management company is closely associated with the hedge fund company. Legal basis is an investment management contract, which clarifies among other items the interactions between the two companies as well as remuneration of the management. Asset management is the main task of the management company. In addition, it is also responsible for daily administration, marketing and distribution. The work of the management company is a fundamental contributor to the success of the hedge fund.

15.6.3 External service providers

In addition to the hedge fund company and the hedge fund management company, external providers are needed to assure daily operations. Among them are prime brokers, custodians and fund administrators.

15.6.3.1 Prime broker

Prime brokers are the leading investment banks (such as Morgan Stanley, Goldman Sachs) and occasionally universal banks (such as Deutsche Bank, UBS). They provide services to the management of the hedge fund. The service range offered is rather broad and adjusted to meet the specific requirements of the hedge fund. Core tasks include the implementation of the strategies of the hedge fund management as well as the proper clearing and settlement of the transactions. Prime brokers also calculate risk figures for the hedge fund, trade in securities and derivatives and manage the accounts. Additional important functions are the provision of lines of credit, called cash lending, and the provision of securities (securities lending) as well as intermediary services when conducting short sales.

15.6.3.2 Custodian bank

The tasks of a custodian bank include administration of the fund assets, control of regulatory and fund specific investment guidelines, issuance and redemption of shares in the fund as well as payment services. Frequently the prime broker also assumes the task of custodian. In this case, the fund assets also serve as collateral.

15.6.3.3 Fund administration

The fund administration is in a neutral position with regard to the hedge fund management, the prime broker or the custodian bank. Responsibilities include fund accounting, modern risk management, fund reporting and performance measurement. It also offers support with regard to the structuring of contracts and tax issues by providing qualified experts. Mostly universal banks and their subsidiaries act as fund administrators.

> The hedge fund Amaranth has made a lot of money with active speculation on the price of gas. Unfortunately, these speculations also ended in the insolvency of the fund in 2006. The expected increase of gas prices following the devastating tornadoes Katrina and Rita did not materialize. On the contrary, the price of gas declined by more than 12 percent. This development resulted in a loss of about USD 5 billion for the fund. Something similar happened to Long-Term Capital Management (LTCM), a fund which was directed among others by *Myron S. Scholes* and *Robert C. Merton*. It took a speculative short position which turned out to be ill advised. A major rescue operation became necessary when the fund declared insolvency during the Russian crisis in 1998. LTCM did not have sufficient equity capital to close their open positions.

15.7 Strategies

Hedge funds usually work with specific strategies which can be put into different categories. Their approaches normally differ from conventional fund strategies, but in some cases can be quite similar or even identical. Obligatory is the use of derivatives. In the following we want to take a brief look at the most common strategies and their implementation.

15.7.1 Convertible bond arbitrage

This strategy usually involves the investment in a convertible bond of a company. The fund manager can focus on different sources of revenue: volatilities, interest rates, credit quality and so forth. The convertible bond allows the hedge fund to be invested in a derivative of the underlying (see Figure 15.2). In most cases the market risk of the underlying is eliminated by entering into a short position. Therefore the investor in the convertible bond is not exposed to any equity risk (see Figure 15.3).

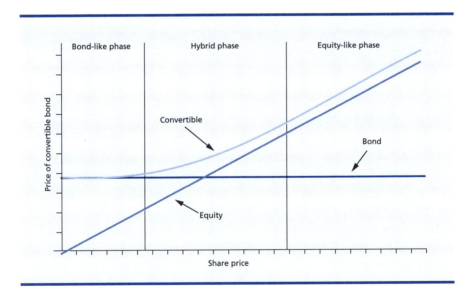

Figure 15.2: Price development of a convertible bond[5]

---

[5] see Wiedemann 2004 S. 5.

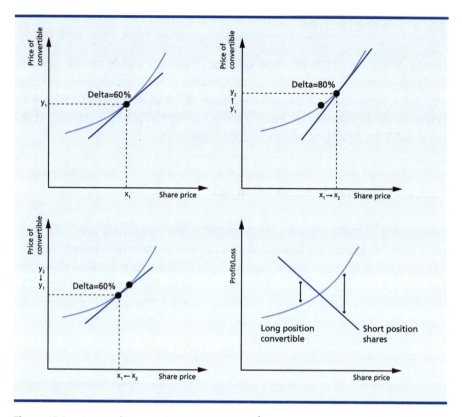

Figure 15.3: Setup of convertible bond arbitrage[6]

15.7.2 Short equity

So called "short sellers" predominantly benefit from falling prices of the shares traded. The manager borrows shares from his broker (securities lending), in order to sell them in the market. If the share price declines as expected, the fund manager repurchases the shares and returns them to the broker. Any difference between the purchase and selling price is his profit. A short equity strategy is thus also a "no equity" strategy, since the investor never actually owned any shares.

Short sales X shares at EUR 100
Repurchase of X shares at EUR 80
Profit = EUR 20 per share

---

[6] Following Peetz 2007a.

15.7.3 Emerging markets

With this strategy, the manager attempts to benefit from the expected attractive returns of equities and bonds in emerging markets. Regulatory difficulties, such as the frequently found prohibition to enter into short positions or a lack of derivatives (such as futures), imply that this frequently is a long only investment and not all instruments can be used by the fund manager. Let us take look at the emerging market of Vietnam in this context. Due to political guidelines, derivatives transactions are prohibited in Vietnam. Major companies are state owned and not listed at an exchange. The shares that can be purchased in the unofficial market are hard to analyze. This example shows the difficulty of implementing a meaningful and profitable strategy.

15.7.4 Market neutral equity

This strategy attempts to make use of the inefficiency of equity markets. This is normally done by simultaneously entering into a long and a short position. In order to be truly market neutral, the size of the position is adjusted in line with the beta of the position. In addition, it must be kept in mind that the sector risk also needs to be eliminated. Often leverage[7] is used in order to achieve corresponding return increases.

15.7.5 Event driven

This strategy attempts to benefit from expected or already announced events at the company level. Examples are restructurings, mergers, divestments of individual business segments or similar activities. The following **event driven strategies** are distinguished:

1. Risk arbitrage/merger arbitrage
Following the announcement of a company takeover, a long position (long equity) is established in the company which was acquired and simultaneously a short position (short equity) is established in the acquiring company. Once the merger is completed, the manager benefits from the spread between the two shares.

---

[7] Leverage; debt financing, equity capital is replaced by debt capital.

2. Distressed investing

In this strategy, the fund manager invests in securities (shares, bonds, securitized credit and so forth) of companies that are experiencing difficulties. In many cases an attempt is made to actively get involved in the management of the company and to engineer a turnaround.

3. Regulation "D"

This refers to securities (mostly convertible bonds[8]), which were issued by smaller companies and under the rules of regulation D can only be sold to certain investors in large denomination (for example specifically issued securities). While they promise to yield a higher return, they are also subject to additional risks due to the credit standing of the issuer and the large volume (concentration risk). Fungibility is rather limited in most cases. Furthermore, they are mostly not transparent and pure long investments.

4. High yield

This strategy entails an investment in poorly rated companies or companies without a rating, which have significant potential for appreciation. The debt issued by these companies is called a high yield bond.

15.7.6 Fixed income arbitrage

A fixed income arbitrageur attempts to profit from valuation differences between related bonds or interest rate derivatives. Most fund managers follow an approach with a global focus and the goal to generate stable returns with minimal volatility. This strategy, among others, makes use of yield curve arbitrage, swap arbitrage as well as arbitrage between (government) bonds and MBS (Mortgage Backed Securities)[9].

15.7.7 Global macro

Global macro managers are positioned either short or long in global financial markets. The positions reflect the opinions and perspectives concerning the expected market development, which are derived from global trends and

---

[8] Debt instrument which entails a conversion right into equity of the company. It is thus a fixed income instrument with an equity component (which has potential).

[9] With the beginning of the subprime crisis/financial crisis in 2007, this market has come to a halt. See Bloss, Ernst, Häcker, Eil 2008.

economic considerations. The portfolios of these managers contain all types of securities, currencies and derivatives. In the past years, many managers are also focusing on emerging markets with their strategies.

15.7.8 Long/short equity

This strategy describes the simultaneous holding of both a long and a short equity portfolio. The goal is not to be 100 percent market neutral, but rather to establish a long portfolio which in increasing markets goes up more than the short portfolio and similarly to have larger profits in the short portfolio in the case of declining markets. Managers can adjust the extent of their "exposure" quickly in line with market developments. For this purpose, many managers also make use of derivatives and strategies discussed in this book.

15.8 Managed futures

Managers who use this strategy exclusively invest in listed commodity or financial futures. These managers are frequently called CTA (Commodity Trading Adviser). The investment strategy can either be directed systematically, with the help of automated computer programs or via discretionary trading decisions. Systematic trading programs predominantly make use of the time series of prices (both intraday and inter day) to reach trading decisions, while discretionary managers also incorporate other (fundamental) elements in their decisions.

Figure 15.4 once again provides a graphical summary of the strategies.

15.9 Single hedge fund versus fund of hedge funds

In the case of a single hedge fund, an investor holds a fund with a specific management. In the case of a fund of hedge funds, he holds a share in an investment vehicle which in turn is invested in a number of single hedge funds (see Figure 15.5). An investor thus only indirectly participates in hedge funds and spreads his assets among a number of managers, which leads to diversification.

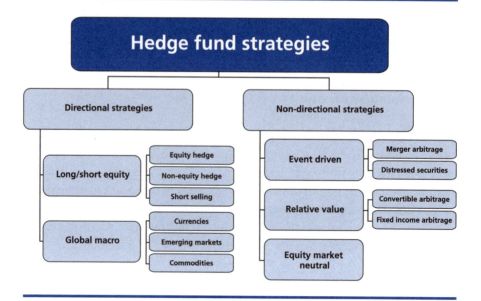

Figure 15.4: Hedge fund strategies

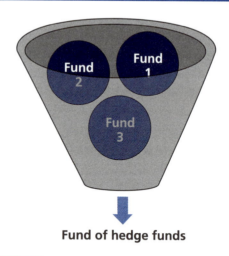

Figure 15.5: Fund of hedge funds

15.10 Hedge funds as golden calf?

Humans continue to dream of the "golden calf"[10]. But hedge funds are also not always and everywhere a source of easy money. Especially during the financial crisis it became apparent that these highly complex constructions are rather fragile. Thus, in difficult times we witness a market consolidation. Only the good funds of high quality remain. Smaller funds, funds with weak finances or problematic funds disappear from the scene. The strategies employed also become apparent in times of crisis. The biggest publicity is usually reserved for those cases where illegal means were used to feign success. Cases of fraud such as the one involving Bernhard L. Madoff[11] are infamous in this regard. But as a basic principle, hedge funds are not objectionable, cruel or reprehensible. But it is also true what has already been said a long time ago with reference to the golden calf: "You shall not worship them or serve them."

The best advice that can be given to an investor is to use these instruments as portfolio additions and not as a major investment block. For most investors, an addition of 5-10% of the entire portfolio volume is more than adequate. Decisive are the risk attitude of the investor and his other activities. It holds for every investor that they should not establish these positions on credit.

---

[10] Created according to the Bible as a graven image while Moses received the 10 commandments on Mount Sinai.
[11] He is the former CEO of the technology exchange NASDAQ. At the end of 2008 he was arrested for running a Ponzi scheme over several decades.

Literature for this chapter

Graef, Andreas: Aufsicht über Hedgefonds im deutschen und amerikansichen Recht. Zugleich ein Beitrag zu den Einflüssen des Anlagemodells auf die Finanzmarktstabilität, 2008

Hauswald, Carina: Hedge Fonds und ihre Rolle für die Stabilität internationaler Finanzmärkte

Sperber, Herbert, Sprink, Joachim: Internationale Wirtschaft und Finanzen, 2007

Questions and answers on this chapter

Question 1:
What is the aim of a hedge fund?

Question 2:
What is address non-payment risk?

Question 3:
What is meant by the term prime broker?

Question 4:
What is involved in the strategy short equity?

Question 5:
What is a fund of hedge funds?

Answer to question 1:

The aim is to generate absolute returns. This means to obtain a positive return independent of the market situation.

Answer to question 2:
Address non-payment risk refers to the risk that one or several contract partners are no longer able to fulfill their contractual obligations.

Answer to question 3:
The leading investment houses are providing their brokerage services to the hedge funds.

Answer to question 4:
The strategy short equity involves short selling of equities with the aim of repurchasing them later at a lower price.

Answer to question 5:
No individual trading is done in a fund of hedge funds. Instead the fund invests in target funds, which in turn conduct individual transactions.

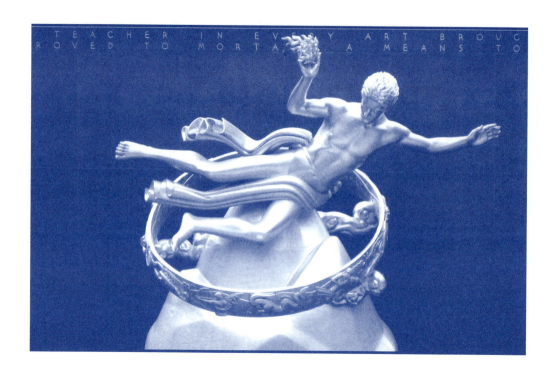

16 Risk controlling and margining

The following chapter covers these issues:

- Why is active risk controlling important?
- How can a targeted risk controlling be implemented?
- What is the meaning of margining?
- What types of margin exist?
- How do I deposit margin?
- What are closing costs?

16.1 Basics of risk controlling

"Common sense can replace almost any degree of education, but no educational degree can replace common sense." This aphorism which is attributed to Arthur Schopenhauer fits well with the topic of risk controlling. In addition to strong technical qualifications, the ability to emotionally assess the counterparty is also required. The importance of an active and targeted risk controlling is demonstrated by the negative examples from the past. Banks and brokers have central staff units that control the risk which results from open derivatives market positions. Nonetheless, it is the task of every investor or advisor to keep an eye on risks at all times. The complete avoidance of risk cannot be the goal, since this would be equivalent to a complete abandonment of all risky transactions. This in turn would severely restrict an investor and his investments would become unbalanced and senseless. Instead the recognition and reduction of risks should be the main tasks. Of primary importance is an active monitoring of the size of the trading book. Frequently it starts to grow uncontrolled, especially when positions are rolled. This should definitely be avoided, especially since it renders impossible the consistent management in

line with the strategy. An initial position of 10 contracts should never grow to a rollover position of 100 contracts. Investors should always be aware of the volume of trading in the underlying. This is the only possibility to get a feeling for the market and its size. It is absolutely recommended to work with trading limits[1]. Without a trading limit, it is impossible to implement adequate risk controlling. The same is true for the provision of a safety deposit in the form of a **margin** payment. In this case in particular, risk is accepted and this absolutely requires that trading volumes are known and understood. Risk controlling must be conducted daily, in complex market situations several times each day. It must be assured that margin payments can be made and that the size of the position is proportional to net wealth. As a basic rule, not more than **20–30%** of liquid net wealth[2] should be allocated to derivatives transactions. The transfer of risk from one position to several positions, which in a worst case scenario can grow to ruinous proportions, must definitely be avoided with the help of active and early intervention. Risk and trading limits should never be adjusted in line with actual use; instead use must be aligned to the existing limits. Investors with highly risky positions require comprehensive and targeted active support, which can only be provided by financial engineers with strong experience and concrete expert knowledge. Since normally every decision is reached in an environment characterized by incomplete information, it must be adjusted quickly and meaningfully on a case by case base to conform to new situations. The experience from applied work shows that frequently too much time goes by between identification of risks as a result of new market developments and implementation of a new strategy. Quick and targeted decisions are required in this case. Often the first loss is the smallest. Especially large private investors are reluctant to cut their losses at this point. But those who wait and hope for a recovery can quickly witness huge losses in the trading book.

The case of Barings Bank

Boasting a history of more than 200 years and a very exclusive group of customers, among them, so it was rumored, also the Queen of England, the British Barings Bank was forced to file for bankruptcy in 1995. This was caused by the trading activities of a single employee in Singapore. Nick Leeson ruined the bank with his unauthorized trading activities and disappeared. He was arrested and convicted. Barings Bank could not absorb the total loss of close to USD one billion and was bankrupt.

---

[1] In most cases these are set by the brokers; for example 50% of net wealth.
[2] Net wealth = Assets minus liabilities; real estate holdings and direct company participations are not taken into account. Only liquid assets are considered.

16.1.1 MaRisk as the basis for risk controlling

The strict separation between risk controlling and trading units must be assured by financial institutions. This is specified in the regulations which are summarized in MaRisk. Persons who are active in trading are not allowed to also hold a controlling function. They must be controlled by a unit that is distinctly separate. A fundamental distinction is made between the following three areas[3]:

Market
Units that initiate transactions and that have a veto right when it comes to credit decisions.

Operative credit function
These units also have a veto right when it comes to credit decisions, but are independent of the market.

Trading
Units that have a strategic responsibility concerning pricing, closing or positioning of trading business as defined by MaRisk. A trader is a person who enters into trading transactions and has room for discretionary action.

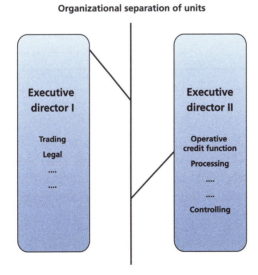

Figure 16.1: Differentiating between various operative units[4]

---

[3] see Eller R., (2005), page 51.
[4] following Sparkassen Finanzgruppe (2007), page 49.

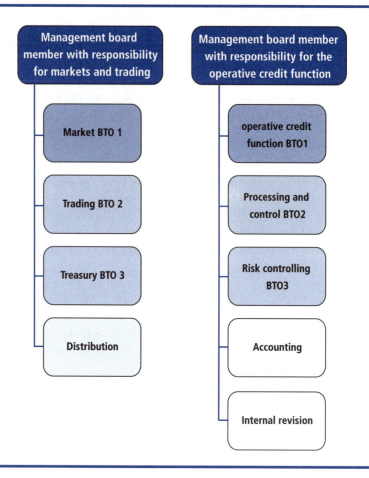

Figure 16.2: Typical organizational setup with two members of the management board[5]

As Figure 16.1 makes clear, a strict organizational separation between the trading function and the independent processing and controlling units is required. Only in exceptional cases, which will be considered in detail later, can the requirement of an organizational separation be relaxed.

Figure 16.2 shows the ideal organizational setup. A distinction is made between BTO 1 (credit business) and BTO 2 (trading activities). Neutral areas are not separated and can be assigned freely. They are not subject to the principle of functional separation. For the functions labeled BTO 1 and BTO 2, a structural separation is required between market and operative credit func-

---

[5] See: Sparkassen Finanzgruppe (2007), S. 71.

tion as well as between trading and risk controlling and processing. This separation must even be implemented at the management board level.

Due to the size of many institutions, it is not possible to work with a management board that only has two members. Therefore a larger number of management board members share responsibility in line with the outline presented above.

In BTO 2.2 one exception is allowed[6]: the general separation of the units that are related to trading can be waived if the trading activities as assessed by volume or relevance for risk are so insignificant that a functional separation would be unreasonable. An escape clause which is based on the credit law exists for small banking institutions with little trading activities. This simplification is permissible if the following prerequisites are met[7]:

- The bank is a non account book institute.
- The focus of trading activities is on long-term assets or the liquidity reserve.
- The volume of trading activities is low compared to the overall business volume.
- The structure of the trading activities is simple. Complexity, volatility and risk of the positions are small.

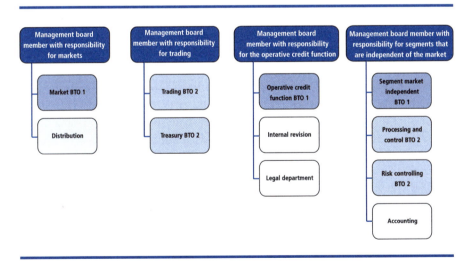

Figure 16.3: Typical organizational setup with four members of the management board[8]

---

[6] See Sparkassen Finanzgruppe (2007), p. 19.
[7] See Sparkassen Finanzgruppe (2007), pages 46 ff.
[8] Sparkassen Finanzgruppe (2007), S. 72.

16.1.2 Risk controlling of wealth management clients

An active daily risk controlling is conducted for wealth management clients[9]. It consists on the one hand of the monitoring of market risks, the checking for margin requirements as well as making sure that the transactions conducted are in line with the business volume of the customer. On the other hand, internal bank data is checked. Were trading limits observed, were losses generated, did the client trade only in products that he was approved for, did he receive the appropriate advice and information about chances and risks? This also includes the controls which are imposed on banks and brokers by the legislator as well as the controlling of the traders. In the case of major derivatives clients, who often post collateral in the form of a settlement line[10], the use of this line must be monitored constantly. In case of an increase in risk, both the client advisor and the client must be informed. This assures seamless controlling.

16.1.3 Risk controlling of financial engineering units

Risk controlling of financial engineering units does not differ hugely from that of classical wealth management clients. Again the margin risk[11] must be controlled. For products that are traded OTC, an individual contract exists with each counterpart[12] which specifies the type of collateral, its volume and extend. Agreed trading agreements and trading limits must be observed and are controlled by a unit which is usually housed in the back office. Computer supported processes are used to control the individual risks. Due to the size of the business transactions, an effective and targeted risk controlling is of paramount importance. The front offices[13] are hedging against the back office units[14]. Specific software is used, which allows effective hedging procedures.

---

[9] Wealth management is the highest client segment of a bank. This is where the wealthiest clients are and usually also the best bank advisers. Due to their complexity, derivatives are often only offered actively in this segment alone. Retail clients are usually trading "execution only." This means that they will not get any active and thorough advice. Since only the order is taken, this can also be considered a brokerage service. Of course, retail clients are treated the same way as wealth management clients by risk controlling. The procedure may even be more rigorous, since the financial background may be different.

[10] A settlement line is a type of credit line, which defines the business volume the client is allowed to conduct.

[11] Controlling of margin calls as well as of collateral for all positions.

[12] The active counterpart in the transaction.

[13] Trading.

[14] Are responsible among other things for hedging.

Contracts provide the necessary legal clarity with regard to counterparts. They are specified by ISDA[15] and used internationally.

> **Lessons from the past**
>
> A lot of negative examples such as the cases of Barings Bank or Société Générale are known. Each individual case is a negative and sobering example. But the important thing is to draw the appropriate lessons. One major insight is the realization that as much risk controlling as is necessary should be used. Never trust your systems blindly and never go against the market. Define clear loss and risk limits and stick with them. Conduct scenario analyses and stress tests and draw your conclusions. Do not think that you can beat the market. If your decisions are correct 60% of the time, you are already very good.

16.2 Unforeseeable market events

In closing we want to share a few thoughts on the topic of unforeseeable market events[16], which can happen at any point in time: of course we do not recommend waiting for those events, but at the same time, every investor should have sufficient degrees of freedom for action. Otherwise a margin call or forced liquidation can quickly be the consequence. And it is also true that such critical market situations can be used to generate profits via active speculation. Basically it must always be considered where the biggest risk of a position is located. Upside, if the underlying (also in combination with the trading book) increases or downside, if the underlying declines. Especially in the case of complex strategies or when considering all positions in combination, this issue should be considered carefully. If the positions are tilted in one direction, large losses can accumulate quickly. A balanced trading book can help in this regard. The same is true for block holdings, which should be avoided in favor of several smaller positions. While these may require an increased management effort, the risk of sudden and unforeseen price changes is reduced.

---

[15] International Swaps and Derivatives Association, Inc.
[16] Black swans – refers to events that were not foreseeable and which can cause massive market fluctuations. Examples are a coup, political unrest, a terrorist attack or for example a surprising insolvency (see bankruptcy of Lehmann Brothers in 2008).

Figure 16.4: Risk controlling

Figure 16.4 again summarizes the main points concerning risk controlling.

The 10 golden rules of risk controlling

1. As much controlling as necessary and not as possible!
2. Never blindly trust a system!
3. Everyone, trader, client or risk controller, must deal daily with the issue of risk.
4. Never let risks "get out of hand."
5. Panic is the enemy of good results. Stay calm and try to make rational decisions.
6. Do not overreact, do not ignore risks.
7. Maintain intensive communication among the parties. Always discuss all risks openly and intensively.
8. Take the chirurgical approach and do not "hit them over the head."
9. Assess chances and risks before entering into a transaction.
10. The risk is gone from the trading book only after the position is closed.

16.3 What is margin?

A margin is a deposit required to enter into a derivatives transaction. Its function is to assure that all financial obligations can be met and that a position which was opened can also be closed again. As a basic rule, a margin payment is required for all exchange traded derivatives transactions. Only long options do not involve a margin payment[17], since only a right is purchased and no obligation can arise[18]. Margin calls have to be met for all open positions by the next business day. In a difficult market environment it is also possible that additional margin must be posted within a trading day.

Banks and brokers provide the collateral to the derivatives exchange in the form of securities or liquid funds (in different currencies – EUR, CHF, USD, GBP) and then block, for every individual client, these securities or funds in the accounts. Normally the amount that clients have to provide to the bank or broker exceeds the margin requirements of the derivatives exchanges by a factor of 1.2 to 2. This "artificial" increase once again serves as protection, both for the client (since his scope for activities is reduced) and the bank or broker.

But what is the composition of the margin requirement? A number of different margin systems exist such as risk based margining[19], SPAN[20], TIMS[21] and so forth.

Using the example of Eurex, we want to elaborate further on risk based margining in the following sections.

> An Eurex margin calculator is available in our download area. It can be used to calculate margins and to simulate their use.

All transactions which are conducted at Eurex exchanges are cleared via Eurex Clearing AG. It guarantees to its business partners and clearing participants that the transactions will be honored. In this context it is also responsible for the calculation of margin.

---

[17] Long positions give rise to a positive margin account when netting all positions.
[18] With the payment of the premium to the short investor all obligations have been met.
[19] Risk Based Margining is the margin system used at Eurex.
[20] Method for the calculation of margin requirements which was developed 1988 by Chicago Mercantile Exchange (CME). It is still used today at CBOE, CME, LIFFE and other exchanges. SPAN is an abbreviation for "Standard Portfolio Analysis of Risk." The SPAN margin is determined with the help of highly complex algorithms which take into consideration all options and futures in a trading account which are either written or purchased. Therefore they reflect the overall portfolio risk. Calculated are the maximum losses and gains for the next trading day of all positions in the account. This serves as the basis for the determination of the margin which needs to be deposited.
[21] Theoretical Inter-market Margin System: System of the Options Clearing Corporation (OCC). OCC was founded in 1973 and is located in Chicago.

16.4 What is risk based margining?

For the investor it is an advantage that he only needs to deposit an amount equal to the risk of losses in his trading book rather than the entire value of the position. When combinations are taken into account, risk is reduced and the provision of excessive margin avoided. Products that make use of (almost) identical underlying instruments are put into the same risk category: as an example all options on DAX® shares as well as ODAX® and FDAX® positions are included in the margin category DAX®. All categories are formed in a similar fashion. All margin deposits and margin requirements of the same category are netted. This procedure is called cross margining. It helps to preserve liquidity since the individual valuation of all positions would in sum lead to a higher margin requirement. The combination of two or more margin categories with similar correlations is called margin group. Within such a group, cross margining is again applied. As an example, the categories Euro Bund Future, Euro Bobl Future and Euro Schatz Future are netted.

The margin is calculated anew each day for every member of the exchange. And during the course of a business day, the calculation of margins continues. Not only current, but also probable future price risks are taken into consideration. Should an exchange member suffer an intraday shortage of margin, a so called intraday margin call is issued, which demands the immediate provision of liquidity.

16.5 Why is the deposit of margin required and how is it calculated?

A margin payment helps to eliminate the risk that one contract party cannot meet its obligations in a worst case scenario.

In a first step all long and short positions which are written on identical contracts and have the same expiration date are **netted** – this gives rise to a net long or a net short position. All net risk positions are aggregated and considered as a combined net risk position.

In order to determine the maximum cost of closing the positions, an attempt is made to draw conclusions about the future development of the prices based on the historic price movements of the contracts (or their underlying). A key role in this regard is played by the volatility or the range of fluctuations: to calculate this figure, Eurex Clearing AG takes a look at the price movements over the past 30 or 250 trading days (which is equal to a trading month or a trading year). Based on these fluctuations, margin parameters are determined, which specify the maximum price movement from one trading day to the next. These parameters can be adjusted if necessary.

With the help of the margin parameters, possible minimum and maximum values for the individual underlying securities are determined and theoretical option prices are calculated. The volatility used in this exercise is the implied volatility which can be extracted from the closing prices of the option.

16.6 Which types of margin exist?

16.6.1 Premium margin

This type of margin is used for all options where the premium must already be paid when the option transaction takes place (see Figure 16.5). The writer of the option must provide relevant collateral (accepted securities or cash). The premium margin covers the loss which would arise if the option writer were to repurchase his positions on the same trading day.

In the case of options on futures[22] no **premium margin** is required. Here the option premium is not paid at the beginning, but rather spread out over the term to maturity using the mark to market procedure.

For long positions there is also no need to deposit a premium margin, since the payment of the option premium only provides a right and no obligation. Corresponding to the short positions, positive values in the margin account in the case of long positions are taken into consideration when the overall margin situation of a trading book is assessed.

16.6.2 Additional margin

Additional margin (see Figure 16.5) serves to cover all possible additional costs of closing a position by the next trading day or also intraday (in a worst case scenario). The **additional margin** is charged on all options and futures positions. In the case of futures positions this is also called (outside of the

---

[22] Future style options.
[23] Exchange traded funds; for example index funds, which are traded on exchanges in the form of special assets. Options can also be written on these securities. Eurex for example

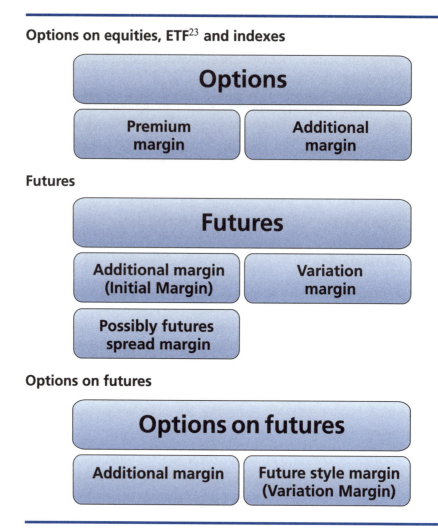

Figure 16.5: An overview of the different types of margin

terminology of Eurex) **initial margin**. When the derivatives transaction is agreed, an initial amount is deposited, which is supposed to cover the worst case scenario of a position.

---

offers options on DAX®-ETF (iShares) in order to offer a version for retail clients that is covered. The market response so far has been muted. CBOE also offers options on ETFs.

16.6.3 Variation margin

Variation margin is the daily adjustment of profits and losses for futures and options on futures. Here the mark to market procedure mentioned above is used: the profits or losses that accrue every day are either credited or debited on the accounts of the clearing members. What is significantly different compared to other types of margin is the fact that variation margin is not the provision of collateral in the form of securities and similar assets, but rather the actual balancing of profits and losses.

If an investor has purchased a futures contract at 100 points and it rises to 110 points on the next day, he will be credited the 10 points – translated into the relevant monetary unit. Meanwhile, the owner of a short position will be debited.

Thus all holdings will be valued daily in the **mark to market procedure.** Even on the last day of trading, only the difference between the value on the previous day and the final settlement price needs to be determined.

Example of variation margin

Date	Closing price	Profit and loss in points	Value per point in EUR[24]	Number of contracts	Variation margin in EUR
11/25	4,705	– 30	25	10	– 7,500
11/26	4,742	+ 37	25	10	+ 9,250
11/27	4,726	– 16	25	10	– 4,000
11/28	4,778	+ 52	25	10	+ 13,000
Sum	–	+ 43	–	–	+ 10,750

The sum of EUR 10,750 is the profit for the client if he closes the futures position.

16.6.4 Futures spread margin

If several futures positions on the same underlying are contained in a trading book, long and short positions can be offset against each other. It is important that the maturities of the contracts are identical. This procedure is called

---

[24] Example of FDAX = EUR 25 per point.

"netting." Remaining long or short positions with differing maturities are also considered. These are called non-spreads that cannot be compensated and are assessed the **futures spread margin**.

16.7 Option margins

16.7.1 Long positions

All financial risk has been eliminated with the payment of the option premium in the case of long positions. Only a right is purchased and no obligation has arisen. But any credit balance in the margin account can be used for netting.

16.7.2 Short positions

An initial distinction must be made between covered and uncovered short positions. In the case of **covered** short positions[25], the investor holds the underlying in his account. For example, if he holds a short call position on X shares, in a covered short call position he possesses the relevant shares at a rate of 1:1 relative to the derivative position. This only works in the case of options with physical delivery, in other words for options not written on futures. Options with cash settlement can only be written uncovered.

If a long investor exercises his options, a corresponding short position is assigned randomly and the underlying is delivered. Delivery times vary by contract and mode of delivery.

In the case of **uncovered** options a deposit is required in the form of a margin payment that has already been discussed. The theoretical option prices which are needed for this are determined with the help of different option pricing models. In combination with an assessment of different price paths for the underlying, the margin is determined.

Figures 16.6 and 16.7 show margin calculations for a trading portfolio. Two different approaches are used: risk based margin (Figure 16.6) and SPAN (Figure 16.7).

---

[25] CCW = Covered Call Writing.

Option margins

```
INST: DTE    METHOD: 22 - DTB Risk Based Meth    CROSS INST GROUP: AT22 - EURX - Klasse DTE
                              INITIAL PORTFOLIO
TRADE  PROMPT                           CONTRACT    OPTION    MARKET      MARKET
TYPE   DATE    SERIES  CONTRACTS        SIZE        PREM      PRICE       VALUE

PUT    DEC/09  11.00   -150             100.0000    2.47      9.67       -37050.00

                              ADDITIONAL MARGIN
TRADE  PROMPT                           <---------- THEO ---------->    UPSIDE/
TYPE   DATE    SERIES  CONTRACTS        RISK        PRICE     VALUE     DOWNSIDE

PUT    DEC/09  11.00   -150             3.288653    8.61      49329.80   DOWNSIDE
                                        2.970412    9.00      44556.20   DOWNSIDE
                                        2.589941    9.50      38849.10   DOWNSIDE
                                        2.237054   10.00      33555.80   UPSIDE
                                        1.931803   10.50      28977.00   UPSIDE
                                        1.792176   10.73      26882.60   UPSIDE

         ACCUMULATED THEO VALUES
UPSIDE/      THEORETICAL    VARIANCE FROM
DOWNSIDE     CONT VALUE     MARKET VALUE

DOWNSIDE     49329.80       12279.80
DOWNSIDE     44556.20        7506.20
DOWNSIDE     38849.10        1799.10
UPSIDE       33555.80       -3494.20
UPSIDE       28977.00       -8073.00
UPSIDE       26882.60      -10167.40

     FINAL TOTALS:                                                PREMIUM MARGIN         37050.00DR
                                                           FUTURES SPREAD MARGIN             0.00
                                  ADDITIONAL MARGIN DISCOUNT/MARKUP OF 100.00%  ADDITIONAL MARGIN     12279.80DR

                                                                         MARGIN         49329.80DR
                                  DISCOUNT/MARKUP OF 100.00%    INITIAL MARGIN         49329.80DR
```

Figure 16.6: Risk based margin calculation for short puts (150) on Deutsche Telekom[26]

```
MARGIN METHOD: 29 - LTOM SPAN Method    CROSS INST GROUP: 29 - LNM
                                                          !SCANNING RISKS- POSITIVE FIGURES SHOW LOSSES, NEGATIVE SHOW GAINS!
        BREAK   TRADE PROMPT                 DELTA  COMP    NET ! <-------- DOWN -------->    NO    <-------- UP -------->  UP EXT !
INST   MONTH   TYPE  DATE    SERIES  LOTS    DIV    DELTA   DELTA !   3/3    2/3    1/3   CHANGE    1/3    2/3    3/3  DN EXT !

LNM            PUT   JUN/09  1000   -2 1000.00 -0.22   0.43!    1599    907    432    -43   -386   -656   -927   -486 !
                                                            !   1599    907    432    -43   -386   -656   -927   1515 !
                                                            !
               CALL  JUN/09  1100   -3 1000.00  0.72  -2.17!   -5443  -3787  -2120    -68   1985   4142   6503   4833 !
                                                            !   -5443  -3787  -2120    -68   1985   4142   6503  -3095 !
                                                            !
         TOTALS FOR LNM                              -1.74!   -3844  -2880  -1688   -111   1599   3486   5576   4347 !
                                                            !   -3844  -2880  -1688   -111   1599   3486   5576  -1580 !

     INTERMONTH SPREAD - METHOD 01           SPOT MONTH SPREAD - METHOD 01              FINAL TOTALS

  NO CHARGE APPLICABLE:         0.00        NO CHARGE APPLICABLE    :     0.00      SCANNING RISK (LINE 11):    5576.00DR
                                                                                    INTERMONTH CHARGE:             0.00
  INTERMONTH CHARGE:            0.00        SPOT MONTH CHARGE:            0.00      SPOT MONTH CHARGE:             0.00

                                                                                    TOTAL CHARGE:              5576.00DR

                            SHORT OPTION LOTS:   -5    SHORT OPTION RATE:    0.00   SHORT OPTION MINIMUM CHARGE:   0.00
                                                                        CUSTOMER SPEC FACTOR :   1.00          5576.00DR
                                                                        INIT/MAINT RATIO :       1.00          5576.00DR

                                                                                    OPTION MARKET VALUE:      12327.50
                                                                                    INITIAL MARGIN:            5576.00DR
```

Figure 16.7: SPAN margin calculation for short calls (3) and short puts (2) on Lonmin[27]

Since there is a risk that the calculated prices are too low for deep out-of-the-money options (since they can react very strongly to an abrupt increase in volatility) a short options adjustment is used. In some cases this can significantly exceed the calculated option prices.

---

[26] Source: Commerzbank ZTB, Rolfe & Nolan.
[27] Source: Commerzbank ZTB, Rolfe & Nolan.

An input required for the calculation is the out-of-the-money minimum which is set by the derivatives exchange. The following formula is used:

$$\text{short option adjustment} = \\ \text{margin parameter}^{28} \times \text{ out of the money } - \text{ minimum} \\ + \text{ daily settlement price}$$

16.8 Margin during the time of delivery

If an option is exercised, margin is still required until delivery has been completed. But this margin relates to the underlying to be delivered and no longer to the option. The difference between exercise price and closing price of the underlying is to be provided as premium margin. The price fluctuations of the underlying enter the overall margin calculation in the form of additional margin.

16.9 Margin for futures

Profits and losses are balanced daily in line with the price movement of the underlying (see Figure 16.8). This procedure, which is called variation margin, prevents that profits or losses accumulate.

In addition to the daily netting of profits and losses it must also be assured that a possible closing on the next trading day does not result in a loss. This additional margin (initial margin[29]) can be provided – in contrast to the variation margin for which cash is always used – either in the form of securities or of cash (in the form of account balances) (see Figure 16.8). Its magnitude is equal to the amount which is required in a worst case scenario to close out the open contracts.

In a first step all long and short positions with the same maturity are offset ("netting"). Net positions (long or short) which may result from this are checked for the possibility of obtaining spreads. On those, a spread margin is assessed which is lower than the additional margin on the remaining net posi-

---

[28] The margin parameters are set by the respective derivatives exchanges and are adjusted in line with the riskiness of the underlying.
[29] Wording outside Eurex.

Margin for futures

```
MARGIN METHOD:  19 - CME SPAN           CROSS INST GROUP:   19 - EC

      BREAK TRADE PROMPT                  COMP    NET  ! SCANNING RISKS - POSITIVE FIGURES SHOW LOSSES, NEGATIVE SHOW GAINS  !
INST  MONTH TYPE  DATE    SERIES   LOTS   DELTA   DELTA!    1/2/3      4/5/6       7/8/9     10/11/12    13/14/15       16  !
EC          FUT   MAR/09             15   1.00    15.00!        0     -22500      -45000       45000       67500      64800!
                                                      !                22500      -45000      -67500       67500           !
                                                      !   -22500       22500       45000      -67500      -64800           !
                                                      !
            TOTALS FOR EC                         30.0000!       0     -22500      -45000       45000       67500      64800!
                                                      !        0       22500      -45000      -67500       67500           !
                                                      !   -22500       22500       45000      -67500      -64800           !

       INTERMONTH SPREAD - METHOD 10          DELIVERY MONTH SPREAD - METHOD 01              FINAL TOTALS
       ----------------------------------     ---------------------------------    ----------------------------------
                                                  NO CHARGE APPLICABLE:   0.00      SCANNING RISK (LINE 13):   67500.00DR
             INTERMONTH CHARGE:      0.00                                                 INTERMONTH CHARGE:       0.00
                                              DELIVERY MONTH CHARGE:      0.00       DELIVERY MONTH CHARGE:       0.00
                                                                                              TOTAL CHARGE:   67500.00DR
             SHORT OPTION LOTS:         0          SHORT OPTION RATE:    23.00    SHORT OPTION MINIMUM CHARGE:     0.00
                                                                                   CUSTOMER SPEC FACTOR :   1.00    67500.00DR
                                                                                      INIT/MAINT RATIO :    1.35    91125.00DR
                                                                                        FORWARD OPTION VALUE:       0.00
                                                                                               INITIAL MARGIN:  91125.00DR
```

Figure 16.8: EUR/USD futures at CME, Span method[30]

```
INST: FDAX   METHOD: 22 - DTB Risk Based Meth   CROSS INST GROUP: AD22 - EURX - Klasse DAX
                                  INITIAL PORTFOLIO
TRADE  PROMPT                          CONTRACT    OPTION    MARKET    MARKET
TYPE    DATE    SERIES  CONTRACTS        SIZE      PREM      PRICE     VALUE
FUT    MAR/09                   -5     25.0000      0.00    4031.50   -503937.50
                                 ADDITIONAL MARGIN
TRADE  PROMPT                    <---------- THEO ---------->   UPSIDE/
TYPE    DATE    SERIES  CONTRACTS    RISK      PRICE    VALUE   DOWNSIDE
FUT    MAR/09                   -5  3586.500000  3586.50  448312.50  DOWNSIDE
                                    3600.000000  3600.00  450000.00  DOWNSIDE
                                    3650.000000  3650.00  456250.00  DOWNSIDE
                                    3700.000000  3700.00  462500.00  DOWNSIDE
                                    3750.000000  3750.00  468750.00  DOWNSIDE
                                    3800.000000  3800.00  475000.00  DOWNSIDE
                                 ADDITIONAL MARGIN
TRADE  PROMPT                    <---------- THEO ---------->   UPSIDE/
TYPE    DATE    SERIES  CONTRACTS    RISK      PRICE    VALUE   DOWNSIDE
                                    3850.000000  3850.00  481250.00  DOWNSIDE
                                    3900.000000  3900.00  487500.00  DOWNSIDE
                                    3950.000000  3950.00  493750.00  DOWNSIDE
                                    4000.000000  4000.00  500000.00  DOWNSIDE
                                    4050.000000  4050.00  506250.00  UPSIDE
                                    4100.000000  4100.00  512500.00  UPSIDE
                                    4150.000000  4150.00  518750.00  UPSIDE
                                    4200.000000  4200.00  525000.00  UPSIDE
                                    4250.000000  4250.00  531250.00  UPSIDE
                                    4300.000000  4300.00  537500.00  UPSIDE
                                    4350.000000  4350.00  543750.00  UPSIDE
                                    4400.000000  4400.00  550000.00  UPSIDE
              ACCUMULATED THEO VALUES
 UPSIDE/     THEORETICAL    VARIANCE FROM
DOWNSIDE     CONT VALUE     MARKET VALUE
DOWNSIDE     456250.00       -47687.50
DOWNSIDE     462500.00       -41437.50
DOWNSIDE     468750.00       -35187.50
DOWNSIDE     475000.00       -28937.50
DOWNSIDE     481250.00       -22687.50
DOWNSIDE     487500.00       -16437.50
DOWNSIDE     493750.00       -10187.50
DOWNSIDE     500000.00        -3937.50
UPSIDE       506250.00         2312.50
UPSIDE       512500.00         8562.50
UPSIDE       518750.00        14812.50
UPSIDE       525000.00        21062.50
UPSIDE       531250.00        27312.50
UPSIDE       537500.00        33562.50
UPSIDE       543750.00        39812.50
UPSIDE       550000.00        46062.50

       FINAL TOTALS:                                                      PREMIUM MARGIN          0.00
                                                                   FUTURES SPREAD MARGIN          0.00
                                  ADDITIONAL MARGIN DISCOUNT/MARKUP OF 100.00%   ADDITIONAL MARGIN     55625.00DR
```

Figure 16.9: Margin calculation FDAX® at Eurex, risk based method[31]

---

[30] Source: Commerzbank ZTB, Rolfe & Nolan.
[31] Source: Commerzbank ZTB, Rolfe & Nolan.

tions. If neither netting nor construction of a spread is possible, the additional margin is assessed.

- When the **spread margin** is computed, a distinction is made between the **spot month spread margin** and the **back month spread margin**. The derivatives contract which is next to mature is called front contract, the corresponding month is called front month; all other months are called back months. The contracts are called **deferred contracts**. The spot margin is related to the front contract (assuming that all contracts are in the same month). The reason for this is simple: the contract which matures next is characterized by the highest volume and also the greatest volatility. One consequence can be that the long and short positions are no longer negatively correlated with regard to risk and that they therefore provide insufficient compensation. The increase of the margin is effective at the beginning of the last trading month.
- If no spreads can be formed, the **additional margin** is assessed as discussed, since the positions are fully exposed to the closing risk until the following trading day. When this book was completed, for an FDAX® position an additional margin[32] of 550 FDAX® points per contract was assessed (equivalent to 550 × EUR 25 = EUR 13,750).

16.10 Margin for future style options

While the usual **premium margin** is due for classical options, this is not the case for **future style options**. The premium payment is included in the mark to market procedure instead (see variation margin 16.6.3). The additional margin, which covers losses until the next trading day or even intraday from closing out positions in a **worst case scenario**, is calculated analogous to classical options.

Future style options are subject to the **future style premium posting**. This means that in the case of exercise or expiration, the remaining unpaid portions of the premium are considered in addition to the daily settlement of profits and losses. Thus the option premium is paid only when the option is exercised or after it has expired. This gives a liquidity advantage to the buyer. **Crediting** or **debiting** is done on the basis of daily option prices. Since the writer of the options relinquishes the interest income from the reinvestment of the option premiums, the premiums of these options are higher than those of classical

---

[32] Initial margin.

options. With this procedure, less capital is tied up. At Eurex it is used for options on futures (for example OGBL).

16.11 How is the margin calculated for option positions?

Should a trading book contain several contracts on the same underlying, a compensation of the risk weights (riskiness) is possible. This is done with the help of the **cross margin approach** used earlier in the chapter.

Basis of the margin calculation is the assumed maximum price movement of the underlying until the next trading day (**margin parameter**). It is determined with the help of a statistical analysis of the underlying and can be added or subtracted from the actual price to arrive at maximum and minimum prices for the underlying. Such an approach reveals whether **upside risk** or **downside risk** is present[33]. Next all strike prices of a margin interval are calculated.

> The current margin parameters can be found on the homepages of the derivatives exchanges. They are adjusted in line with risk assessments. You can also find the margin parameters in our download area.

16.12 Calculating the costs of closing a position

The effect of cross margining increases as the number of option combinations in the trading book goes up. If several **margin classes** can be combined into a margin group, it is again assessed based on similar risks. Initially the upper and lower half of the additional margin is calculated for each margin class. If a negative margin results, it is usually multiplied with the so called **offset percent**. Since it is usually set at zero, these positions drop out. Following that, all margins for the upper half are added. The result is called **upside additional margin** of a **margin group**. The same is done for the lower half;

---

[33] Upside = in case the underlying moves up; downside = in case the underlying moves down.

in this way the downside additional margin of the group is determined. The two values are compared and the higher one is assessed as **additional margin** for the margin group.

16.13 How to provide margin

Margin can be deposited in the form of **cash** or **securities**. In principle, different currencies are allowed, but it must be taken into consideration that **currency risk** can reduce the value of these assets. At the same time, discounts from the nominal values of the securities can be calculated in order to increase the margin of safety. Banks and brokers collectively provide the required collateral to the derivatives exchanges for all their customers and then block the client holdings in their individual accounts.

16.14 Settlement price

The **settlement price** is the last price of the trading day. If no price is available for a product, a series or a contract, Eurex Clearing AG will calculate a settlement price. The settlement price of the last trading day is called final settlement price.

Margin for U.S. options at CBOE

The margin for uncovered options at the CBOE is calculated as follows:

The larger value from the following calculations is chosen:

- **100% of the premium payment plus 20% of the price of the underlying minus the amount that the option is out of the money, if applicable.**

or

- **100% of the premium payment plus 10% of the price of the underlying (in the case of call options) or 10% of the strike price (in the case of put options)**

For index options only 15% instead of 20% are used.

16.15 What is a margin call?

In this section an example of a **margin call** from the perspective of the investor is provided. If an investor is unable to meet his liabilities (provision of collateral)[34], he will receive a formal **margin call** from his bank or broker. In this letter (see Figure 16.10), he will be asked to add an additional amount to his margin account. At the same time, he is threatened with a **forced closing**, the so called **liquidation** of the positions. If the investor does not fulfill the additional margin requirements, the holdings will be liquidated at the specified time. In practice it is the exception that investors are unwilling to heed this request. In order to avoid this scenario, banks and brokers have put monitoring systems in place which require early reactions of the investors. The broker or the bank will try to find a solution jointly with the client. If it is possible to find an agreement concerning the margin call, no additional steps are taken. Only if these talks are not successful, will a **formal margin call** be issued. In a **forced liquidation**, positions will be closed until the actual margin is again in line with the required margin.

Dear Sir or Madam,

As a result of the current valuation of your positions of financial derivatives transactions, additional margin payments in the amount of EUR 150,000.00 have become necessary.

We therefore ask you to add to the existing collateral the above mentioned amount by July 22, 2010, 2p.m., either in the form of a cash deposit or a verified transfer to your subaccount /76. If you plan to transfer securities from another bank to the account maintained at our institution, this must be organized by the date stated above and a written confirmation of the transferring bank must be provided. Please bear in mind that certain valuation adjustments are used in the case of securities. Your advisor can give you additional information on that issue.

Alternatively, it is possible that you reconcile the actual level of your margin account with the margin requirement by selling short positions or buying long positions that help to offset the margin requirement. Please keep in mind that the purchases of these options may be charged against existing balances which are currently used as collateral and consequently reduce these balances. Again your advisor will be happy to support you in this regard.

If you are unable to meet the deadline specified above, we will completely or partly terminate your positions and cancel all open orders for financial derivatives transactions that may still be registered with us. Should market developments lead to an increase of the margin requirements beyond the value specified above, any closings will be adjusted accordingly.

Sincerely yours,

Figure 16.10: Margin call

---

[34] He falls below the maintenance level.

16.16 Forced liquidation from the perspective of the bank or the broker

In the worst case scenario of a forced liquidation, all steps must be carefully documented by the bank or the broker. Business relations with the client should be terminated if possible. There is a great danger that a situation of an **insufficient margin account** will be repeated or that the investor becomes **insolvent**. Here the bank or the broker have an obligation to act with due diligence and prevent further investments by the client at derivatives exchanges. It must also be stressed that only that number of positions should be closed which is needed to rebalance the margin account. Closings should be distributed homogeneously across the entire trading book – this means not one big position, but several partial holdings instead. Otherwise it could happen that investors are making profits on some of the closed positions while they are suffering losses on positions that are still open – this would be indefensible. If possible, the liquidation should be done in cooperation with the investor. If the investor is unwilling to contribute, a forced liquidation must be initiated and the investor must be confronted promptly with the results and the decisions taken. He must immediately receive this information, so that he can react.

Underlying	Position prior to forced closing (contracts)	Position after forced closing (contracts)
Short call	500	250
Short put	500	250
Short futures	10	5

Concluding assessment of a forced liquidation

The relationship between client and bank or broker will suffer noticeably in the case of a forced liquidation. Most clients will terminate their banking relation in reaction to such a closing. At least this must be anticipated in practice. It must further be assumed that a bank will massively reduce or terminate the business volume with a client who was faced with a forced liquidation for risk reasons. Thus a forced liquidation will almost always result in the termination of the business relation. Important in this regard is the insight that business considerations should not be given more weight than the rules of risk controlling. This would have fatal and ruinous consequences.

Robert C. Merton once said *"It is an error to think that only because we have measured risk, we can eliminate it."* Every financial engineer should always be aware of this perspective on risk.

Literature for this chapter

Hull, John: Options, Futures and Other Derivatives, 7th edition, 2009

Jabbour, George; Budwick, Philipp: The Option Trader Handbook, 2004

Saliba, Anthony J.: The Options Workbook, 2nd edition, 2002

Questions and answers on this chapter

Question 1:
What is meant by margining?

Question 2:
What is variation margin?

Question 3:
Do different margin systems exist?

Question 4:
What is a margin call?

Question 5:
Can a bank or broker simply exercise a forced liquidation?

Answer to question 1:
Margining means the provision of collateral for open derivatives transactions.

Answer to question 2:
It is the daily accounting for profits and losses using the mark to market procedure for futures.

Answer to question 3:
Yes, a first differentiation is made between the various systems of the different derivatives exchanges. Additionally the systems which are used for the various types of derivatives are distinguished.

Answer to question 4:
A formal margin call is a letter which demands that the investor provides additional collateral (and a forced liquidation is threatened).

Answer to question 5:
If an investor is unable to provide the requested additions to the margin account, the broker or the bank can execute a forced closing of the positions and thus reestablish conformity with the rules.

In closing

The strategies, approaches and explanations provided in this book aim at characterizing the comprehensive field of financial engineering. Financial engineering spans a range between simple and highly complex products. The following figure once again summarizes the product world of the financial engineer.

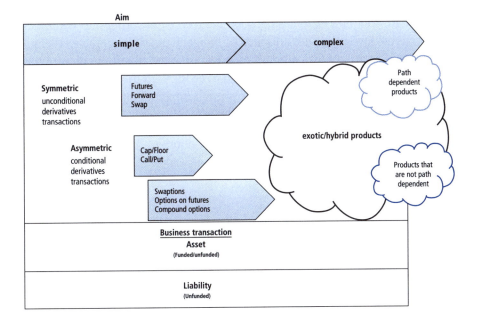

Financial engineering products can be used both on the asset and the liability side. The **simple financial engineering products** can be either symmetric or asymmetric in nature. Among the **symmetric and unconditional derivatives** are futures, forwards and swaps. The **asymmetric and conditional derivatives transactions** can be structured at a first level in a product group with caps and floors and with calls and puts. At a second level, more complex products, consisting of swaptions, options on futures and compound options can be distinguished.

The transition to **financial engineering products** is gradual and it gets harder to identify the products along clear criteria. While a number of these products were presented in this book, they only represent a small sample of possible attributes. Due to the lack of delineation, we get a grouping which contains **exotic** and **hybrid** products. The complex solutions can be separated into products that are **path-dependent** and others that are **not path-dependent**. The products which are **not path-dependent** can usually be separated into individual products which are valued with the help of simpler pricing models. The **path-dependent** products can most efficiently be valued using simulation methods.

Financial engineering is among the most exiting business areas a universal or investment bank has to offer. The creation of new instruments with the help of derivatives and the possibility to satisfy customer demand with the help of tailor-made solutions explain the uniqueness of financial engineering. At the same time these solutions play an important economic role: they allow the transfer and valuation of specific risks. Financial engineering thus combines quantitative knowledge with all kinds of financial questions. Financial engineering is a discipline which draws on a pool of derivatives, but above all is subject to constant renewal as a reaction to changes in the overall economy, the demands of clients and the regulatory environment. Financial engineering is thus an evolving discipline that continues to advance.

With this book, we hope to have opened the doors to the exciting world of financial engineering for you.

Michael Bloss
Dietmar Ernst
Joachim Häcker
Daniel Sörensen

17 | Appendix

Typical exam questions and problems

Problem 1:

Which is not part of a reverse floater?

A: Caps
B: Swaps
C: Floater
D: Floor

Answer 1

Answer D

Problem 2:

The strategy put volatility trade does not involve:

A: Long underlying
B: Short underlying
C: Long put
D: Short put

Answer 2

Answers B and D

Problem 3:

Is it true that the discounted cash flow model (DCF) works with compounded company values?

Answer 3

Not true

Problem 4:

The determination of volatility in the case of real options can also be done with the help of alternative approaches

A: Iteration procedure
B: Monte-Carlo simulation
C: Peer group analysis
D: Calculation of the cash flow

Answer 4

Answers B and C

Problem 5:

Is this statement correct? A zero bond always has a duration which is equal to its remaining term to maturity.

Answer 5

Correct

Problem 6:

Is this statement correct? A reverse convertible has the same payoff as a discount certificate.

Answer 6

Correct

Problem 7:

Is this statement correct? Multiple callable bonds usually provide a termination right to the investor.

Answer 7

Incorrect

Problem 8:

Is it correct that the funding rate is frequently a floating rate?

Answer 8

Correct

Problem 9:

Is this statement correct? Alpha can be generated with the strategy CCW.

Answer 9

Correct

Problem 10:

Is this statement correct? Only liquidity denominated in euro can be used to meet margin obligations.

Answer 10

Incorrect

Problem 11:

Which positions are required to synthetically replicate a short position in EURO STOXX futures?

A: Short call and long put with identical exercise price in EURO STOXX options
B: Short position in EURO STOXX portfolio and cash investment for the term to maturity of the EURO STOXX futures
C: Short position in EURO STOXX portfolio and borrowing for the term to maturity of the EURO STOXX futures
D: Long call and long put with identical exercise price but different maturities in EURO STOXX options

Answer 11

Answers A and B

Problem 12:

On November 25 you enter into a long position of 17 DAX® futures contracts at a price of 4,735 points. Please calculate the variation margin for the daily settlement prices until the closing of the position on November 28. Please also state the total profit or loss of the position.

Date	Settlement price	Profit and loss in points	Value in EUR per point	Number of contracts	Variation margin in EUR
11/25	4,705				
11/26	4,742				
11/27	4,726				
11/28	4,778				
Sum	—		—		

Answer 12

Date	Settlement price	Profit and loss in points	Value in EUR per point	Number of contracts	Variation Margin in EUR
11/25	4,705	− 30	25	17	− 12,750
11/26	4,742	+ 37	25	17	+ 15,725
11/27	4,726	− 16	25	17	− 6,800
11/28	4,778	+ 52	25	17	+ 22,100
Sum	—	+ 43	—	—	+ 18,275

Problem 13:

How are combined orders with the restriction IOC (Immediate or Cancel) treated?

A: Execution of the same volume for both parts
B: Execution at the set price range or better
C: Cancellation of the part which was not traded
D: Simultaneous execution of both parts

Answer 13

Answers A, B, C and D

Problem 14:

Which market expectations are expressed with the sale of put options on the DAX?

A: Expectation of falling prices of the index
B: Expectation of a reduction in implied volatility
C: Expectation of an increase in implied volatility
D: Expectation of declining interest rates over the term to maturity of the put

Answer 14

Answer B

Problem 15:

What is expressed by the statistical measure "volatility?"

Answer 15

It is a statistical measure for the degree of variability of an investment object. The measure is not concerned with the direction of change, but only with its intensity. A statement about the riskiness of an investment can be derived with the help of this measure.

Problem 16:

What is measured with the hedge ratio?

Answer 16

The hedge ratio states the number of contracts required to form a hedge. The hedge ratio can be a variable position. This implies that the number of contracts must be adjusted over time.

Problem 17:

Explain the importance of the leverage effect in derivatives investments.

Answer 17

The leverage effect enables investors to trade a large volume (for example futures on an index) with little capital (initial margin). This enables him to increase the investment volume at his disposal.

Problem 18:

An investor takes a short position in a Swiss equity option at a quote of 23.00–25.00. A few days later he closes out his position at a quote of 26.00–28.00. What is the result of this transaction if he trades 3 contracts (contract size 10, not taking into account fees)?

Answer 18
He suffers a loss of CHF 150.

Problem 19:
What is the name for the difference between the price of the futures contract on an equity index and the spot index and how is it calculated?

Answer 19
It is called base and is calculated as the difference between futures price and price of underlying.

Problem 20:
An investor compares several possibilities for an investment of EUR 50,000: (A) Purchase of an equity portfolio which is equivalent to the DAX index in its composition. (B) Depositing this amount as additional margin in order to enter into a corresponding long position in DAX futures. Which statement(s) is (are) correct?

A: In case A the investor at most risks the loss of EUR 5,000
B: In case B the investor is potentially required to provide additional funds (margin)
C: Case B allows a significantly larger gain if the price develops favorably
D: The only difference between case A and case B are the fees for the transaction

Answer 20
Answers B and C

Problem 21:
Is the value of a call option influenced by increasing interest rates?

Answer 21
Yes, the call option gains in value. This results from the fact that the direct investor does not have higher interest income from the increase in interest rates. Meanwhile, the call investor who holds his remaining liquidity in the form of interest bearing securities does benefit. This differential is reflected in the price of the call.

Problem 22:

A cross hedge is characterized among others by which of the following attributes?

A: Basis risk
B: Difference between term to maturity of the hedging instrument and the period during which the underlying is held
C: Incomplete match between the underlying to be hedged and the hedging instrument
D: A cross hedge is always a perfect hedge

Answer 22

Answers A, B and C

Problem 23:

The current market price of an underlying with a volatility of 25% is currently EUR 1,000.00. What are the upper and lower bounds for the market price of the underlying in one year with a probability of about 68%?

A: EUR 250.00 and EUR 1,750.00
B: EUR 750.00 and EUR 1,250.00
C: EUR 900.00 and EUR 1,100.00
D: EUR 975.00 and EUR 1,025.00

Answer 23

Answer B

Problem 24:

Which of the following transactions is the synthetic equivalent to taking out a loan?

A: Conversion
B: Reversal
C: Long box
D: Long butterfly

Answer 24

Answer B

Problem 25:
The capital structure of a company has changed. Will this affect the options which are already in circulation?

Answer 25
Yes, the options will be adjusted in line with the changes in the capital structure. The version number of the adjusted options will be increased by one.

Problem 26:
What is the position of an investor who has conducted the following transactions? Purchase 10 Sept 6000 puts, sale 20 DAX Sept 6100 puts, purchase 10 DAX 6200 puts.

A: Long butterfly
B: Short butterfly
C: Long condor
D: Short condor

Answer 26
Answer A

Problem 27:
In one month you will receive a payment from your life insurance company in the amount of EUR 200,000. You plan to invest this amount in German 10-year government bonds. Which position is needed to lock in the current level of interest rates?

Answer 27
You purchase two Euro Bond futures contracts or purchase call options on the Euro Bond futures contract. This will guarantee the current level of interest rates.

Problem 28:
An investor is unable to provide the required margin payment for his futures position. What do you do?

Answer 28
You seek an intensive discussion aimed at solving the problem. If the investor is able to provide additional collateral, the problem has been solved. If this is

not the case, the management of his positions needs to be discussed. If he is not willing to cooperate and does not want to adjust his holdings, you issue a formal margin call. If the client still does not react, you enforce the margin call and liquidate the positions of the investor. The necessary closings need to be distributed homogeneously across the complete trading book.

Problem 29:

An investor has written covered calls on his holding of X shares. What is his maximum loss?

Answer 29

The maximum loss is related to the necessity to sell the shares at the strike price. If the share price increases above that value plus the option premium received, the investor no longer participates and thus foregoes a profit.

Problem 30:

The owner of a call SMI May 6,850, which was purchased at a price of 132.00 is exercising the option in April. What is the net result of the transaction if the SMI is currently trading at 6,964 (ignoring transaction costs)?

A: CHF 280.00
B: CHF −180.00
C: CHF 275.00
D: The owner of the call is not allowed to exercise the option in April.

Answer 30

Answer D

Problem 31:

What are the characteristics of an exotic option of the type Bermuda?

Answer 31

The exercise right of the option is special. The exercise date or period is structured and agreed individually. This means that it can fall for example on every 12th day of the month or always on January 1st of every year.

Problem 32:

What is the price structure of a compound option in relation to a plain vanilla option?

Answer 32

The compound option is less expensive, as it is merely an option on an option and thus a right to obtain a right.

Problem 33:

What is meant by put call parity?

Answer 33

It describes the relationship between the price of a put and the price of a call on the same underlying with the same expiration date and strike price. The put can be considered to be an "insurance premium" of the call (the right to purchase).

Problem 34:

You are holding a portfolio valued at USD 20 million with a beta of 1.2. For hedging purposes you want to trade futures contracts on the XY index. The index stands at 1,020 and every futures point has a value of USD 50. How many contracts are required?

Answer 34

The required number of contracts can be calculated as follows:

$$1.2 \cdot \frac{20,000,000}{1020 \cdot 50} = 470.58$$

After rounding, 471 contracts are needed.

Problem 35:

What is meant by the term convenience yield?

Answer 35

The convenience yield is the benefit obtained from physically holding an asset. It is used when pricing commodity futures. The convenience yield is something which the owner of the good obtains and therefore it must be included in the calculation.

Problem 36:

A futures contract is trading in "contango." Provide an explanation and make a recommendation for action.

Answer 36

Contango means that the futures contracts with a longer term to maturity have a higher price than the ones with shorter maturities. This means that futures prices are increasing with maturity. This can be negative for a long futures investor, since he needs to pay more with every rollover.

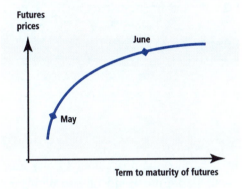

Problem 37:

What is the relevance of the swap rate?

Answer 37

The swap rate equilibrates the interest rate differences between two currencies.

Problem 38:

What is involved in a payer swaption?

Answer 38

In a payer swaption the investor becomes payer in the swap once he exercises the option.

Problem 39:

What is a chooser option and how is it structured?

Answer 39

A chooser option provides a choice between call and put. These options are more expensive than comparable plain vanilla options. The higher price is justified by the extended choices which the option provides.

Problem 40:

An investor establishes a long position in DAX futures of 5 contracts which are quoted at 5,192.0–5192.5. To limit his losses, he enters a stop loss order with a trigger price of 15 points below the purchase price. The market declines and the stop loss order is triggered. 2 contracts are traded at the trigger price and the remaining contracts are traded one tick below. What is the resulting profit or loss (ignoring transaction costs)?

Answer 40

The loss amounts to EUR 1,912.50

Problem 41:

Which market expectation is behind the following positioning? Long Euro Bund futures with short maturity and short Euro Bund futures with long maturity.

A: Increase in bond yields
B: Decline in bond yields
C: Steepening of the yield curve
D: Flattening of the yield curve

Answer 41

Answer C

Problem 42:

Are you aware of the strategy for extending a position which is preferred in this book?

Answer 42

Pyramiding. The individual contract positions are added in a way that resembles a pyramid. The pyramid must be built the right way: the largest number of contracts serves as the base and a smaller number of contracts are added on.

x
xx
xxx

Problem 43:

An investor expects both a decline in volatility and falling prices for the DAX index. Which trading strategy is appropriate for such an outlook?

A: Bull call spread DAX option
B: Short call DAX option
C: Bear call spread DAX option
D: Long jelly roll

Answer 43

Answers B and C

Problem 44:

Which transaction(s) are required by an investor who holds a long position in Euro Bobl futures when the transaction is settled?

A: Acceptance of a deliverable bond and payment of the futures price
B: Delivery of a deliverable bond and receipt of the invoice amount
C: Acceptance of a deliverable bond and payment of the invoice amount
D: Closing by entering into a short position with longer term to maturity

Answer 44

Answer C

Problem 45:

On June 17 you enter into a long position of 25 Dow Jones STOXX 50 futures September at a level of 3,117. The additional margin parameter for that asset class is set at EUR 2,700. What is the amount of additional margin to be deposited and what is the leverage effect (value of the position relative to capital employed)?

On June 18 you are selling 25 Dow Jones STOXX 50 futures December against your existing position. Please calculate the spread margin for this position. The spread margin parameter for this asset class is EUR 150.

Answer 45

Calculation of additional margin:
Additional margin = number of contracts × margin parameter in EUR = 25 × EUR 2,700 = EUR 67,500

Calculation of the value of 25 Dow Jones STOXX 50 futures and the leverage effect:
Value of the position = number of contracts × futures price × index multiplier
= 25 × 3,117 × EUR 10 = EUR 779,250

$$\text{Leverage effect} = \frac{\text{Value of position}}{\text{Capital employed}} = \frac{779{,}250}{67{,}500} = 11.54$$

With a margin requirement of EUR 67,500, a leverage factor (value of the position relative to capital employed) of 11.54 results.

Calculation of spread margin:
Spread margin = number of spreads × margin parameter in EUR = 25 × EUR 150 = EUR 3,750

The spread margin is equal to EUR 3,750.

Problem 46:

An investor enters into a short Euro Bund futures position at a price of EUR 102.50. A few days later the market value is 104.40. What is the accumulated profit or loss per contract in the margin account (not taking into consideration fees)?

A: EUR 4,750.00
B: EUR −4,750.00
C: EUR 1,900.00
D: EUR −1,900.00

Answer 46

Answer D

Problem 47:

You own an at-the-money call option on XY shares. The XY share is starting to move higher. Will the value of the call option continue to increase in absolute amounts that are as large as before if the share moves higher?

Answer 47

Due to the positive gamma, the delta goes up as the share price moves higher. This means that the price of the option increases by more than the price of an at-the-money option per unit of share price increase.

Problem 48:

An investor observes the following market prices: Euro Bund futures March 108.02–108.03, Euro Bund futures call option March 108.00 1.13–1.15, Euro Bund futures put option March 108.00 1.19–1.21. What is the profit in ticks for one contract which the investor can make at these prices if he applies the optimal arbitrage strategy (ignoring fees)?

Answer 48

6 ticks.

Problem 49:

The quarterly figures for Y company are expected shortly. Your equity analyst is of the opinion that the quarterly figures will be significantly worse than expected by the market consensus. What is the best option strategy to benefit from this outlook?

Answer 49

You purchase puts on Y shares that are in the money or sell futures on Y shares.

Problem 50:

An investor sells a call on ABC company with an exercise price of EUR 52.50 and a premium of EUR 2.10. For which prices of the underlying will the investor make the maximum profit?

Answer 50

For prices of EUR 52.50 or below, the option will not be exercised by the buyer and the seller obtains the maximum profit of EUR 2.10.

Glossary

Additional margin The additional margin serves to cover additional costs of closing out a position which might arise in an unfavorable market environment.

American option An American option can be exercised on any trading day during the life of the option.

Arbitrage Arbitrage makes use of price differences between two trading locations on the same trading day (time of trading). Arbitrage involves the simultaneous buying and selling of a security.

Arbitrageur Investor who realizes a risk-free return.

Asian option An option with a payoff that depends on the average price of the underlying during a specific time period.

Ask Price at which a market participant is willing to sell.

Assignment The exercise of a long option requires that a short investor fulfills his contractual obligation.

At-the-money The strike price of an option is approximately equal to the current market price.

Averaging Averaging is an attempt to achieve a favorable purchase price for long-term holdings. This is particularly relevant for the expansion of positions. But since the volume traded is equal to that of the original position, risk is substantially increased. Strategies to lower the average price should be considered a last resort.

Backwardation The futures price is lower than the spot price.

Barrier option An option with a path-dependent payoff.

Basis convergence Futures and spot price are equal. This is the case on the last day of trading.

Basis Difference between value of the underlying and futures price. The basis can be either negative, positive or zero.

Beta Measures the sensitivity of an individual security or portfolio with regard to the overall market.

Bid Price at which a market participant is willing to buy.

Bid-ask spread Measures the difference between the bid price and the ask price. Ask is always above bid. The bid-ask spread is either specified as an absolute value or as a percentage value (absolute value divided by ask price).

Binomial model Model which was developed by Cox, Ross and Rubinstein for the determination of option prices.

Black-Scholes model Continuous time model for the calculation of theoretical option values. Developed by Black and Scholes.

Boston option Option with delayed payment date.

Break even The "point" at which the risk profile of a trade is equal to zero.

Broker Person who conducts transactions against payment of a commission.

Call option The right, but not the obligation to purchase an underlying at a predetermined point in time at a pre-specified price.

Callable bond Bond which can be repaid by the issuer at a specific point in time. In financial engineering, the callable bond (from the perspective of the investor) is constructed by purchasing a straight bond and simultaneously being short a call on the bond.

Cap Upper limit on interest rates.

Caplet Component of a cap.

Cash settlement Case where a derivatives transaction is not closed out via physical delivery, but settled in cash instead (index futures for example).

Cash-and-carry arbitrage Sale of futures and simultaneous purchase in the spot market.

CCW "Covered Call Writing." A call which is covered by the underlying is sold. The investor holds the shares which possibly have to be delivered.

Chooser option Option where a choice between call and put exists.

Clearinghouse A central counterpart that guarantees the settlement of exchange listed derivatives transactions.

Closing A derivatives transaction is terminated by entering into an offsetting transaction.

Collar Combination of cap and floor.

Combinations In a combination at least two different, but connected derivatives transactions are conducted. They should not be terminated individually and should always be considered as an overall position.

Commodity derivatives transactions Derivatives transactions that use commodities as underlying. Thus they are subject to different volatilities and value drivers than financial derivatives.

Contango The futures price is higher than the spot price.

Contract Minimum size or quantity of a derivatives transaction.

Convenience yield Yield obtained from physically holding the underlying. It is included in the calculation of the commodity futures price.

Correlation coefficient Indicates the degree of co-movement of two values.

Cost of Carry (CoC) Premium on the financing cost of the futures price. COC is equal to the basis.

Counterparty Opposite party in a derivatives transaction.

Credit default swap CDS, credit derivative.

Credit derivative Derivative which is subject to credit risk. Can be traded OTC, securitized or at derivatives exchanges.

Cross rate Trading of a third currency via two other currencies.

CTD "Cheapest to Deliver." The bond which can be delivered at the lowest cost.

Currency derivatives Derivatives which use currencies as underlying.

Daily settlement price Price used for the valuation of all options and futures.

Delta Value of change in the option price for a change in the underlying by one unit.

Derivative The value of derivatives is derived from spot market prices. The underlying is not traded directly.

Digital option Option with payoffs that are not continuous.

Discount Price reduction in the case of a currency transaction.

Dividend Cash payment to shareholders.

Due date / expiration date States the day on which the derivatives transaction expires. This is usually the third Friday of the month.

European option Option which can only be exercised on the last day of trading (for example index options).

Exchange minimum margin The minimum amount which is specified by the derivatives exchange excluding premiums. In the case of deep-out-of-the-money options the minimum margin payment that is required.

Exotic options Options where additional rights have been added or no longer exist. They serve as the basis for structured products and are traded OTC.

Expiration date Date on which a derivatives contract becomes worthless. Usually the third Friday of the month.

Fiduciary call Consists of the purchase of a call and the simultaneous purchase of a riskless bond which matures on the same date as the call and has the same nominal value as the strike price of the call.

Floor Lower limit on interest rates.

Floorlet Component of a floor.

Forced liquidation Liquidation of derivatives positions as a result of insufficient margin and an inability or unwillingness of the investor to provide additional funds.

Forward rate agreement Unconditional derivatives transaction on interest rates which is not exchange traded.

Funding The funding or the funding level of a financial engineering department states which internal or external rate of return on capital received is returned to the financial engineering department from the treasury of the issuer. It thus directly affects the pricing of a new product (ex costs).

Futures spread margin Margin required on futures spread positions.

Future style options Options which are written on futures and entail the daily settlement of profits and losses.

Futures price Settlement price of a futures transaction.

Futures Unconditional derivatives transactions.

Gamma "Delta of delta," also called convexity. States the change in the delta for a one unit change in the underlying.

Hard commodities Commodity derivatives transactions on hard commodities such as gold and silver. The counterpart are soft commodities.

HDD Heating degree days.

Hedge ratio Number of contracts required to establish a hedging strategy.

Hedger Investor who wants to protect against market developments.

Hedging Protection of existing holdings or of holdings which are to be established in the future.

Implied volatility Volatility which is reflected in the option price. Price at which volatility is traded.

In the money An option is in the money if the price of the underlying exceeds the strike price in the case of a call and if the price of the underlying is below the strike price in the case of a put.

Initial margin Margin which must be deposited with the clearing house for a futures contract in order to be able to open a position. Frequently this is also called additional margin.

Intensity of default Measures the probability of non-payment.

Inter-contract spread Two futures with different contract specifications are traded against each other.

Inter-market spread The investor is buying and selling identical contracts at two different exchanges and in that way is utilizing price differences between the two exchanges.

Intra-contract spread Futures on the same underlying with different expiration dates are traded.

Intrinsic value Difference between spot price and exercise price of the option. The intrinsic value is always greater than or equal to zero.

Leverage Effect which results when small amounts of capital are used to move large volumes.

Lognormal distribution The logarithm of a variable follows a normal distribution.

Long position Derivatives position purchased.

Lookback option Payment depends on a particular asset price during the term to maturity.

Low Exercise Price Options Options that are deep in the money. Traded at Eurex, they have the advantage of mirroring the price development of the underlying.

Margin call Formal request to add to the margin account. This is coupled with the threat to close positions if the margin call is not met.

Margin Deposit which is required for derivatives transactions. A distinction is made between different types of margin and different ways of calculating margin.

Marking to market Daily revaluation of futures and options on futures in order to determine daily accruals to profits or losses.

Martingale Stochastic process with zero drift.

Monte-Carlo simulation Procedure for the simulation of changes of market variables in the context of the valuation of derivatives.

Netting Certain positions can be compared and cancelled out.

Normal distribution Bell-shaped standard distribution from statistics.

Open interest Number of open contracts in circulation.

Open outcry Trading system that uses verbal bids and offers in the trading pits.

Option Conditional derivatives transaction which provides the acquirer with a right to choose.

Option price Also called premium. The price which must be paid for an option.

Option writer Short investor. He has sold an option and collected the premium.

OTC "Over the Counter." Refers to an individual transaction that takes place outside an exchange.

Out-of-the-money The strike price is away from the current market price. For a call it is below and for a put it is above the current market price.

Plain vanilla Term for a simple product with completely standardized features.

Premium Additional payment which must be made. For options, the time value is measured by the premium. In a currency derivatives transaction, it refers to the price differential between forward rate and spot rate.

Premium based model Margin model used by U.S. derivatives exchanges. Does not consider compensating holdings.

Premium margin Must be deposited by the option writer. It is supposed to cover the costs of closing out the position.

Premium Positive price differential in a currency derivatives transaction.

Premium See option price.

Present value Current value of one or several future payment streams.

Protective put This position consists of the purchase of a share and the simultaneous purchase of a put in that share. Protective put is a static hedging strategy, which has its origins in put-call parity.

Put option The right, but not the obligation to sell an underlying at a predetermined point in time at a pre-specified price.

Putable bond Bond which gives the investor the right to return it to the issuer at a predetermined point in time and at a pre-specified price. The putable bond consists of a straight bond and a long put on the bond.

Putable swap Swap which can be terminated prematurely by one of the parties.

Put-call parity Relationship between the price of a European call and the price of a European put for an identical strike price and expiration date (see fiduciary call and protective put).

Pyramiding Use of an approach that resembles a pyramid in order to establish holdings. Recommended extension strategy.

Quanto The payoff of the derivative is in a different currency than the nominal. The amount of the payoff depends on variables which are denominated in the original currency.

Real options Options which are related to real assets and which are frequently used for the valuation of investment decisions.

Return Yield of an investment project.

Reverse cash and carry arbitrage Purchase of futures and spot sale.

Rho States the influence of interest rates on the option price.

Risk based margining Margin system used at Eurex. Compensation of certain positions is possible.

Risk controlling Active controlling of existing risks in the trading book of an investor.

Risk-free rate of interest Interest income which can be obtained without incurring risk.

Rollover Prolongation of a derivatives transaction past the initial due date. The original transaction is closed and a new transaction, which is directly related to the old one, is opened up.

Settlement Fulfillment of a derivatives obligation. Either physical delivery or cash payment are possible.

Settlement price The price at which a derivatives transaction is settled.

Short option adjustment Way to calculate the exchange minimum margin.

Short position Derivatives position sold.

Soft commodities Term for commodity derivatives transactions which are written on soft commodities such as coffee, orange juice, wheat, corn and so forth. In contrast hard commodities such as gold, silver and so forth also exist.

Speculation The aim of speculation is to make a profit. The speculator is willing to accept risk in the process.

Spread position Option combination which involves the simultaneous purchase and sale of option contracts.

Spreader Investor who trades spreads.

Straddle Option combination which involves the simultaneous purchase or sale of an identical number of calls and puts on the same underlying, the same expiration date and the same strike price.

Strangle Option combination which involves the simultaneous purchase or sale of an identical number of calls and puts on the same underlying and with the same expiration date, but different strike prices.

Strike price (= exercise price) Price at which an option is exercised.

Swap Bilateral financial contract which covers the exchange of streams of payments.

Swap rate Interest rate at which two banks are willing to exchange fixed interest payments which are tied to that rate against variable interest payments. In the currency area, the swap rate relates to the interest rate difference between two currencies.

Swaption Option which is written on a swap.

Synthetic positions Combinations which replicate the profile of chances and risks of a basic position.

Term structure of interest rates Relationship between interest rates and term to maturity.

Theta Measures the influence of the time value on the price of an option.

Time value Component of the option price which is related to the remaining time to maturity and the possibility that the option will end up in the money. With declines in the time to maturity, time value declines at an accelerating rate.

Triple witching day The third Friday of the last month of the quarter. On this date, options on single stocks, options on indexes and futures expire simultaneously.

Underlying The underlying is the basis for the derivatives transaction (examples are equities or indexes).

Variation margin Daily accounting of profits and losses for futures and options on futures. This valuation is done with the help of the mark to market procedure.

Vega Measures the influence of volatility on the price of the option.

Volatility Extent of actual or expected fluctuations of a financial instrument (is only concerned with the intensity of fluctuations and not with their direction). Can be calculated either as historical or implied volatility.

Volatility smile Variation of implied volatility with regard to the price of the underlying.

Weather derivatives Derivatives which are related to weather or weather changes.

Wiener process Stochastic process which grows at increments that are independent and normally distributed.

Zero bond Bond that never makes a coupon payment.

Table of standard normal distribution

z-values	0	0.01	0.02	0.03	0.04	0.05	0.06	0.07	0.08	0.09
				Part 2 of z-values						
-2.9	0.00190	0.00180	0.00180	0.00170	0.00160	0.00160	0.00150	0.00150	0.00140	0.00140
-2.8	0.00260	0.00250	0.00240	0.00230	0.00230	0.00220	0.00210	0.00210	0.00200	0.00190
-2.7	0.00350	0.00340	0.00330	0.00320	0.00310	0.00300	0.00290	0.00280	0.00270	0.00260
-2.6	0.00470	0.00450	0.00440	0.00430	0.00410	0.00400	0.00390	0.00380	0.00370	0.00360
-2.5	0.00620	0.00600	0.00590	0.00570	0.00550	0.00540	0.00520	0.00510	0.00490	0.00480
-2.4	0.00820	0.00800	0.00780	0.00750	0.00730	0.00710	0.00690	0.00680	0.00660	0.00640
-2.3	0.01070	0.01040	0.01020	0.00990	0.00960	0.00940	0.00910	0.00890	0.00870	0.00840
-2.2	0.01390	0.01360	0.01320	0.01290	0.01250	0.01220	0.01190	0.01160	0.01130	0.01100
-2.1	0.01790	0.01740	0.01700	0.01660	0.01620	0.01580	0.01540	0.01500	0.01460	0.01430
-2	0.02280	0.02220	0.02170	0.02120	0.02070	0.02020	0.01970	0.01920	0.01880	0.01830
-1.9	0.02870	0.02810	0.02740	0.02680	0.02620	0.02560	0.02500	0.02440	0.02390	0.02330
-1.8	0.03590	0.03510	0.03440	0.03360	0.03290	0.03220	0.03140	0.03070	0.03010	0.02940
-1.7	0.04460	0.04360	0.04270	0.04180	0.04090	0.04010	0.03920	0.03840	0.03750	0.03670
-1.6	0.05480	0.05370	0.05260	0.05160	0.05050	0.04950	0.04850	0.04750	0.04650	0.04550
-1.5	0.06680	0.06550	0.06430	0.06300	0.06180	0.06060	0.05940	0.05820	0.05710	0.05590
-1.4	0.08080	0.07930	0.07780	0.07640	0.07490	0.07350	0.07210	0.07080	0.06940	0.06810
-1.3	0.09680	0.09510	0.09340	0.09180	0.09010	0.08850	0.08690	0.08530	0.08380	0.08230
-1.2	0.11510	0.11310	0.11120	0.10930	0.10750	0.10560	0.10380	0.10200	0.10030	0.09850
-1.1	0.13570	0.13350	0.13140	0.12920	0.12710	0.12510	0.12300	0.12100	0.11900	0.11700
-1	0.15870	0.15620	0.15390	0.15150	0.14920	0.14690	0.14460	0.14230	0.14010	0.13790
-0.9	0.18410	0.18140	0.17880	0.17620	0.17360	0.17110	0.16850	0.16600	0.16350	0.16110
-0.8	0.21190	0.20900	0.20610	0.20330	0.20050	0.19770	0.19490	0.19220	0.18940	0.18670
-0.7	0.24200	0.23890	0.23580	0.23270	0.22960	0.22660	0.22360	0.22060	0.21770	0.21480
-0.6	0.27430	0.27090	0.26760	0.26430	0.26110	0.25780	0.25460	0.25140	0.24830	0.24510
-0.5	0.30850	0.30500	0.30150	0.29810	0.29460	0.29120	0.28770	0.28430	0.28100	0.27760
-0.4	0.34460	0.34090	0.33720	0.33360	0.33000	0.32640	0.32280	0.31920	0.31560	0.31210
-0.3	0.38210	0.37830	0.37450	0.37070	0.36690	0.36320	0.35940	0.35570	0.35200	0.34830
-0.2	0.42070	0.41680	0.41290	0.40900	0.40520	0.40130	0.39740	0.39360	0.38970	0.38590
-0.1	0.46020	0.45620	0.45220	0.44830	0.44430	0.44040	0.43640	0.43250	0.42860	0.42470
0	0.50000	0.49600	0.49200	0.48800	0.48400	0.48010	0.47610	0.47210	0.46810	0.46410
0	0.50000	0.50400	0.50800	0.51200	0.51600	0.51990	0.52390	0.52790	0.53190	0.53590
0.1	0.53980	0.54380	0.54780	0.55170	0.55570	0.55960	0.56360	0.56750	0.57140	0.57530
0.2	0.57930	0.58320	0.58710	0.59100	0.59480	0.59870	0.60260	0.60640	0.61030	0.61410
0.3	0.61790	0.62170	0.62550	0.62930	0.63310	0.63680	0.64060	0.64430	0.64800	0.65170
0.4	0.65540	0.65910	0.66280	0.66640	0.67000	0.67360	0.67720	0.68080	0.68440	0.68790
0.5	0.69150	0.69500	0.69850	0.70190	0.70540	0.70880	0.71230	0.71570	0.71900	0.72240
0.6	0.72570	0.72910	0.73240	0.73570	0.73890	0.74220	0.74540	0.74860	0.75170	0.75490
0.7	0.75800	0.76110	0.76420	0.76730	0.77030	0.77340	0.77640	0.77940	0.78230	0.78520
0.8	0.78810	0.79100	0.79390	0.79670	0.79950	0.80230	0.80510	0.80780	0.81060	0.81330
0.9	0.81590	0.81860	0.82120	0.82380	0.82640	0.82890	0.83150	0.83400	0.83650	0.83890
1	0.84130	0.84380	0.84610	0.84850	0.85080	0.85310	0.85540	0.85770	0.85990	0.86210
1.1	0.86430	0.86650	0.86860	0.87080	0.87290	0.87490	0.87700	0.87900	0.88100	0.88300
1.2	0.88490	0.88690	0.88880	0.89070	0.89250	0.89440	0.89620	0.89800	0.89970	0.90150
1.3	0.90320	0.90490	0.90660	0.90820	0.90990	0.91150	0.91310	0.91470	0.91620	0.91770
1.4	0.91920	0.92070	0.92220	0.92360	0.92510	0.92650	0.92790	0.92920	0.93060	0.93190
1.5	0.93320	0.93450	0.93570	0.93700	0.93820	0.93940	0.94060	0.94180	0.94290	0.94410
1.6	0.94520	0.94630	0.94740	0.94840	0.94950	0.95050	0.95150	0.95250	0.95350	0.95450
1.7	0.95540	0.95640	0.95730	0.95820	0.95910	0.95990	0.96080	0.96160	0.96250	0.96330
1.8	0.96410	0.96490	0.96560	0.96640	0.96710	0.96780	0.96860	0.96930	0.96990	0.97060
1.9	0.97130	0.97190	0.97260	0.97320	0.97380	0.97440	0.97500	0.97560	0.97610	0.97670
2	0.97720	0.97780	0.97830	0.97880	0.97930	0.97980	0.98030	0.98080	0.98120	0.98170
2.1	0.98210	0.98260	0.98300	0.98340	0.98380	0.98420	0.98460	0.98500	0.98540	0.98570
2.2	0.98610	0.98640	0.98680	0.98710	0.98750	0.98780	0.98810	0.98840	0.98870	0.98900
2.3	0.98930	0.98960	0.98980	0.99010	0.99040	0.99060	0.99090	0.99110	0.99130	0.99160
2.4	0.99180	0.99200	0.99220	0.99250	0.99270	0.99290	0.99310	0.99320	0.99340	0.99360
2.5	0.99380	0.99400	0.99410	0.99430	0.99450	0.99460	0.99480	0.99490	0.99510	0.99520
2.6	0.99530	0.99550	0.99560	0.99570	0.99590	0.99600	0.99610	0.99620	0.99630	0.99640
2.7	0.99650	0.99660	0.99670	0.99680	0.99690	0.99700	0.99710	0.99720	0.99730	0.99740
2.8	0.99740	0.99750	0.99760	0.99770	0.99770	0.99780	0.99790	0.99790	0.99800	0.99810
2.9	0.99810	0.99820	0.99820	0.99830	0.99840	0.99840	0.99850	0.99850	0.99860	0.99860

Rating scales

Moody's		S&P		Fitch		
Long Term	Short Term	Long Term	Short Term	Long Term	Short Term	
Aaa		AAA		AAA		Prime
Aa1		AA+	A-1+	AA+	A1+	
Aa2	P-1	AA		AA		High grade
Aa3		AA-		AA-		
A1		A+	A-1	A+	A1	
A2		A		A		Upper Medium grade
A3	P-2	A-	A-2	A-	A2	
Baa1		BBB+		BBB+		
Baa2	P-3	BBB	A-3	BBB	A3	Lower Medium grade
Baa3		BBB-		BBB-		
Ba1		BB+		BB+		Non-Investment grade speculative
Ba2		BB		BB		
Ba3		BB-	B	BB-	B	
B1		B+		B+		
B2		B		B		Highly Speculative
B3		B-		B-		
Caa	Not Prime	CCC+				Substantial risks
Ca		CCC	C	CCC	C	Extremely speculative
C		CCC-				In default with little prospect for recovery
/				DDD		
		D	/		/	In default

Bond return and rating in context

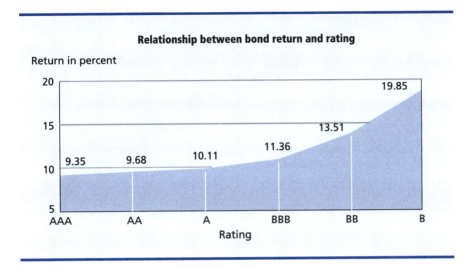

Figure 17.1: Relationship between bond return and rating[1]

Table 17.1: Average cumulative rates of default (%) 1970–2006[2]

	1	2	3	4	5	7	10
Aaa	0.000	0.000	0.000	0.026	0.099	0.251	0.521
Aa	0.008	0.019	0.042	0.106	0.177	0.343	0.522
A	0.021	0.095	0.220	0.344	0.472	0.759	1.287
Baa	0.181	0.506	0.930	1.434	1.938	2.959	4.637
Ba	1.205	3.219	5.568	7.958	10.215	14.005	19.118
B	5.236	11.296	17.043	22.054	26.794	34.771	43.343
Caa-C	19.476	30.494	39.717	46.904	52.622	59.938	69.178

[1] Source: Moody's.
[2] Source: Basisinformationen über Vermögensanlage in Wertpapiere, Bank-Verlag Köln.

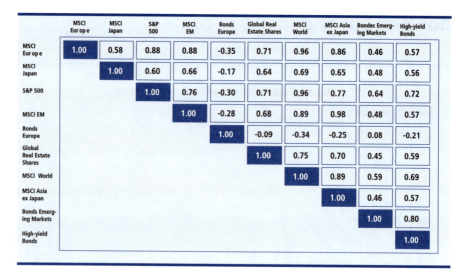

Figure 17.2: Correlation of individual markets (Date: July 2009)[3]

---

[3] Source: JP Morgan.

Internet addresses

Download area for this book:
http://www.certified-financial-engineer.com

Options master of Eurex
http://www.EUREXchange.com/education/tools/option_master_en.html

Market data of Eurex (delayed))
http://www.EUREXchange.com/market_en.html

Products at Eurex
http://www.EUREXchange.com/trading/products_en.html

Final settlement prices at Eurex
http://www.EUREXchange.com/market/clearing/finalsettlement_en.html

Trading calendar of Eurex
http://www.EUREXchange.com/trading/calendar/

Trading times at Eurex
http://www.EUREXchange.com/trading/hours/INT_en.html

Trading fees and prices
http://www.EUREXchange.com/trading/fees_en.html

Derivatives exchanges globally and their internet addresses

Name	Homepage
Abuja Securities & Commodity Exchange	http://www.abujacomex.com/
Agricultural Futures Exchange of Thailand	http://www.afet.or.th/v081/english/
Amsterdam Power Exchange (APX)	http://www.apxgroup.com/index.php?id=1
ASX Limited (Australian Securities Exchange, Derivatives)	http://www.asx.com.au/
Athens Exchange Derivatives (ADEX)	http://www.adex.ase.gr/AdexHomeEN/ns/index.html
Baumwollbörse Bremen	http://www.baumwollboerse.de/
BIFFEX	http://www.balticexchange.com
Bombay Stock Exchange	http://www.bseindia.com/
Boston Options Exchange (BOX)	www.bostonoptions.com/
Brazilian Mercantile & Futures Exchange	www.bmf.com.br/IndexEnglish.asp
Budapest Stock Exchange (BSE)	http://www.bse.hu/
Bursa Malaysia	www.klse.com.my/
Canadian Derivatives Exchange	http://www.m-x.ca/accueil_en.php
CBOE Futures Exchange (CFE)	http://cfe.cboe.com/
Central Japan Commodity Exchange	http://www.c-com.or.jp/public_html_e/index/index.php
Chicago Board Option Exchange (CBOE)	http://www.cboe.com/
Chicago Climate Futures Exchange (+ Montreal climate exchange)	http://www.ccfe.com/
Chicago Mercantile Exchange (CME) (GLOBEX) incl. CBOT	www.cmegroup.com

China Financial Futures Exchange	http://www.cffex.com.cn
Dalian Commodity Exchange (DCE) in China	www.dce.com.cn
Dubai Gold & Commodities Exchange	http://www.dgcx.ae/AboutUs.aspx
Dubai Mercantile Exchange	www.dubaimerc.com
ELX Electronic Liquidity Exchange	http://www.elxfutures.com/
EUREX	http://www.EURExchange.com
Euronext	www.euronext.com
European Climate Exchange	http://www.ecx.eu/
European Energy Derivatives Exchange	http://www.endex.nl/
European Energy Exchange: EEX	http://www.eex.com/de/
Hong Kong Futures Exchange (HKFE)	www.hkex.com.hk/
Hong Kong Mercantile Exchange	http://www.hkmerc.com/hkmex/index.php?&lang=english
IMAREX	http://www.imarex.com/
Indonesia Stock Exchange	http://www.idx.co.id/
Intercontinental Exchange (NYSE; ICE), New York Board of Trade (NYBOT)	www.nybot.com
International Securities Exchange (ISE)	http://www.ise.com/
Italian Stock Exchange – La Borsa Valori Italiana	www.borsaitaliana.it/
Jakarta Futures Exchange	http://www.bbj-jfx.com/
JSE Limited Südafrika	http://www.jse.co.za/
Kansai Commodities Exchange (KANEX)	http://www.kanex.or.jp/other/bei_eng.html
Kansas City Board of Trade	www.kcbt.com
Korea Exchange (KRX)	http://www.krx.co.kr/
Kuwait Stock Exchange	http://www.kuwaitse.com/PORTAL/DEFAULT.ASPX
Lahore Stock Exchange	http://www.lahorestock.com/Default.htm

London Metal Exchange	www.lme.co.uk
London Stock Exchange	http://www.londonstockexchange.com/home/homepage.htm
MEFF: mercado oficial español de futuros y opciones	www.meff.es/
Mercado a Término de Buenos Aires	http://www.matba.com.ar/INGLES/default.asp
Mercantile Exchange Nepal Limited	http://www.mexnepal.com/
Mexican Derivatives Exchange	www.mexder.com.mx/.../Derivatives_Exchange.html
Minneapolis Grain Exchange	www.mgex.com
Moscow Interbank Currency Exchange	http://www.micex.com/
Multi Commodity Exchange of India	http://www.mcxindia.com/
NADEX North American Derivatives Exchange	http://www.nadex.com/
Nasdaq OMX Group	www.nasdaqomx.com
Nasdaq OMX Nordic	http://www.nasdaqomxnordic.com/
National Commodity and Derivatives Exchange (indien)	http://www.ncdex.com/
National Multi Commodity Exchange of India	http://www.nmce.com/
National Stock Exchange of India (NSE)	www.nseindia.com/
New York Mercantile Exchange NYMEX	www.nymex.com/
New Zealand Futures	www.nzx.com/
NYSE Euronext	www.euronext.com/
OneChicago	www.onechicago.com/
Osaka Mercantile Exchange	www.osamex.com/
Osaka Securities Exchange	http://www.ose.or.jp/e/
Oslo Stock Exchange	http://www.oslobors.no/ob_eng/
Powernext SA	http://www.powernext.fr

Prague Stock Exchange	http://www.pse.cz/
RMX Risk Management Exchange	www.rmx.eu
Rosario Futures Exchange	http://www.rofex.com.ar/default.asp
Russian Exchange	www.rts.ru/en/
Shanghai Future Exchange	http://www.shfe.com.cn/Ehome/index.jsp
SIBEX SIBIU MONETARY	http://www.sibex.ro/?l=en
Singapore Commodity Exchange (SICOM)	www.sicom.com.sg/
Singapore Exchange	www.sgx.com/
Singapur Mercantile Exchange	http://www.smx.com.sg/
SIX Swiss Exchange	http://www.scoach.ch/DE/showpage.aspx?pageID=19
South African Futures	www.safex.co.za/
Sydney Futures Exchange (SFE) Corporation Limited	http://www.asx.com.au/about/sfe/index.htm
Sydney Futures Exchange Ltd.	www.asx.com.au/
Taiwan Futures Exchange	http://www.taifex.com.tw/eng/eng_home.htm
Taiwan Stock Exchange	http://www.twse.com.tw/en/
Tel Aviv Stock Exchange	www.tase.co.il/TASEEng/Homepage.htm
Thailand Future Exchange	http://www.tfex.co.th/en/index.html
TMX Montreal Exchange	http://www.tmx.com/en/index.html
Tokyo Commodity Exchange (TCOM)	www.tocom.or.jp/
Tokyo Financial Exchange inc (TFX, ehemals: TIFFE)	http://www.tfx.co.jp/en/index.shtml
Tokyo Grain Exchange (TGE)	www.tge.or.jp/
Tokyo Stock Exchange	http://www.tse.or.jp/english/
Turkish Derivatives Exchange	http://www.turkdex.org.tr/VOBPortalEng/DesktopDefault.aspx
Warsaw Stock Exchange	http://www.gpw.pl/index.asp
Österreichische Termin- und Optionen Börse (ÖTOB)	http://www.wienerborse.at/
Zhengzhou Commodity Exchange	http://english.czce.com.cn/

References

Beike, Rolf; Barckow, Andreas: Risk – Management mit Finanzderivaten, 3rd edition, Boston 2002.
Bloss, Ernst, Häcker, Hass, Röck: Financial Modelling, Stuttgart 2010.
Bloss, Michael; Ernst, Dietmar: Derivate – Handbuch für Finanzintermediäre und Investoren, München 2007.
Bloss, Michael; Eil, Nadine; Ernst, Dietmar; Fritsche, Harald; Häcker, Joachim: Währungsderivate, München 2009.
Bloss, Michael; Ernst, Dietmar; Häcker, Joachim; Eil, Nadine: Von der Subprime-Krise zur Finanzkrise, München 2008.
Bloss, Michael; Ernst, Dietmar; Häcker, Joachim; Eil, Nadine: Von der Wallstreet zur Mainstreet, München 2009.
Buckley, Adrian: Multinational Finance, 4th edition, Harlow 2000.
Choudhry, Moorad: The Bond & Money Markets, Burlington 2001.
Choudry, Moorad; Pereira, Richard; Pienaar, Rod; Joannas, Didier: Capital Market Instruments, London 2002.
Copeland, Thomas E.; Weston J. Fred; Shastri, Kuldeep: Finanzierungstheorie und Unternehmenspolitik, 4th edition, München 2008.
Das, Senjiv Ranjan: Credit Risk Derivatives in The Journal of Derivatives 3/1995, pp. 7–23.
DeRosa, David F.: Options on Foreign Exchange, 2nd edition, New York, 2000.
DeRosa, David: Currency Derivatives, New York 1998.
Dicks, James: Forex Made Easy, London 2004.
Eilenberger, Guido: Währungsrisiken, Währungsrisikomanagement und Devisenkurssicherung von Unternehmen, 4th edition, Frankfurt am Main 2004.
Ernst, Schneider, Thielen: Unternehmensbewertungen erstellen und verstehen, 3rd edition, München 2008.
Fabozzi, Frank J.: The Handbook of Financial Instruments, New Jersey 2002.
Fastrich, Hedrik; Hepp, Stefan: Währungsmanagement international tätiger Unternehmen, Stuttgart 1991.
Friberg, Richard: Exchange Rates and the Firm, New York 1999.

Gamper, Philipp Ch.: Währungs-Exposure Management, Hrsg.: Bern; Stuttgart; Wien 1995.

Gastineau, Gerry L.; Kritzman, Mark P.: Dictionary of Financial Risk Management, New Hope 1999.

Giddy, Ian H.: Global Financial Markets, Lexington 1994.

Graef, Andreas: Aufsicht über Hedgefonds im deutschen und amerikanischen Recht. Zugleich ein Beitrag zu den Einflüssen des Anlagemodells auf die Finanzmarktstabilität, Berlin 2008.

Hager, Peter: Corporate Risk Management: Cash Flow at Risk und Value at Risk, Frankfurt am Main 2004.

Hackl, Peter: Einführung in die Ökonometrie, München 2005.

Hauswald, Carina: Hedge Fonds und ihre Rolle für die Stabilität internationaler Finanzmärkte, Bochum 2007.

Hee, Christian, Hoffmann, Lutz: Wetterderivate Grundlagen, Exposure, Anwendung und Bewertung, Wiesbaden 2006.

Hicks, Alan: Managing Currency Risk Using Foreign Exchange Options, o.O. 2000.

Hull, John C.: Fundamentals of Futures and Options Markets, 5th edition, New Jersey 2005.

Hull, John C.: Options, Futures and Other Derivatives, 7th edition, New Jersey 2009.

Jabbour, George; Budwick, Phillip: The Option Trader Handbook: Strategies and Trade Adjustments, New Jersey 2004.

Jarrow, Robert A.; Turnbull, Stuart M.: Pricing derivatives on financial securities subject to credit risk, The Journal of Finance 1/1995, 53-85.

Jarrow, Robert A.; Lando, David; Turnbull, Stuart M.: A Markov model for the term structure of credit risk spreads; Working Paper, University of Coppenhagen, Institute of Mathematical Statistics 1995.

Kolb, Robert W.; Overdahl, James A.: Financial Derivatives, 3rd edition, New Jersey 2002.

Krugman, Paul R.; Obstfeld, Maurice: International Economics, 6th edition, London 2003.

Lando, David: Three Essays on Contingent Claims Pricing; Dissertation, Cornell University (New York) 1994.

Lando, David: A continuous time Markov model of the term structure of credit risk spreads; Working Paper, Cornell University (New York) 1994.

Longstaff, Francis A.; Schwartz, Eduardo S.: A simple approach to valuing risky fixed and floating rate debt; The Journal of Finance 3/1995, 789-819.

Longstaff, Francis A.; Schwartz, Eduardo S.: Valuing credit derivatives; The Journal of Fixed Income 6/1995, 6-12.

Lyuu, Yuh-Dauh, Financial Engineering and Computation - Principles, Mathematics, Algorithms, Cambridge, 2002.

Madura, Jeff: Financial Markets ans Institutions, Cienciennati 2001.

Madura, Jeff: International Financial Management, 6th edition, High Holborn 2004.

Maier, Kurt M.: Risikomanagement im Immobilien- und Finanzwesen, 2nd edition, Frankfurt am Main 2004.

McCafferty Thomas A.: All About Options, 2nd edition, New York 1998.

McEachern, William A.: Macroeconomics, a Contemporary Introduction, 6th edition, Connecticut 2003.

McInish, Thomas H.: Capital Markets, Oxford 2000.

Nelken, Israel: The Handbook of Exotic Options – Instruments, Analysis and Applications, New York 1996.

Perridon, Louis; Steiner, Manfred: Finanzwirtschaft der Unternehmung, 14th edition, München 2007.

Rieck, Christian: Spieltheorie, 8th edition, 2008.

Rubinstein Reuven Y.; Kroese Dirk P.: Simulation and the Monte Carlo Method, 2nd edition, New Jersey 2008.

Rudolph, Bernd; Schäfer, Klaus: Derivative Finanzmarktinstrumente, Berlin 2005.

Saliba, Anthony J.: The Options Workbook, 2nd edition, Chicago 2002.

Sarno, Lucio; Taylor, Mark P.: The Economics of Exchange Rates, Cambridge 2002.

Schirm, A.: Wetterderivate – Einsatzmöglichkeiten und Bewertung, Research in Capital Markets and Finance, Ludwig-Maximilians-Universität, München 2001.

Seethaler, Peter; Steitz, Markus: Praxishandbuch Treasury-Management, Wiesbaden 2007.

Sercu, Piet; Uppal, Raman: International Financial Markets and the firm, London 1995.

Shamah, Shani: A Currency Options Primer, West Sussex 2004.

Shapiro, Alan C.; Balbirer, Sheldon D.: Modern Corporate Finance, New Jersey 2000.

Sherris, Michael: Money & Capital Markets: Pricing, Yields & Analysis, 2nd edition, Crows Nest 1996.

Shim, Jae K; Constas, Michael: Encyclopedia Dictionary of International Finance and Banking, Boca Raton 2001.

Shimpi, P. / Turner, S.: Weather Risk Management. In: Shimpi, P., 2000. Integrating Corporate Risk Management, 2nd edition, Swiss Re New Markets, New York.

Shoup Gary.: Currency Risk Management, Chicago 1998.

Smithson, Charles W.: Managing Financial Risk: A Guide to Derivative Products, Financial Engineering, and Value Maximization, 3rd edition, New York, 1998.
Sörensen, Daniel: The Automotive Development Process, Wiesbaden 2006.
Sperber, Herbert: Wirtschaft verstehen, 2nd edition, Stuttgart 2007.
Sperber, Herbert; Sprink, Joachim: Internationale Wirtschaft und Finanzen, München 2007.
Spremann, Klaus, Gantenbein, Pascal: Zinsen, Anleihen, Kredite, München, 4th edition, 2007.
Spremann, Klaus: Finance, München, 3rd edition, 2007.
Steinbrenner, Hans- Peter: Professionelle Optionsgeschäfte, Frankfurt 2001.
Steinbrenner, Hans-Peter: Optionsrechte in der Praxis – Von Plain Vanilla bis zu Rainbow-Optionen, Stuttgart 2002.
Steiner, Bob: Foreign Exchange and Money Markets, Oxford, Woburn 2002.
Steiner, Manfred; Bruns, Christoph: Wertpapiermanagement, 9th edition, Stuttgart 2007.
Stephens, John J.: Managing Currency Risk Using Financial Derivatives, o.O. 2001.
Thompson, Henry: International Economics: Global Markets and International Competition, London 2001.
Uszczapowski, Igor: Optionen und Futures verstehen, München 2008.
Walmsley, Julian: New Financial Instruments, 2nd edition, o.O., 1998.
Ward, Keith; Bender, Ruth: Corporate Financial Strategy, 6th edition, Oxford 2002.
Werner, E.: Wetter als Börsenprodukt, Versicherungswirtschaft 55, Nr.22.
Wiedemann, Arnd: Bewertung von Finanzinstrumenten, 4the edition, Frankfurt 2007.
Wilmott, Paul: Paul Wilmott introduces Quantitative Finance, 2nd edition, Chichester 2007.
Williams, Michael; Hoffman, Amy: Fundamentals of Options Market, New York 2001.
Wöhe, Günter, Bilstein, Jürgen, Ernst, Dietmar, Häcker, Joachim: Grundzüge der Unternehmensfinanzierung, 10th edition, München 2009.
Wöhe, Günter, Döring, Ulrich: Einführung in die Allgemeine BWL, 23rd edition, München 2008.
Zhang, Peter G.: Exotic Options – A Guide to Second Generation Options, 2nd edition, Singapore, 1998.
Zimmermann, H., Jaeger, S., Jovic, D.: Bedeutung, Bewertung und Einsatz von Wetterderivaten, 2001.

Disclaimer

Deutsche Börse AG (DBAG), Clearstream Banking AG (Clearstream), Eurex Frankfurt AG, Eurex Clearing AG (Eurex Clearing) as well as Eurex Bonds GmbH (Eurex Bonds) and Eurex Repo GmbH (Eurex Repo) are corporate entities and are registered under German law. Eurex Zürich AG is a corporate entity and is registered under Swiss law. Clearstream Banking S.A. is a corporate entity and is registered under Luxembourg law. U.S. Exchange Holdings, Inc. and International Securities Exchange Holdings, Inc. (ISE) are corporate entities and are registered under U.S. American law. Eurex Frankfurt AG (Eurex) is the administrating and operating institution of Eurex Deutschland. Eurex Deutschland and Eurex Zürich AG are in the following referred to as the "Eurex Exchanges".

All intellectual property, proprietary and other rights and interests in this publication and the subject matter hereof (other than certain trademarks and service marks listed below) are owned by DBAG and its affiliates and subsidiaries including, without limitation, all patent, registered design, copyright, trademark and service mark rights. While reasonable care has been taken in the preparation of this publication to provide details that are accurate and not misleading at the time of publication DBAG, Clearstream, Eurex, Eurex Clearing, Eurex Bonds, Eurex Repo as well as the Eurex Exchanges and their respective servants and agents (a) do not make any representations or warranties regarding the information contained herein, whether express or implied, including without limitation any implied warranty of merchantability or fitness for a particular purpose or any warranty with respect to the accuracy, correctness, quality, completeness or timeliness of such information, and (b) shall not be responsible or liable for any third party's use of any information contained herein under any circumstances, including, without limitation, in connection with actual trading or otherwise or for any errors or omissions contained in this publication.

This publication is published for information purposes only and shall not constitute investment advice respectively does not constitute an offer, solicitation or recommendation to acquire or dispose of any investment or to engage in any other transaction. This publication is not intended for solicitation purposes but only for use as general information. All descriptions, examples and calculations contained in this publication are for illustrative purposes only.

Eurex and Eurex Clearing offer services directly to members of the Eurex exchanges respectively to clearing members of Eurex Clearing. Those who desire to trade any products available on the Eurex market or who desire to offer and sell any such products to others or who desire to possess a clearing license of Eurex Clearing in order to participate in the clearing process provided by Eurex Clearing, should consider legal and regulatory requirements of those jurisdictions relevant to them, as well as the risks associated with such products, before doing so.

Eurex derivatives (other than EURO STOXX 50® Index Futures contracts, EURO STOXX® Select Dividend 30 Index Futures contracts, STOXX® Europe 50 Index Futures contracts, STOXX® Europe 600 Index Futures contracts, STOXX® Europe

Large/Mid/Small 200 Index Futures contracts, EURO STOXX® Banks Futures contracts, STOXX® Europe 600 Banks/Industrial Goods & Services/Insurance/Media/Personal & Household Goods/Travel & Leisure/Utilities Futures contracts, Dow Jones Global Titans 50 Index^{SM} Futures contracts, DAX® Futures contracts, MDAX® Futures contracts, TecDAX® Futures contracts, SMIM® Futures contracts, SLI Swiss Leader Index® Futures contracts, Eurex inflation/commodity/weather/property and interest rate derivatives) are currently not available for offer, sale or trading in the United States or by United States persons.

Trademarks and Service Marks

Buxl®, DAX®, DivDAX®, eb.rexx®, Eurex®, Eurex Bonds®, Eurex Repo®, Eurex Strategy Wizard^{SM}, Euro GC Pooling®, FDAX®, FWB®, GC Pooling®, GCPI®, MDAX®, ODAX®, SDAX®, TecDAX®, USD GC Pooling, VDAX®, VDAX-NEW® and Xetra® are registered trademarks of DBAG.

Phelix Base® and Phelix Peak® are registered trademarks of European Energy Exchange AG (EEX).

The service marks MSCI Russia and MSCI Japan are the exclusive property of MSCI Barra.

iTraxx® is a registered trademark of International Index Company Limited (IIC) and has been licensed for the use by Eurex. IIC does not approve, endorse or recommend Eurex or iTraxx® Europe 5-year Index Futures, iTraxx® Europe HiVol 5-year Index Futures and iTraxx® Europe Crossover 5-year Index Futures.

Eurex is solely responsible for the creation of the Eurex iTraxx Credit Futures contracts, their trading and market surveillance. ISDA® neither sponsors nor endorses the product's use. ISDA® is a registered trademark of the International Swaps and Derivatives Association, Inc.

IPD UK Annual All Property Index is a registered trademark of Investment Property Databank Ltd. IPD and has been licensed for the use by Eurex for derivatives.

SLI®, SMI® and SMIM® are registered trademarks of SIX Swiss Exchange AG.

The STOXX® indexes, the data included therein and the trademarks used in the index names are the intellectual property of STOXX Limited and/or its licensors Eurex derivatives based on the STOXX® indexes are in no way sponsored, endorsed, sold or promoted by STOXX and its licensors and neither STOXX nor its licensors shall have any liability with respect thereto.

Dow Jones Dow Jones Global Titans 50 Index^{SM} and Dow Jones Sector Titans Indexes^{SM} are service marks of Dow Jones & Company, Inc. Dow Jones-UBS Commodity Index^{SM} and any related sub-indexes are service marks of Dow Jones & Company, Inc. and UBS AG. All derivatives based on these indexes are not sponsored, endorsed, sold or promoted by Dow Jones & Company, Inc. or UBS AG, and neither party makes any representation regarding the advisability of trading or of investing in such products.

All references to London Gold and Silver Fixing prices are used with the permission of The London Gold Market Fixing Limited as well as The London Silver Market Fixing Limited, which for the avoidance of doubt has no involvement with and accepts no responsibility whatsoever for the underlying product to which the Fixing prices may be referenced.

PCS® and Property Claim Services® are registered trademarks of ISO Services, Inc.

Korea Exchange, KRX, KOSPI and KOSPI 200 are registered trademarks of Korea Exchange Inc.

BSE and SENSEX are trademarks/service marks of Bombay Stock Exchange (BSE) and all rights accruing from the same, statutory or otherwise, wholly vest with BSE. Any violation of the above would constitute an offence under the laws of India and international treaties governing the same.

The names of other companies and third party products may be trademarks or service marks of their respective owners.

Index

A
Additional margin, 125, 511, 518
Address non-payment risk, 486
American-style, 163
Arbitrageur, 99, 494
Asian options, 348
Assignment, 166, 444
At-the-money, 173
Auto-callable, 472
Average options, 348
Averaging, 439, 440, 443, 454

B
Back office, 4
Back spread, 239
Backwardation, 281, 282, 285
Barrier options, 338, 339
Basis convergence, 137, 159
Basket options, 337, 345
Behavioral economics, 64
Behavioral finance, 66, 68
Bermuda options, 342
Beta factor, 35, 62, 153, 154
β hedge, 223, 224
Binomial model, 202, 208, 209
Black-76 model, 249, 304
Black-Scholes formula, 198
Black-Scholes model, 22, 25, 26
Black-Scholes-Merton model, 199
Bonus certificates, 463, 464
Boston options, 348, 560
Box, 239–241
Burn analysis, 396
Burning cost method, 396
Butterfly, 235–238

C
Calender spread, 241, 242
Call, 112, 161, 162, 173, 177, 178, 184, 186–188, 190, 193, 195, 213, 214, 216, 217, 219, 221, 223, 225, 226, 228, 233, 234, 236–242, 248, 249, 251–254, 288, 333, 334, 338, 341, 346, 383, 390, 444, 450, 460, 461, 463, 464, 514, 520, 522, 525
Call volatility trade, 473, 474
Cancel former, 115
Capital asset pricing modell, 58
Caplets, 301, 302, 304
Caps, 301, 303, 390
Cash settlement, 164, 335, 363, 366
Cash-and-Carry arbitrage, 150
CDS, 362–366, 368, 369
Certificates, 6, 467
Cheapest to Deliver, 131, 141
Chooser options, 342
Classical decision theory, 45
Clearing, 110, 111, 120, 490, 509, 510, 513, 520
Cliquet options, 346
Close out, 169
Closing, 112, 115, 127, 169, 170, 275, 444, 446, 508
Club deal, 5
CMS, 309, 354
Collar, 304, 305, 375
Combo, 474, 475
Combo versus long underlying, 474, 475
Commodity futures, 123
Commodity Futures Trading Commission (CFTC), 109
Compound option, 435
Compound options, 342, 343
Condor, 237
Confirmation, 331
Contango, 281, 282, 284

Contract, 129, 130, 165, 185, 248, 252, 401, 518
Convenience yield, 281, 283
Conversion, 131, 476, 477
Conversion versus underlying, 476, 477
Convertible bond arbitrage, 491
Core capital, 358, 360
Corporate actions, 184, 185
Correlation, 30, 33, 55, 305, 558
Correlation coefficients, 33, 35
Cost of Carry, 136, 148
Costs of closing a position, 519
Counterpart, 116, 506
Counterparty risk, 486
Country risk, 486
Covariance, 33, 36, 41, 61
covariance, 34
credit derivate, 452
Credit derivatives, 357, 361, 362, 365, 366
Credit Linked Notes (CLN), 366
Credit ratings, 360
Credit risk, 358, 486
Credit risk of the issuer, 366
Cross rate, 267, 268
Currency derivatives transactions, 266, 268
Currency options, 269, 567
Currency spot transactions, 264
Currency swap, 310
Custodian, 490

D

Daily simulation method, 398
Default, 313, 358, 362–366, 561
Degree day, 377–379, 381, 397, 400
Delta, 39, 41, 186–188, 193, 222, 223
Digital options, 340
Discount certificate, 254, 460, 462
Dividend payments, 183

E

Emerging markets, 493, 495
Equity-linked bonds, 256
European-style, 163
Event driven, 493
Exchange options, 348, 566
Exchange supervision, 109
Execution of orders, 114
Exercise, 168
Exotic options, 211, 338

Expansion option, 435
Extraordinary dividends, 185

F

Fill and kill, 113
Fill or kill, 113, 120
Fixed income arbitrage, 494
Fixed income futures, 107, 117, 123
Flat term structure, 102
Floor, 303–305
Floorlets, 303, 304
Flow products, 9
Forced liquidation, 522
Forward, 91, 94, 120, 123, 266, 301, 305, 310
Frequentist probability, 19
Front office, 4
Fund administration, 490
fund of hedge funds, 495
Funding cost, 459
Future spread margin, 513
Future style options, 518
Futures, 13, 70, 91, 104, 109, 112, 117–120, 123–139, 141–148, 151, 153–155, 158, 159, 171, 244, 246–253, 258, 262, 270–273, 275, 276, 278, 281, 284, 285, 288, 290, 291, 294, 295, 300, 353, 365, 371, 375, 381, 390, 393, 394, 400, 411, 433, 442, 443, 450–453, 510, 511, 513, 516–519, 522, 524, 533, 560–563, 566, 568

G

Game theory, 46, 48, 49, 70
Gamma, 39, 188, 193
Garman-Kohlhagen, 269
Global macro, 494
Greeks, 186, 193

H

Hebel products, 451
Hedge funds, 484–488, 490, 495–499, 566
Hedgefonds, 486
Hedger, 98, 99, 101
HGB, 451, 454
Historical volatility, 179

I

IFRS, 451
Immediate or cancel, 113

In-the-money, 173
Index value simulation method, 398
Inflation swaps, 314
Initial margin, 512, 516
Insurance derivatives, 409
Inter contract spread, 149
Inter market spread, 149
Interest rate swap, 308
Interest structure curve, 139
Intra contract spread, 149
Intrinsic value, 172, 301
Inverted term structure, 103
ISDA, 309, 331, 363, 410, 507
Issuer risk, 486
Itō process, 25, 200
iTraxx, 365

L

Ladder options, 346
Laplace probability, 18
Legal department, 4
LEPO, 168, 460
Leveraged floater, 470
Leveraged products, 465
Limit order, 112
Liquidity risk, 487
Long call, 341
Long future, 288
Long put, 214, 223, 450
Long/short equity, 495
Lookback options, 346
Loss of time value, 175

M

Managed futures, 495
Manager risk, 487, 488
Margin, 125, 130, 248, 271, 509–511, 513–516, 518, 520, 525, 534
Margin call, 521
Margining, 501, 508–510, 519, 525
Mark-to-market, 129
Market if touched, 115
Market interest rate, 183, 186
Market neutral equity, 493
Market order, 112, 212
Market psychology, 64
Market risks, 485
Markov process, 22
Martingale, 28, 71

Master agreements, 331
Matching, 104, 114
Mezzanine, 358
Middle office, 4
Mistrade rules, 116
Monte-Carlo simulation, 211, 399, 471, 472
Multi callable bonds, 469
Multi putable bonds, 469
Multifactor options, 348

N

Netting, 516
Normal term structure, 102
Not held, 115

O

Offshore companies, 485
One cancels the other, 115
Open outcry system, 120
Opening, 95, 107, 112, 115, 127, 275, 444, 447
Operational risk, 487
Option, 92, 112, 161–163, 169, 170, 182, 184, 186, 190, 192, 249, 251, 253, 266, 270, 301, 332, 336, 339, 342, 343, 346, 347, 354, 383, 385–388, 409, 468, 469, 524, 560, 566
Option bonds, 466
Options on futures, 109, 400, 513
Order systems, 116
OTC, 117, 161, 247, 261, 266, 269, 270, 299, 300, 336, 349, 372, 412, 486, 506
Out-of-the-money, 173
Outperformance options, 346

P

Pay-off, 152, 153, 464
Payer, 309, 313–317, 333, 334
Payoff, 341, 461, 464
Placement of orders, 116
Plain vanilla, 213, 269, 292, 568
Play theory, 567
Portfolio insurance, 224
Portfolio management, 63, 64
Portfolio selection modell, 55, 56
Position management, 442
Premium, 166
Premium margin, 511
Price factor, 140

Prime broker, 487, 489, 490, 499
Private placements, 8
Product desks, 4, 14
Protective put, 223, 477, 478
Public offering, 8
Put, 112, 161, 162, 169, 170, 173, 184, 186–188, 190, 193, 195, 214, 219–221, 223, 225, 226, 228, 229, 233, 234, 236, 237, 239–242, 246, 248, 249, 252, 253, 288, 295, 333, 334, 336, 338, 339, 346, 386, 387, 390, 450, 461–464, 522
Put spread versus underlying, 476
Put volatility trade, 474, 475
Put-call parity, 195
Pyramiding, 439, 454

Q

Quanto options, 343
Quotes, 213

R

Rainbow options, 344, 568
Random walk, 23, 28, 396
Range options, 341
Ratio spread, 238
Real options, 435
Receiver, 309, 313, 314, 316, 317, 333, 334
Replication, 39
Report, 265
Reverse floater, 469, 470
Rho, 189, 190, 193
Risk based margining, 510
Risk controlling, 54, 501, 506, 508
Risk reversal, 242, 243, 259
Rollover, 171, 444–446

S

Securities and Exchange Commission (SEC), 109
Securities lending, 465, 490
Settlement, 118, 142, 164, 270, 275–277, 335, 490, 520, 559
Short call, 187, 214
Short equity, 492, 499
Short future, 127, 143
Short put, 187, 214
Shout options, 347
Single callable bonds, 468
Single index model, 57
Single putable bonds, 467

Soft commodities, 278, 285, 286
Speculator, 99
Spread options, 346
Spread order, 113
Spreader, 99
Spreads, 148, 229, 230, 239, 240, 242, 273, 365
Standard deviation, 37, 59, 179
Standard normal distribution, 270
Stop order, 112
Straddle, 225, 226, 228, 234, 244, 254, 375
Strangle, 228, 229, 234, 254, 375
Straps, 227, 259
Strategic risk, 488
Strips, 227
Subjective probabilities, 19
Swap, 306–318, 320, 322, 323, 325–328, 330–332, 344, 354, 362, 363, 365, 375, 410, 494
Swap rate, 307
Swaptions, 332, 334
Synthetic derivatives market position, 253

T

Take time, 115
Term sheet, 6
Term spread, 103
Theta, 190, 191, 193
Tier, 358, 359
Time spread, 147, 241
Time to maturity, 186
Time value, 172, 174
Tobin tax, 268
Trading phase, 107, 108
Trees, 203

U

Underlying, 95, 100, 110, 112, 114, 117, 118, 126, 129, 132, 150, 159, 168, 172, 173, 175, 178, 183, 186, 188, 203, 217, 220, 221, 223, 245, 285, 312, 338, 381, 447, 449, 450, 459, 462, 491, 507, 510, 520, 522
Universal banks, 489
Upside, 507
Upside additional margin, 519

V

Value at risk, 40–42, 70, 485, 566

Variance, 25, 33, 36, 37, 41, 45, 51, 56, 57, 61
Variation margin, 513, 518
Vega, 39, 190, 193
Volatility, 37, 179, 181, 186, 190, 198–200, 208, 209, 211, 221, 244, 245, 259, 305
Volatility smile, 208, 209

W

Weather derivatives, 375, 382, 390, 399, 400, 402, 404, 406, 407, 566, 567
Weather indexed bond, 375
Weather indexed interest rate forward, 375
Weather indexed loan, 375
Weekly options, 117, 168
Wiener process, 22, 23
Window options, 342

Y

Yields, 567

Z

Zero bond, 459
Zero strike call, 460

Safety, efficiency, diversity.

Just some of the things we're bringing to derivatives.

Eurex Group provides more opportunities across a growing range of products – from pre- to post-trading, in major markets around the world.

We help create a safer market where risks are managed more effectively.

And we offer more efficient processes based on innovative and proven technology.

For over 10 years, we have been successfully shaping the future of the derivatives industry.

Today, we have a global liquidity pool trading about 12 million derivatives contracts every day. And we offer ground-breaking clearing services through Europe's leading central counter-party for securities and derivatives transactions.

Eurex Group includes Eurex Exchange, the International Securities Exchange (ISE), European Energy Exchange (EEX), Eurex Clearing, Eurex Bonds and Eurex Repo.

Eurex Group is part of Deutsche Börse Group.

Find out more at **www.eurexgroup.com**.